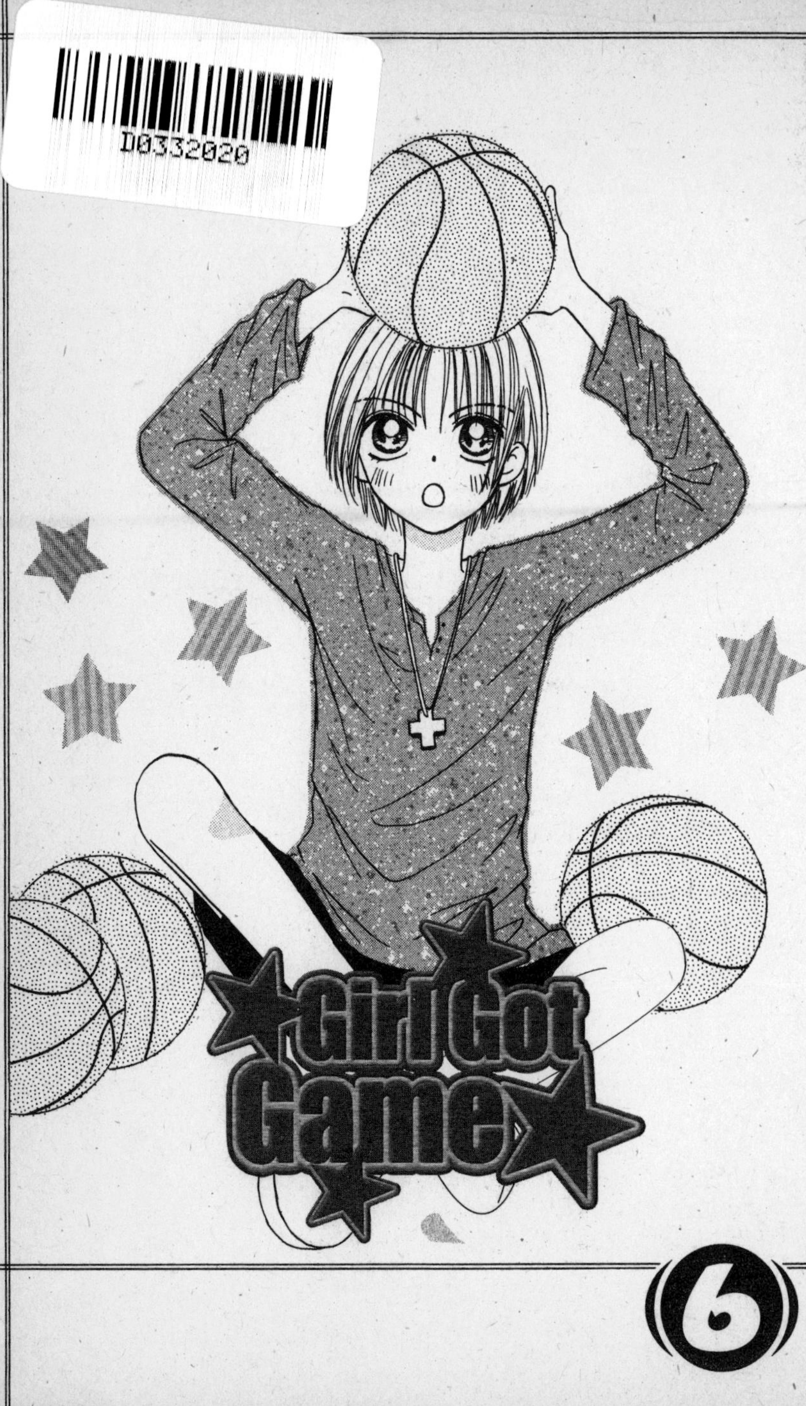
Girl Got Game
6

Girl Got Game Vol. 6
created by Shizuru Seino

Translation - Aya Matsunaga
English Adaptation - Kelly Sue DeConnick
Copy Editor - Suzanne Waldman
Retouch and Lettering - Norine Lukaczyk
Production Artist - Eva Han, James Dashiell
Cover Design - Anna Kernbaum

Editor - Rob Tokar
Digital Imaging Manager - Chris Buford
Pre-Press Manager - Antonio DePietro
Production Managers - Jennifer Miller and Mutsumi Miyazaki
Art Director - Matt Alford
Managing Editor - Jill Freshney
VP of Production - Ron Klamert
President and C.O.O. - John Parker
Publisher and C.E.O. - Stuart Levy

A **TOKYOPOP** Manga

TOKYOPOP Inc.
5900 Wilshire Blvd. Suite 2000
Los Angeles, CA 90036

E-mail: info@TOKYOPOP.com
Come visit us online at www.TOKYOPOP.com

ISBN: 1-59182-701-9

First TOKYOPOP printing: November 2004
10 9 8 7 6 5 4 3
Printed in the USA

Girl Got Game

by Shizuru Seino
Volume 6

HAMBURG // LONDON // LOS ANGELES // TOKYO

The Story So Far

Some people will do anything to realize their dreams...even if it means disguising a girl as a boy so she can play on a famous boys' basketball team. If you don't believe it, just imagine how Kyo Aizawa feels--her dad's the one who cooked up this crazy scheme!

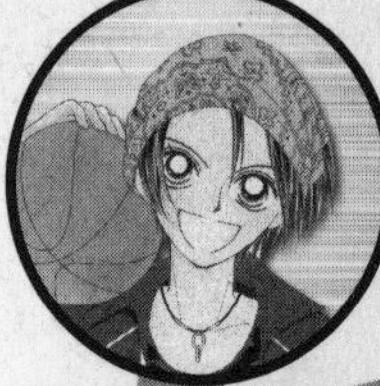

Kyo Aizawa

Kyo's father was once a great basketball player who aspired to play for the NBA. Unfortunately, an injury ended his career before it even started. Despite his disappointment, he passed his love of the game--and his moves--to his daughter.

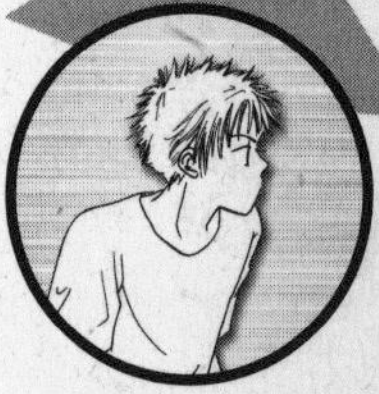

Chiharu Eniwa

Kyo wanted to *date* a boy, not *become* one, and she was not happy about her father's kooky plan...until she met Chiharu Eniwa, the boy who was to be her teammate on the court...and her roommate in the dorms!

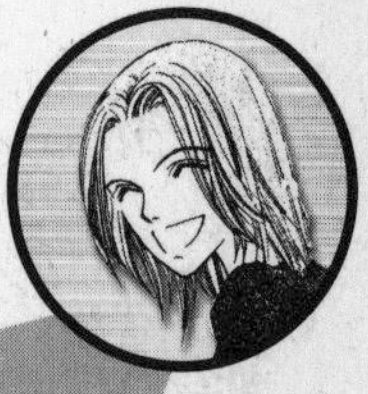

Hisashi Imai

As luck would have it, Kyo and Chiharu got on each other's nerves right from the start, but Kyo's attempts to get past Chiharu's gruff, sullen exterior eventually made the two of them friends. In turn, Chiharu's thoughtful kindness also swept Kyo off her feet...and she wondered if she might have some serious feelings for him.

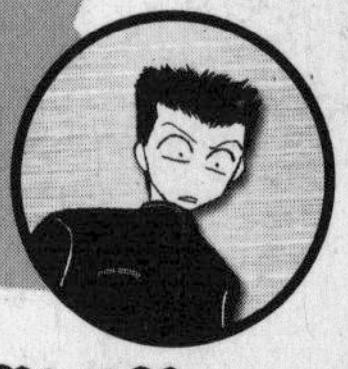

Shinji Hamaya

Kyo and Chiharu's peaceful coexistence was cut painfully short when an old friend of Kyo's named Tsuyaka Himejima arrived on the scene. Tsuyaka knew Kyo from her previous school and transferred to Seisyu so they could play on the same team again. When Tsuyaka learned Kyo was masquerading as a boy, she was willing to protect Kyo's secret...until Kyo proved she was unwilling to leave the boys' team. Attempting to force the issue, Tsuyaka tore open Kyo's shirt in front of Chiharu, revealing Kyo's breasts! Though Chiharu didn't tell Kyo's secret, he did have a tough time adjusting to the idea of a female roommate.

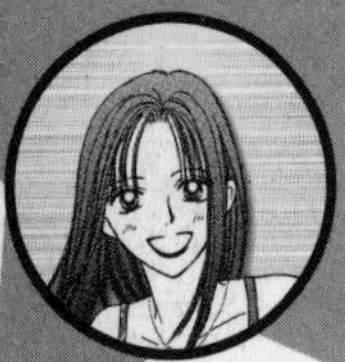

Ayaha

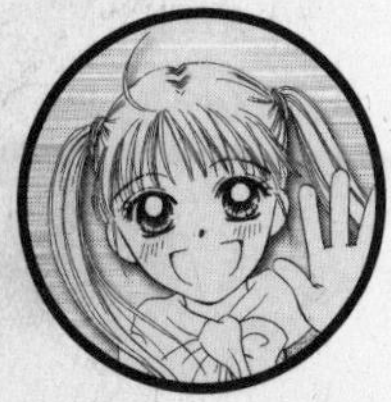

Akari Tojo

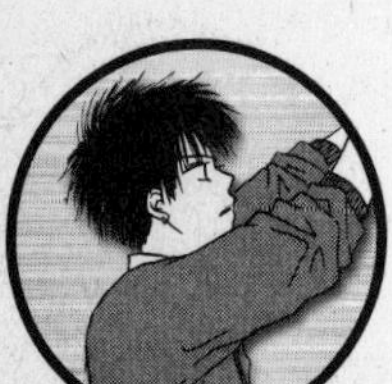

Kensuke Yura

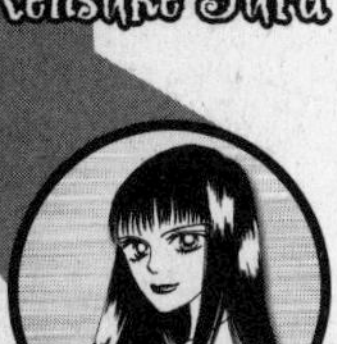

Tsuyaka Himejima

Just as life seemed like it was going to return to "normal," Kyo literally stumbled across Kensuke Yura on her way to practice. Yura, it turns out, is one of the best players on the Seisyu High basketball team, but he hasn't shown up for practice or any games since before Kyo became a member. However, once Yura met Kyo, he started showing up for practice again...though none of the other boys seemed happy about it.

Though Yura's skills on the court are impressive, he is a very poor team player whose steadfast refusal to rely on others alienates his teammates. Unfortunately, Yura's "loner" behavior also extends to his personal life, and it's in large part due to his photographic memory. Yura's perfect, unfailing memory makes school a breeze...and life a pain. He remembers every detail about every bad thing that's ever been said or done to him, and it's left the gifted young man bitter, angry and friendless.

Recently, Kyo tried to save Yura from three of their teammates who were trying to bully Yura into leaving the team. Yura turned the tables on his attackers and left them begging him for mercy instead. As frightening as that was, Kyo was even more horrified when Yura told her that he once poisoned a former classmate in order to scare the other boy into confessing that he abused Yura's trust. Almost as disturbing as the story itself was Yura's follow-up question to Kyo: "It's their own fault, right?"

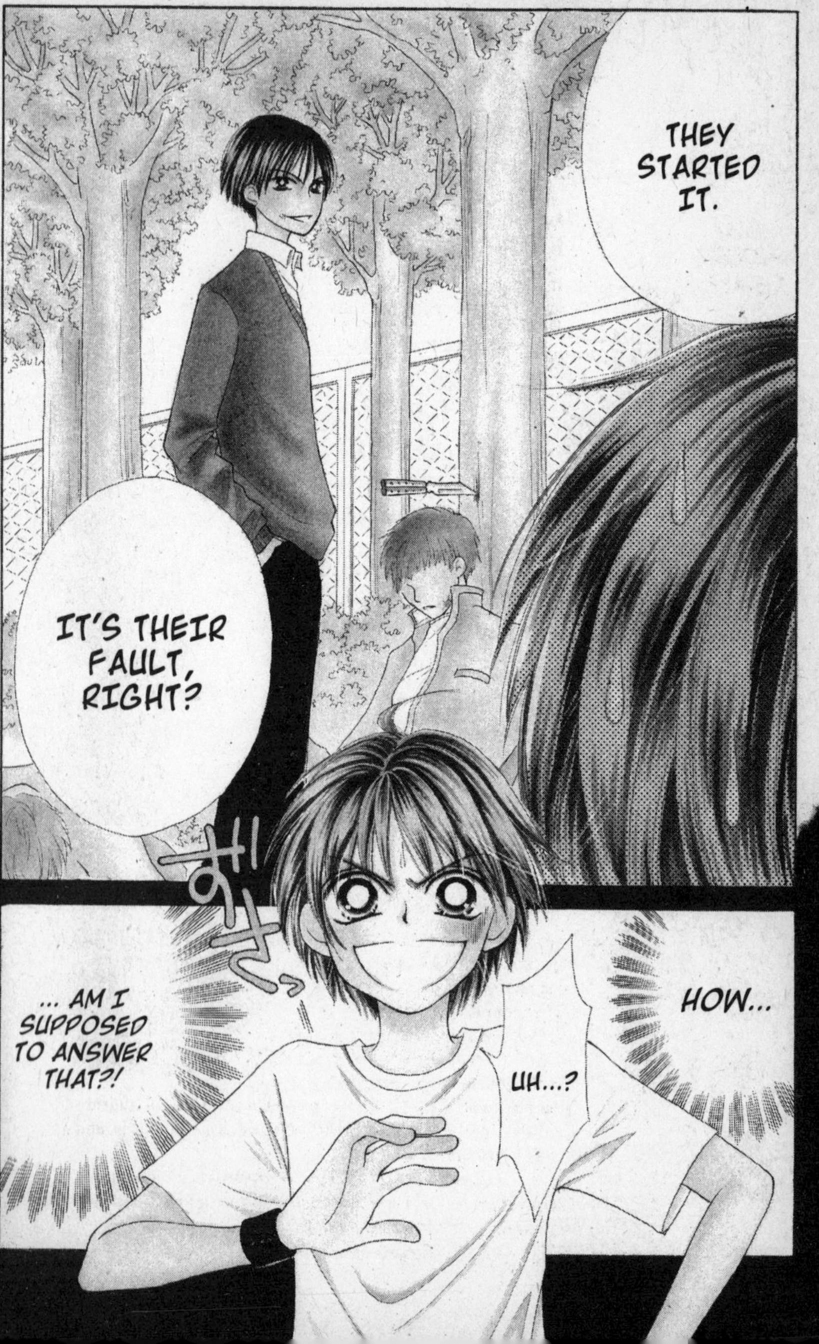
THEY STARTED IT.
IT'S THEIR FAULT, RIGHT?
HOW...
UH...?
... AM I SUPPOSED TO ANSWER THAT?!

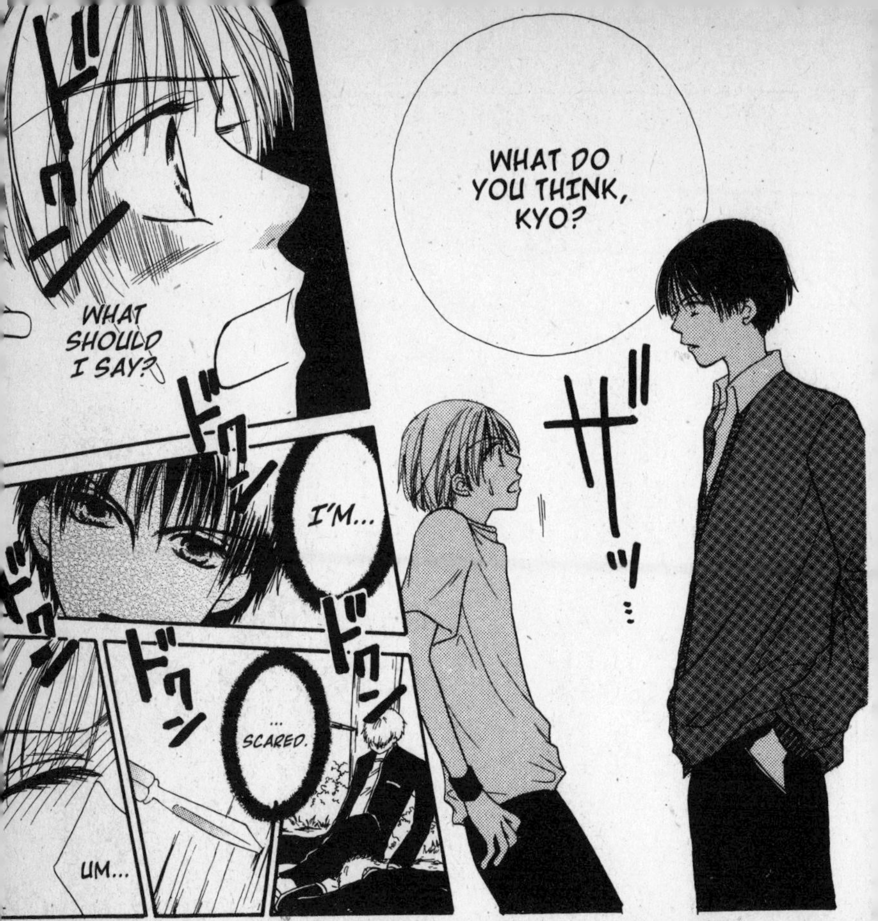
WHAT DO YOU THINK, KYO?
ザッ
ドクン
WHAT SHOULD I SAY?
ドクン
I'M...
ドクン
ドクン
... SCARED.
UM...

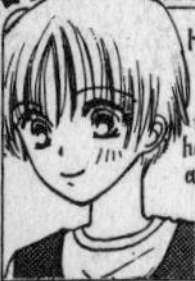

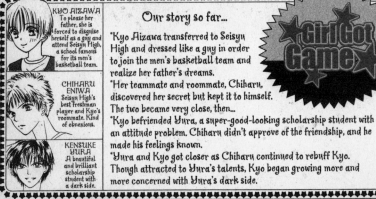

KYO AIZAWA
To please her father, she is forced to disguise herself as a guy and attend Seisyu High, a school famous for its men's basketball team.

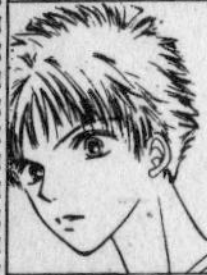

CHIHARU ENIWA
Seisyu High's best freshman player and Kyo's roommate. Kind of obnoxious.

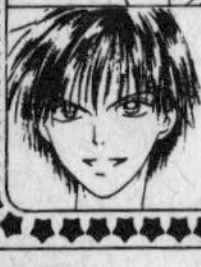

KENSUKE YURA
A beautiful and brilliant scholarship student with a dark side.

Girl Got Game

Our story so far...

*Kyo Aizawa transferred to Seisyu High and dressed like a guy in order to join the men's basketball team and realize her father's dreams.

*Her teammate and roommate, Chiharu, discovered her secret but kept it to himself. The two became very close, then...

*Kyo befriended Yura, a super-good-looking scholarship student with an attitude problem. Chiharu didn't approve of the friendship, and he made his feelings known.

*Yura and Kyo got closer as Chiharu continued to rebuff Kyo. Though attracted to Yura's talents, Kyo began growing more and more concerned with Yura's dark side.

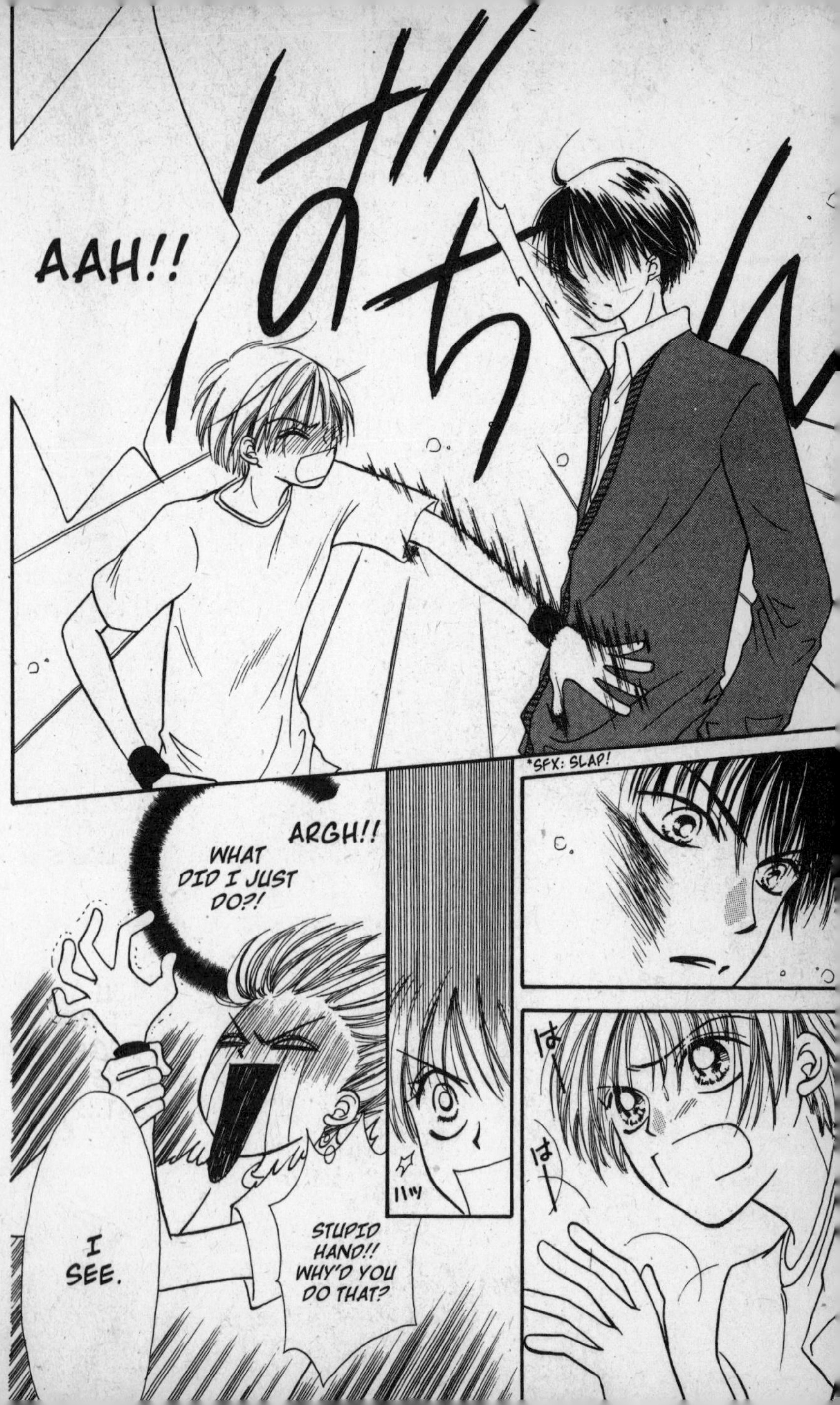
ばちん
AAH!!
*SFX: SLAP!
はーはー
ハッ
ARGH!!
WHAT DID I JUST DO?!
STUPID HAND!! WHY'D YOU DO THAT?
I SEE.

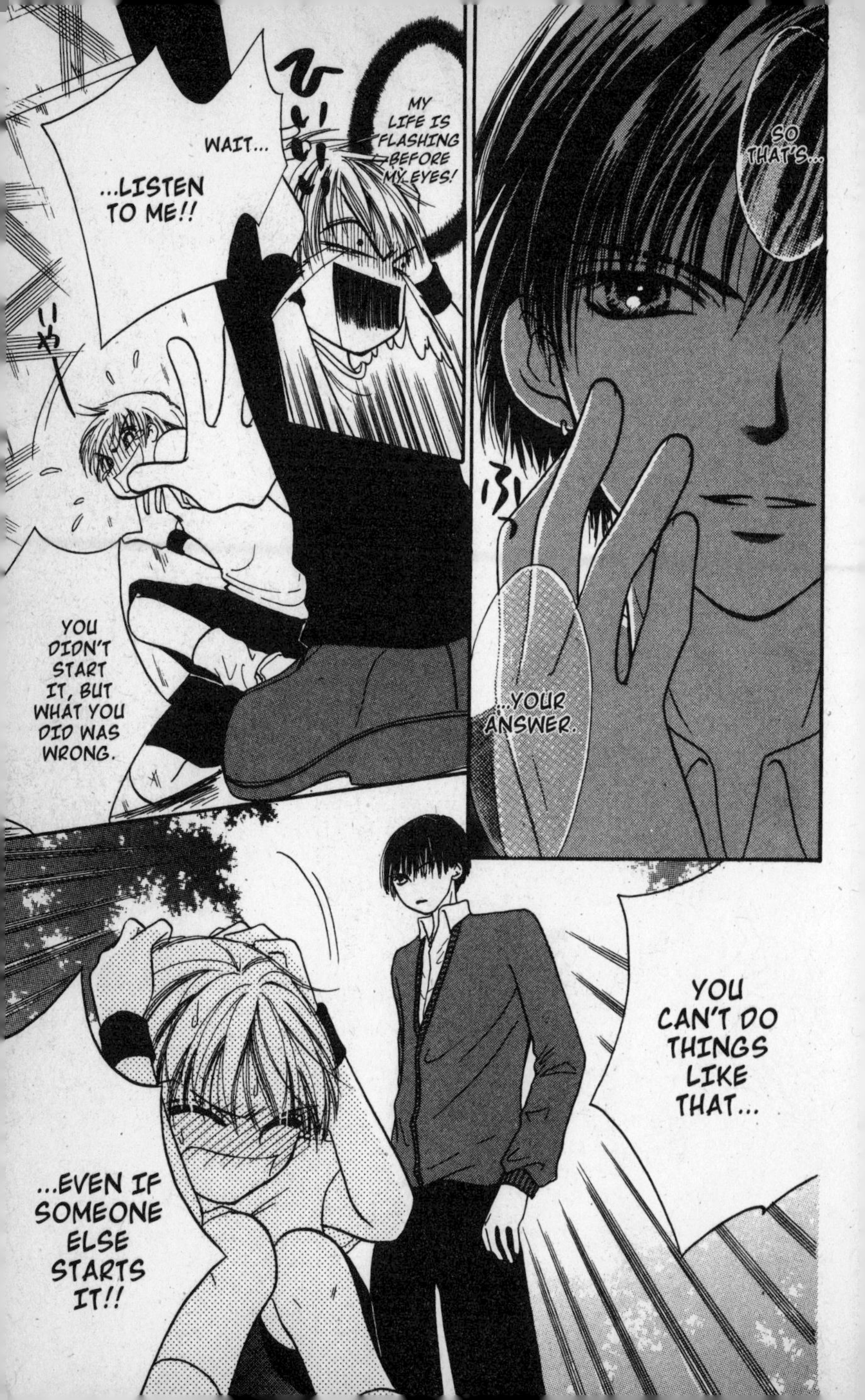
SO THAT'S...
...YOUR ANSWER.
MY LIFE IS FLASHING BEFORE MY EYES!
WAIT...
...LISTEN TO ME!!
YOU DIDN'T START IT, BUT WHAT YOU DID WAS WRONG.
YOU CAN'T DO THINGS LIKE THAT...
...EVEN IF SOMEONE ELSE STARTS IT!!

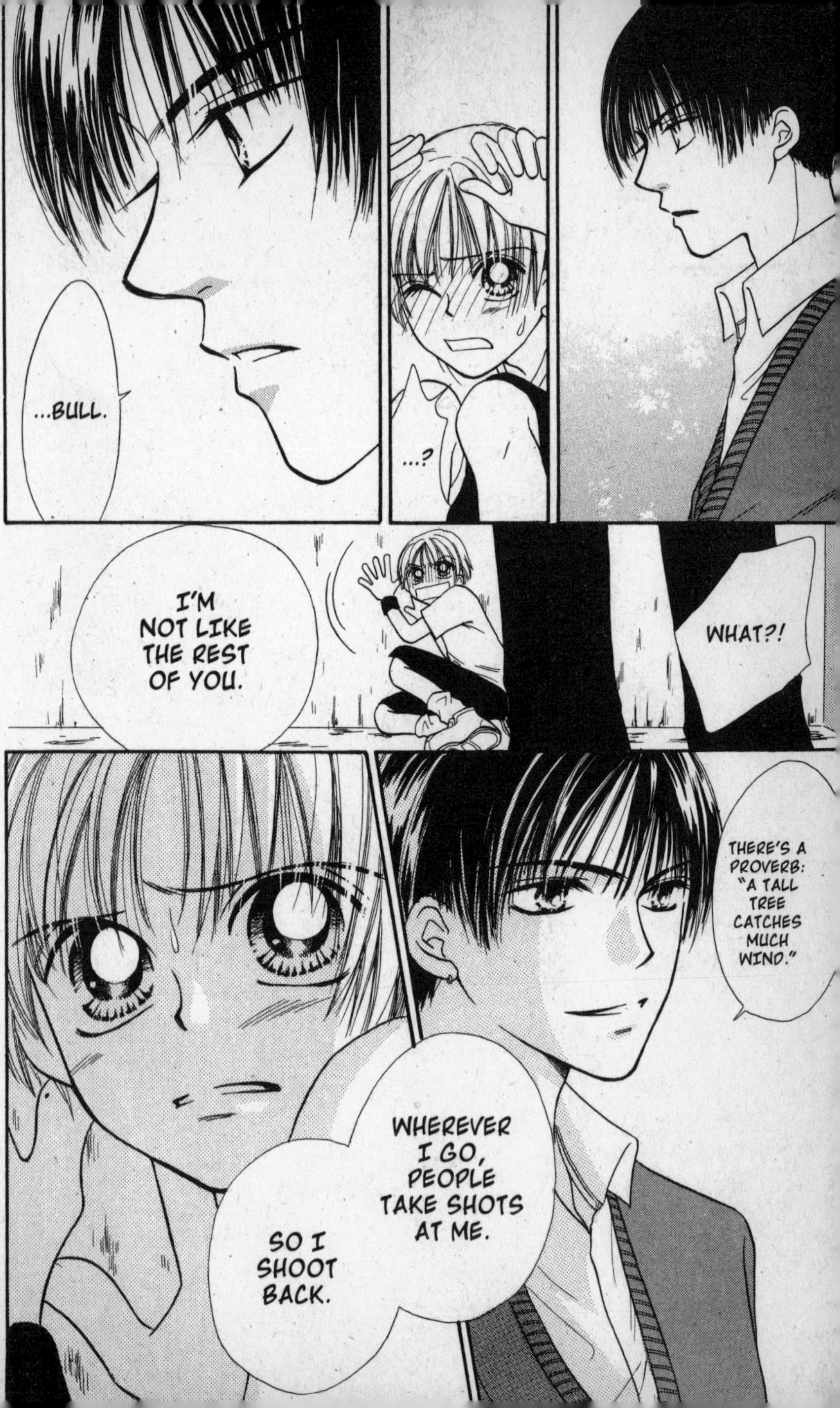
...?
...BULL.
WHAT?!
I'M NOT LIKE THE REST OF YOU.
THERE'S A PROVERB: "A TALL TREE CATCHES MUCH WIND."
WHEREVER I GO, PEOPLE TAKE SHOTS AT ME.
SO I SHOOT BACK.

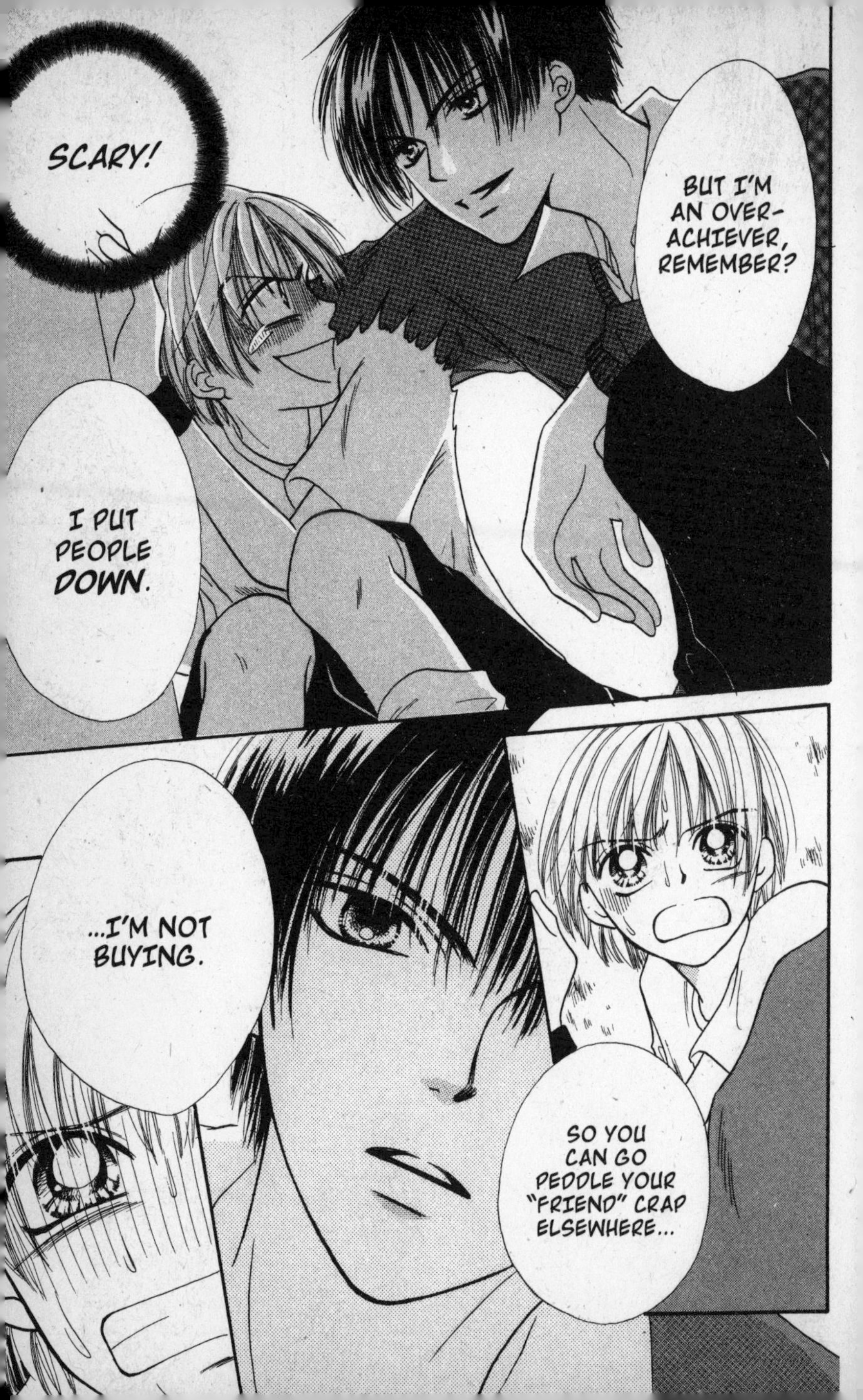
BUT I'M AN OVER-ACHIEVER, REMEMBER?
I PUT PEOPLE DOWN.
SCARY!
SO YOU CAN GO PEDDLE YOUR "FRIEND" CRAP ELSEWHERE...
...I'M NOT BUYING.

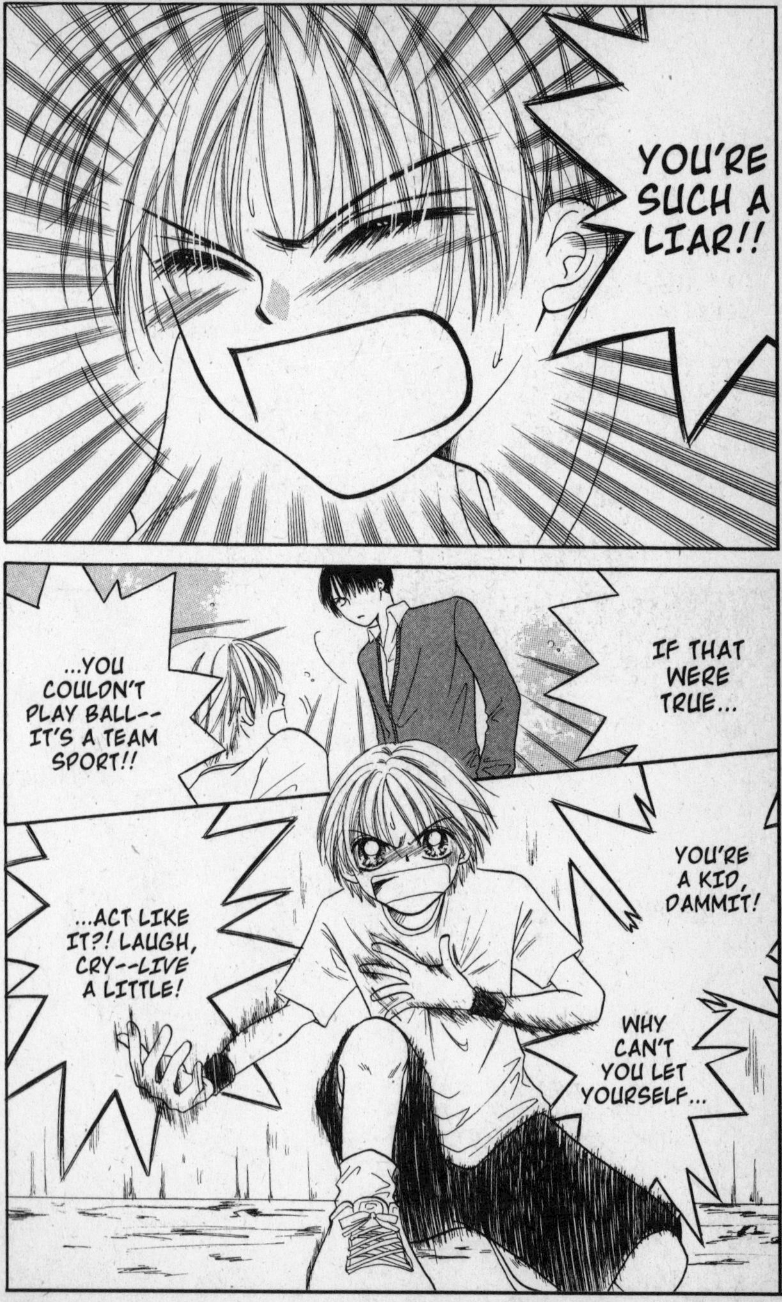
YOU'RE SUCH A LIAR!!
IF THAT WERE TRUE...
...YOU COULDN'T PLAY BALL--IT'S A TEAM SPORT!!
YOU'RE A KID, DAMMIT!
WHY CAN'T YOU LET YOURSELF...
...ACT LIKE IT?! LAUGH, CRY--LIVE A LITTLE!

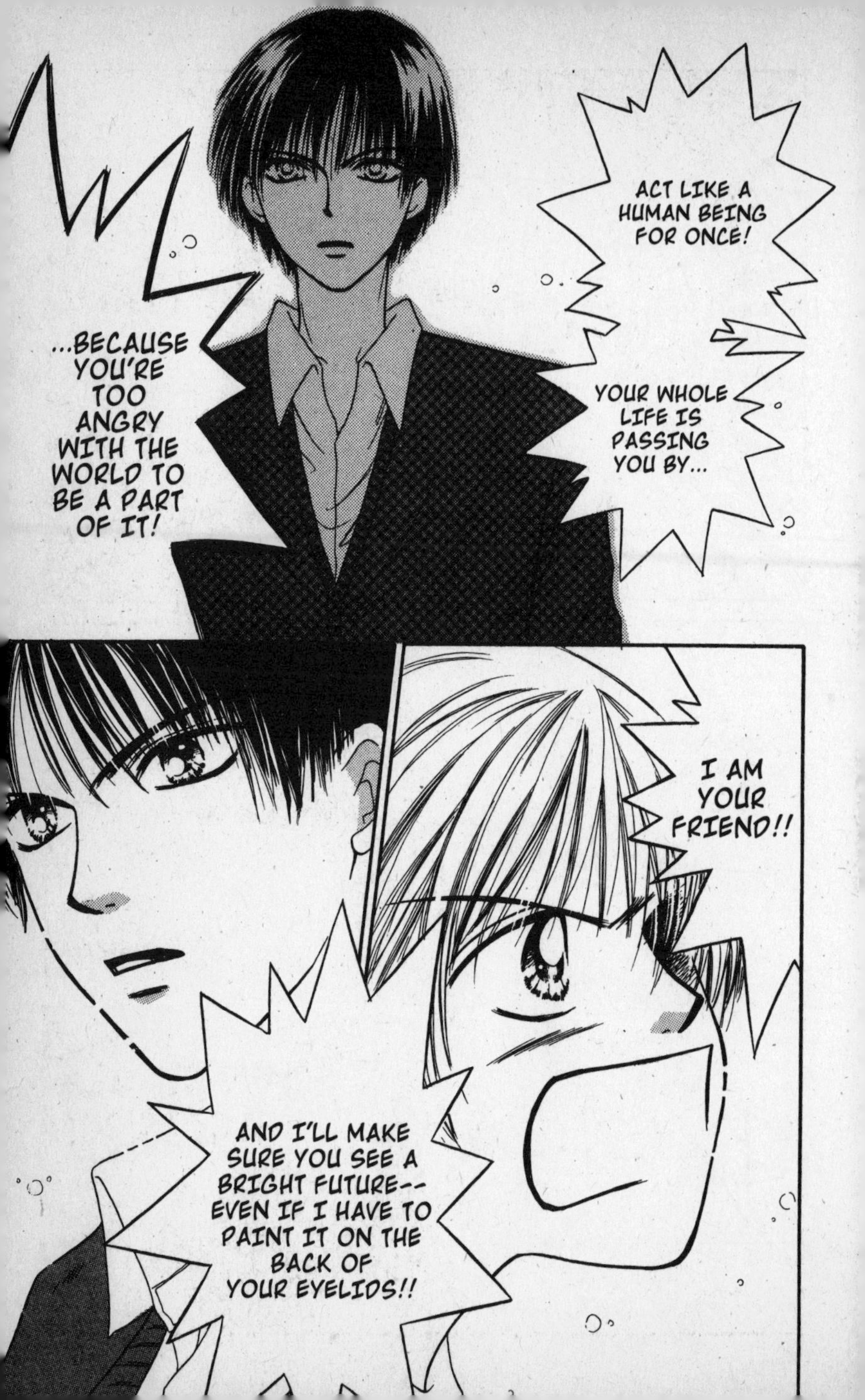
ACT LIKE A HUMAN BEING FOR ONCE!
YOUR WHOLE LIFE IS PASSING YOU BY...
...BECAUSE YOU'RE TOO ANGRY WITH THE WORLD TO BE A PART OF IT!
I AM YOUR FRIEND!!
AND I'LL MAKE SURE YOU SEE A BRIGHT FUTURE--EVEN IF I HAVE TO PAINT IT ON THE BACK OF YOUR EYELIDS!!

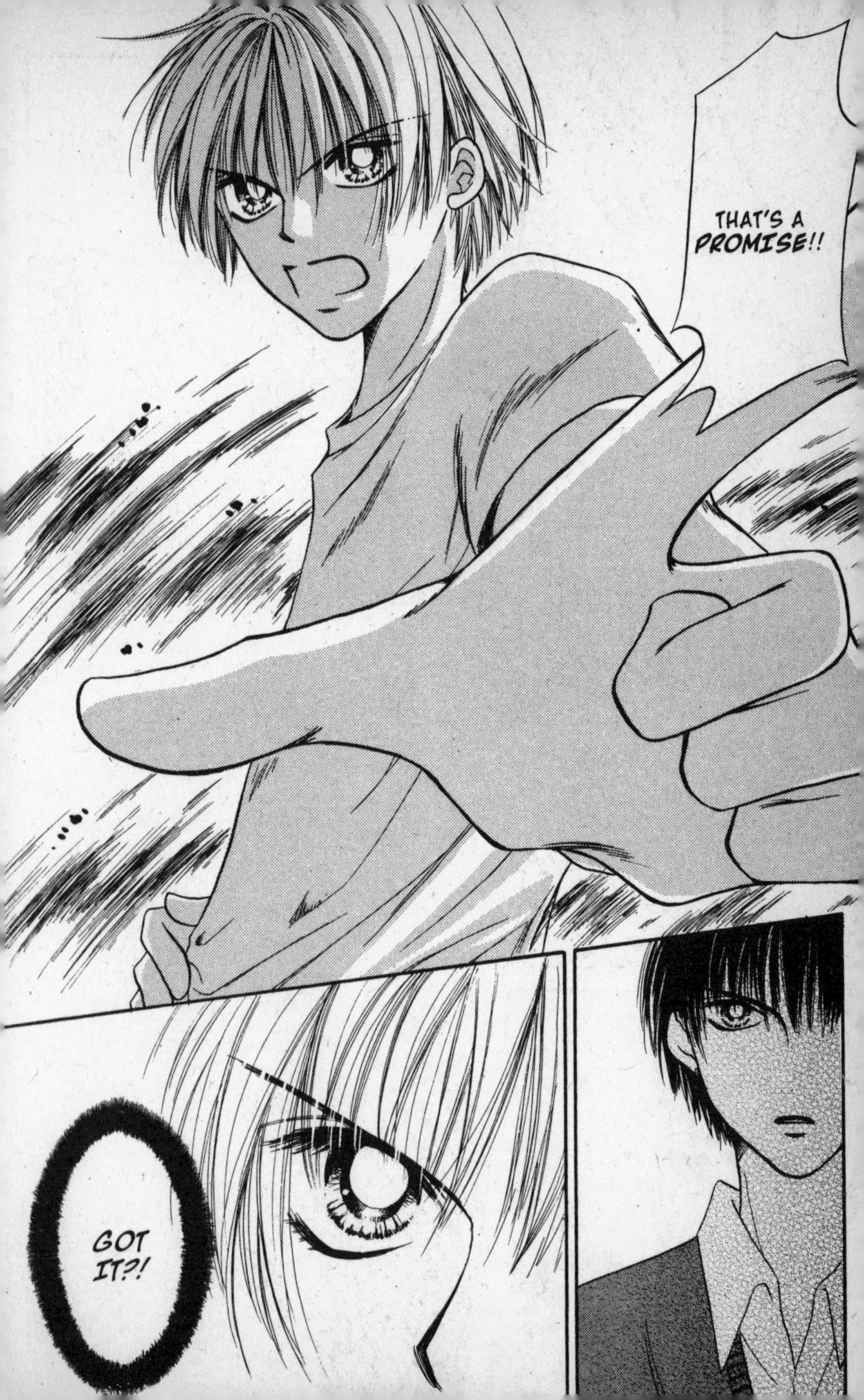
THAT'S A PROMISE!!
GOT IT?!

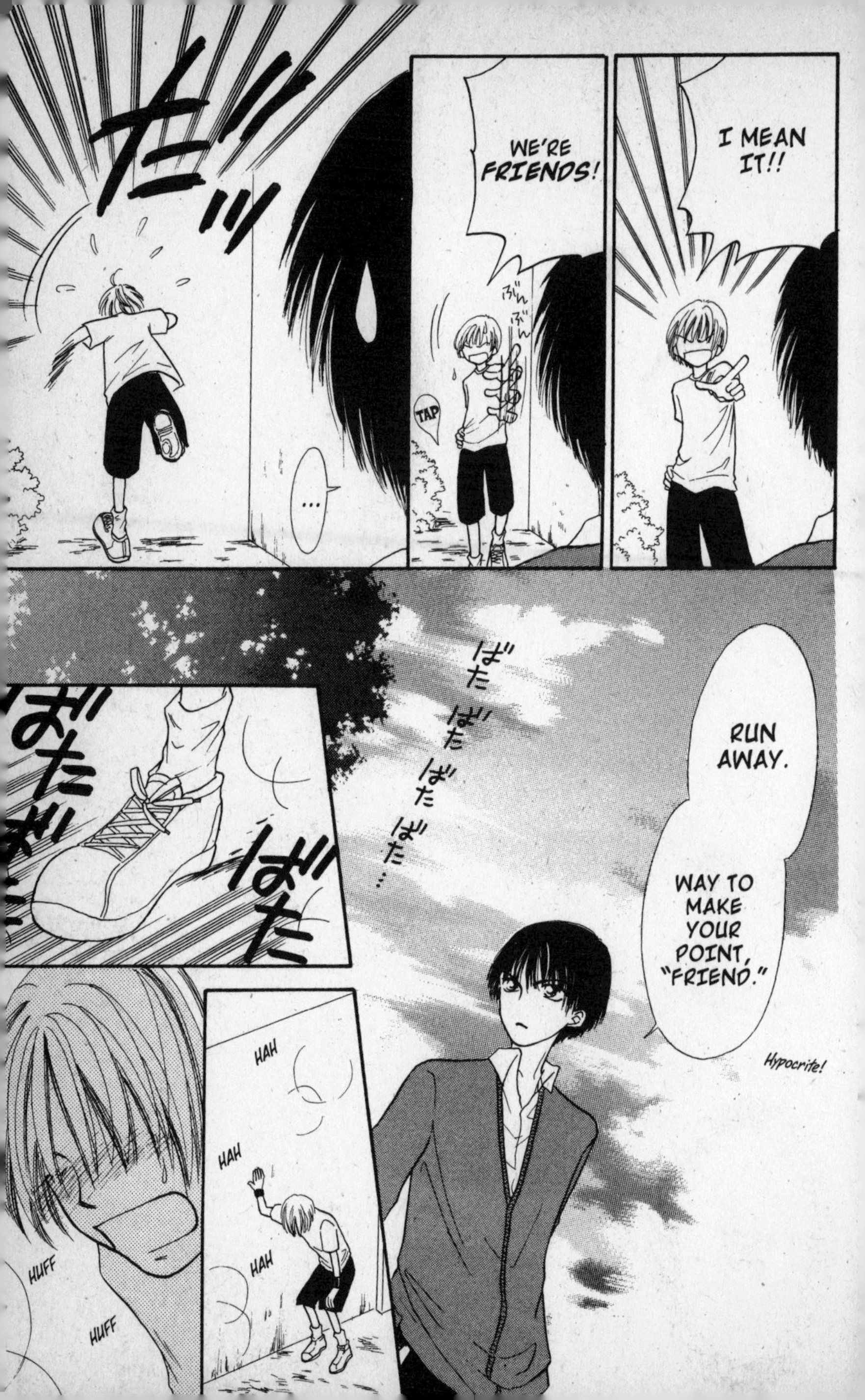

I MEAN IT!!
WE'RE FRIENDS!
ぶんぶん
TAP
たッ
...
RUN AWAY.
WAY TO MAKE YOUR POINT, "FRIEND."
Hypocrite!
ばたばたばたばた…
ばたばた
HAH
HAH
HAH
HUFF
HUFF

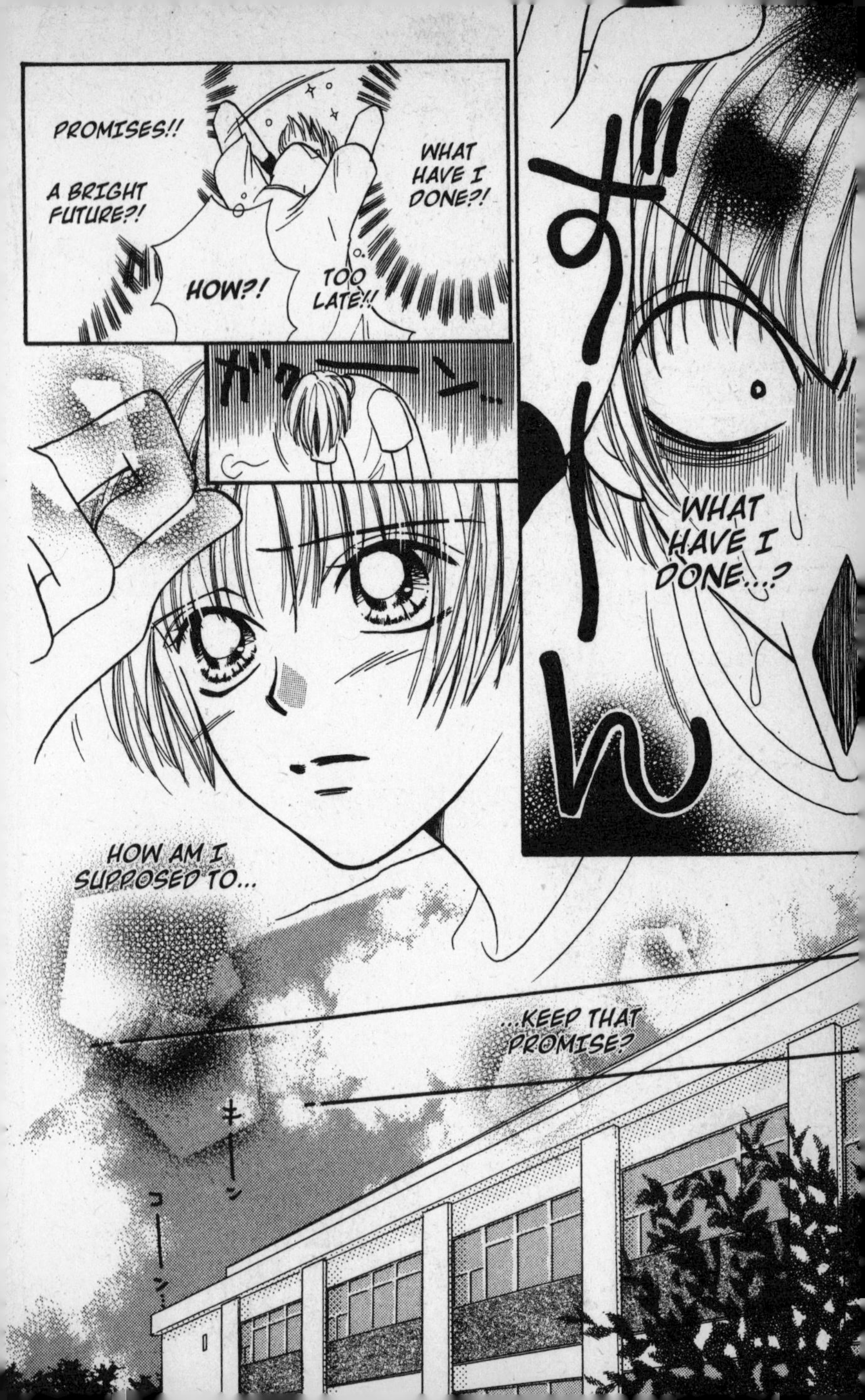
WHAT HAVE I DONE...?
WHAT HAVE I DONE?!
PROMISES!!
A BRIGHT FUTURE?!
TOO LATE!!
HOW?!
HOW AM I SUPPOSED TO...
...KEEP THAT PROMISE?

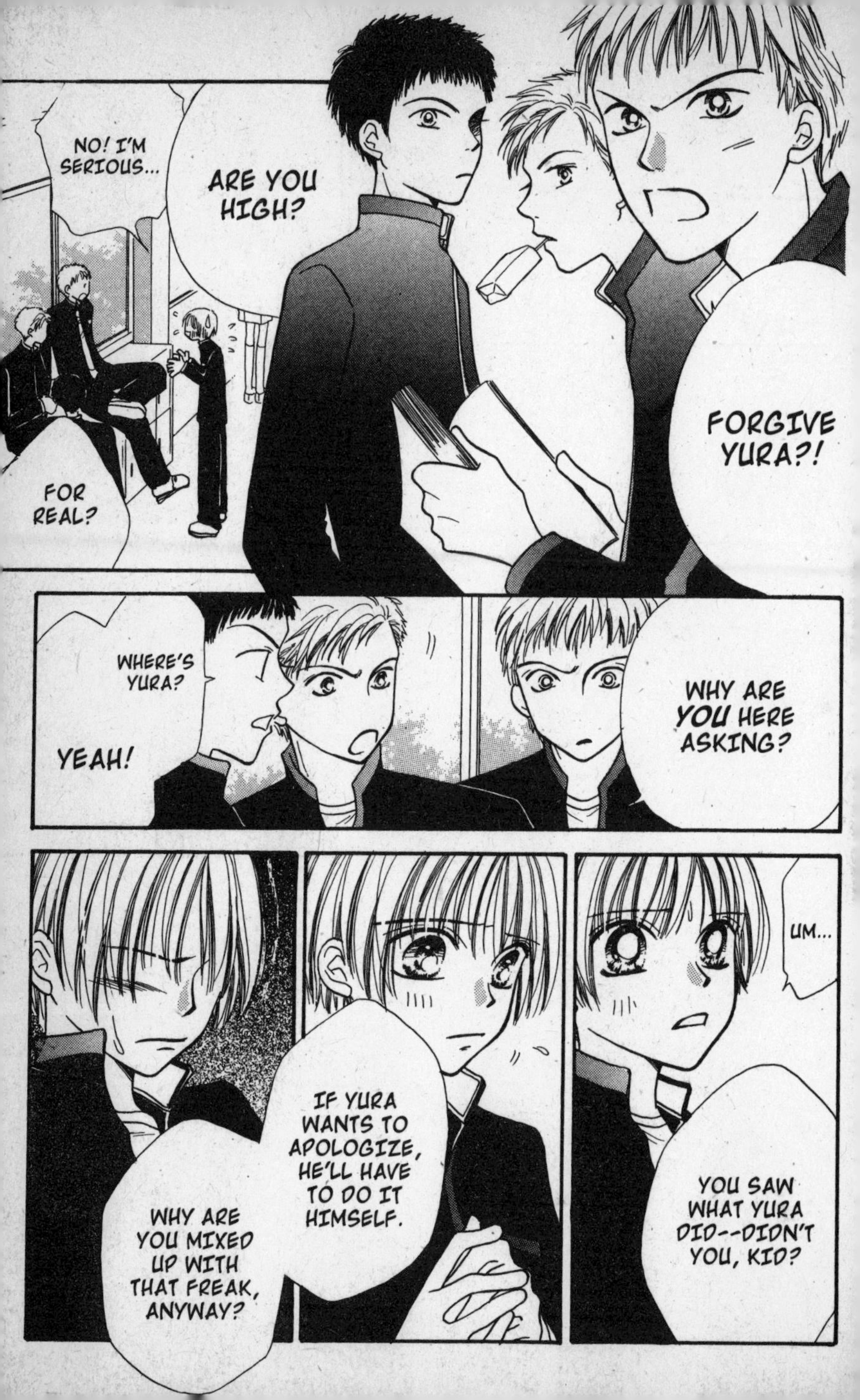
FORGIVE YURA?!
ARE YOU HIGH?
NO! I'M SERIOUS...
FOR REAL?
WHY ARE YOU HERE ASKING?
WHERE'S YURA?
YEAH!
UM...
YOU SAW WHAT YURA DID--DIDN'T YOU, KID?
IF YURA WANTS TO APOLOGIZE, HE'LL HAVE TO DO IT HIMSELF.
WHY ARE YOU MIXED UP WITH THAT FREAK, ANYWAY?

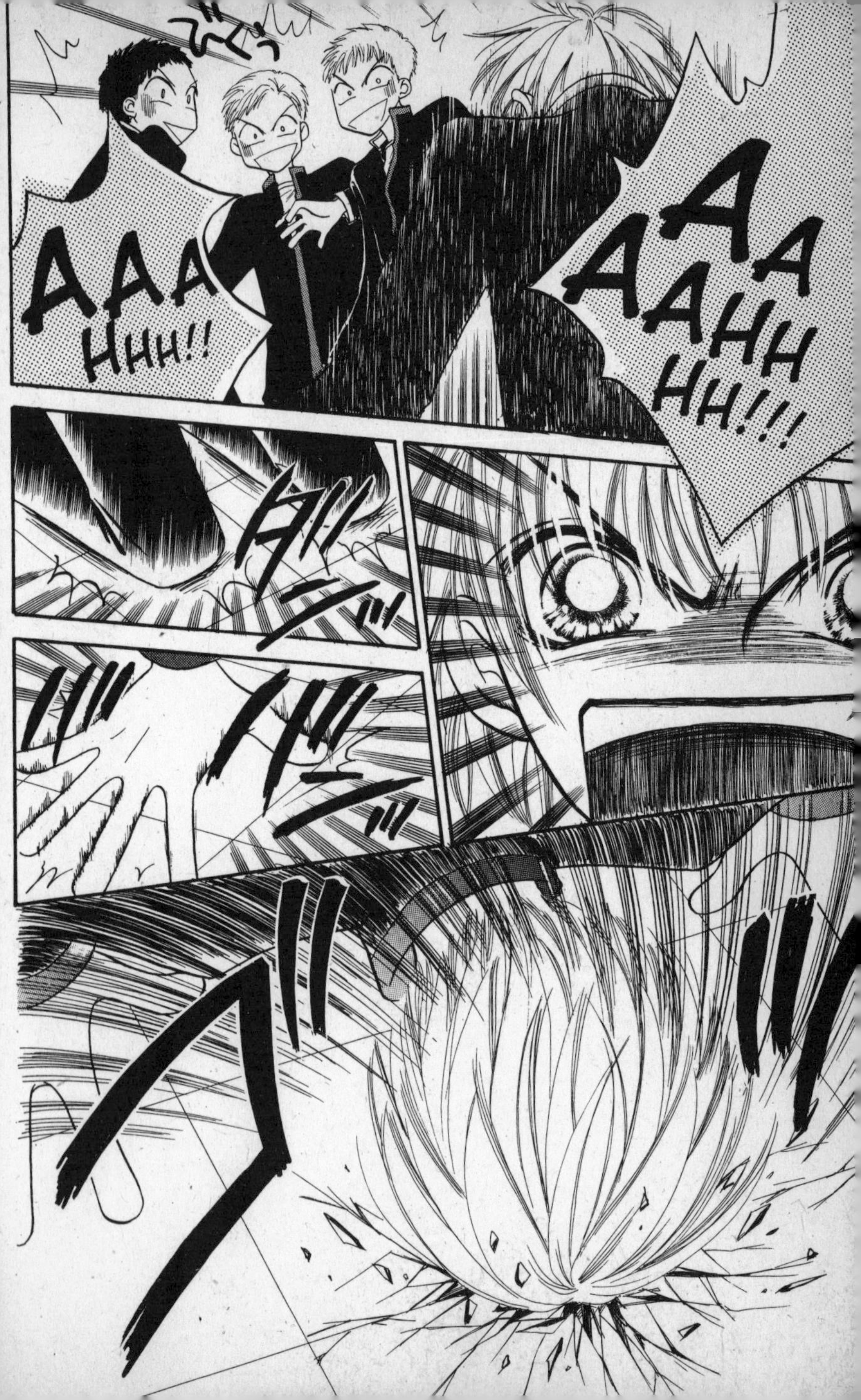
AAAAAHHHH!!!
びくっ
AAAHHH!!

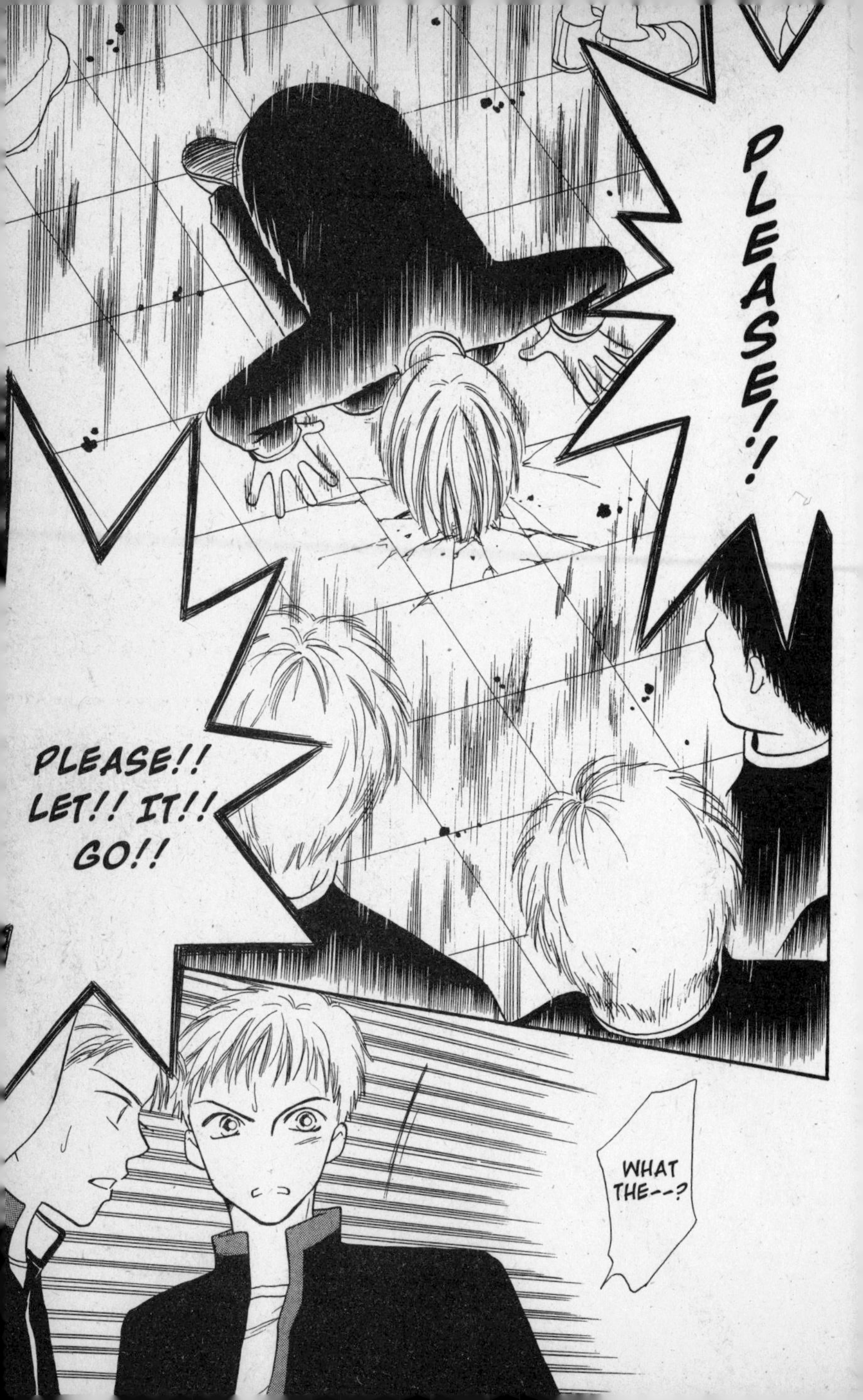
PLEASE!!
PLEASE!! LET!! IT!! GO!!
WHAT THE--?

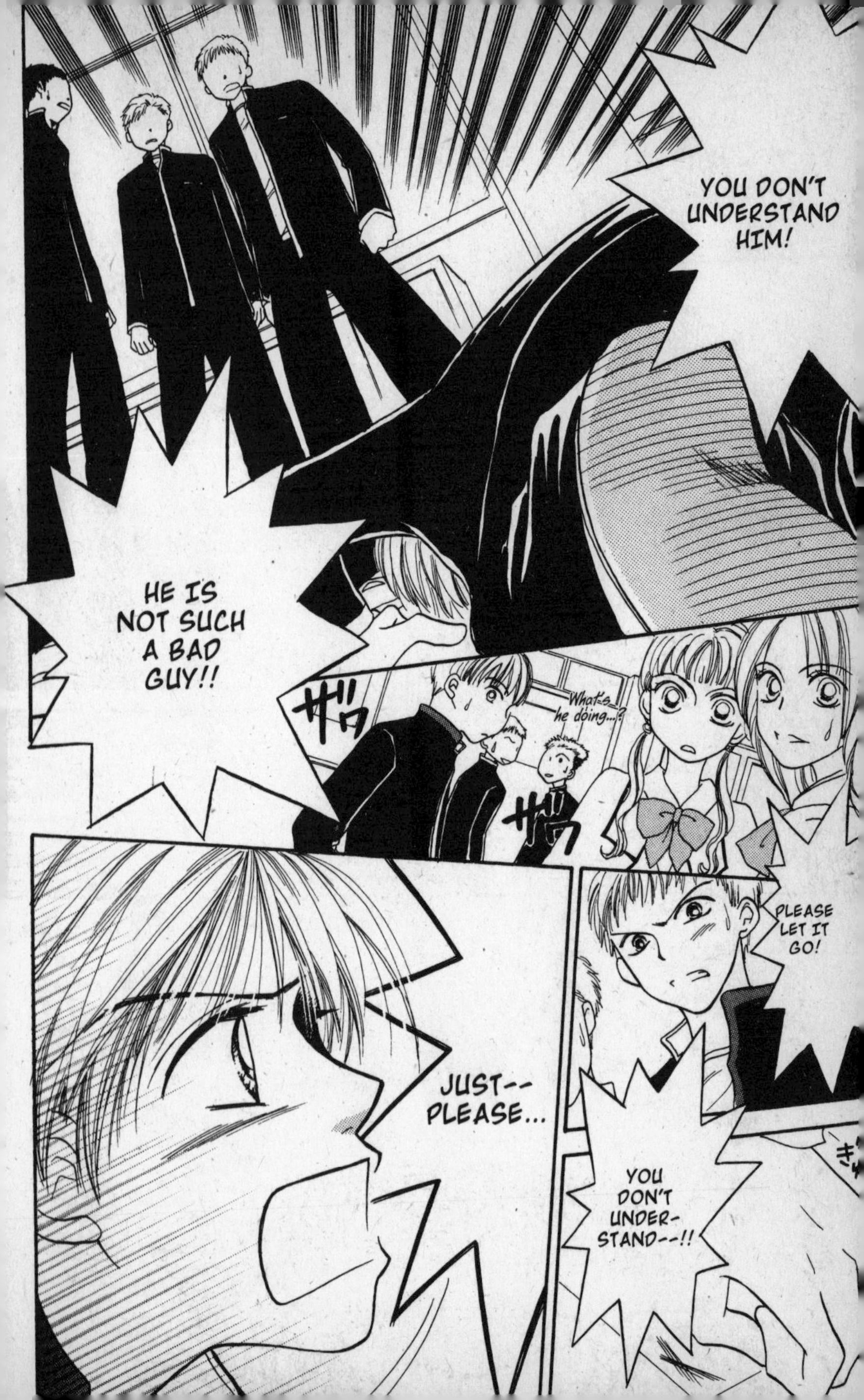
YOU DON'T UNDERSTAND HIM!
HE IS NOT SUCH A BAD GUY!!
ザワ
What's he doing...?
ザワ
PLEASE LET IT GO!
YOU DON'T UNDER-STAND--!!
JUST-- PLEASE...

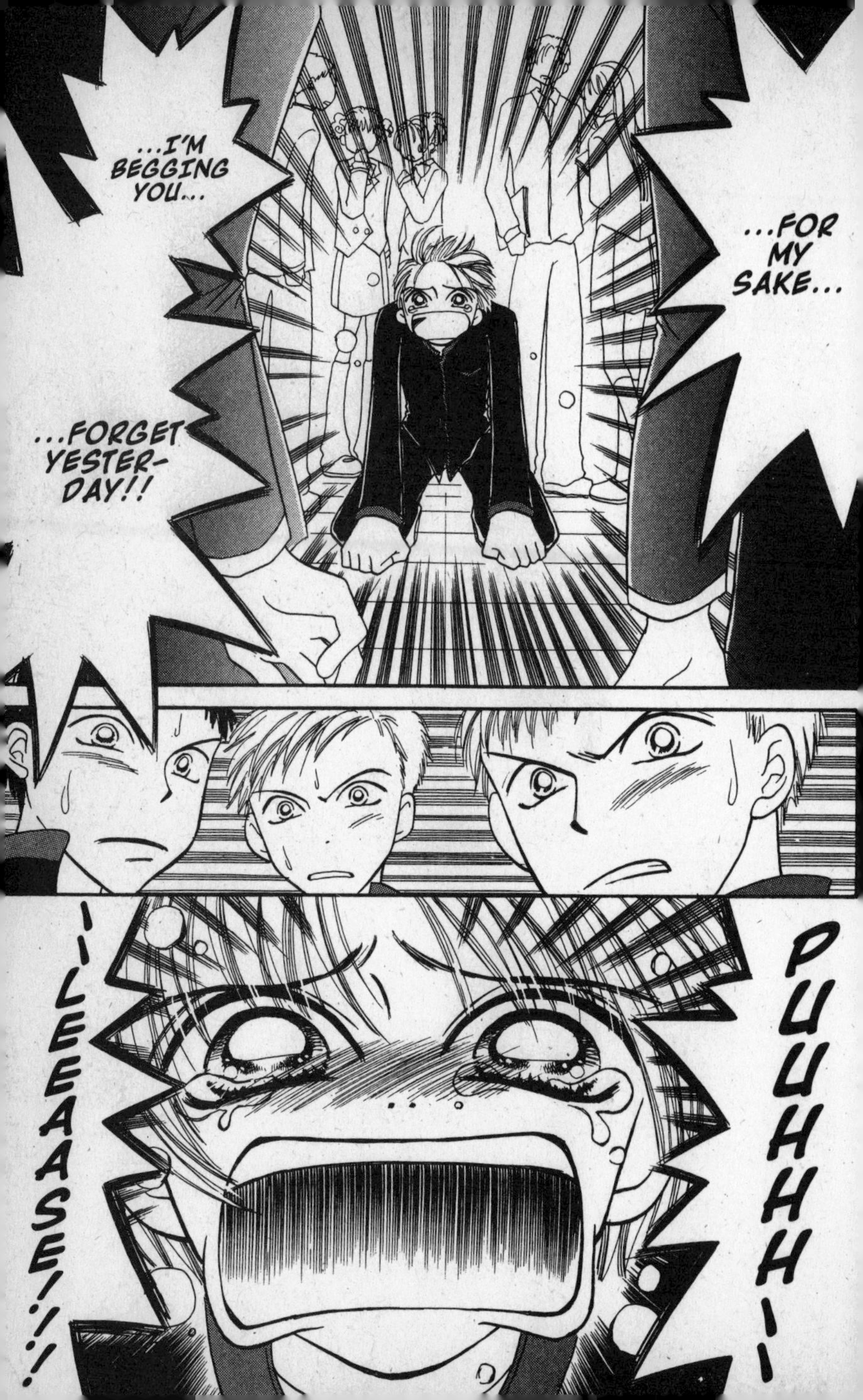
...FOR MY SAKE...
...I'M BEGGING YOU...
...FORGET YESTER-DAY!!
PUUHHH--
--LEEAASE!!!

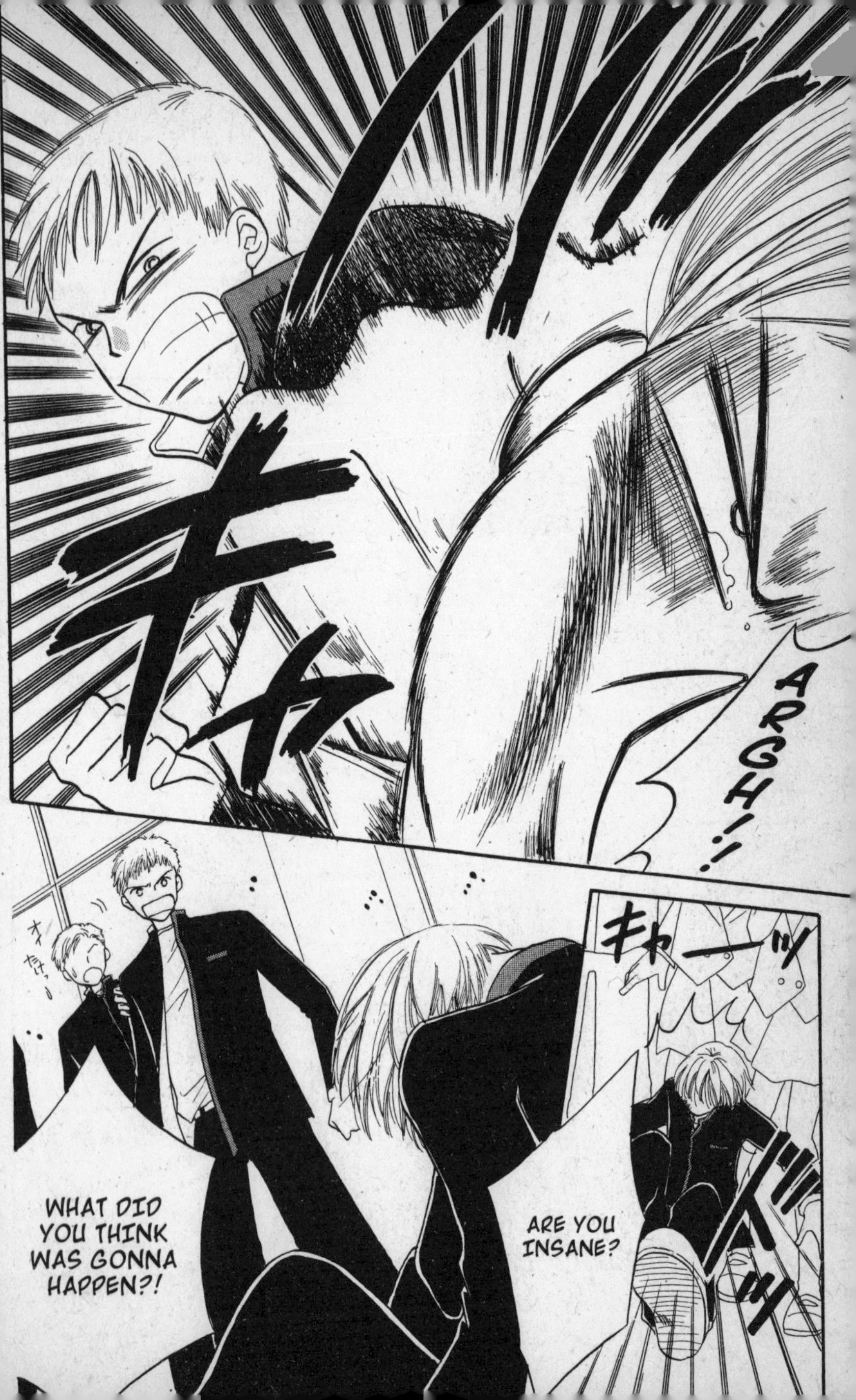
ARGH!!!
キャーーッ
ARE YOU INSANE?
WHAT DID YOU THINK WAS GONNA HAPPEN?!

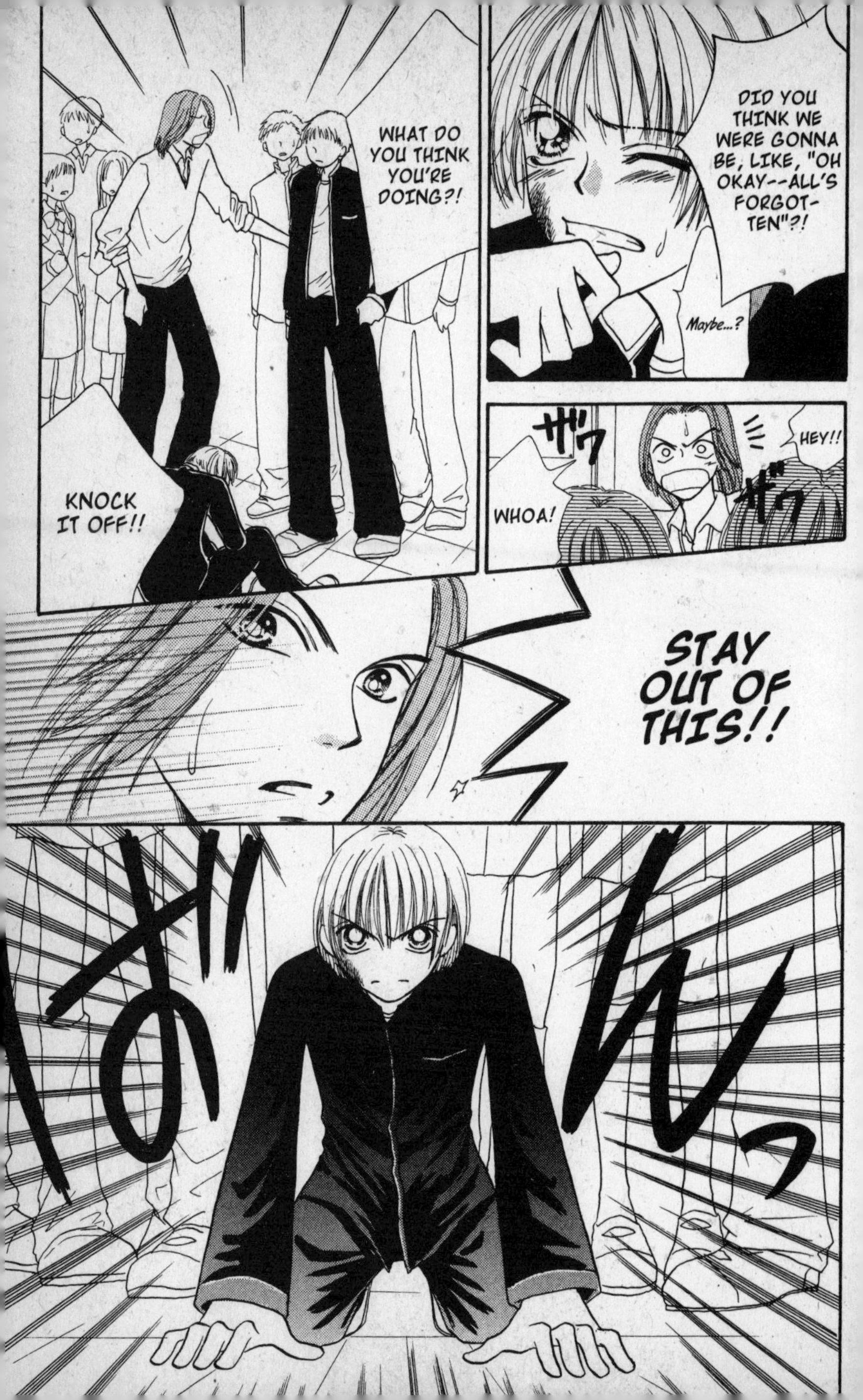
DID YOU THINK WE WERE GONNA BE, LIKE, "OH OKAY--ALL'S FORGOT-TEN"?!
Maybe...?
HEY!!
ザワ
WHOA!
ザワ
WHAT DO YOU THINK YOU'RE DOING?!
KNOCK IT OFF!!
STAY OUT OF THIS!!

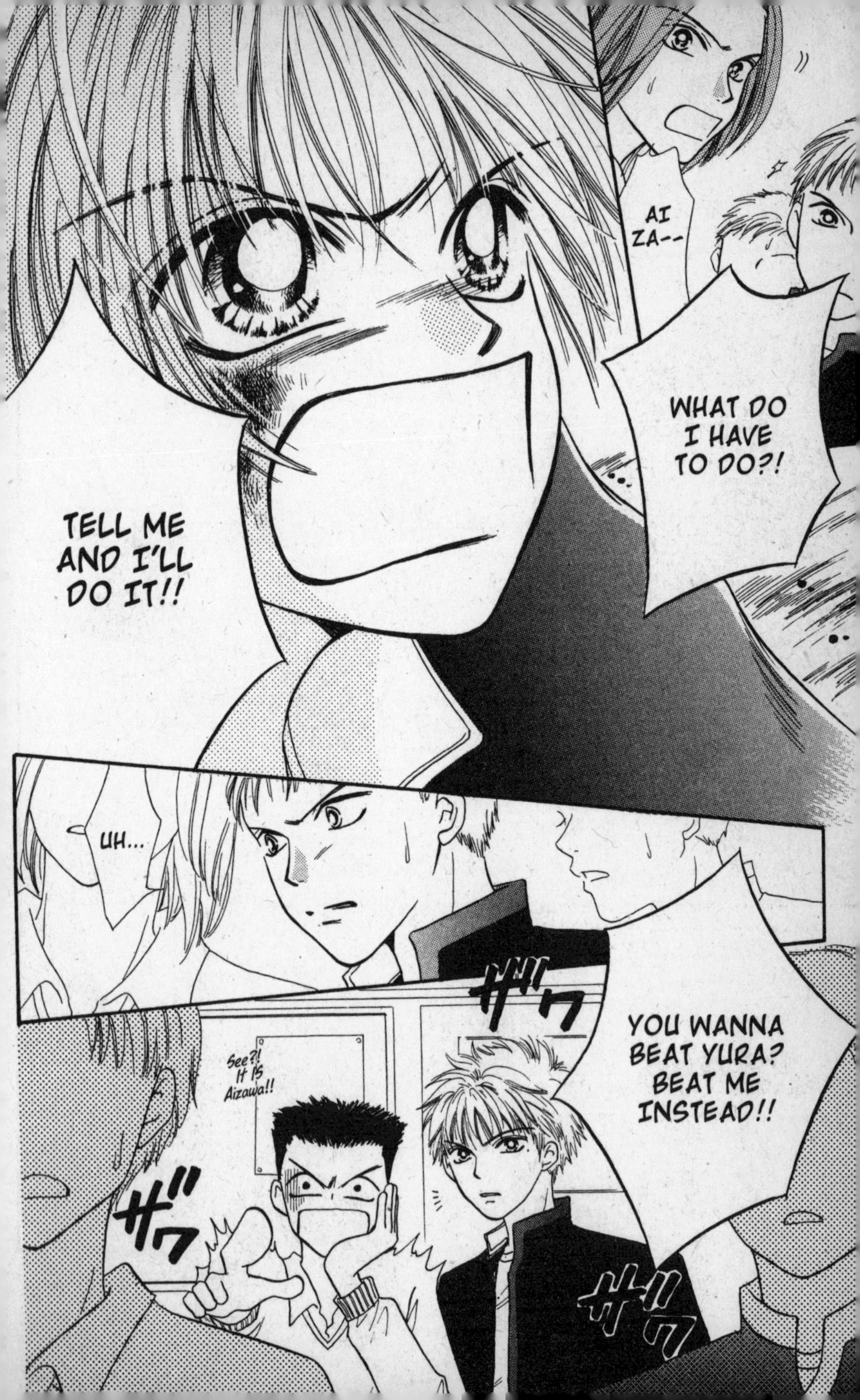
AI ZA--
WHAT DO I HAVE TO DO?!
TELL ME AND I'LL DO IT!!
UH...
ザワ
YOU WANNA BEAT YURA? BEAT ME INSTEAD!!
See?! It IS Aizawa!!
ザワ
ザワ

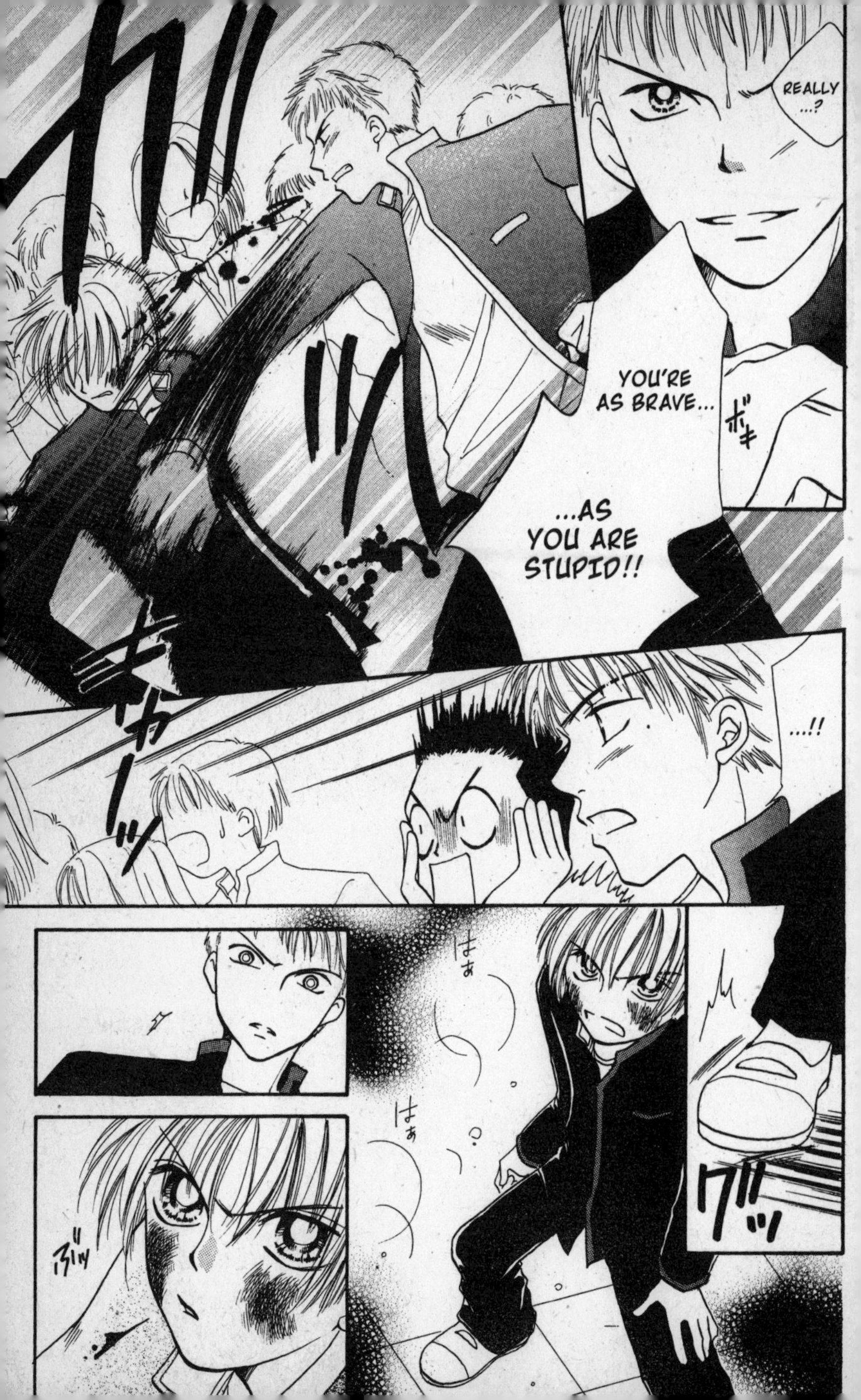
REALLY ...?
YOU'RE AS BRAVE...
ボキ
...AS YOU ARE STUPID!!
ガッ
...!!
ガターン
ワッ
はぁ
はぁ
ぶりッ

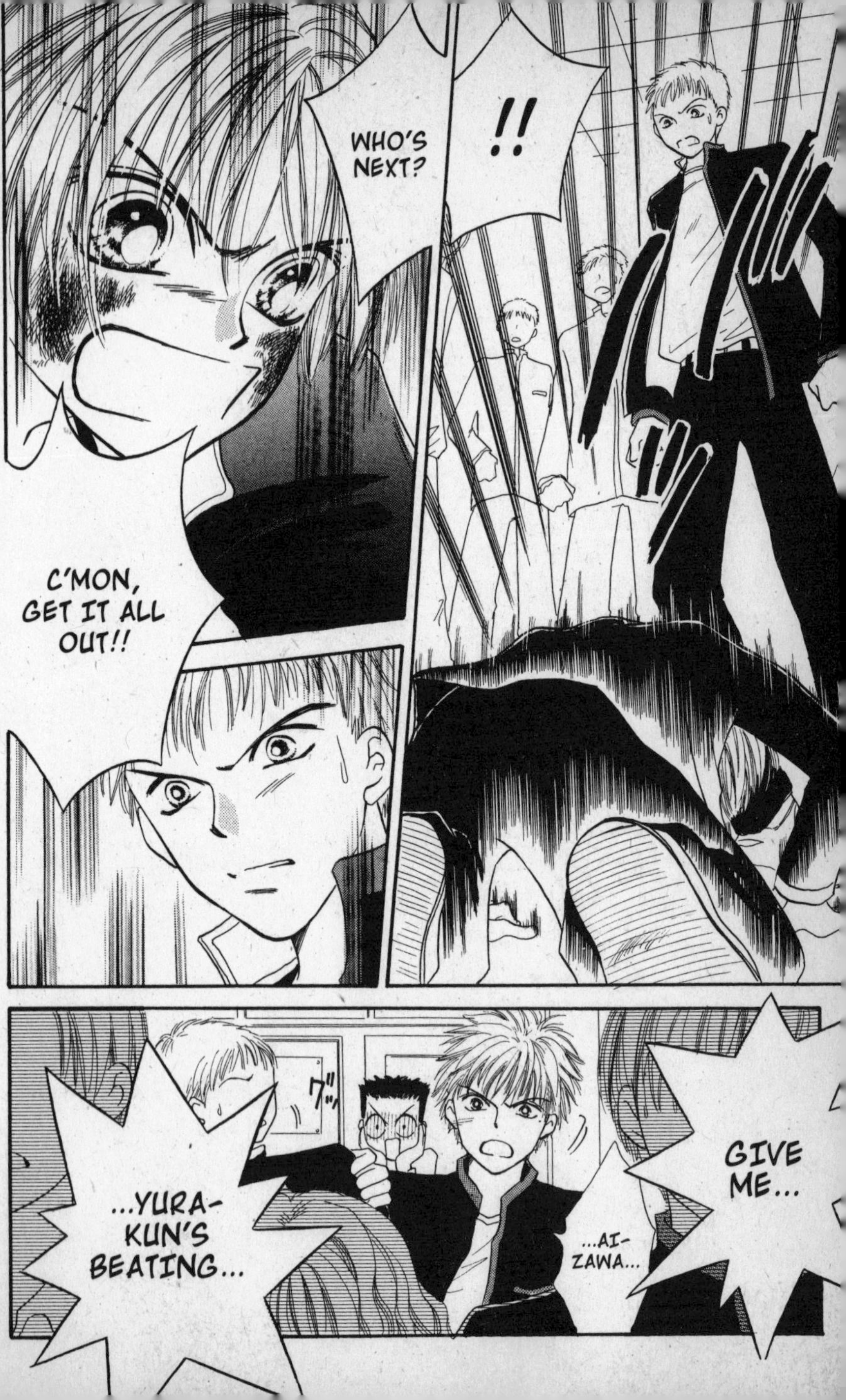
!!
WHO'S NEXT?
C'MON, GET IT ALL OUT!!
GIVE ME...
...AI-ZAWA...
...YURA-KUN'S BEATING...

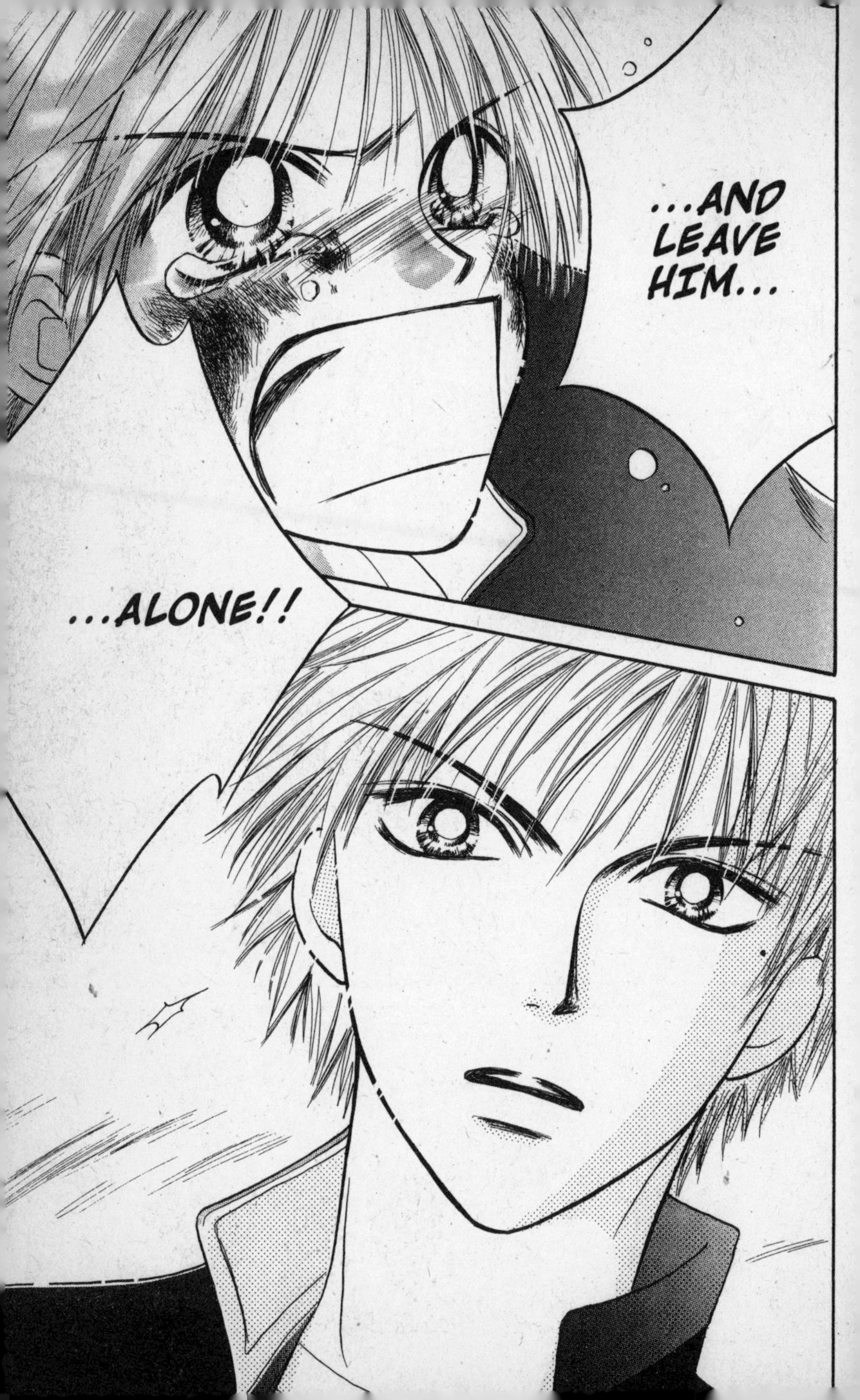
...AND LEAVE HIM...
...ALONE!!

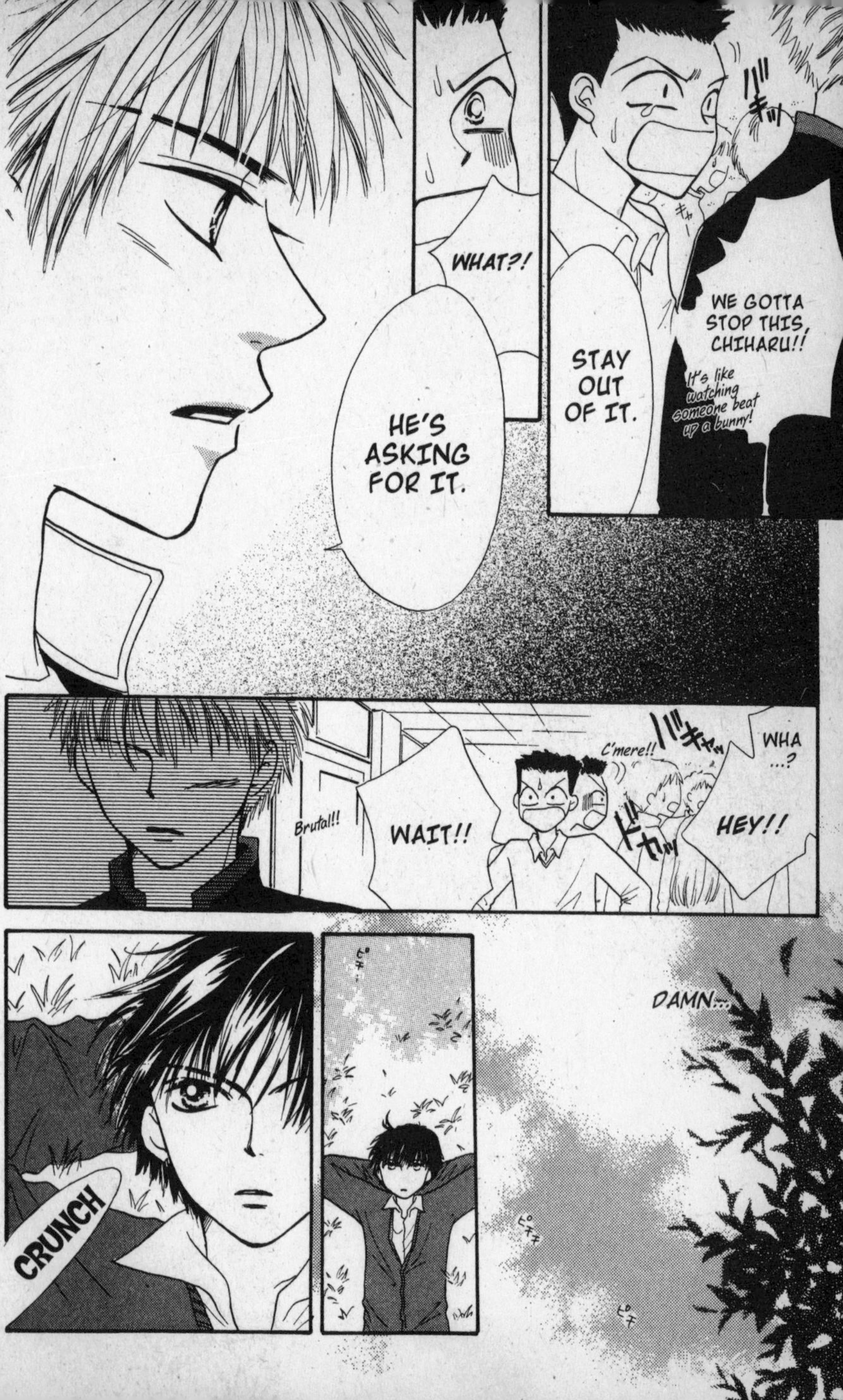
WE GOTTA STOP THIS, CHIHARU!!
It's like watching someone beat up a bunny!
STAY OUT OF IT.
WHAT?!
HE'S ASKING FOR IT.
WHA ...?
HEY!!
C'mere!!
WAIT!!
Brutal!!
DAMN...
CRUNCH

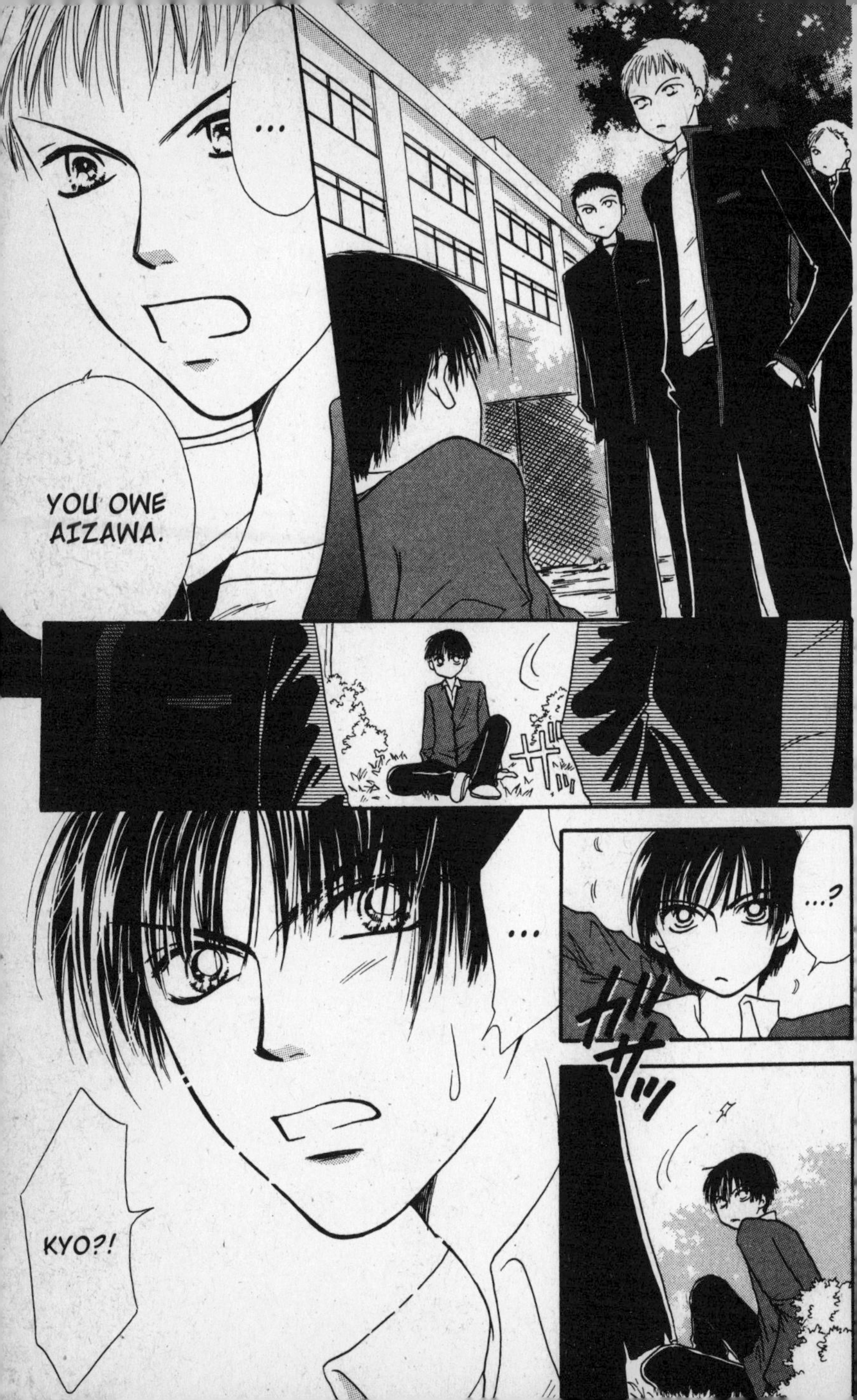
...
YOU OWE AIZAWA.
...?
...
KYO?!

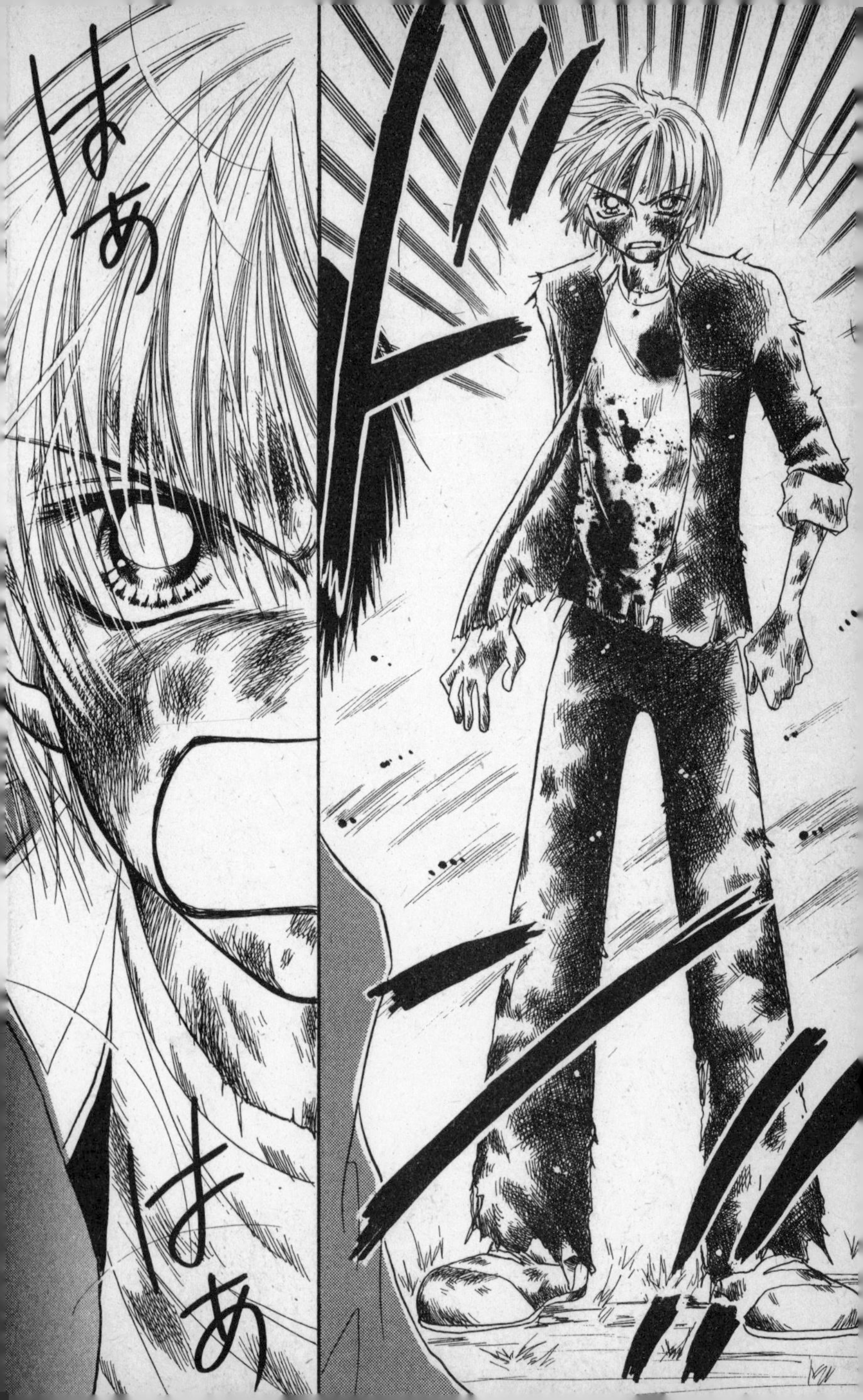
ド
はぁ
はぁ

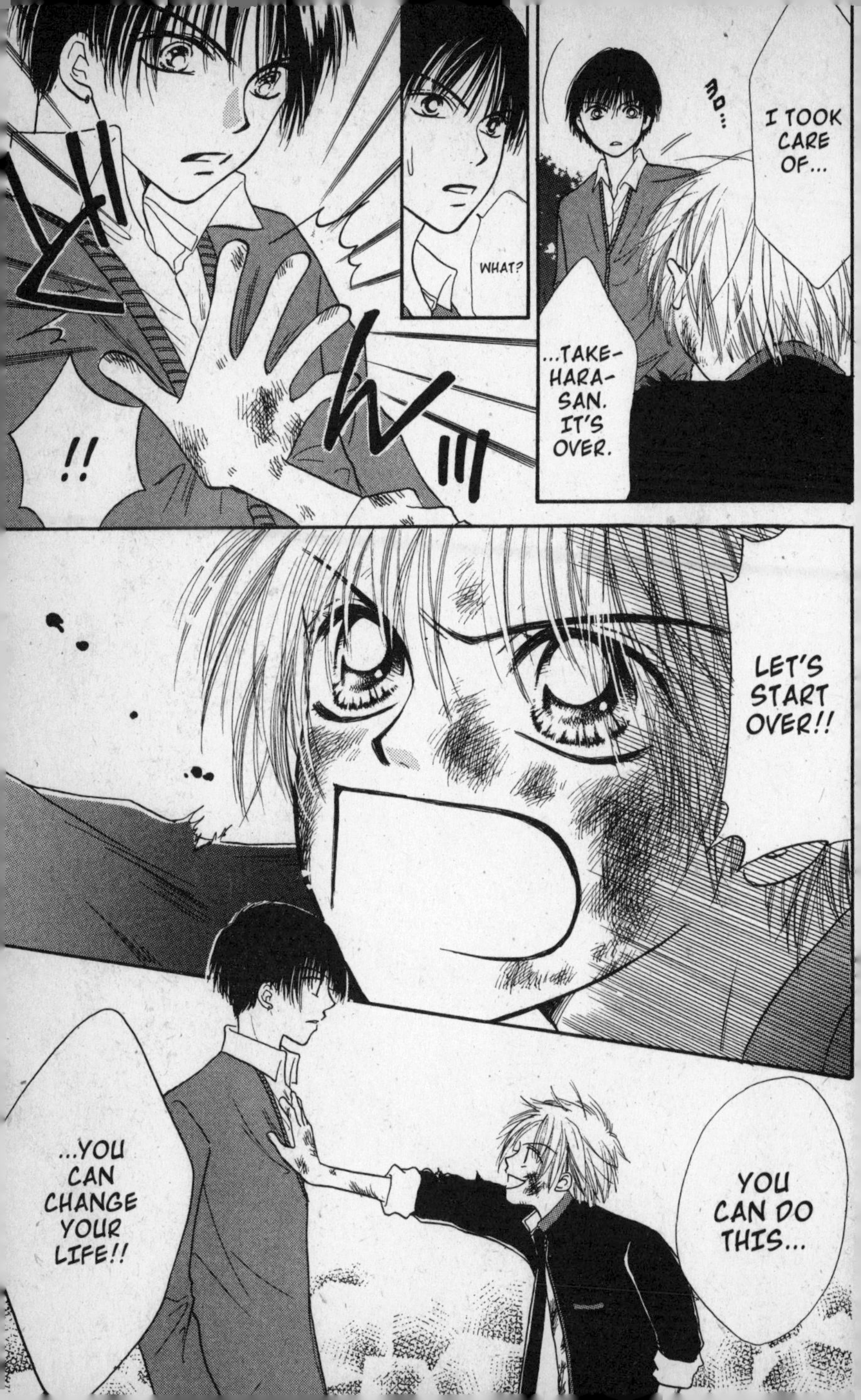
I TOOK CARE OF...
...TAKE-HARA-SAN. IT'S OVER.
WHAT?
!!
LET'S START OVER!!
YOU CAN DO THIS...
...YOU CAN CHANGE YOUR LIFE!!

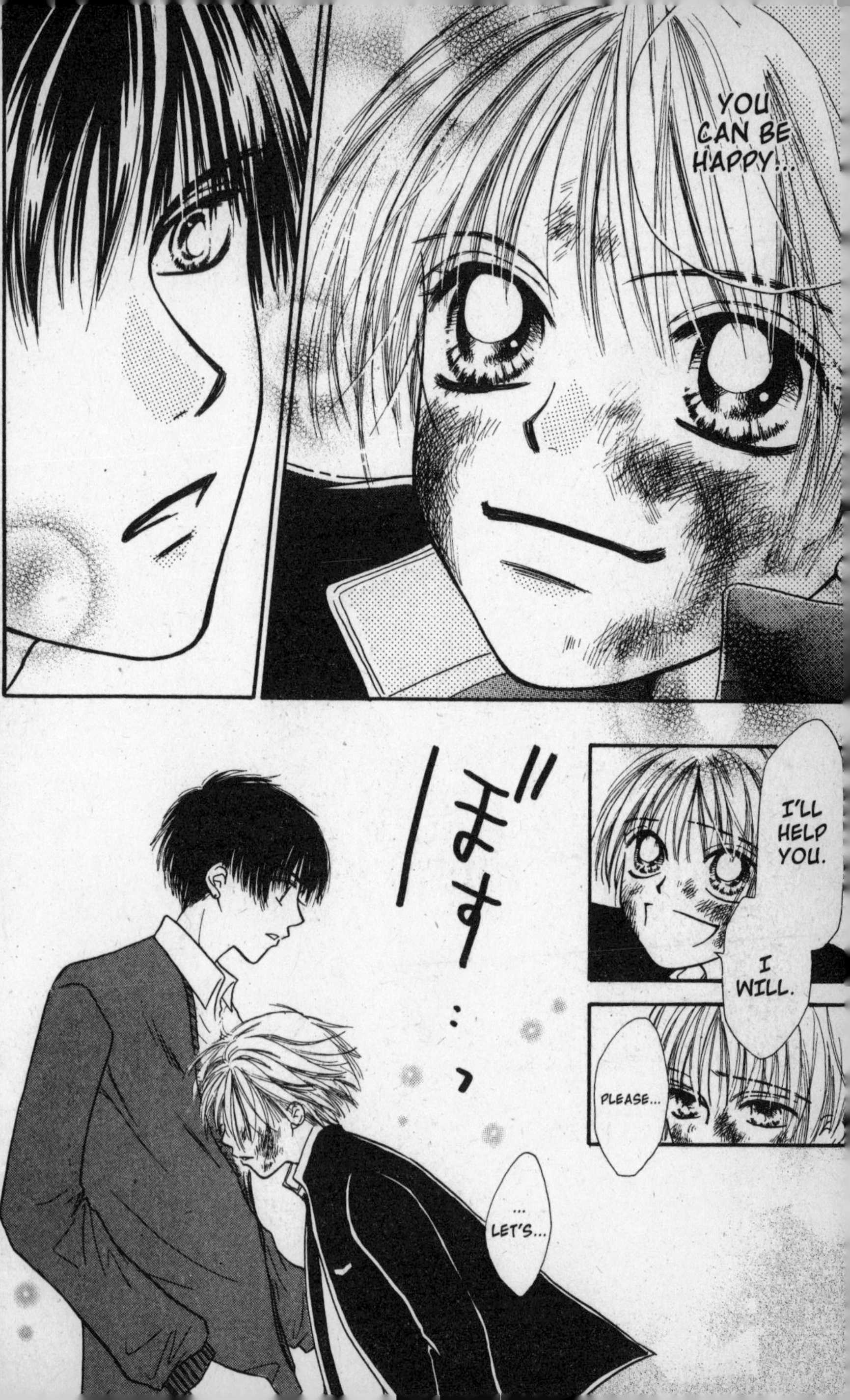

YOU CAN BE HAPPY!...
I'LL HELP YOU.
I WILL.
PLEASE...
ぼす…っ
...LET'S...

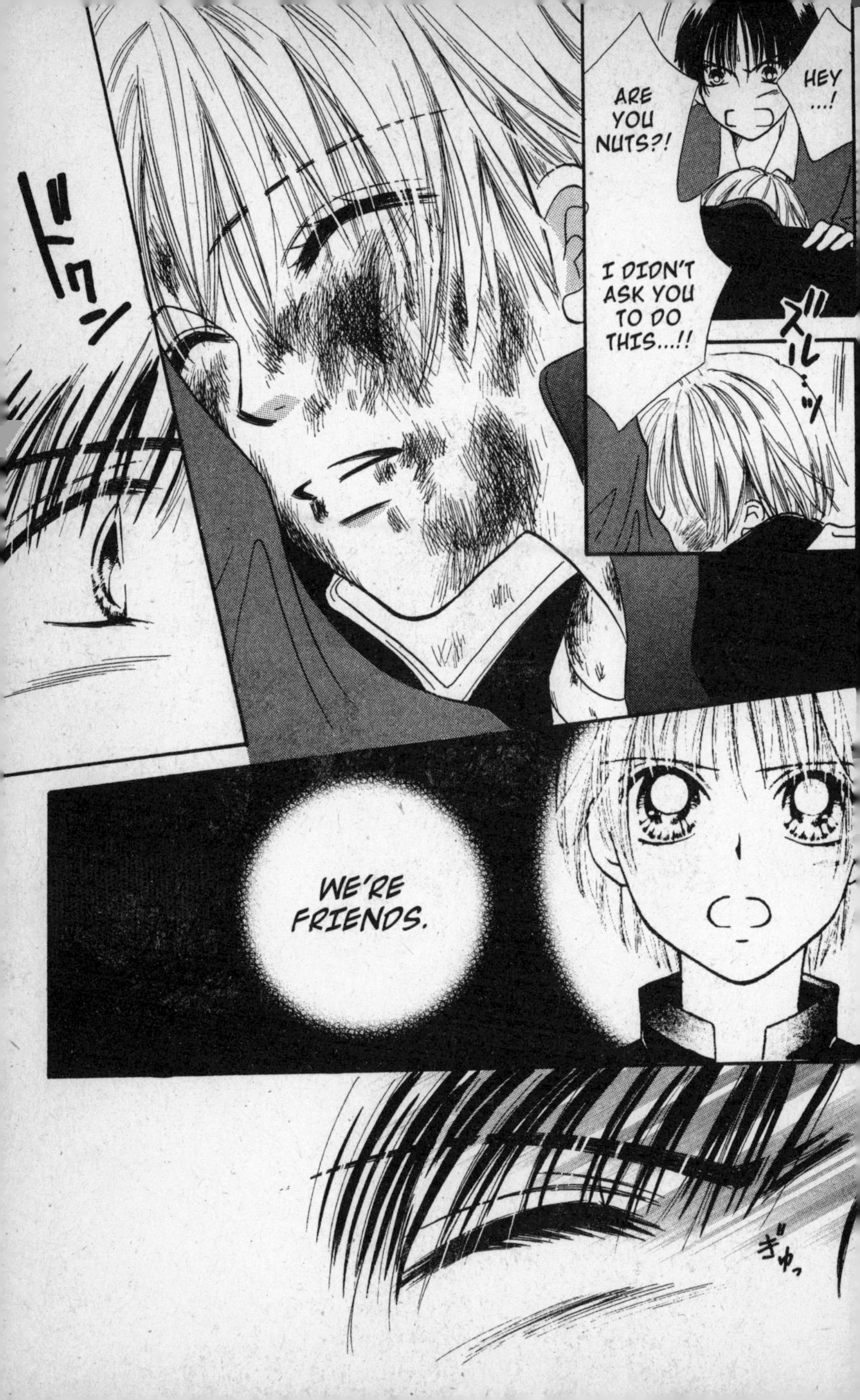
HEY ...!
ARE YOU NUTS?!
I DIDN'T ASK YOU TO DO THIS...!!
ズル…ッ
ドクン
WE'RE FRIENDS.
ぎゅっ

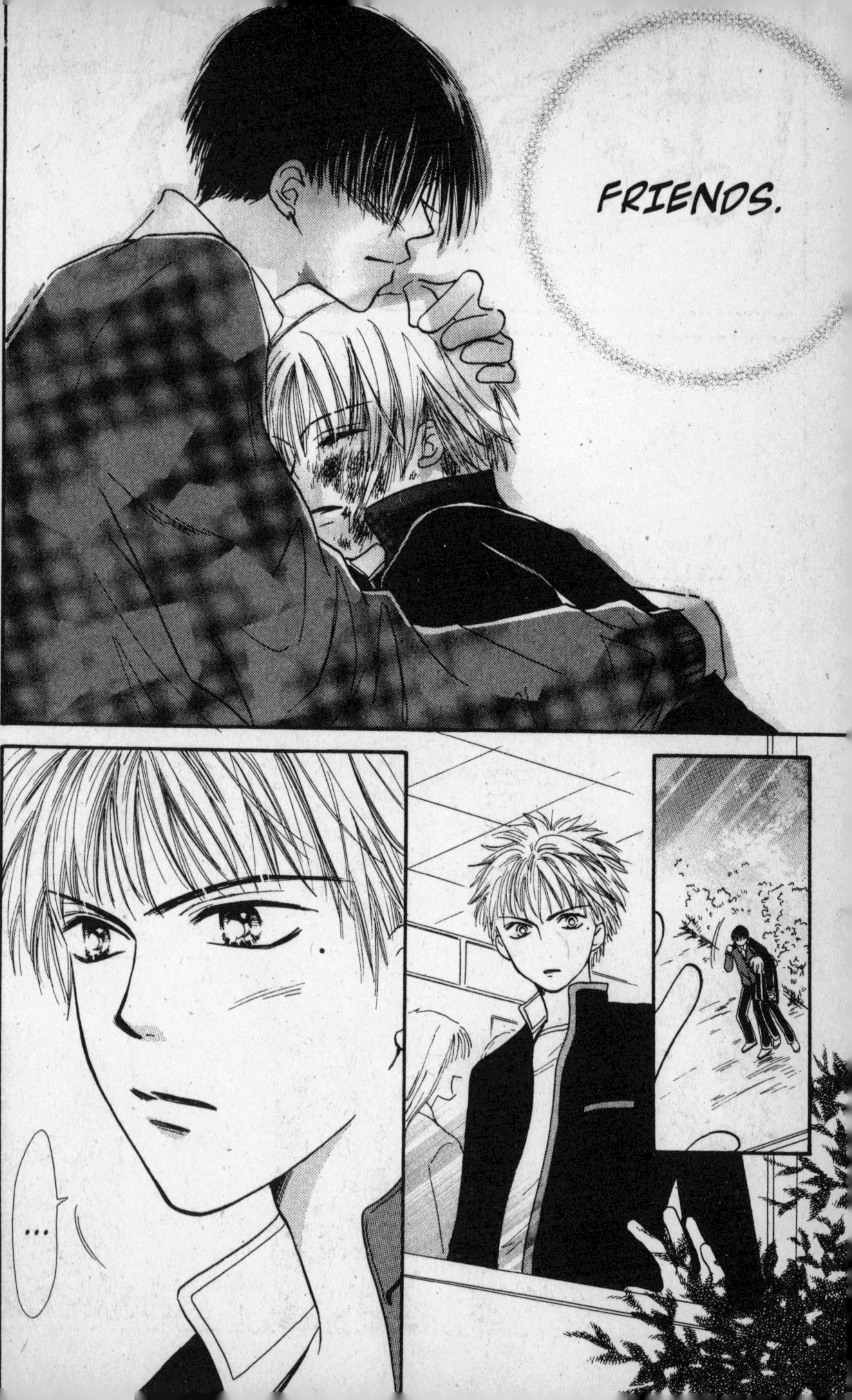
FRIENDS.
...

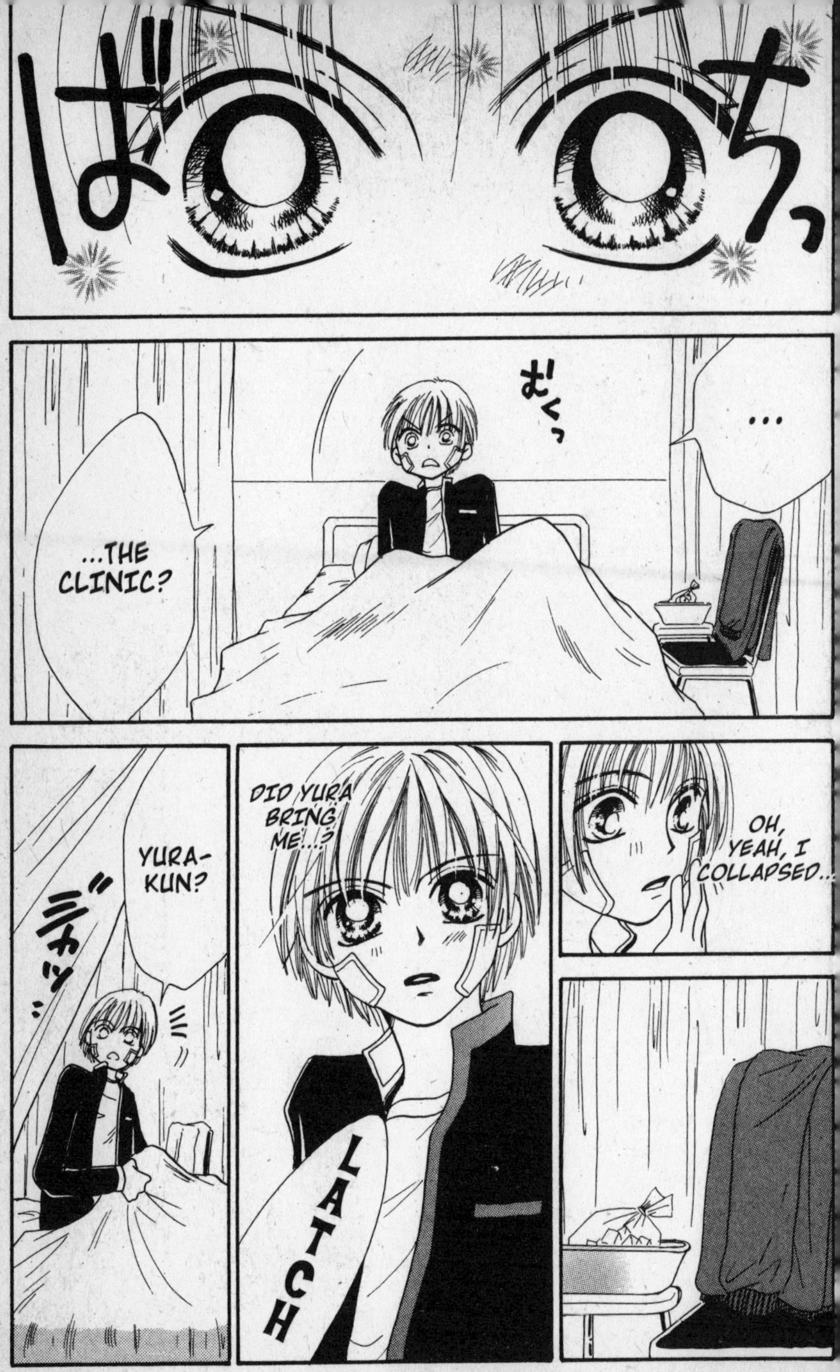
ぱちっ
...
むくっ
...THE CLINIC?
OH, YEAH, I COLLAPSED...
DID YURA BRING ME...?
LATCH
YURA-KUN?
ジャッ

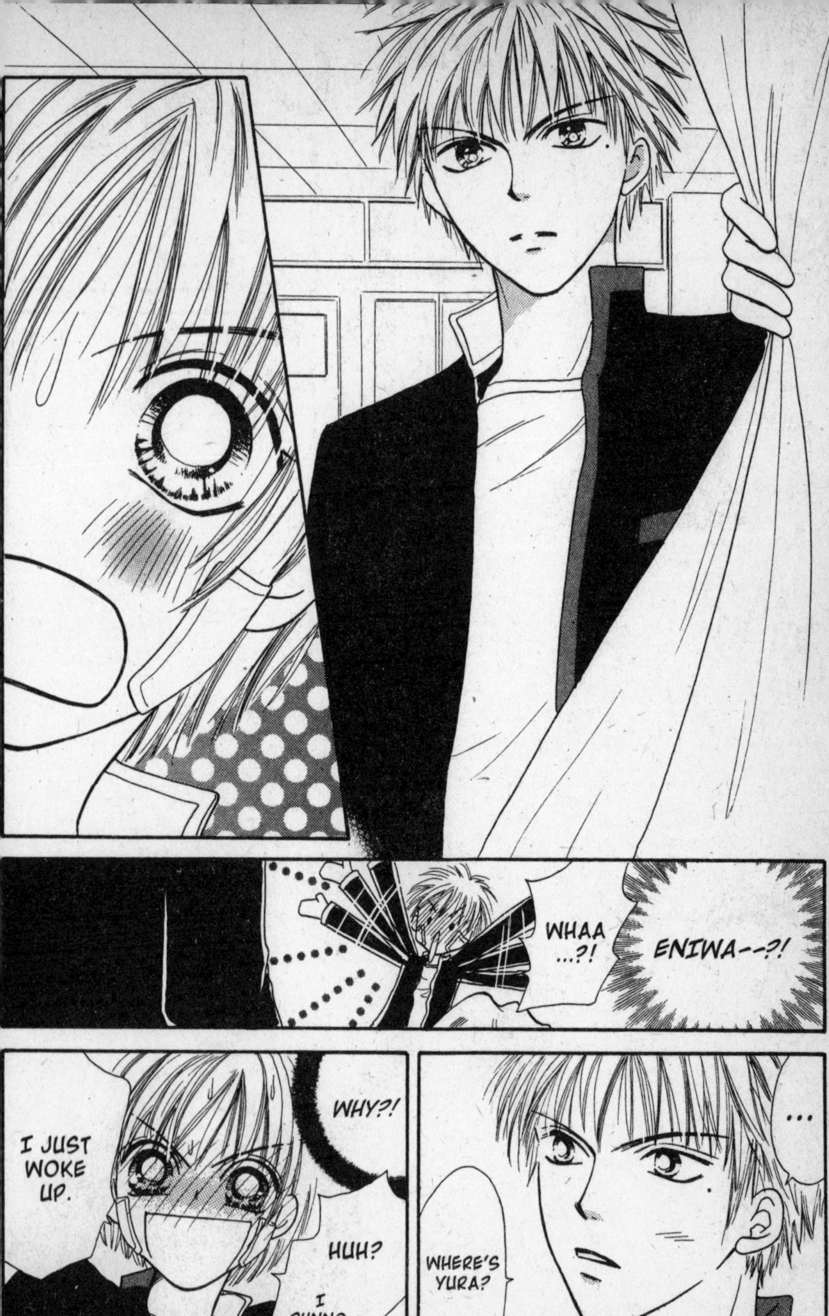
ENIWA--?!
WHAA ...?!
...
WHERE'S YURA?
WHY?!
HUH?
I DUNNO.
I JUST WOKE UP.

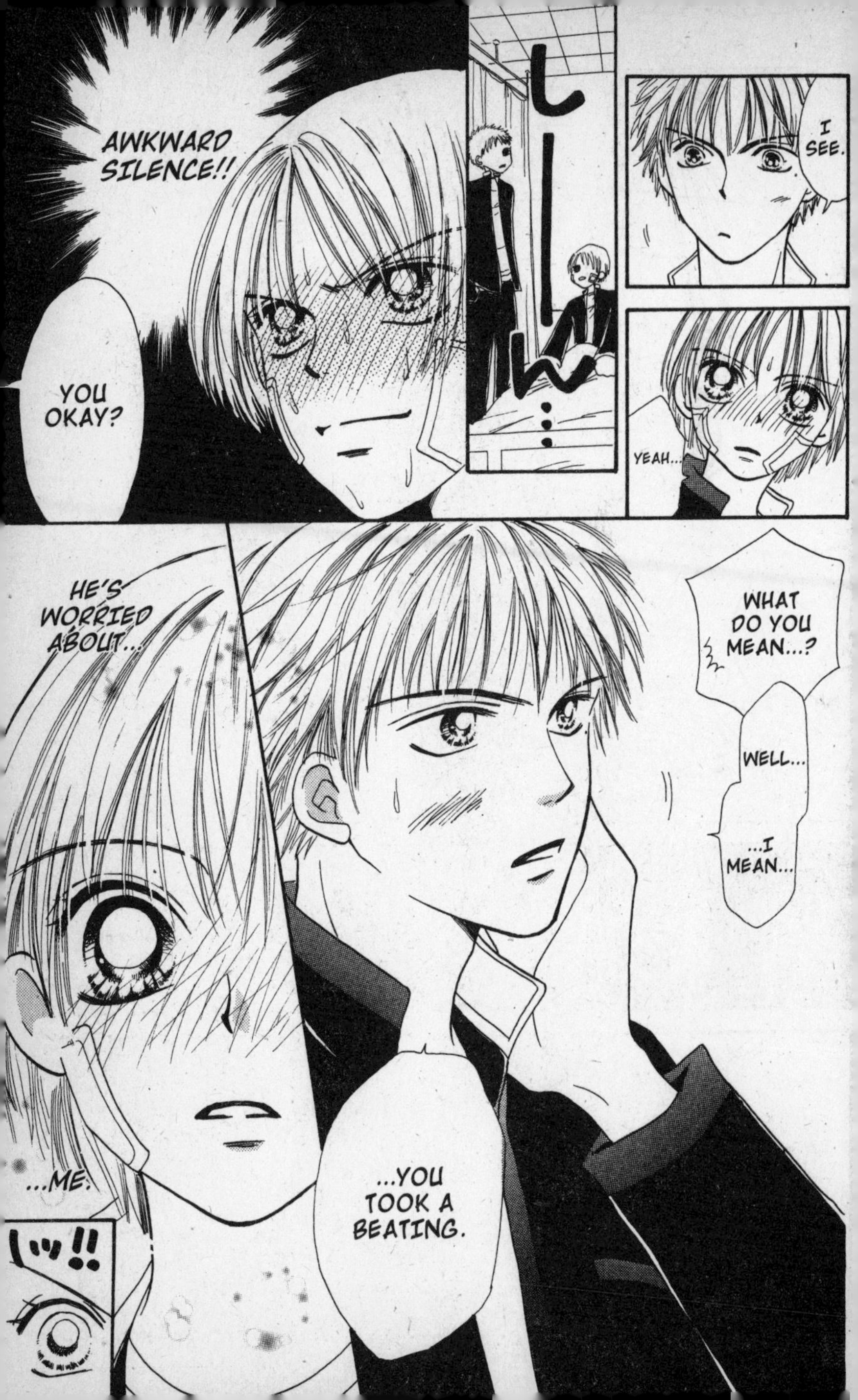
I SEE.
YEAH...
しーん…
AWKWARD SILENCE!!
YOU OKAY?
WHAT DO YOU MEAN...?
WELL...
...I MEAN...
...YOU TOOK A BEATING.
HE'S WORRIED ABOUT...
...ME.
ハッ!!

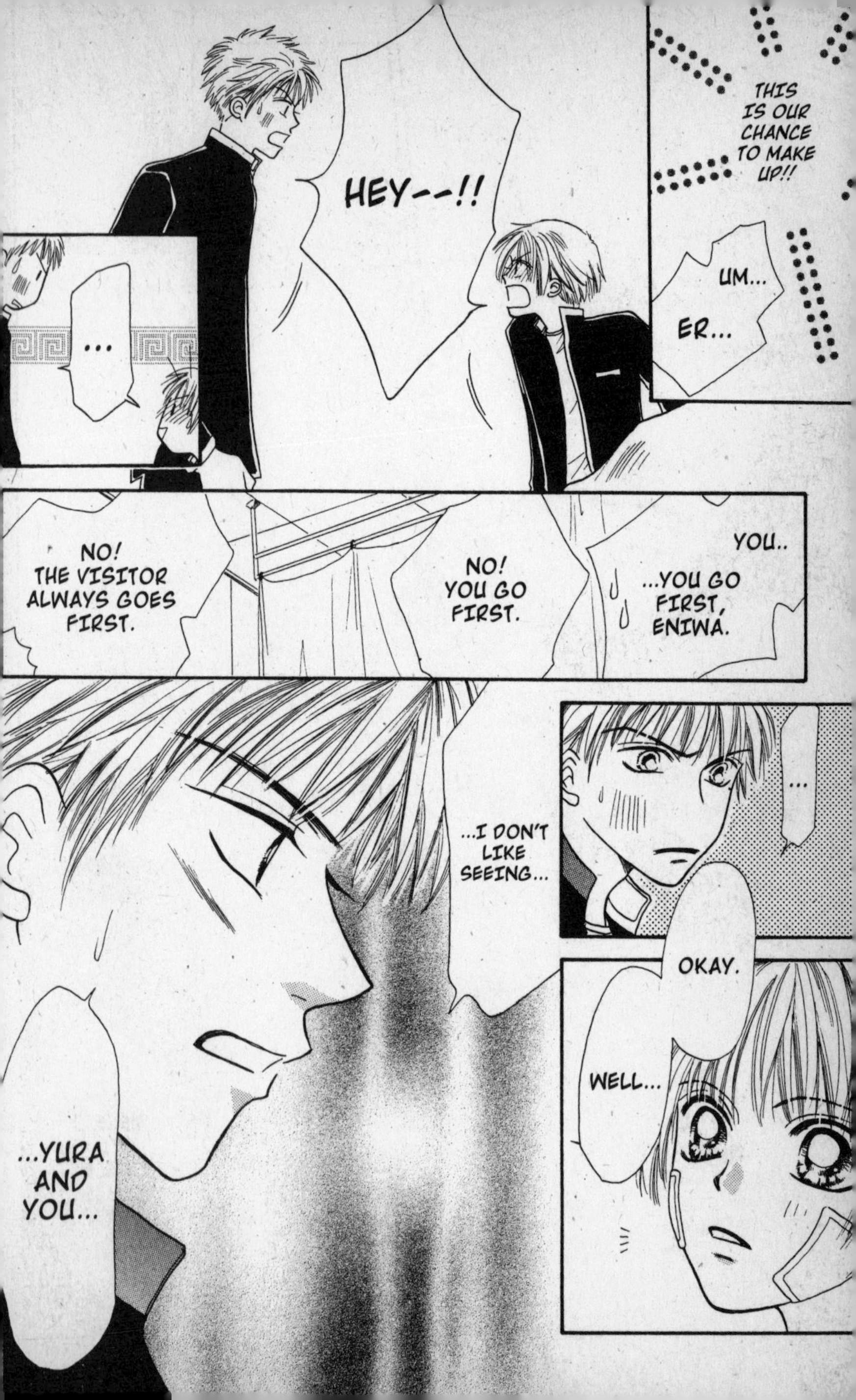
THIS IS OUR CHANCE TO MAKE UP!!
UM... ER...
HEY--!!
...
YOU.. ...YOU GO FIRST, ENIWA.
NO! YOU GO FIRST.
NO! THE VISITOR ALWAYS GOES FIRST.
...
OKAY.
WELL...
...I DON'T LIKE SEEING...
...YURA AND YOU...

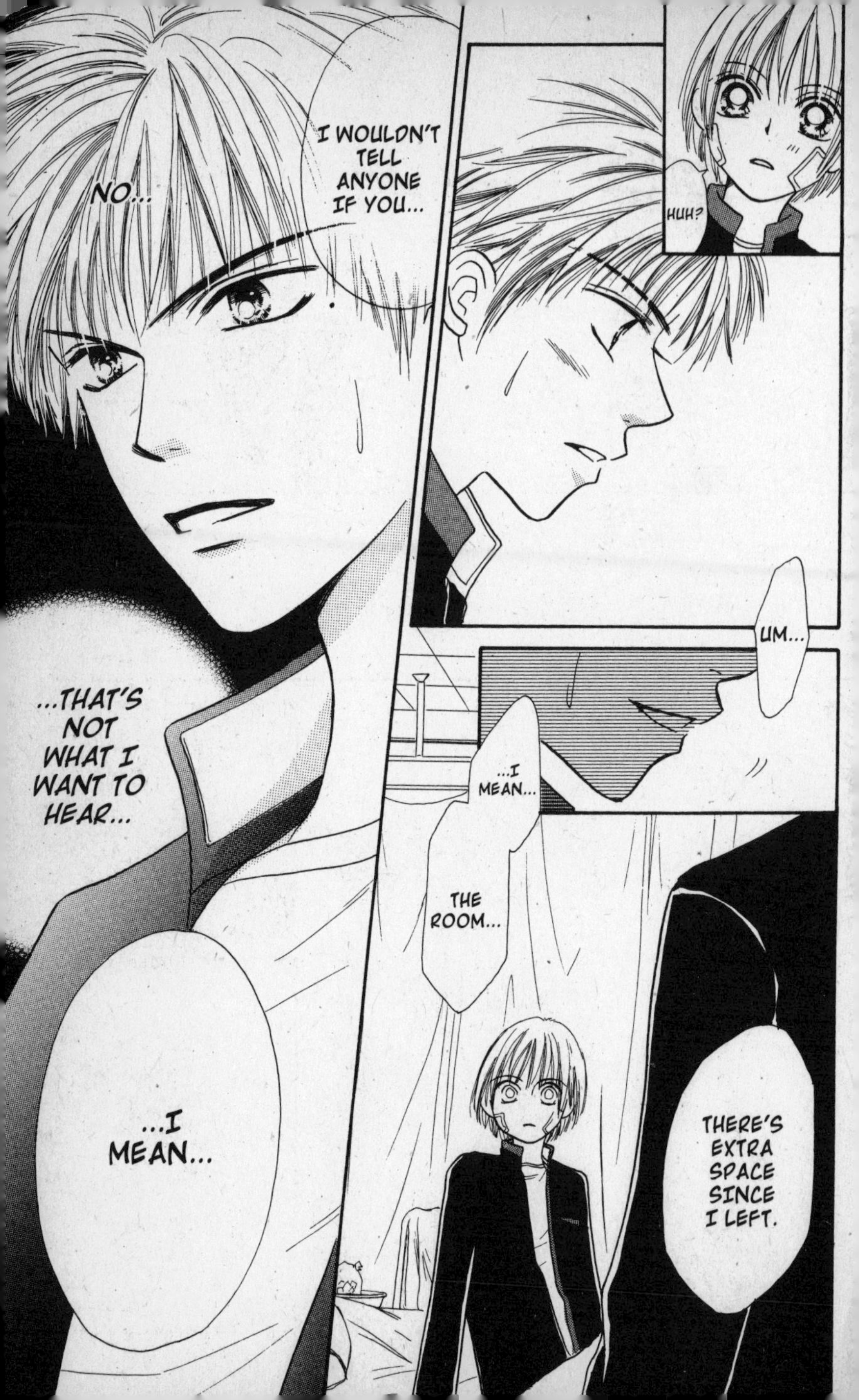
HUH?
UM...
...I MEAN...
THE ROOM...
THERE'S EXTRA SPACE SINCE I LEFT.
I WOULDN'T TELL ANYONE IF YOU...
NO...
...THAT'S NOT WHAT I WANT TO HEAR...
...I MEAN...

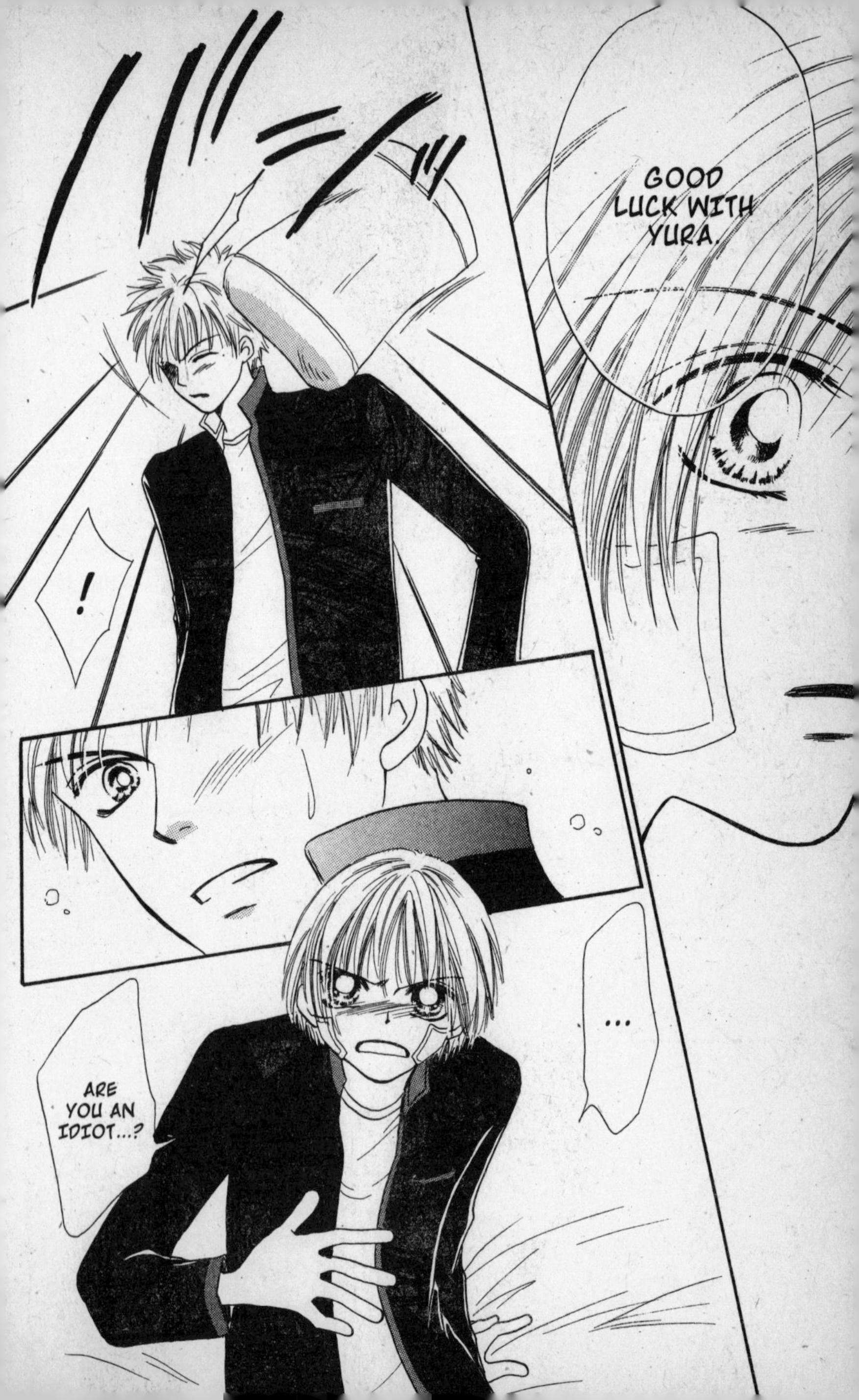
GOOD LUCK WITH YURA.
!
...
ARE YOU AN IDIOT...?

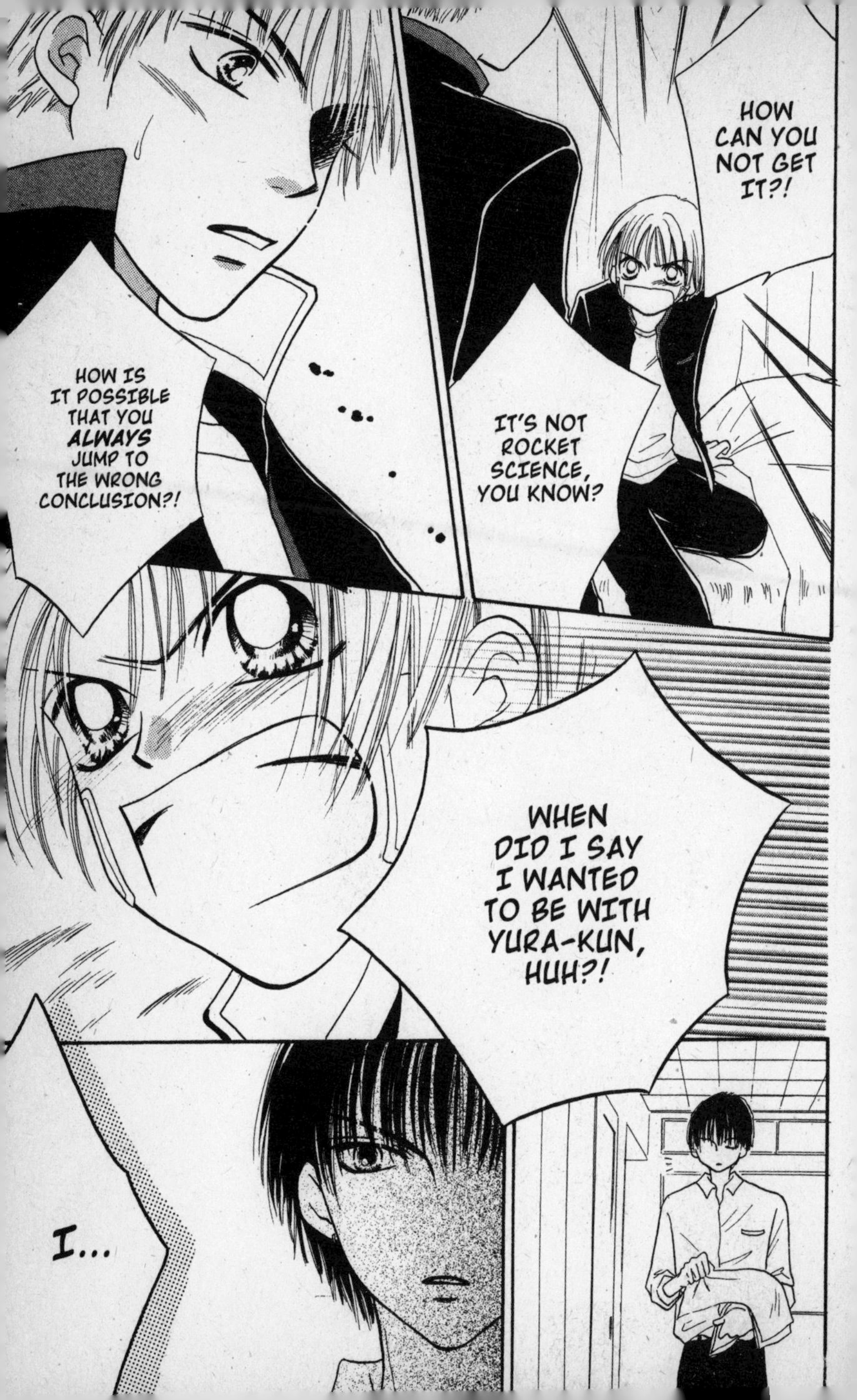
HOW CAN YOU NOT GET IT?!
IT'S NOT ROCKET SCIENCE, YOU KNOW?
HOW IS IT POSSIBLE THAT YOU **ALWAYS** JUMP TO THE WRONG CONCLUSION?!
WHEN DID I SAY I WANTED TO BE WITH YURA-KUN, HUH?!
I...

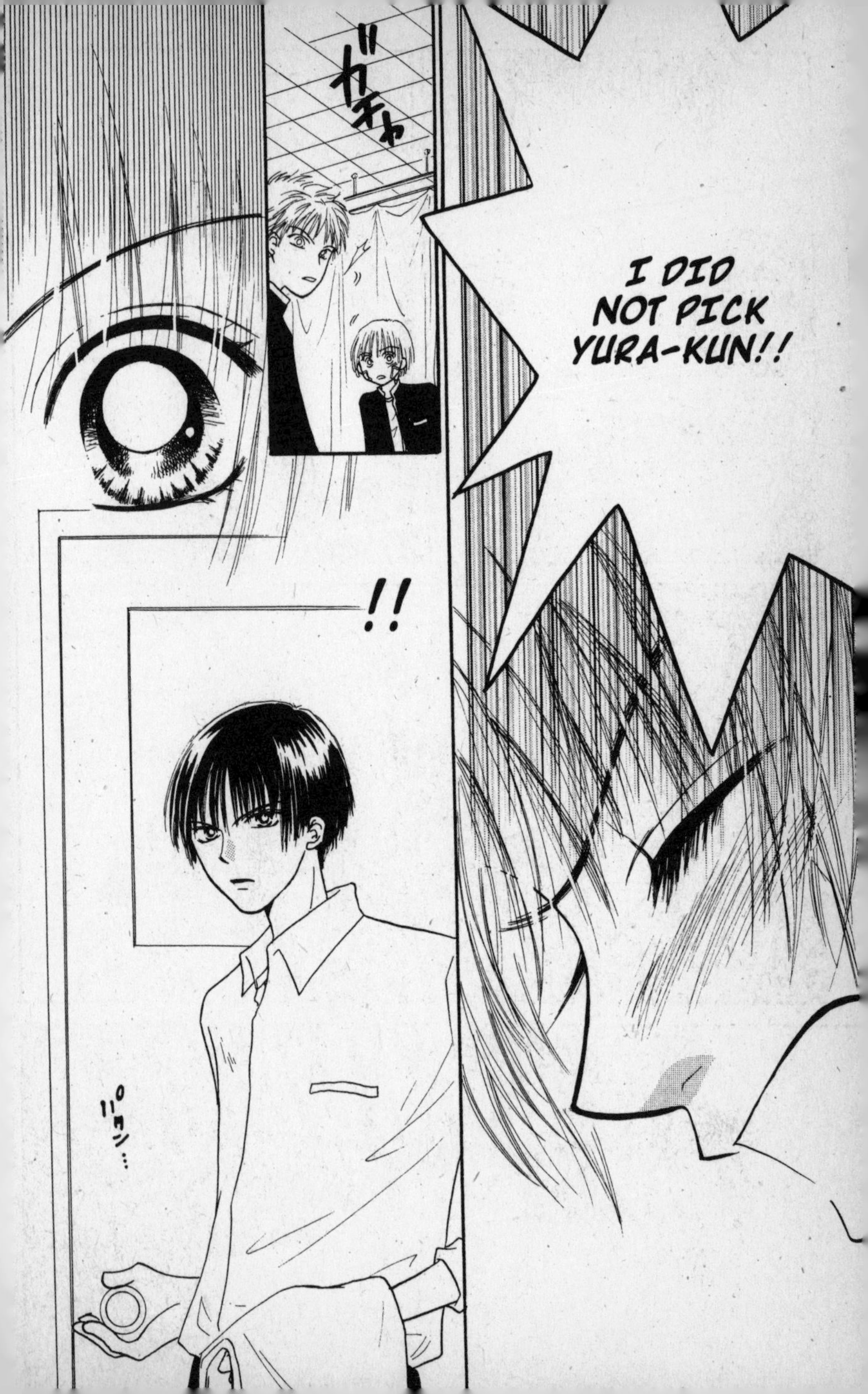
I DID NOT PICK YURA-KUN!!
ガチャ
!!
パタン…

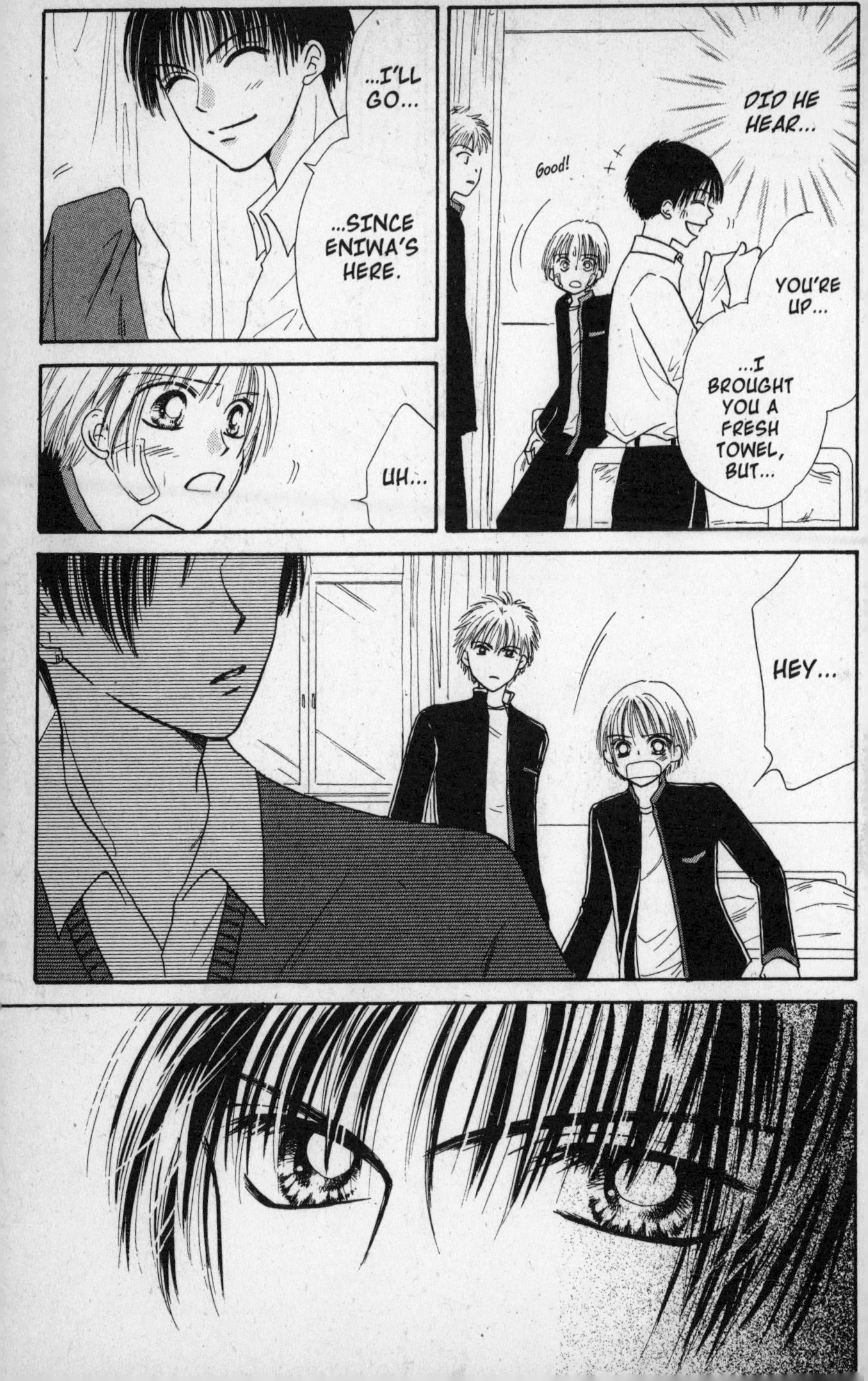
DID HE HEAR...
Good!
YOU'RE UP...
...I BROUGHT YOU A FRESH TOWEL, BUT...
...I'LL GO...
...SINCE ENIWA'S HERE.
UH...
HEY...

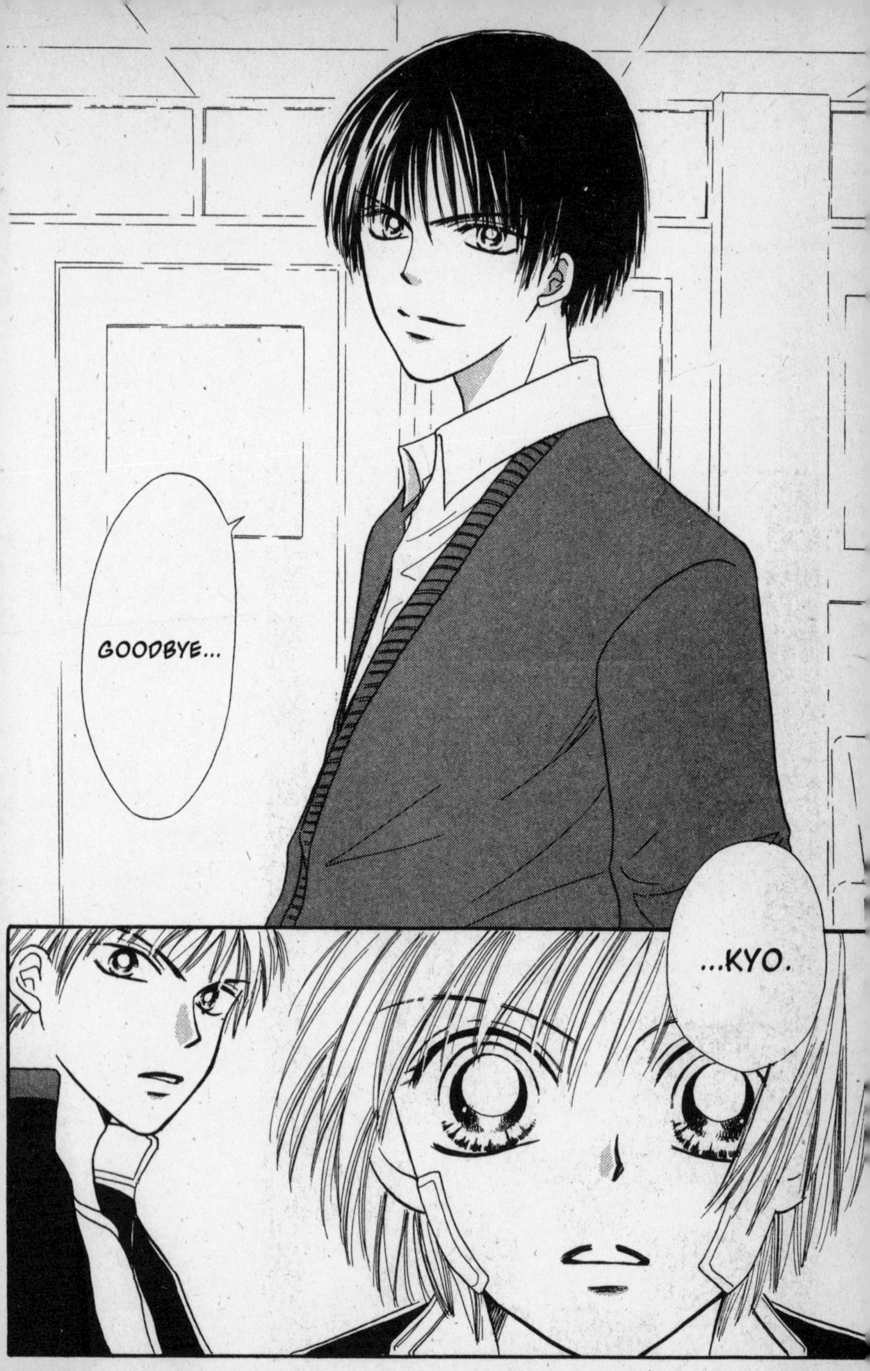
GOODBYE...
...KYO.

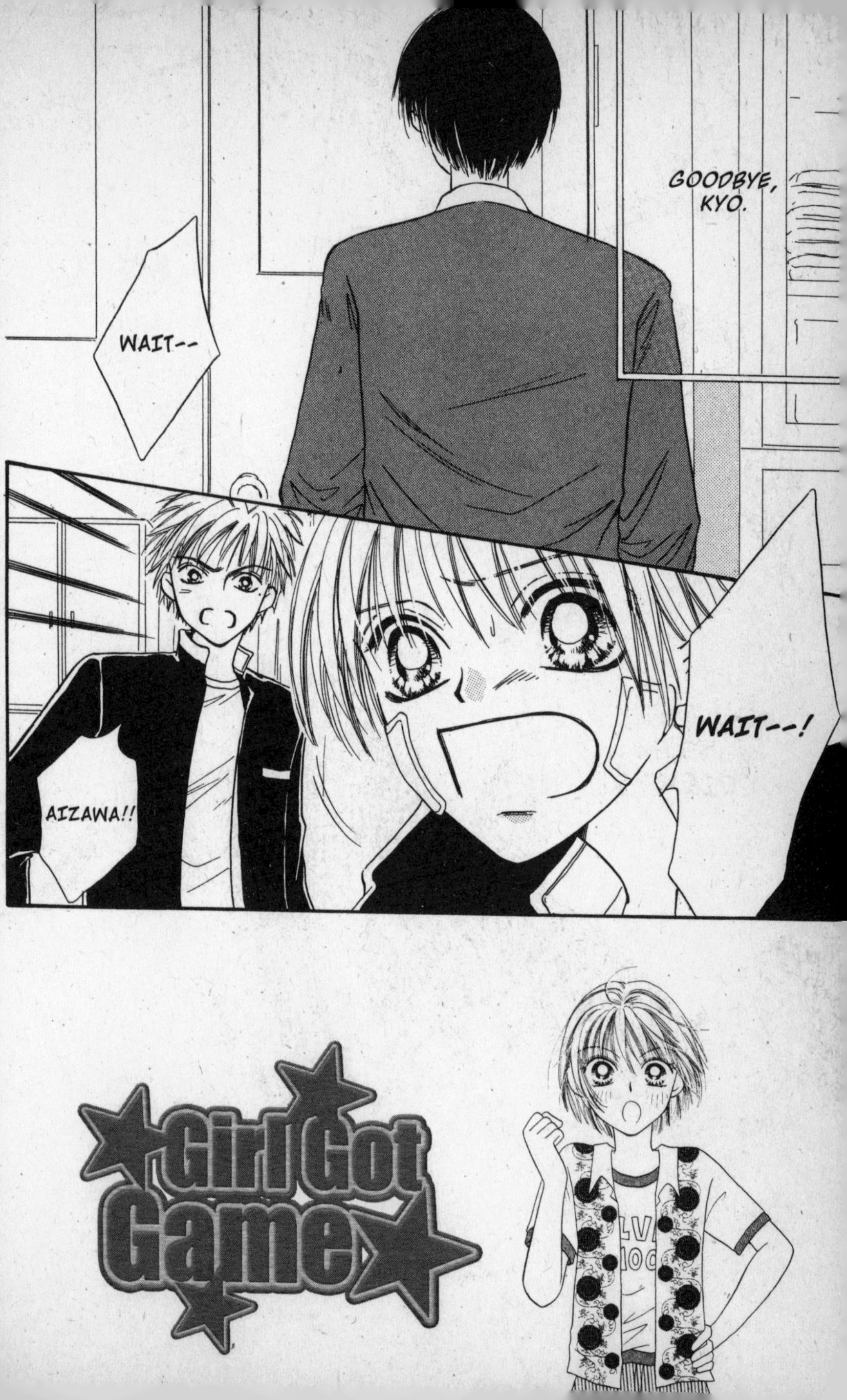
GOODBYE, KYO.
WAIT--
WAIT--!
AIZAWA!!
Girl Got Game

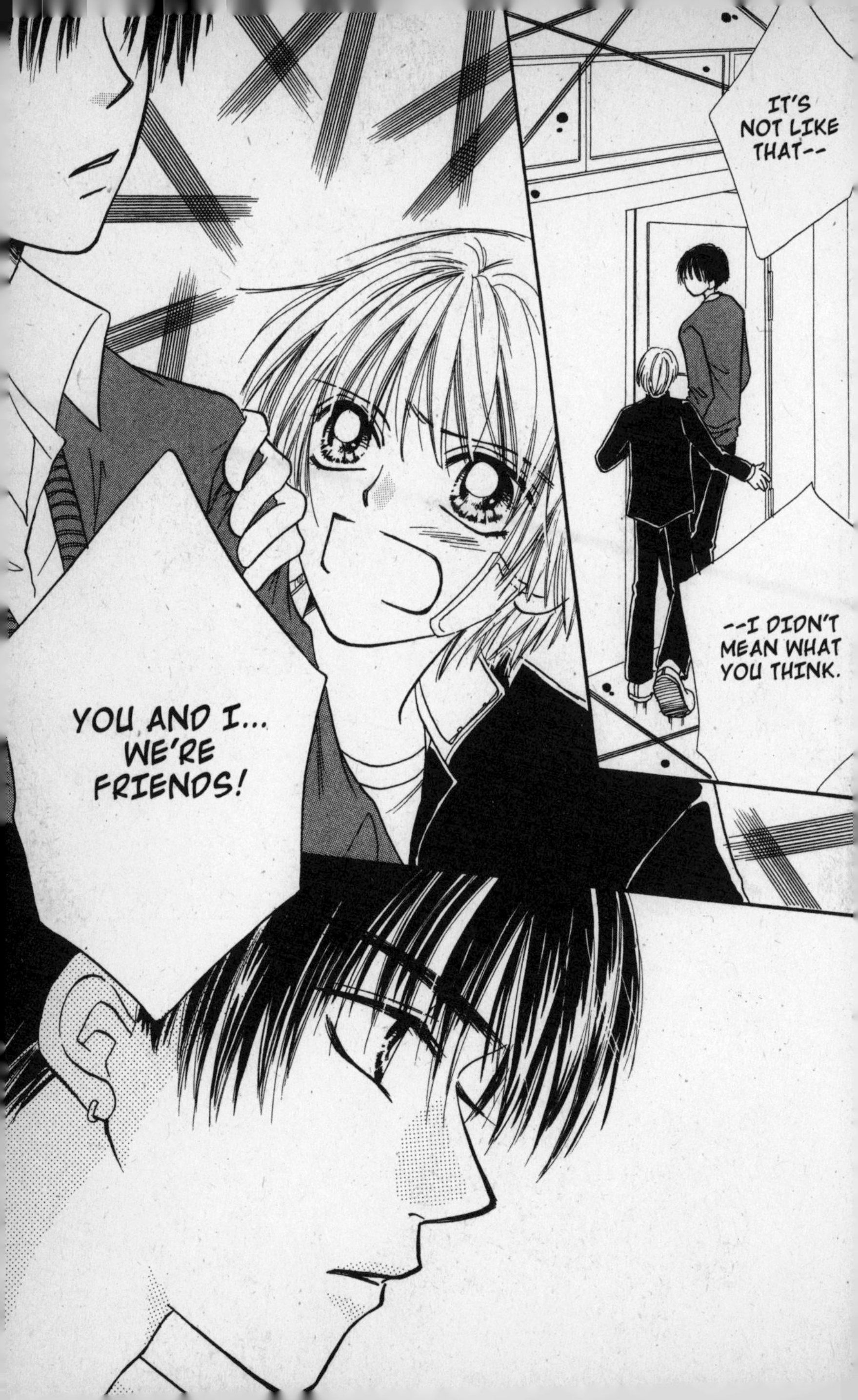
IT'S NOT LIKE THAT--
--I DIDN'T MEAN WHAT YOU THINK.
YOU AND I... WE'RE FRIENDS!

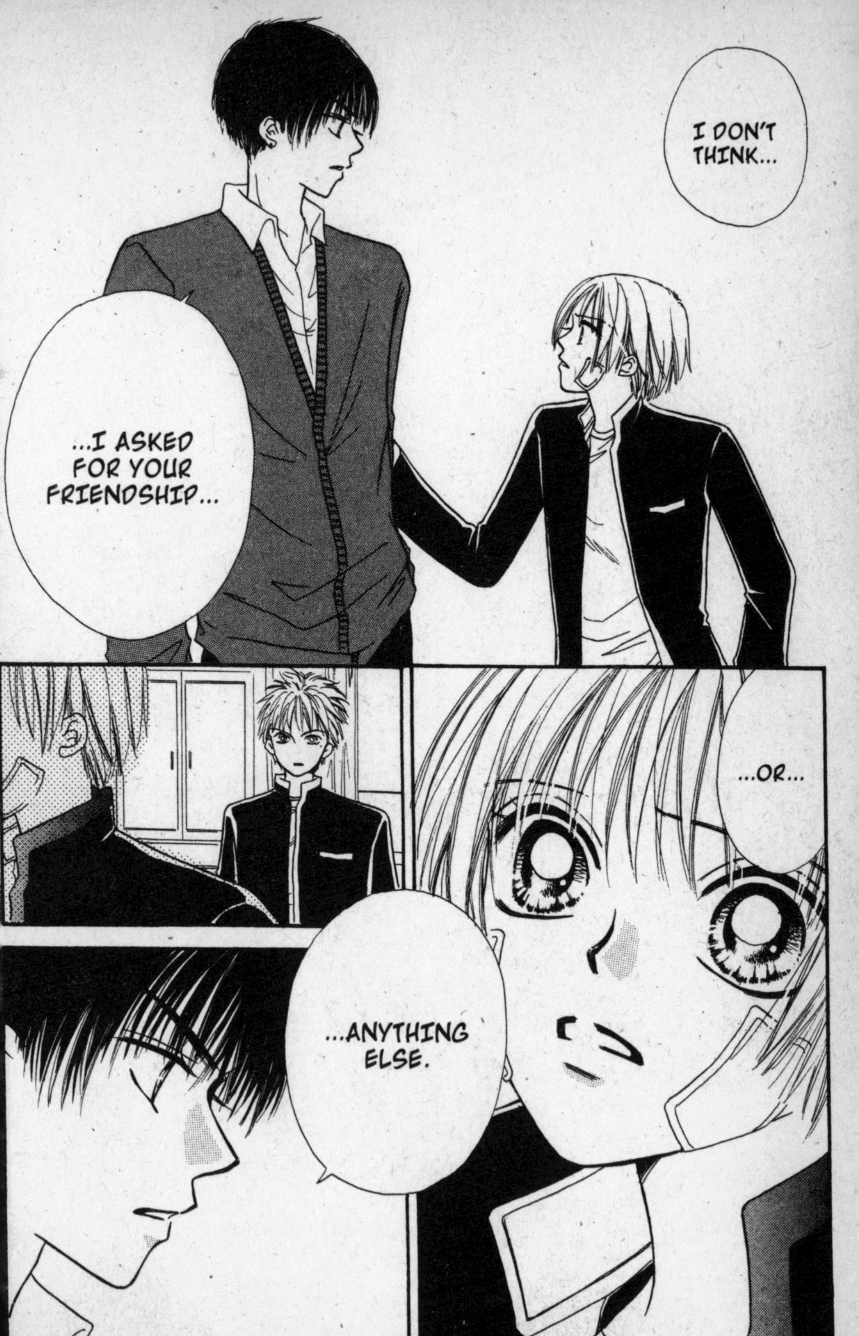
I DON'T THINK...
...I ASKED FOR YOUR FRIENDSHIP...
...OR...
...ANYTHING ELSE.

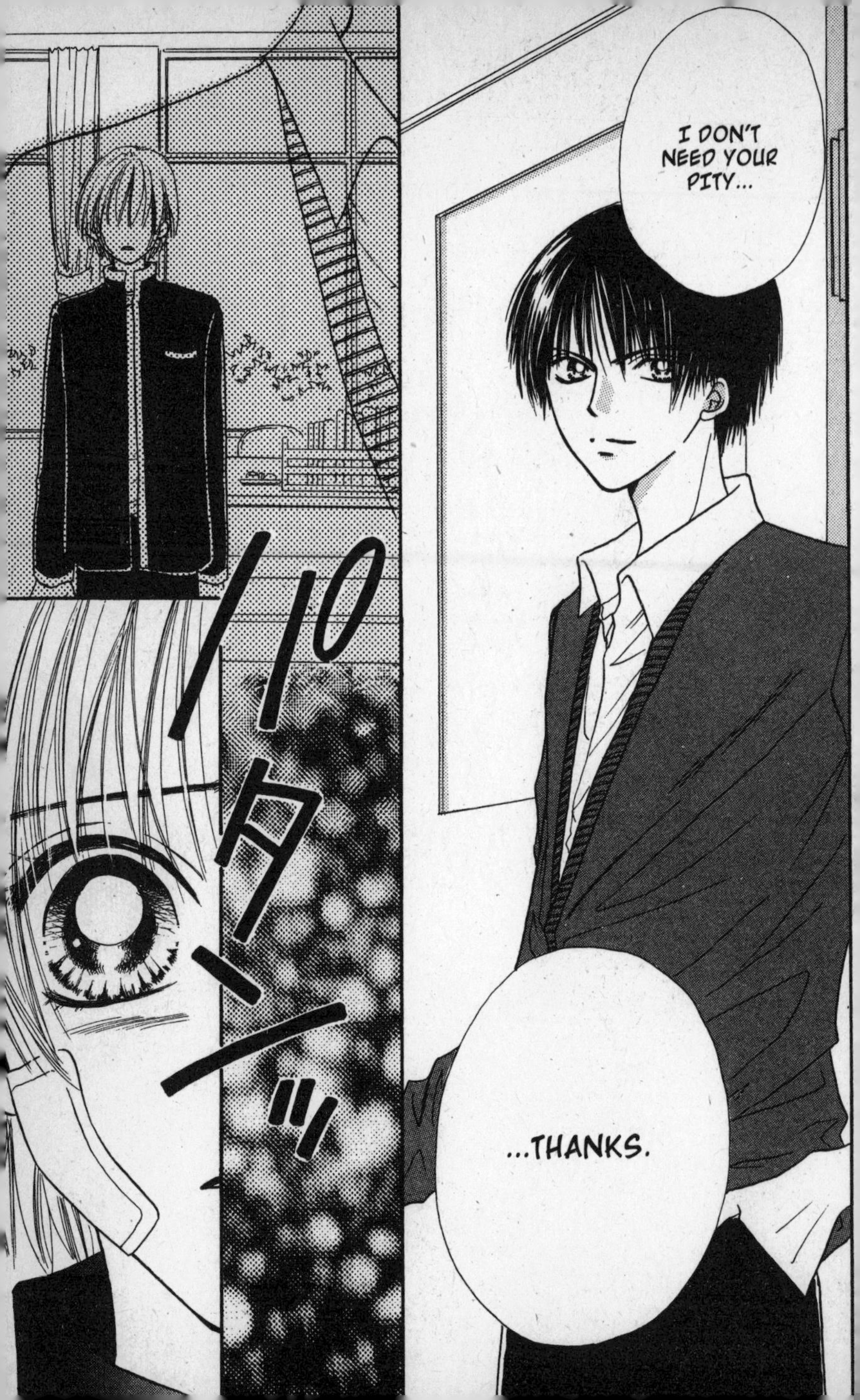
I DON'T NEED YOUR PITY...
...THANKS.
パタンッ

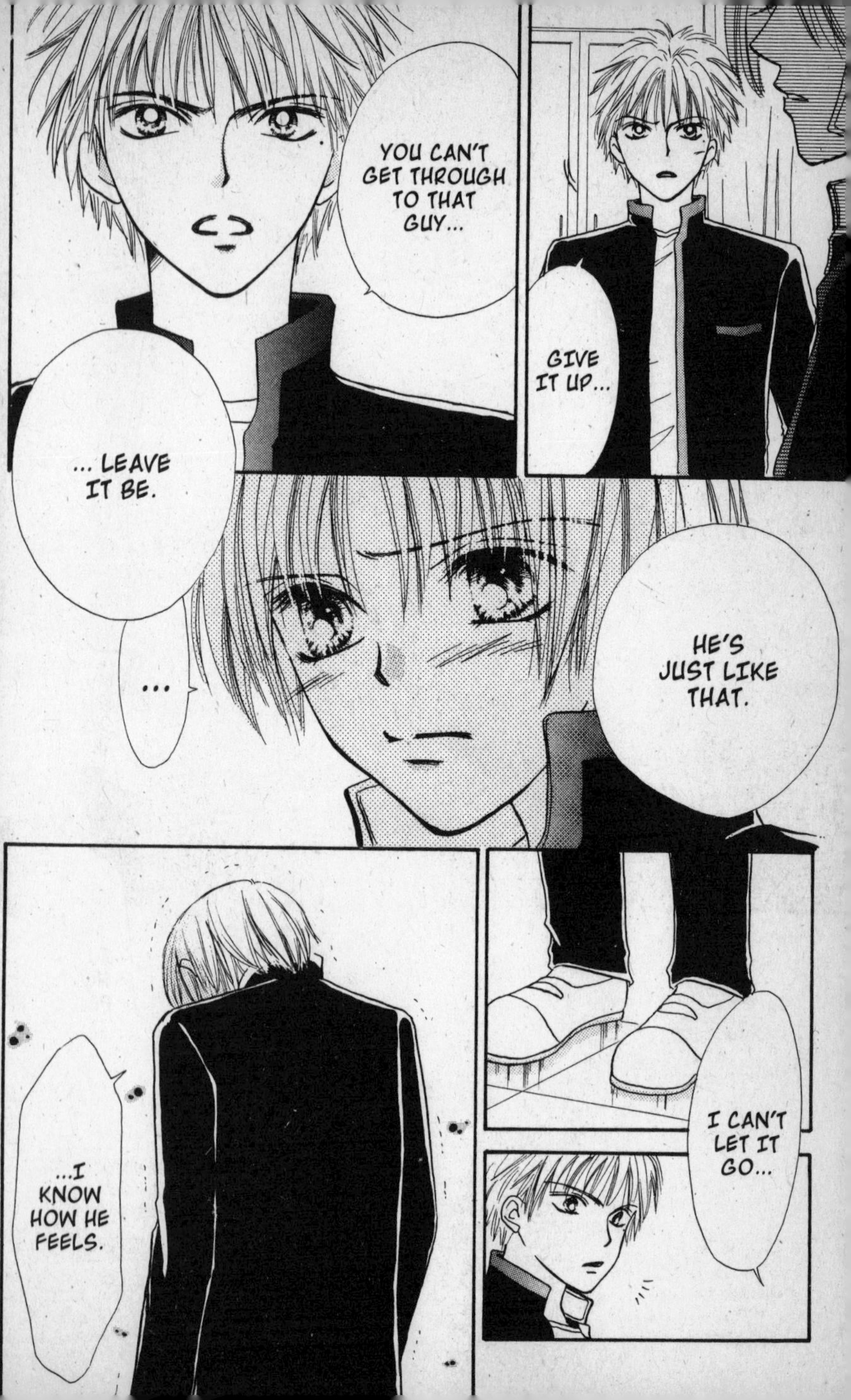
YOU CAN'T GET THROUGH TO THAT GUY...
GIVE IT UP...
... LEAVE IT BE.
HE'S JUST LIKE THAT.
...
I CAN'T LET IT GO...
...I KNOW HOW HE FEELS.

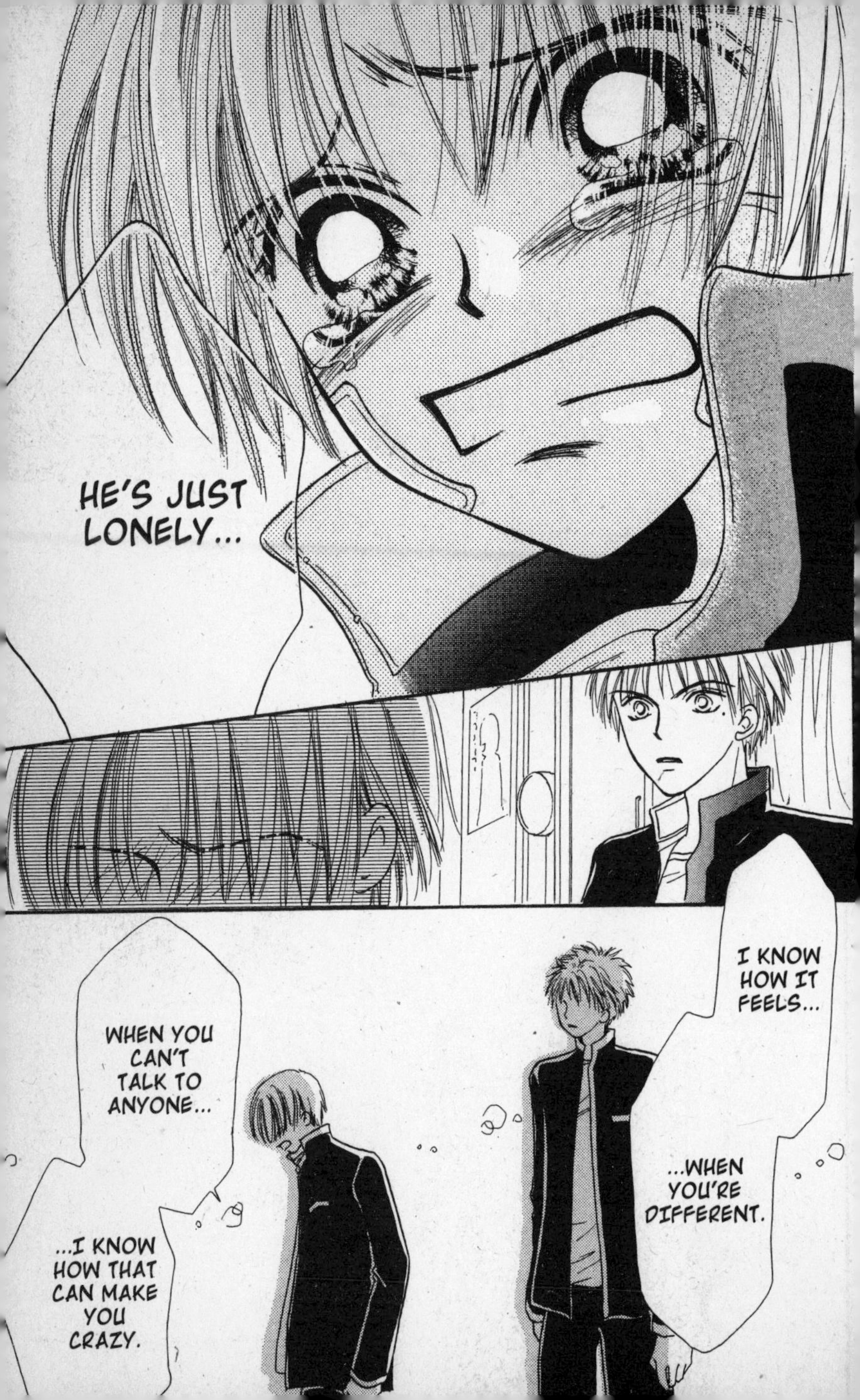
HE'S JUST LONELY...
I KNOW HOW IT FEELS...
...WHEN YOU'RE DIFFERENT.
WHEN YOU CAN'T TALK TO ANYONE...
...I KNOW HOW THAT CAN MAKE YOU CRAZY.

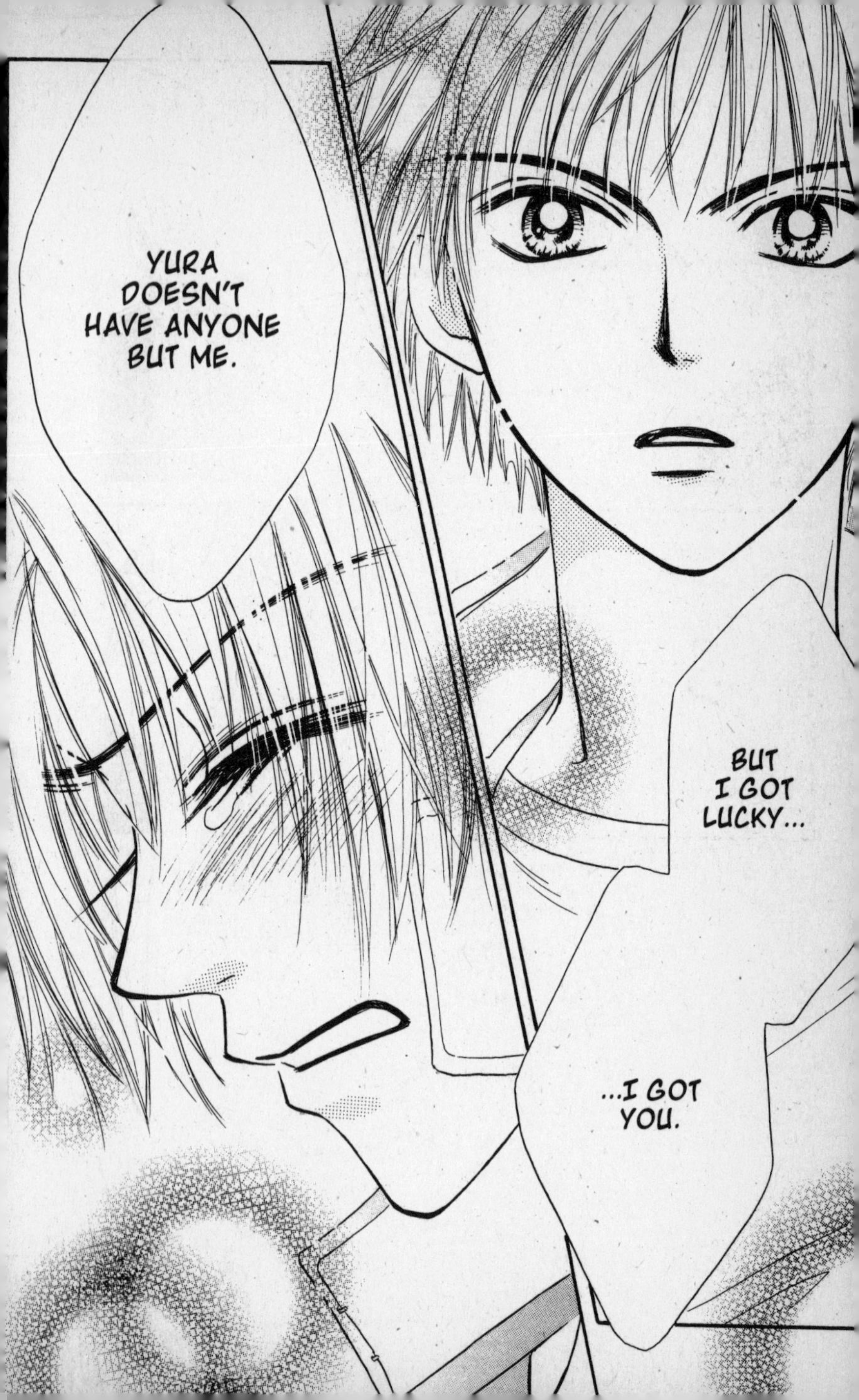
YURA DOESN'T HAVE ANYONE BUT ME.
BUT I GOT LUCKY...
...I GOT YOU.

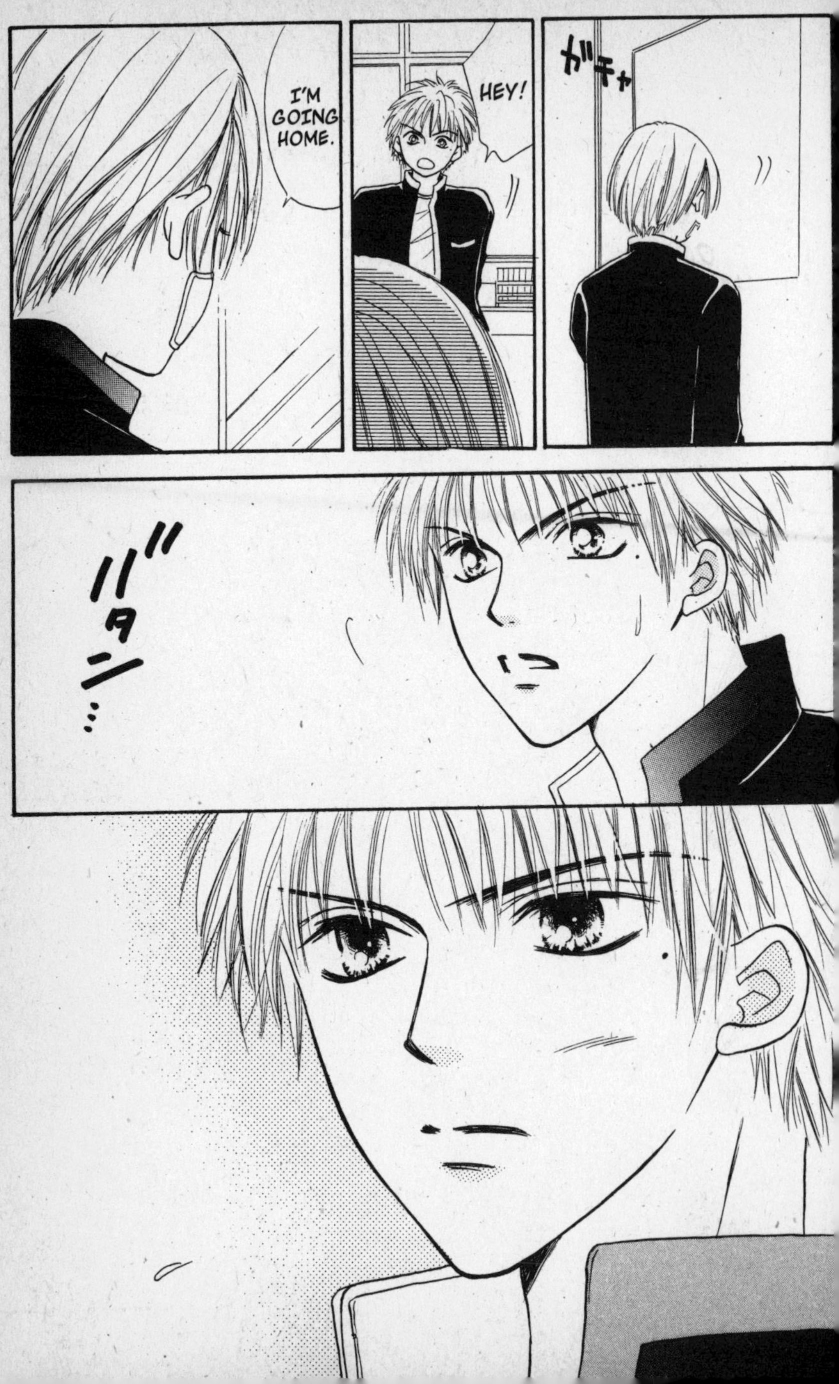
ガチャ
HEY!
I'M GOING HOME.
バタン…

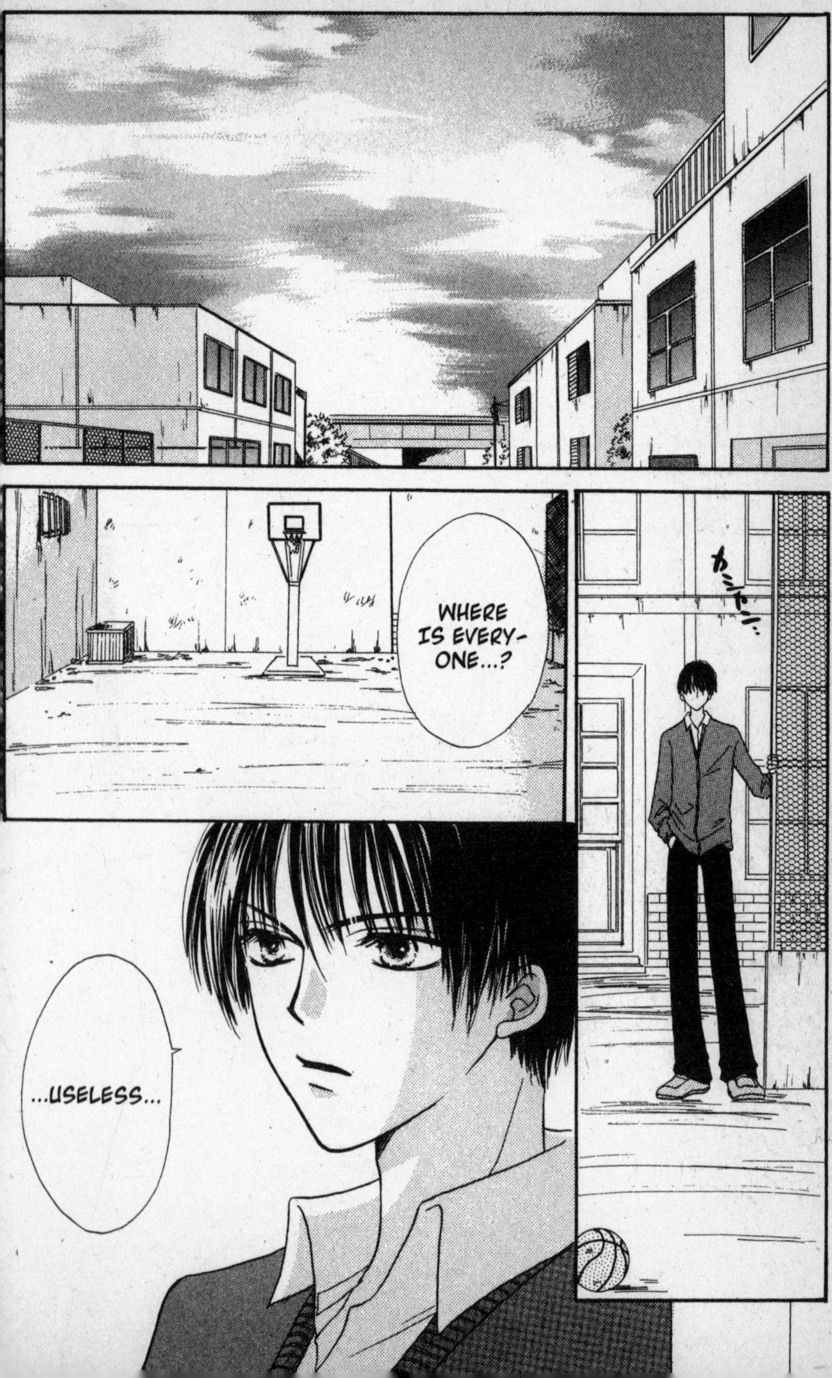
カシャン..
WHERE IS EVERY-ONE...?
...USELESS...

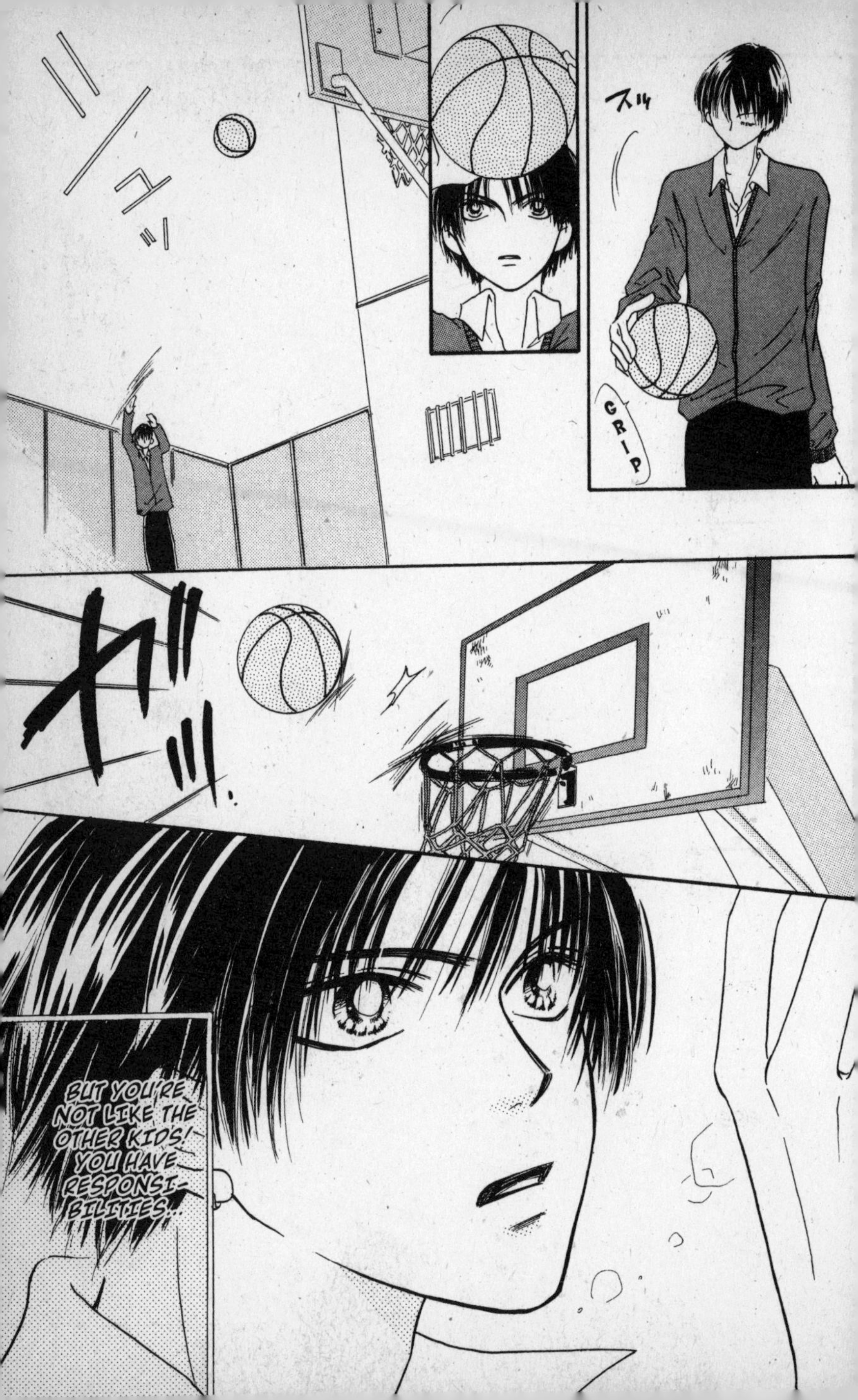
GRIP
BUT YOU'RE NOT LIKE THE OTHER KIDS! YOU HAVE RESPONSI-BILITIES...

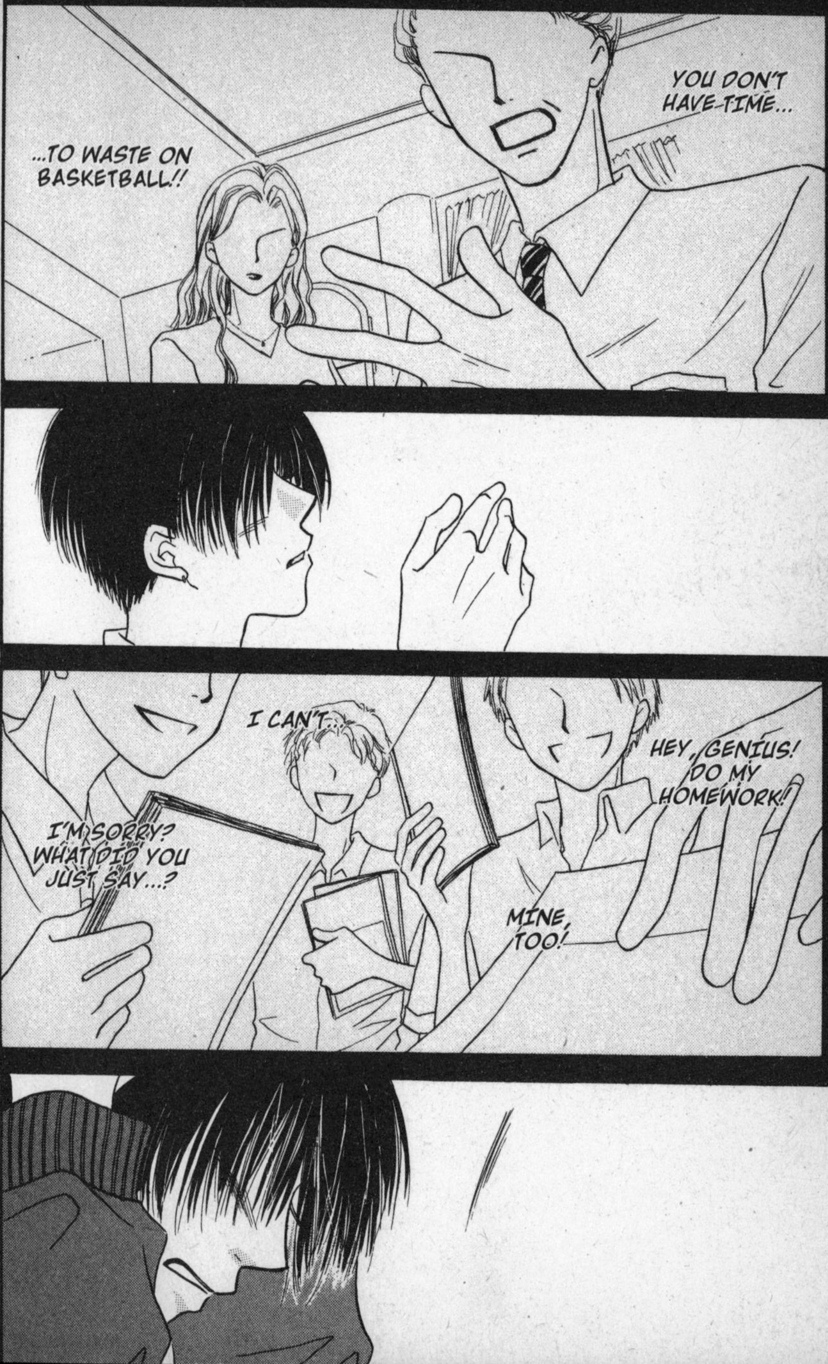
YOU DON'T HAVE TIME...
...TO WASTE ON BASKETBALL!!
HEY, GENIUS! DO MY HOMEWORK!
MINE, TOO!
I CAN'T...
I'M SORRY? WHAT DID YOU JUST SAY...?

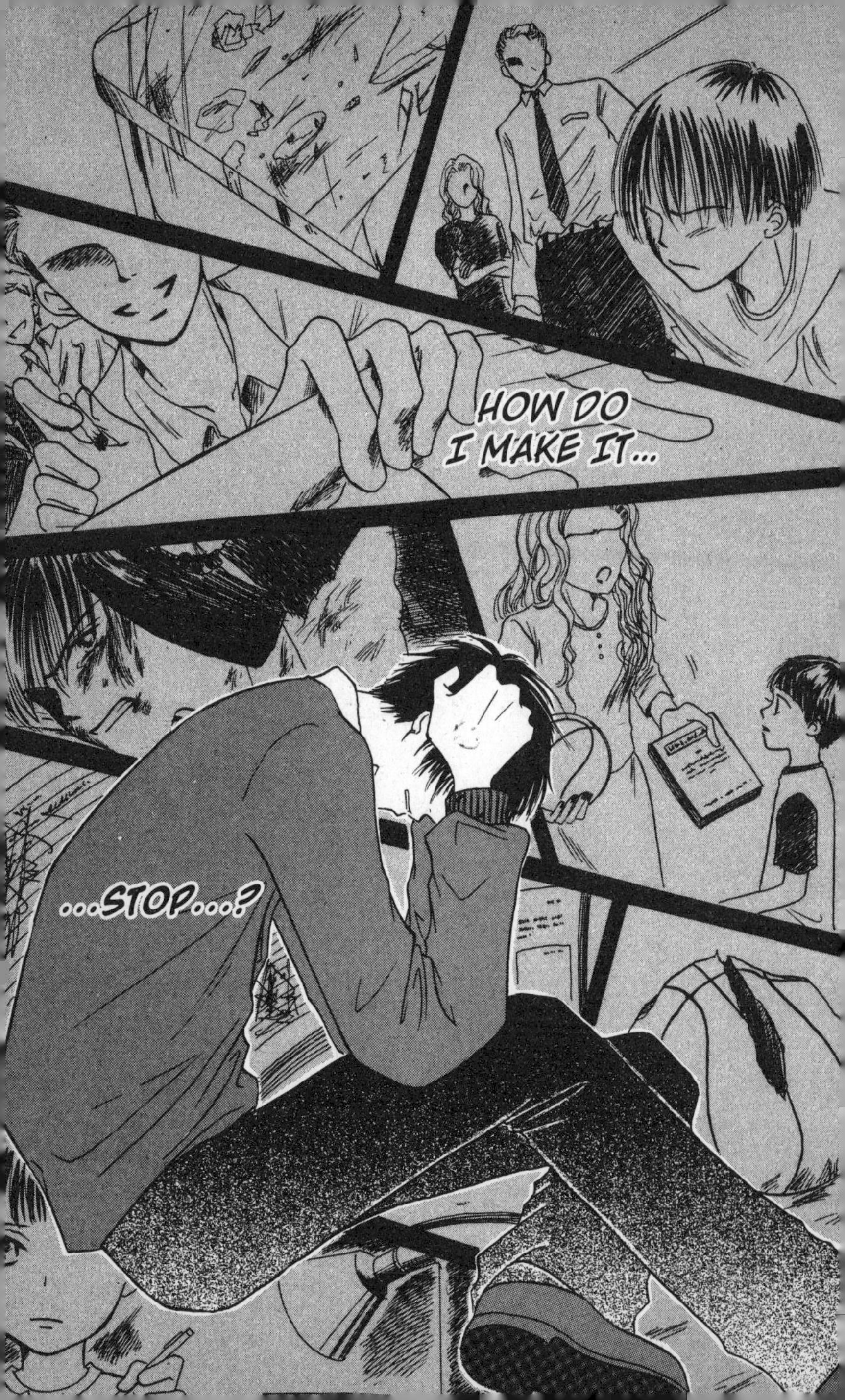
HOW DO I MAKE IT...
...STOP...?

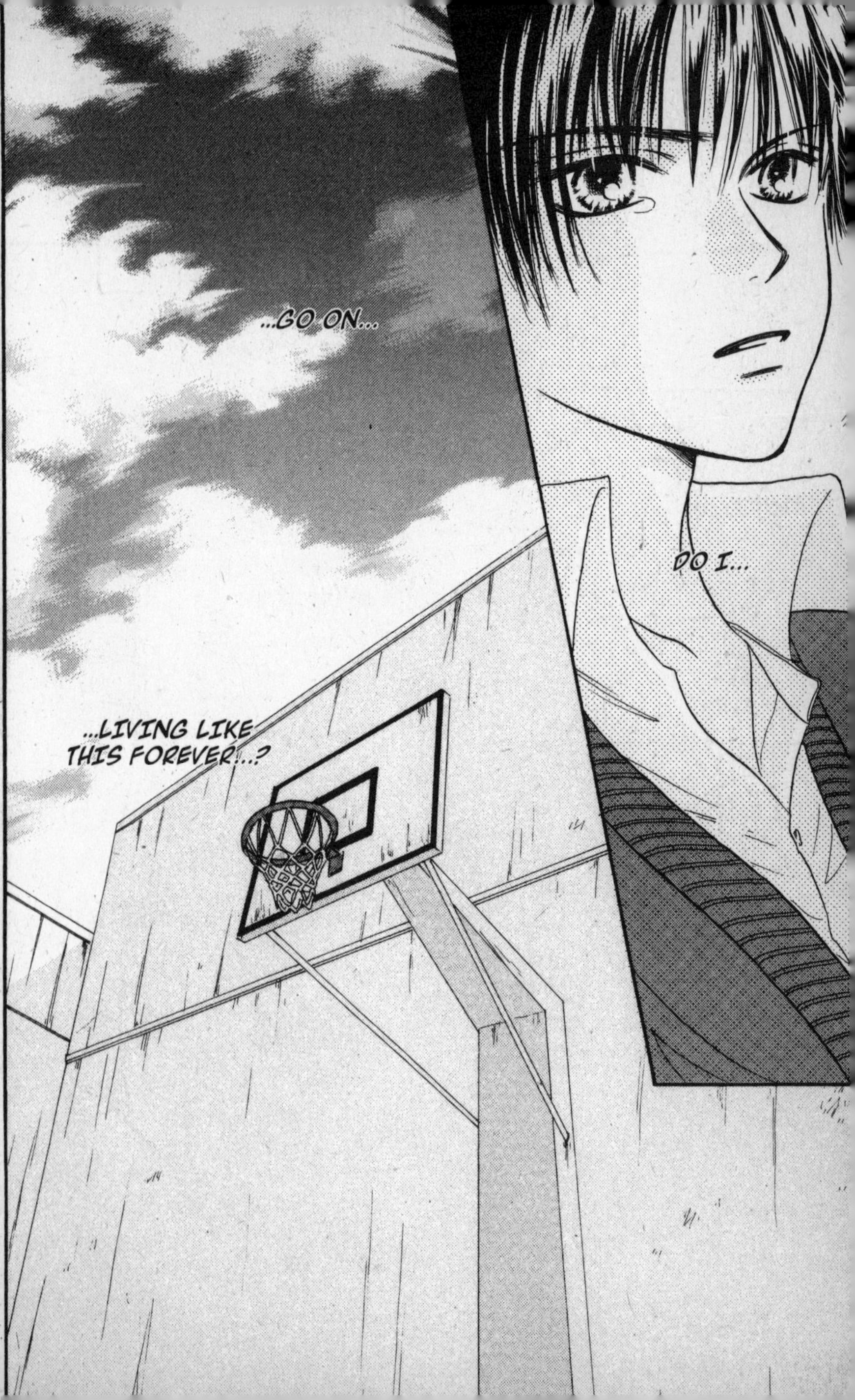
DO I...
...GO ON...
...LIVING LIKE THIS FOREVER...?

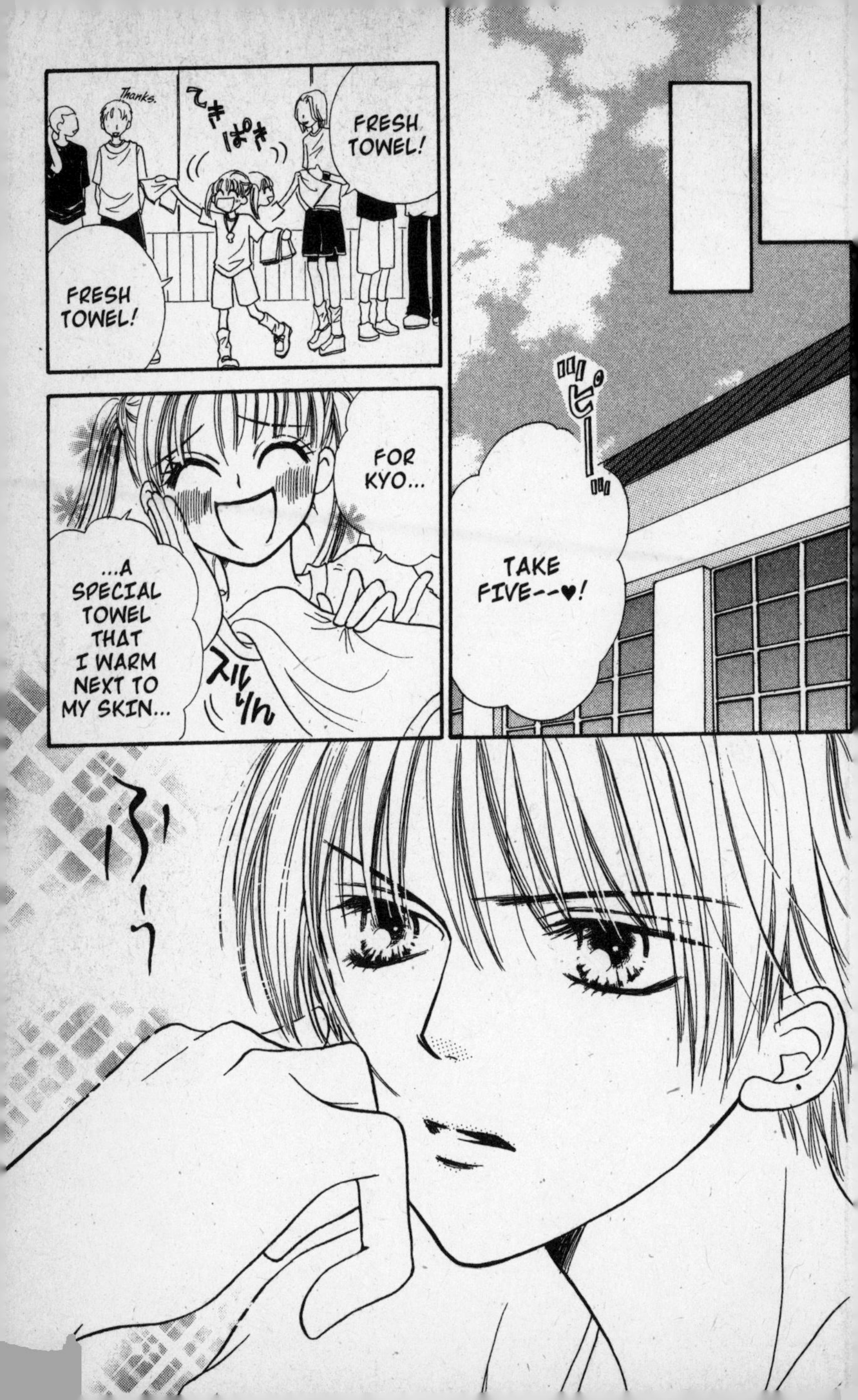
ピー
TAKE FIVE--♥!
FRESH TOWEL!
てきぱき
Thanks.
FRESH TOWEL!
FOR KYO...
...A SPECIAL TOWEL THAT I WARM NEXT TO MY SKIN...
スルりん
ふぅ

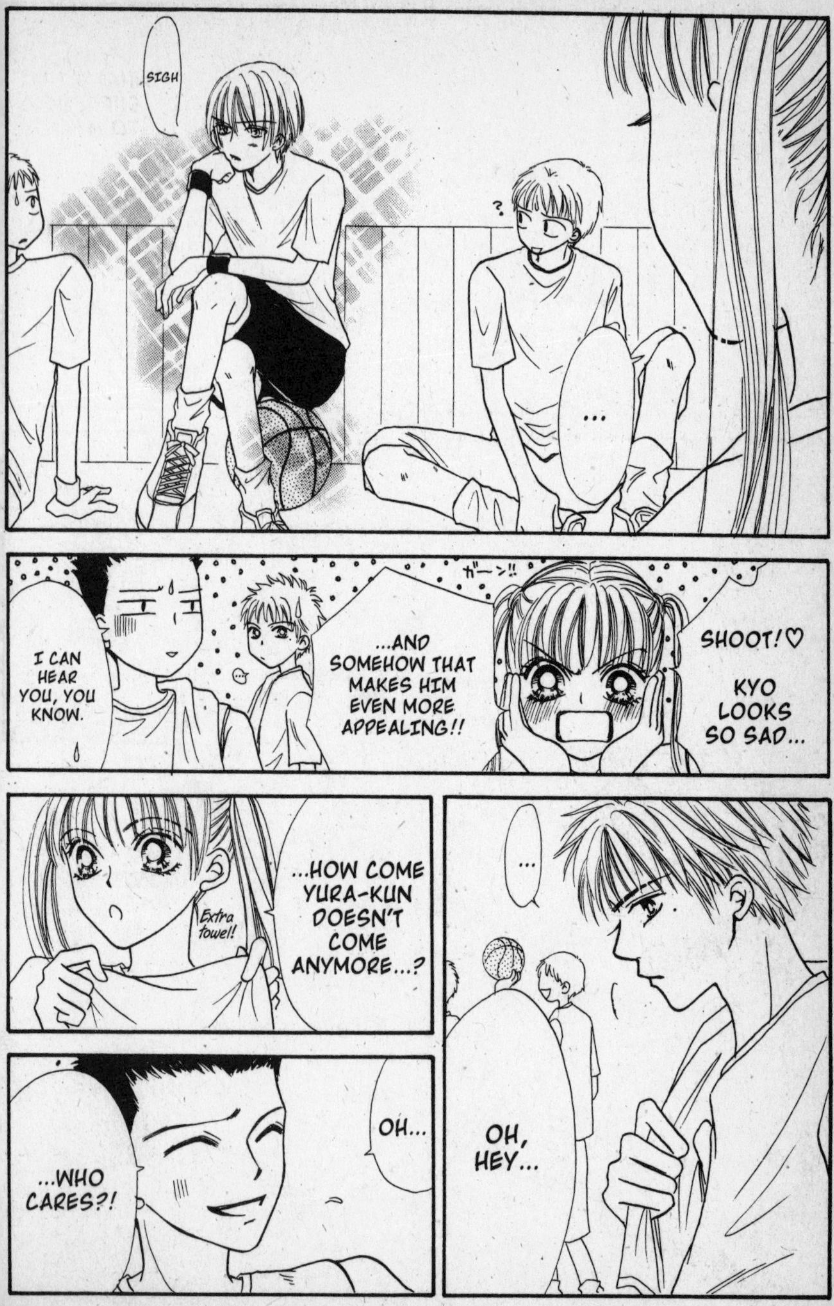
SIGH
...
SHOOT!♡
KYO LOOKS SO SAD...
ガーン!!
...AND SOMEHOW THAT MAKES HIM EVEN MORE APPEALING!!
...
I CAN HEAR YOU, YOU KNOW.
...
OH, HEY...
...HOW COME YURA-KUN DOESN'T COME ANYMORE...?
Extra towel!
OH...
...WHO CARES?!

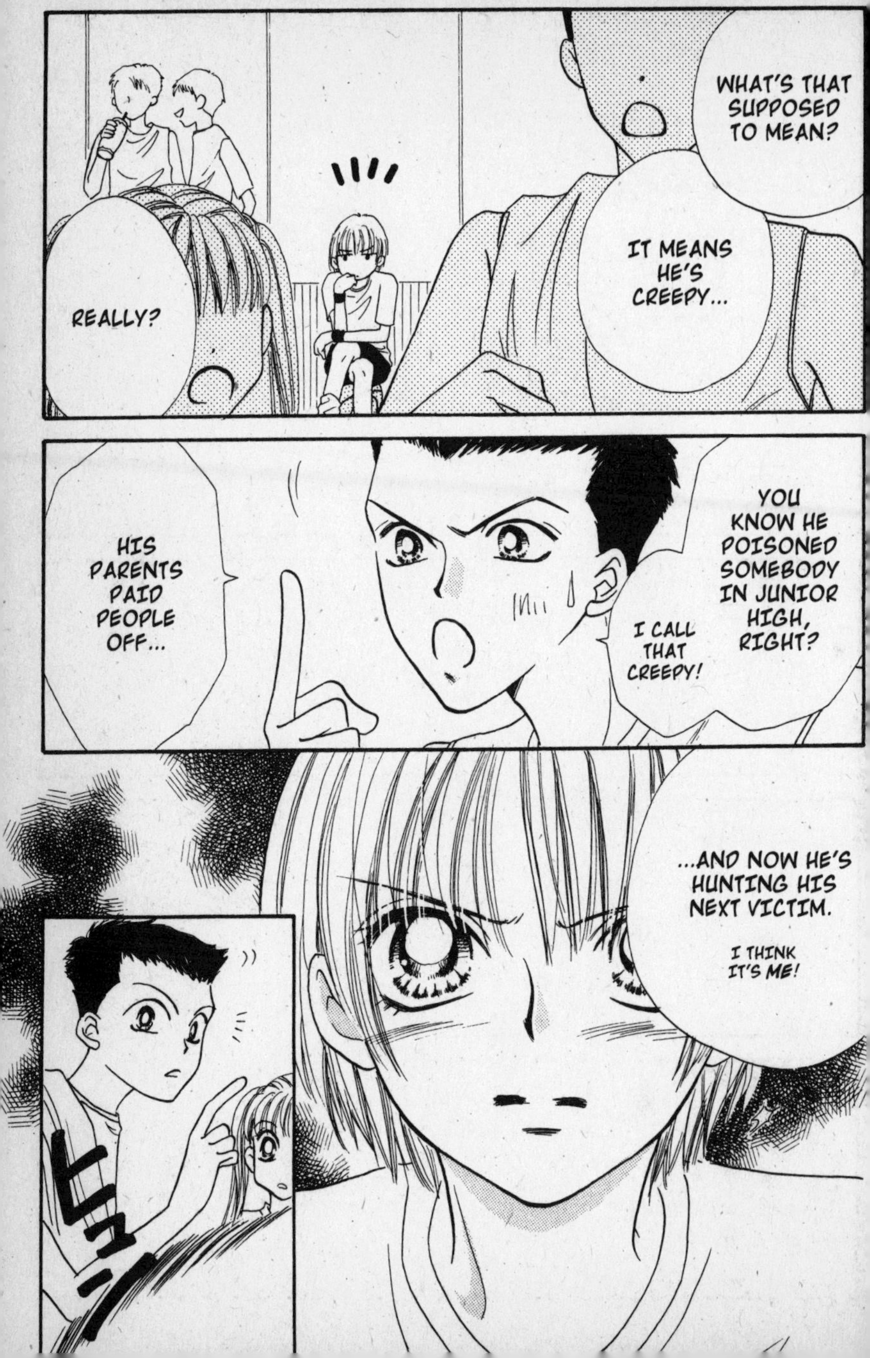
WHAT'S THAT SUPPOSED TO MEAN?
IT MEANS HE'S CREEPY...
REALLY?
YOU KNOW HE POISONED SOMEBODY IN JUNIOR HIGH, RIGHT?
I CALL THAT CREEPY!
HIS PARENTS PAID PEOPLE OFF...
...AND NOW HE'S HUNTING HIS NEXT VICTIM.
I THINK IT'S ME!

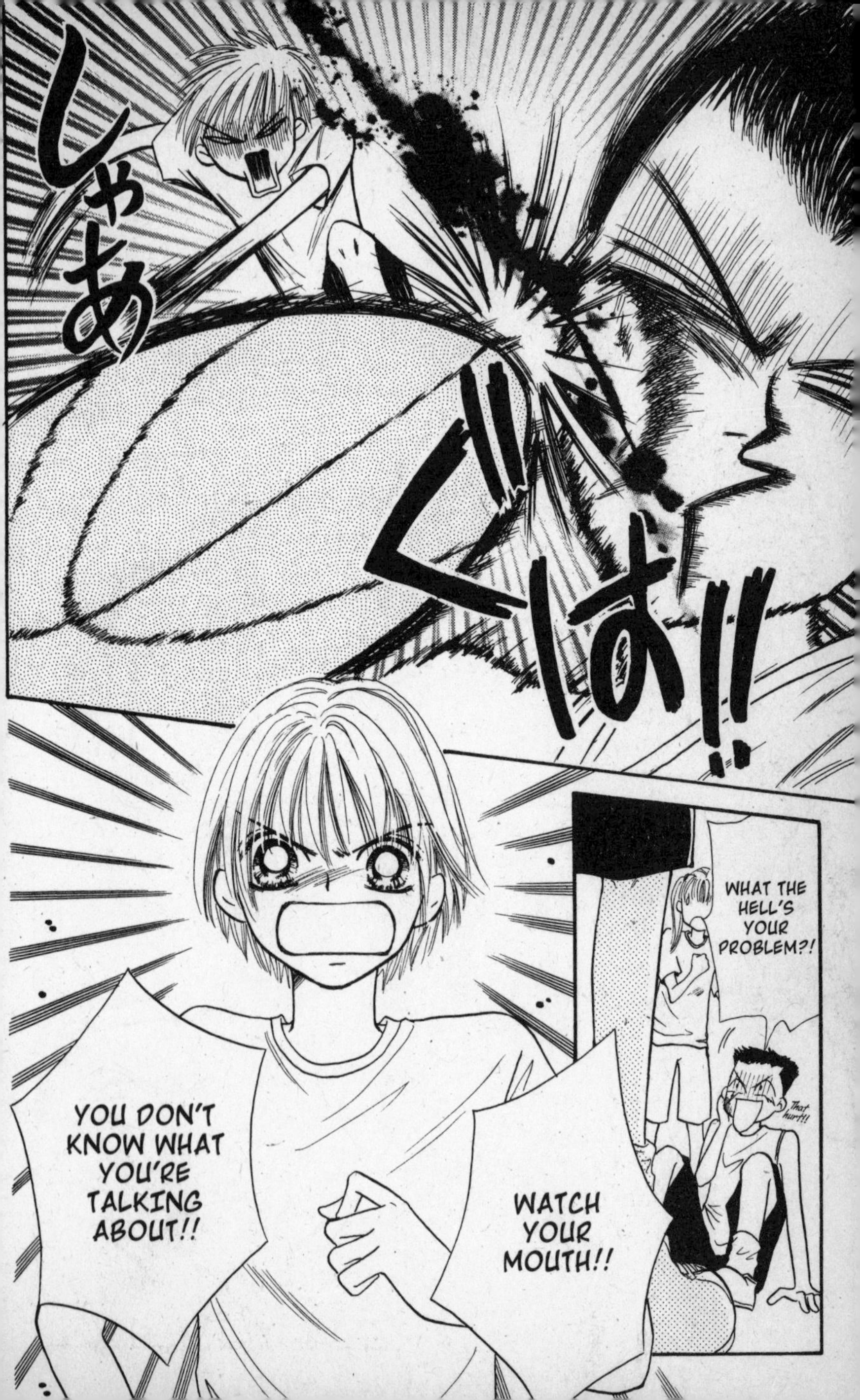
ぐは!!
しゃあ
WHAT THE HELL'S YOUR PROBLEM?!
That hurt!!
WATCH YOUR MOUTH!!
YOU DON'T KNOW WHAT YOU'RE TALKING ABOUT!!

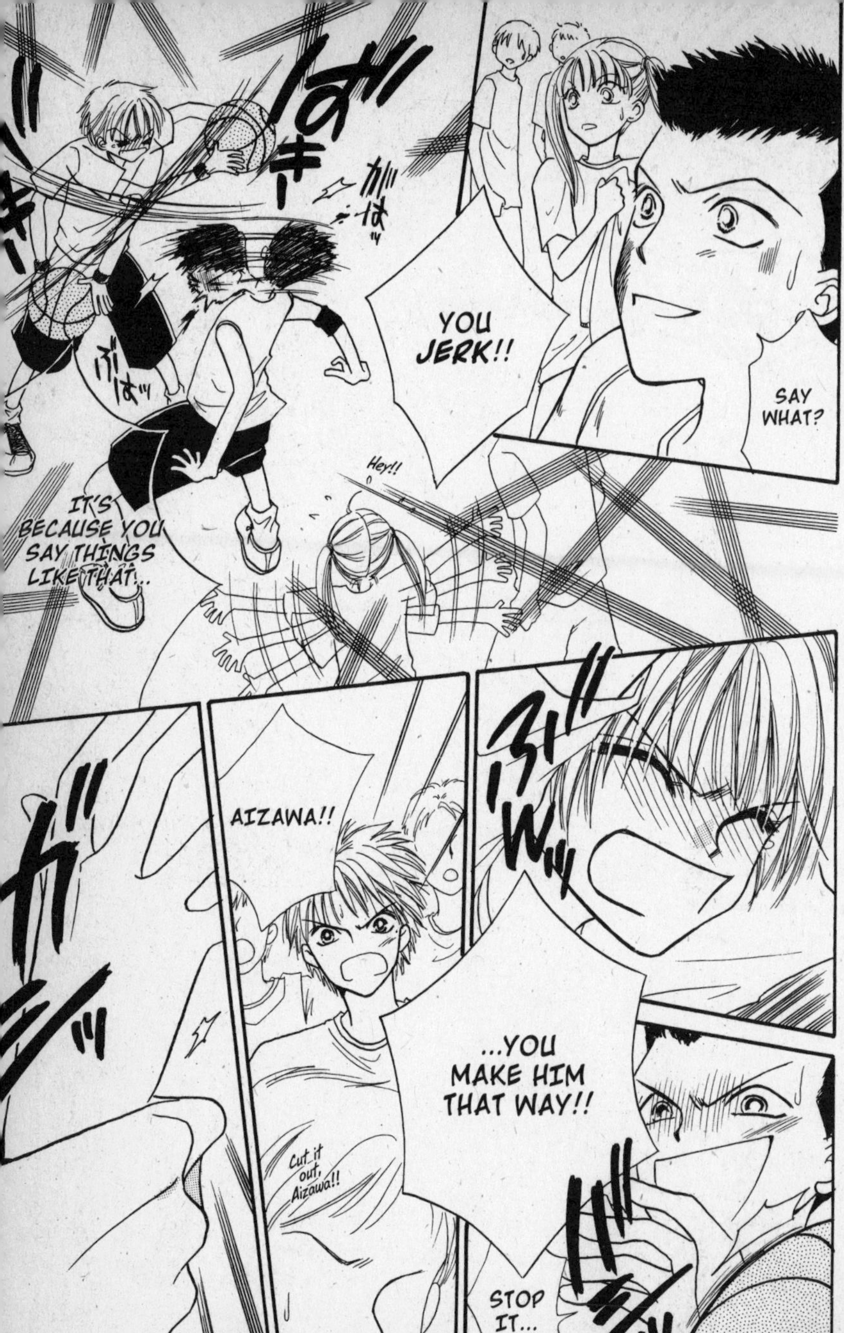
SAY WHAT?
YOU JERK!!
ばきー
がはッ
ぶはッ
Hey!!
IT'S BECAUSE YOU SAY THINGS LIKE THAT...
ふいッ
...YOU MAKE HIM THAT WAY!!
STOP IT...
AIZAWA!!
Cut it out, Aizawa!!
ガシッ

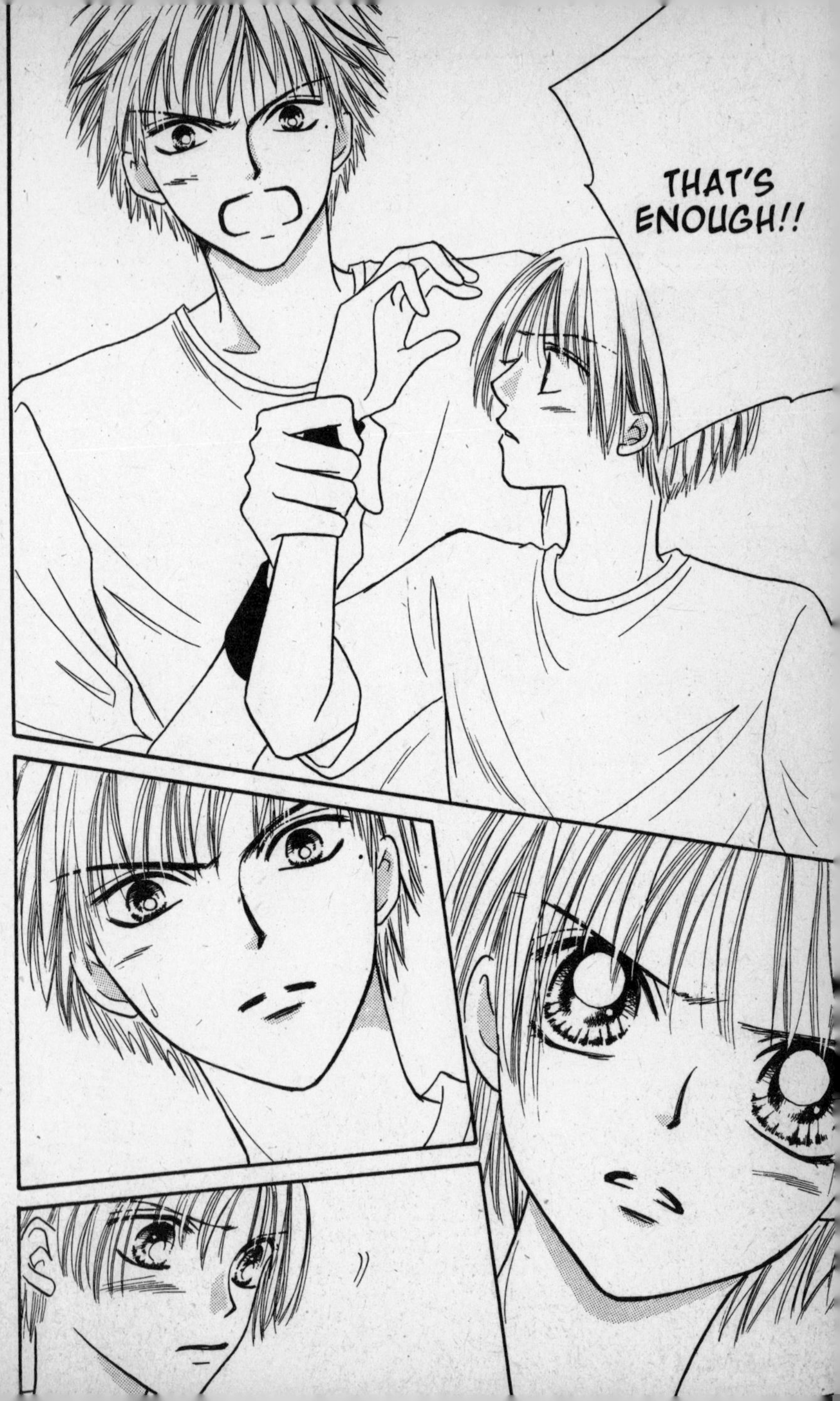
THAT'S ENOUGH!!

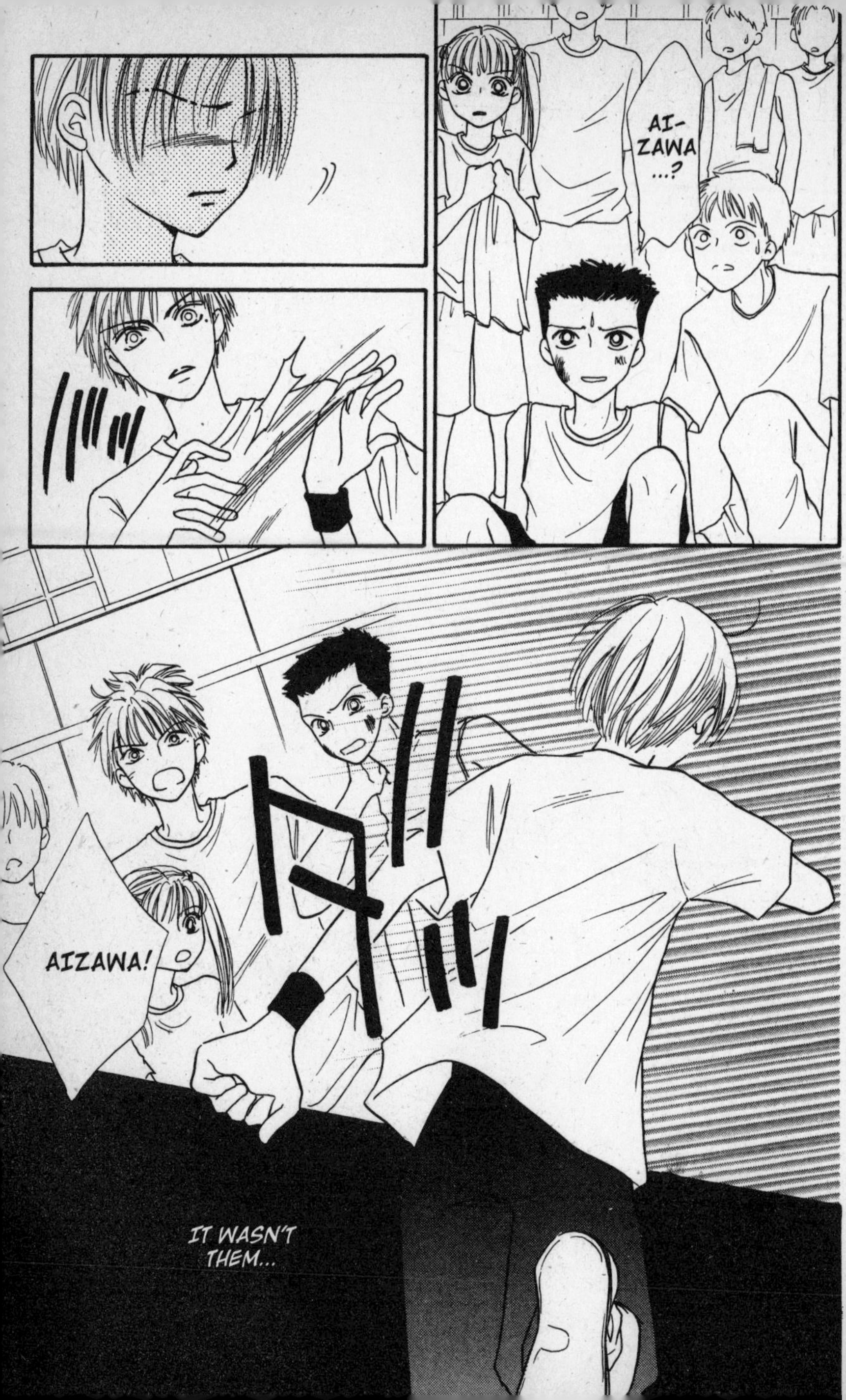
AI-ZAWA...?
AIZAWA!
IT WASN'T THEM...

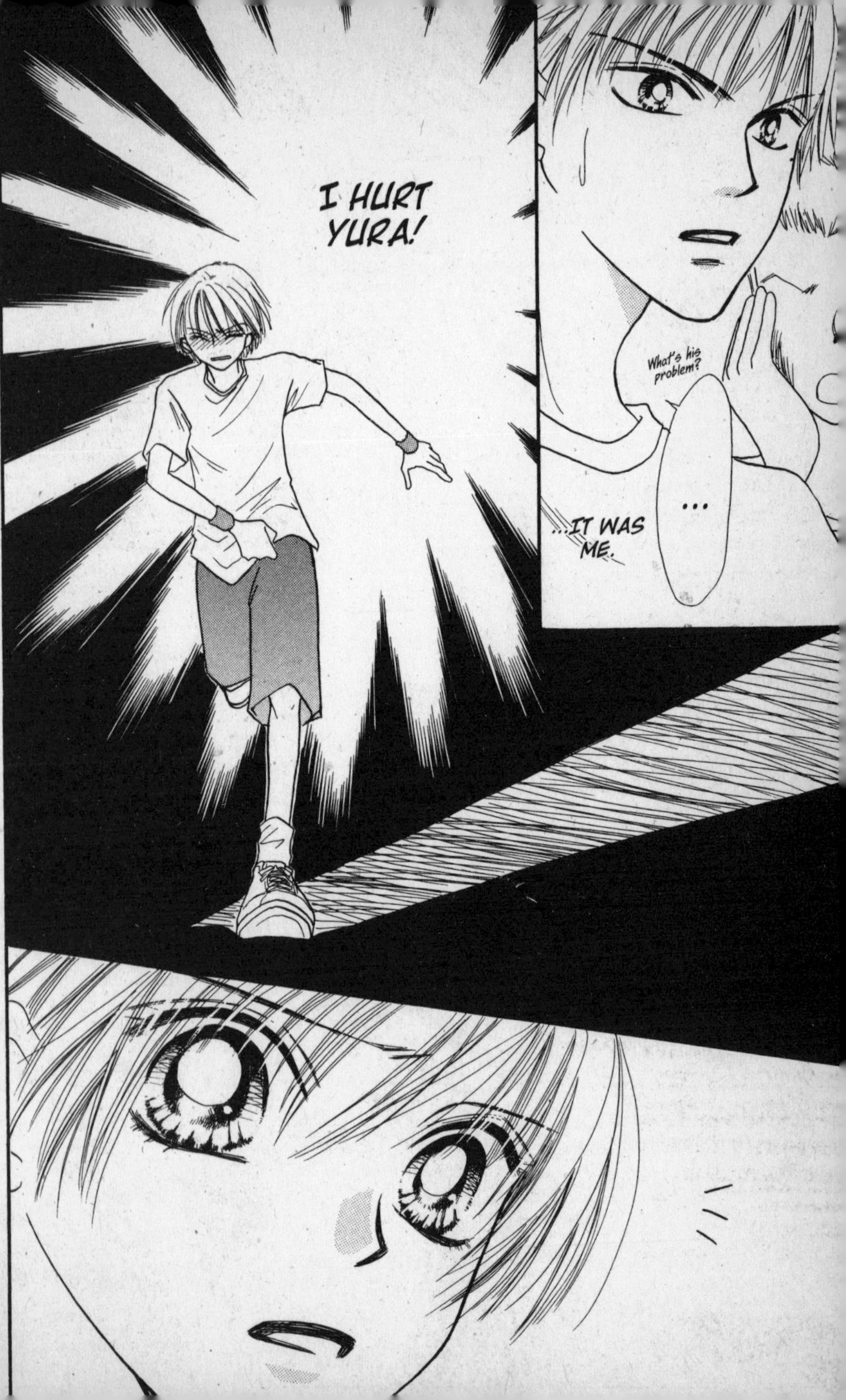
What's his problem?
...
...IT WAS ME.
I HURT YURA!

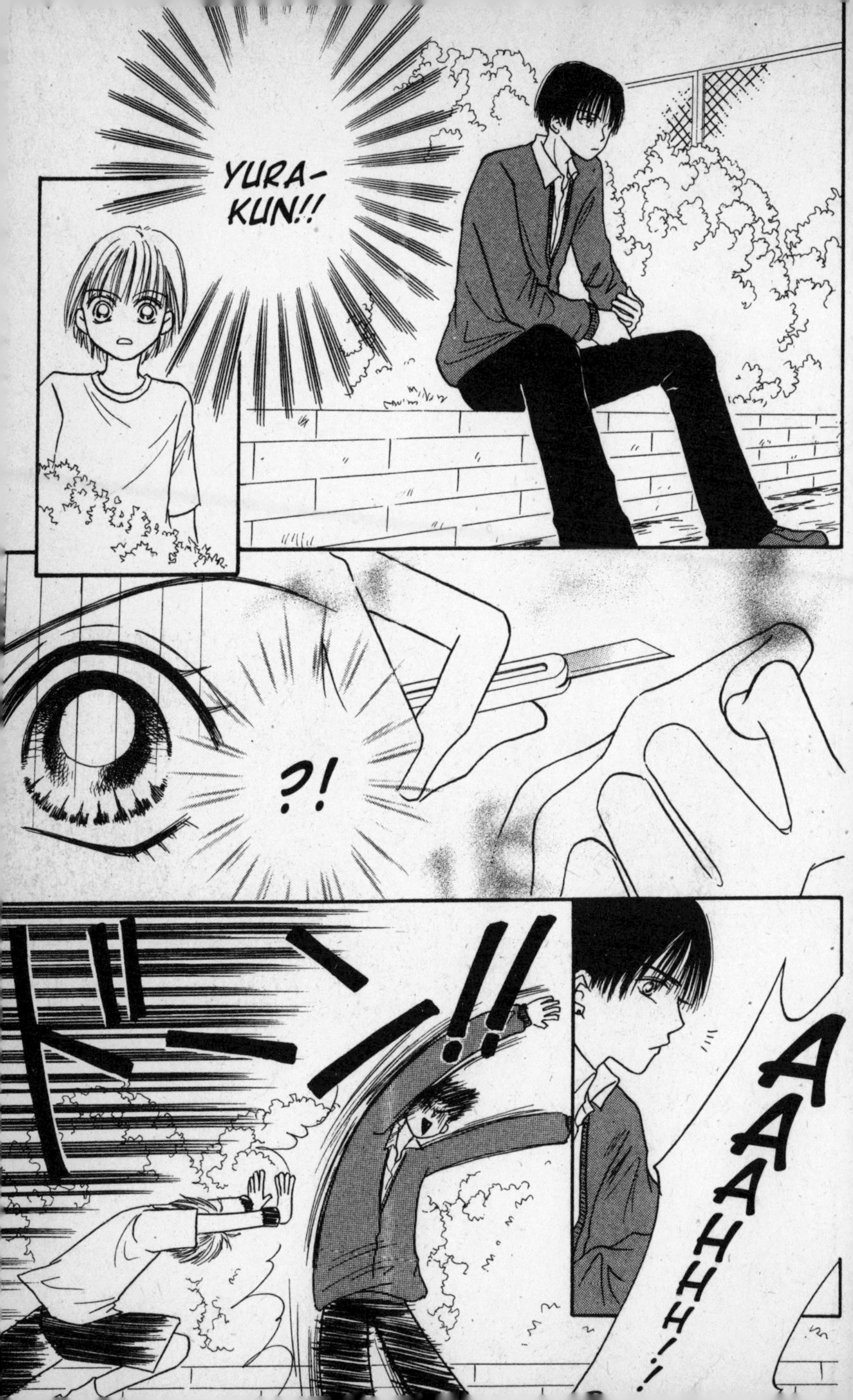
YURA-KUN!!
?!
!!
AAAAHHH-!

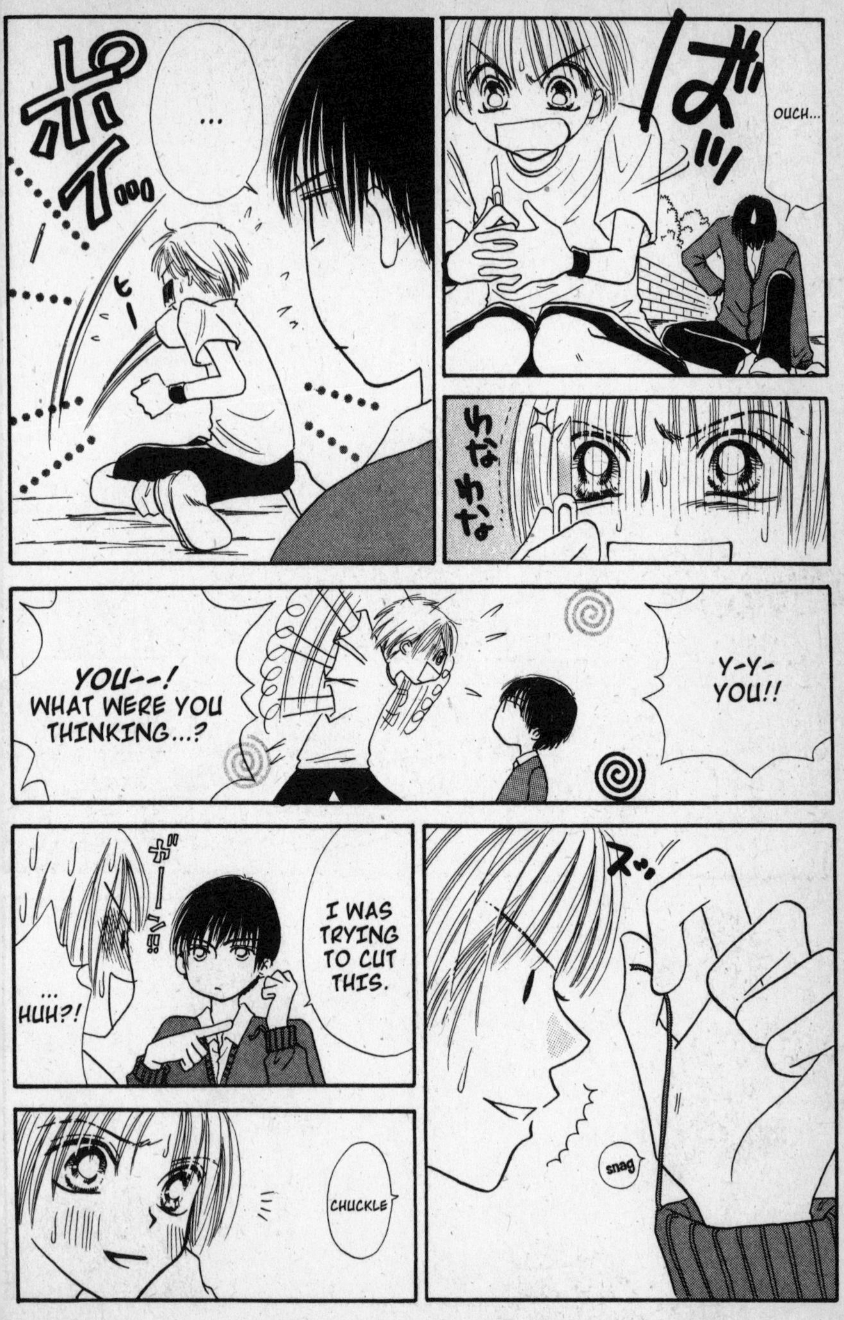
ばッ
OUCH...
わなわな
...
ポイ
ヒー
Y-Y-YOU!!
YOU--! WHAT WERE YOU THINKING...?
ズッ
snag
I WAS TRYING TO CUT THIS.
ガーン!!
...HUH?!
CHUCKLE

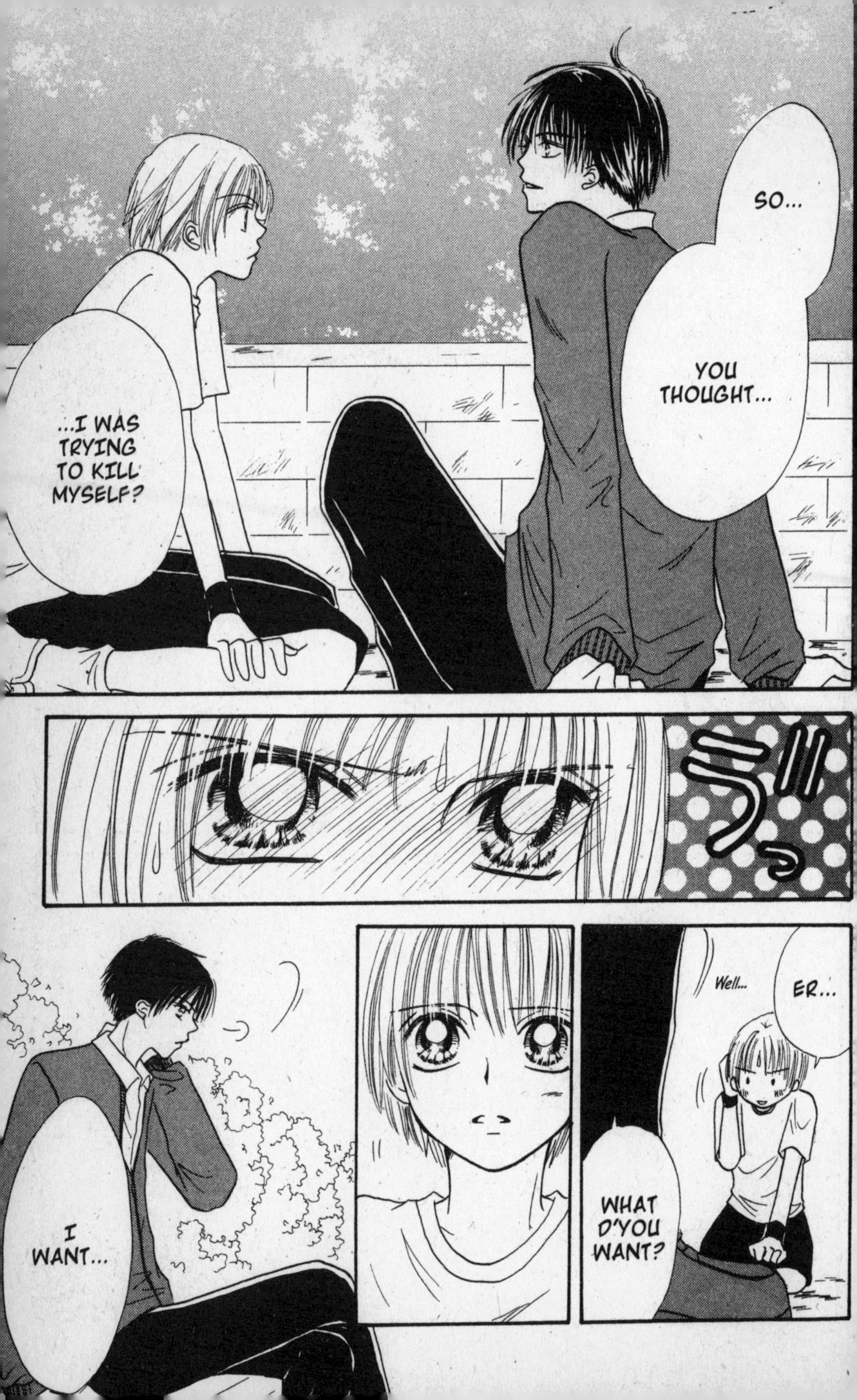
SO...
YOU THOUGHT...
...I WAS TRYING TO KILL MYSELF?
ER...
Well...
WHAT D'YOU WANT?
I WANT...

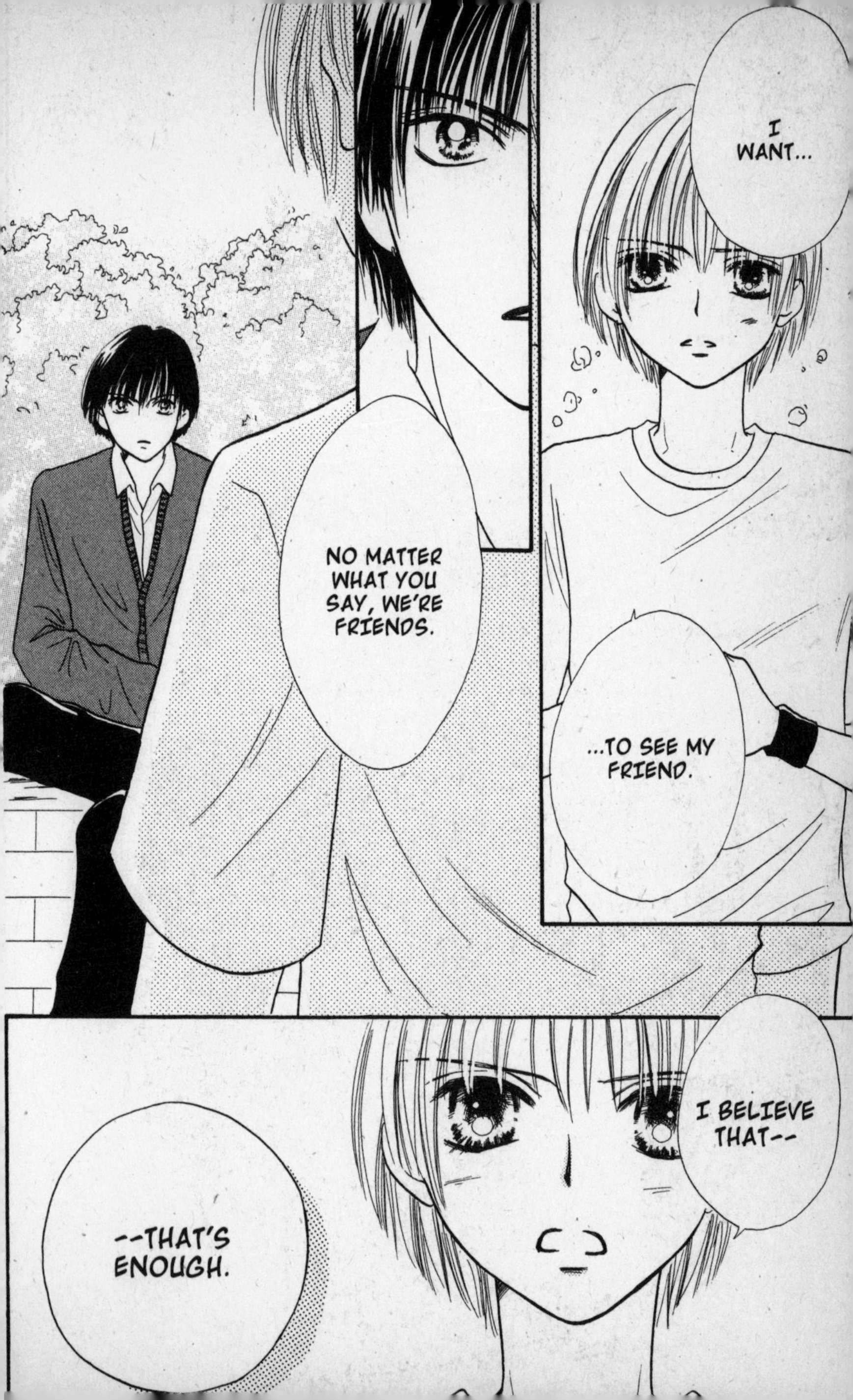
I WANT...
...TO SEE MY FRIEND.
NO MATTER WHAT YOU SAY, WE'RE FRIENDS.
I BELIEVE THAT--
--THAT'S ENOUGH.

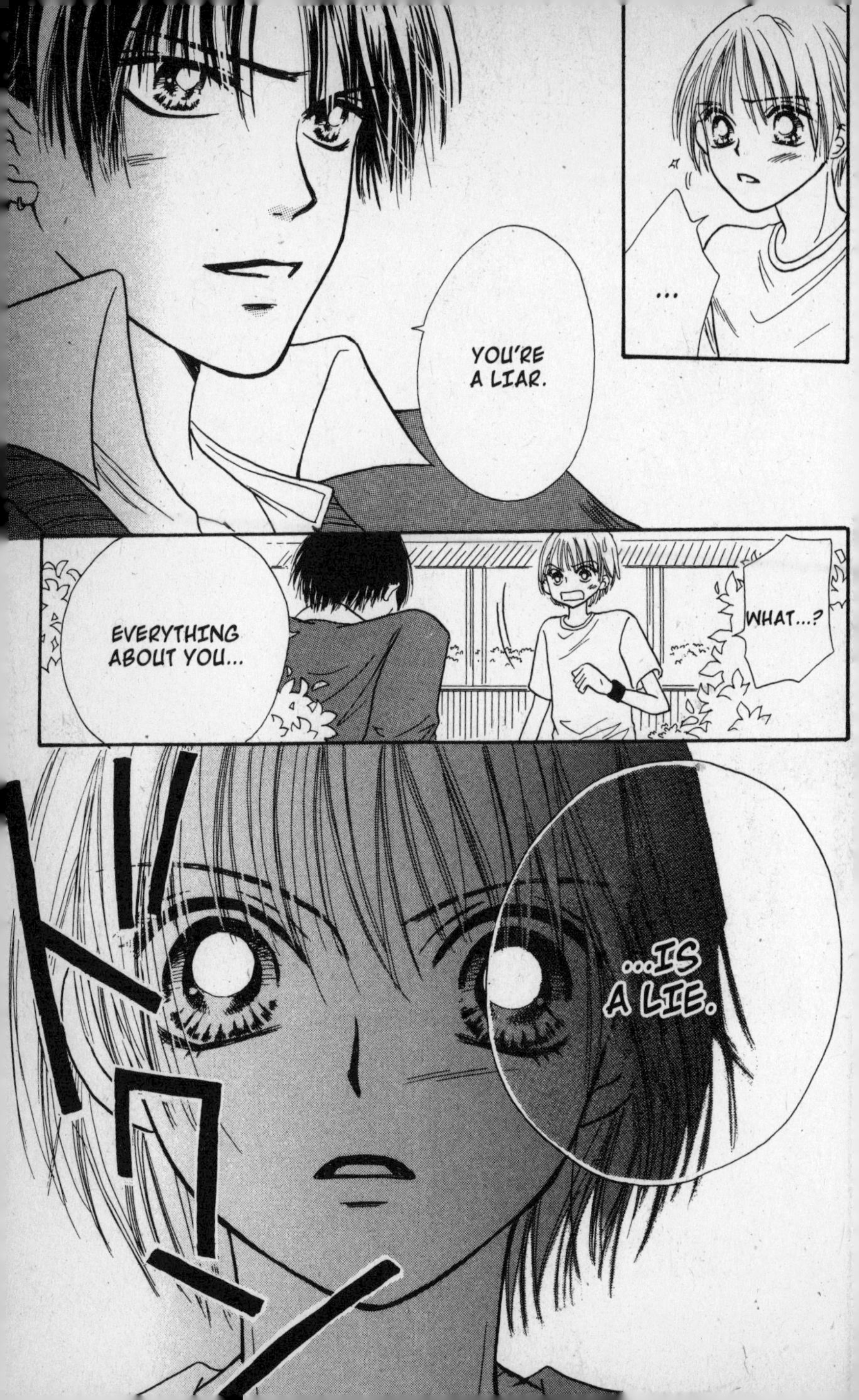
...
YOU'RE A LIAR.
WHAT...?
EVERYTHING ABOUT YOU...
...IS A LIE.

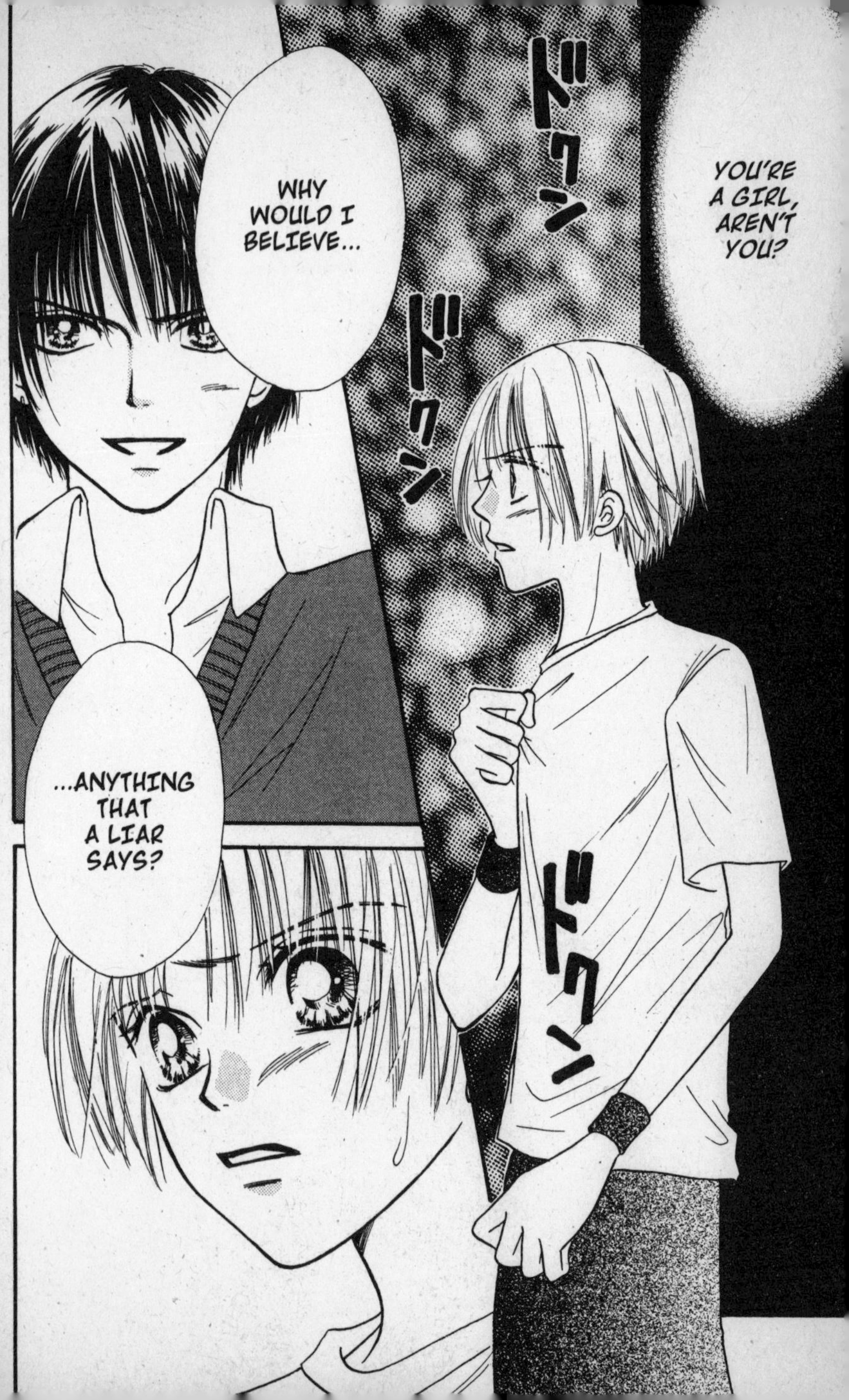
YOU'RE A GIRL, AREN'T YOU?
ドクン
ドクン
ドクン
WHY WOULD I BELIEVE...
...ANYTHING THAT A LIAR SAYS?

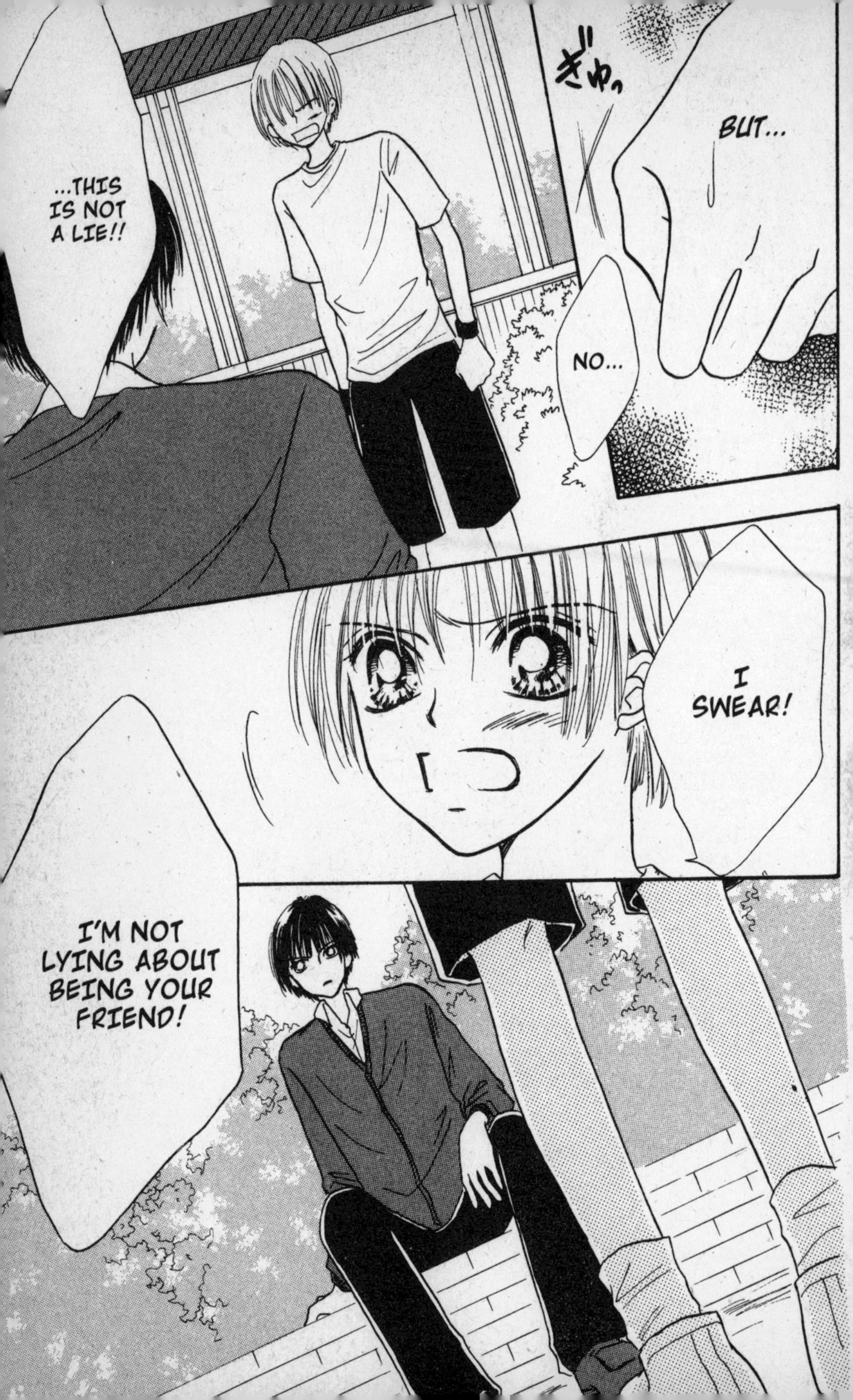
ぎゅっ
BUT...
NO...
...THIS IS NOT A LIE!!
I SWEAR!
I'M NOT LYING ABOUT BEING YOUR FRIEND!

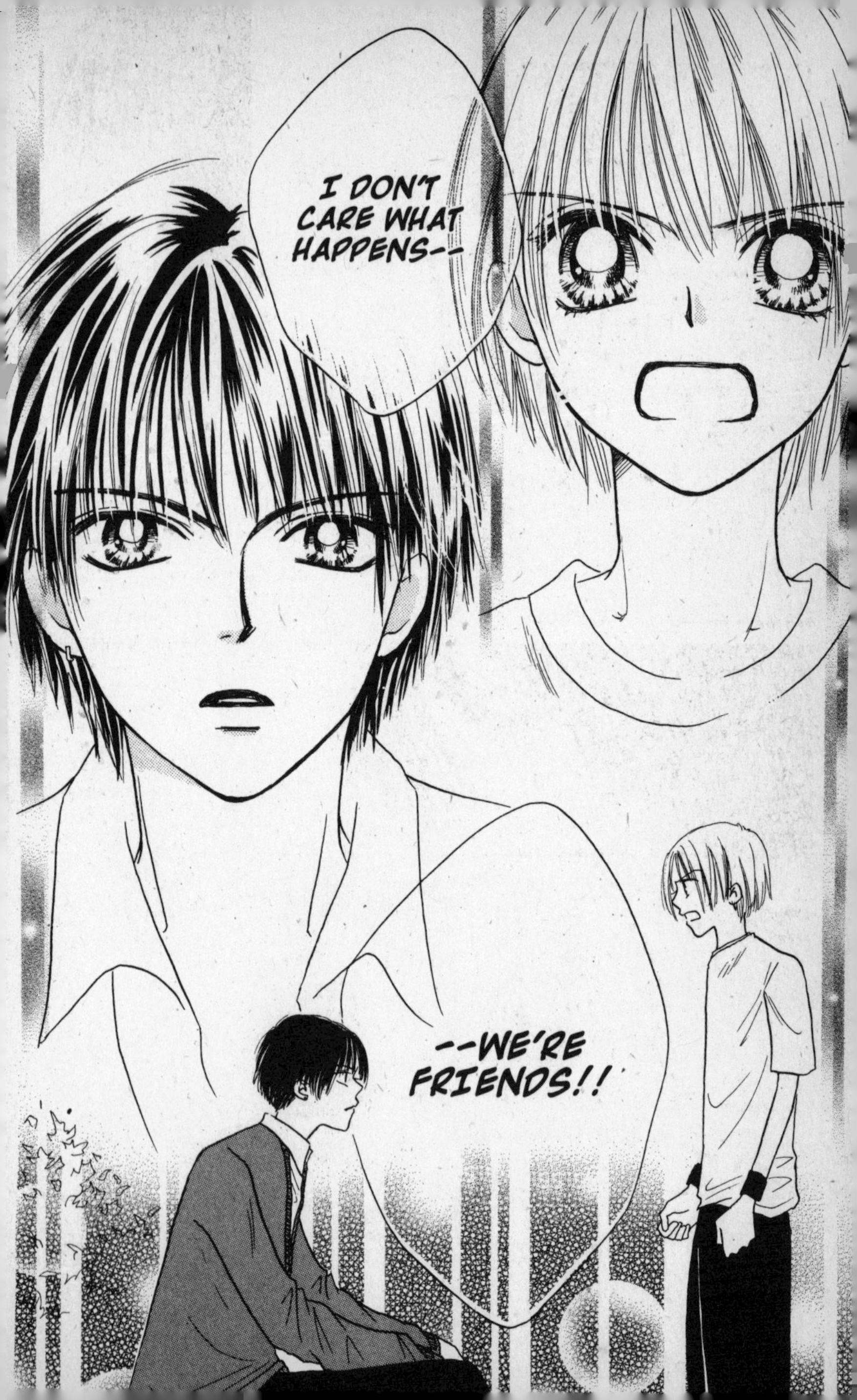
I DON'T CARE WHAT HAPPENS--
--WE'RE FRIENDS!!

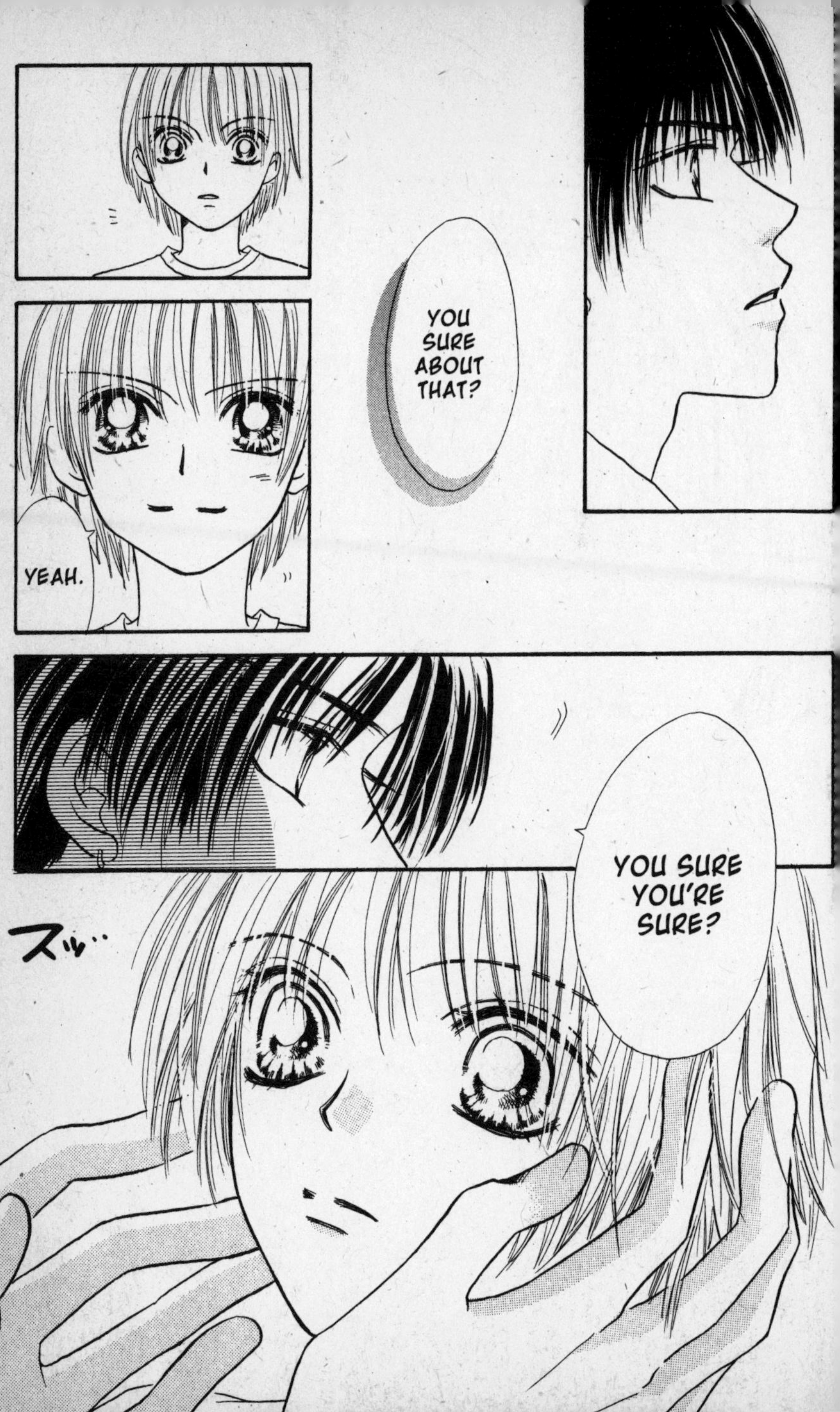
YOU SURE ABOUT THAT?
YEAH.
YOU SURE YOU'RE SURE?
スッ‥

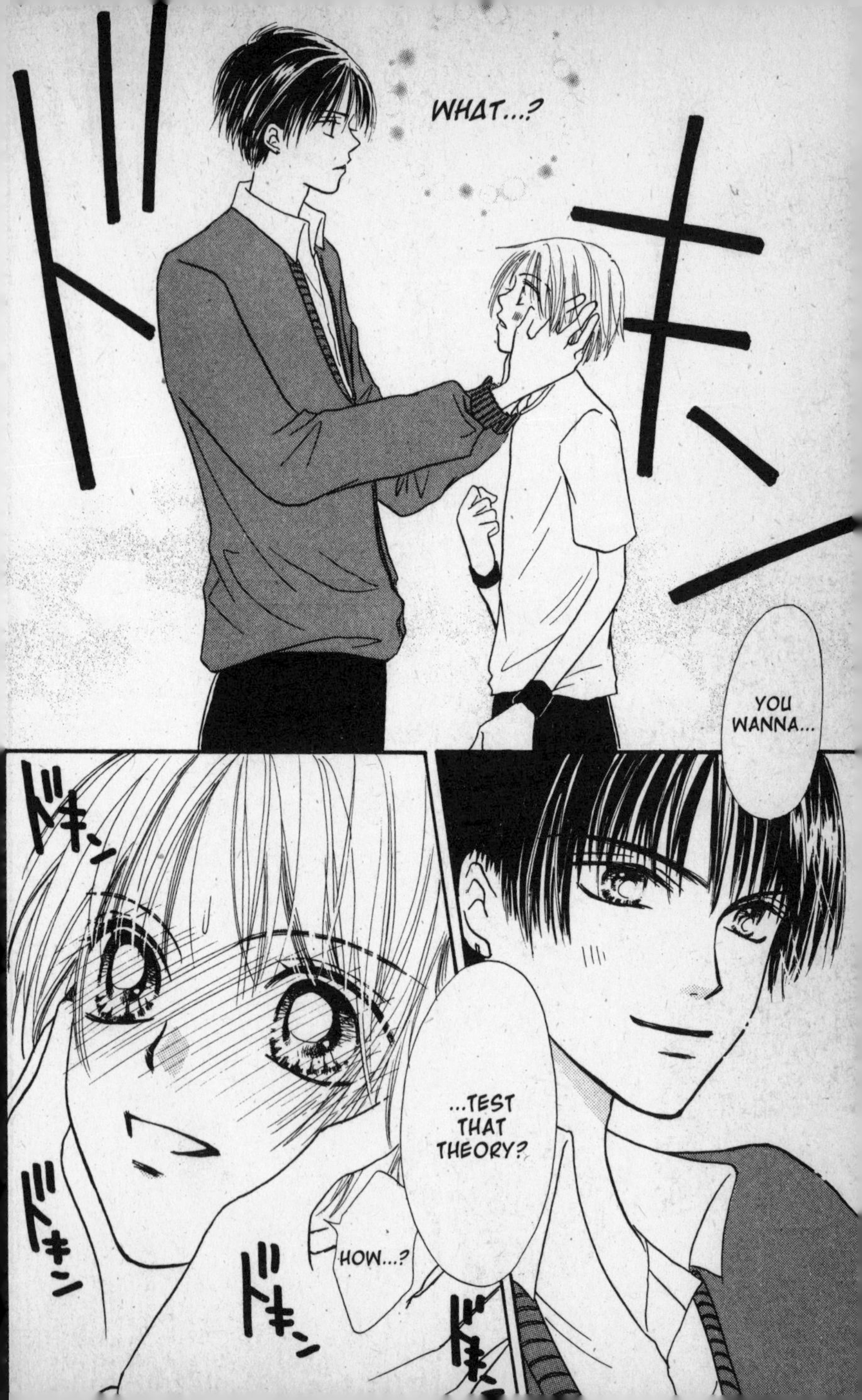

ドキン
WHAT...?
YOU WANNA...
...TEST THAT THEORY?
ドキン
ドキン
HOW...?
ドキン
ドキン

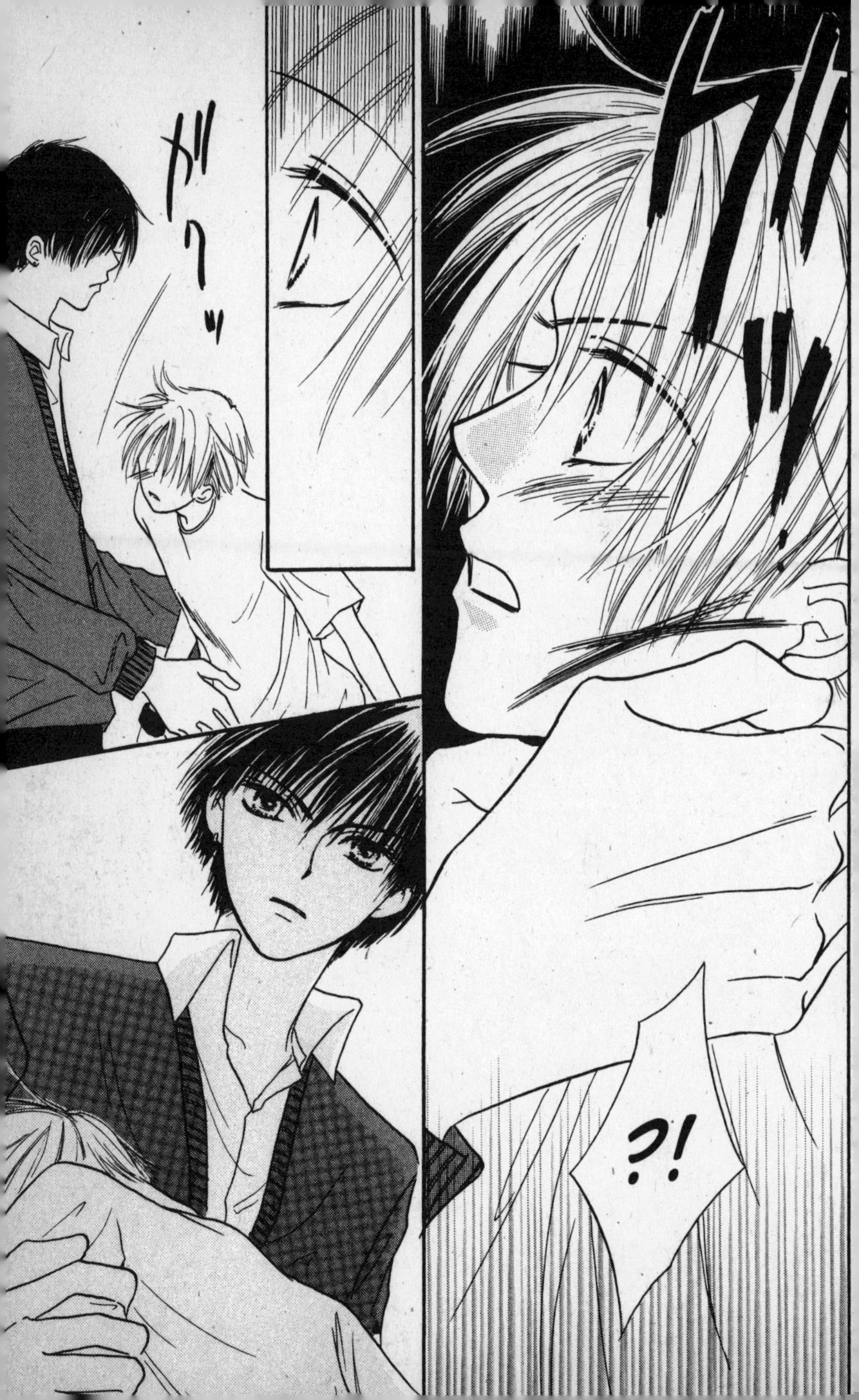
?!

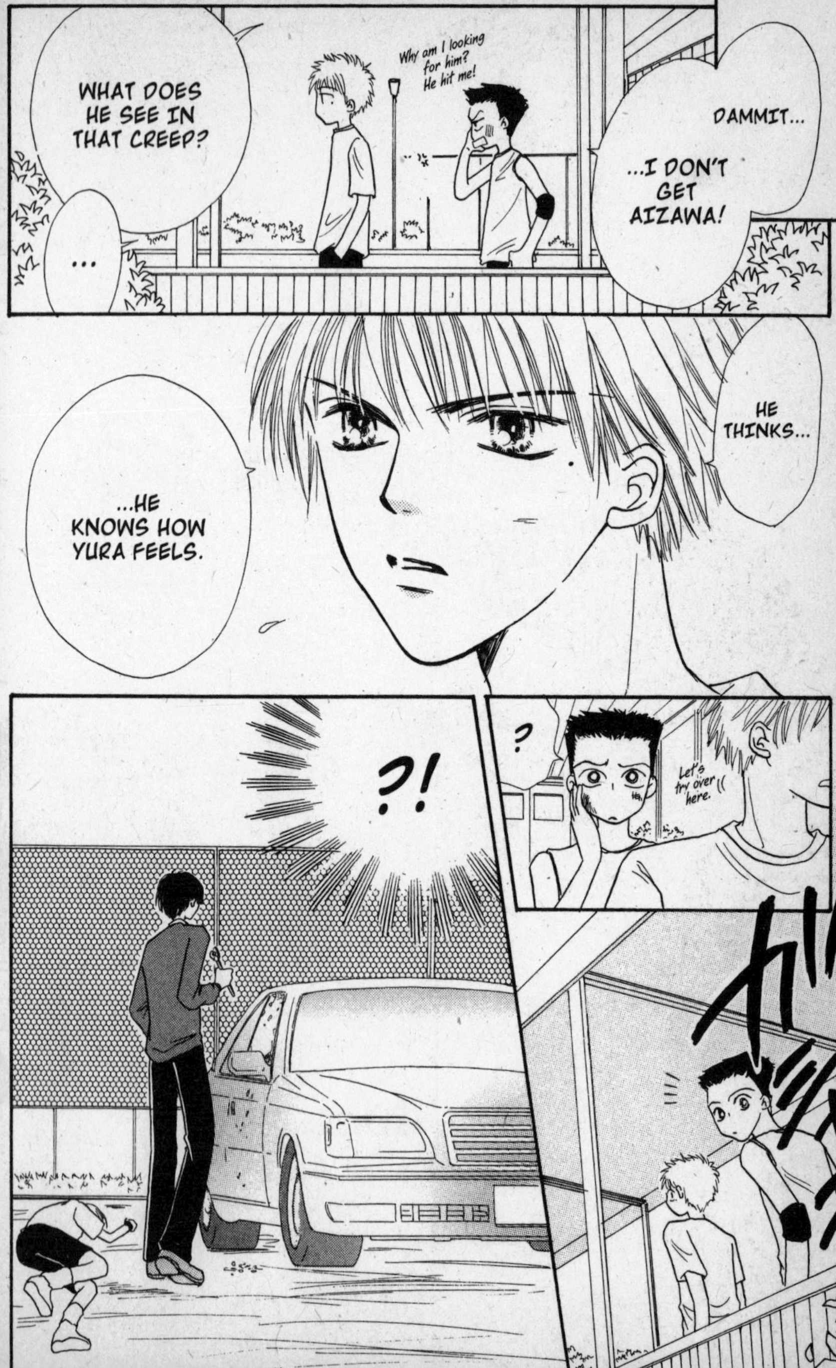
DAMMIT...
...I DON'T GET AIZAWA!
Why am I looking for him? He hit me!
WHAT DOES HE SEE IN THAT CREEP?
...
HE THINKS...
...HE KNOWS HOW YURA FEELS.
?
Let's try over here.
?!

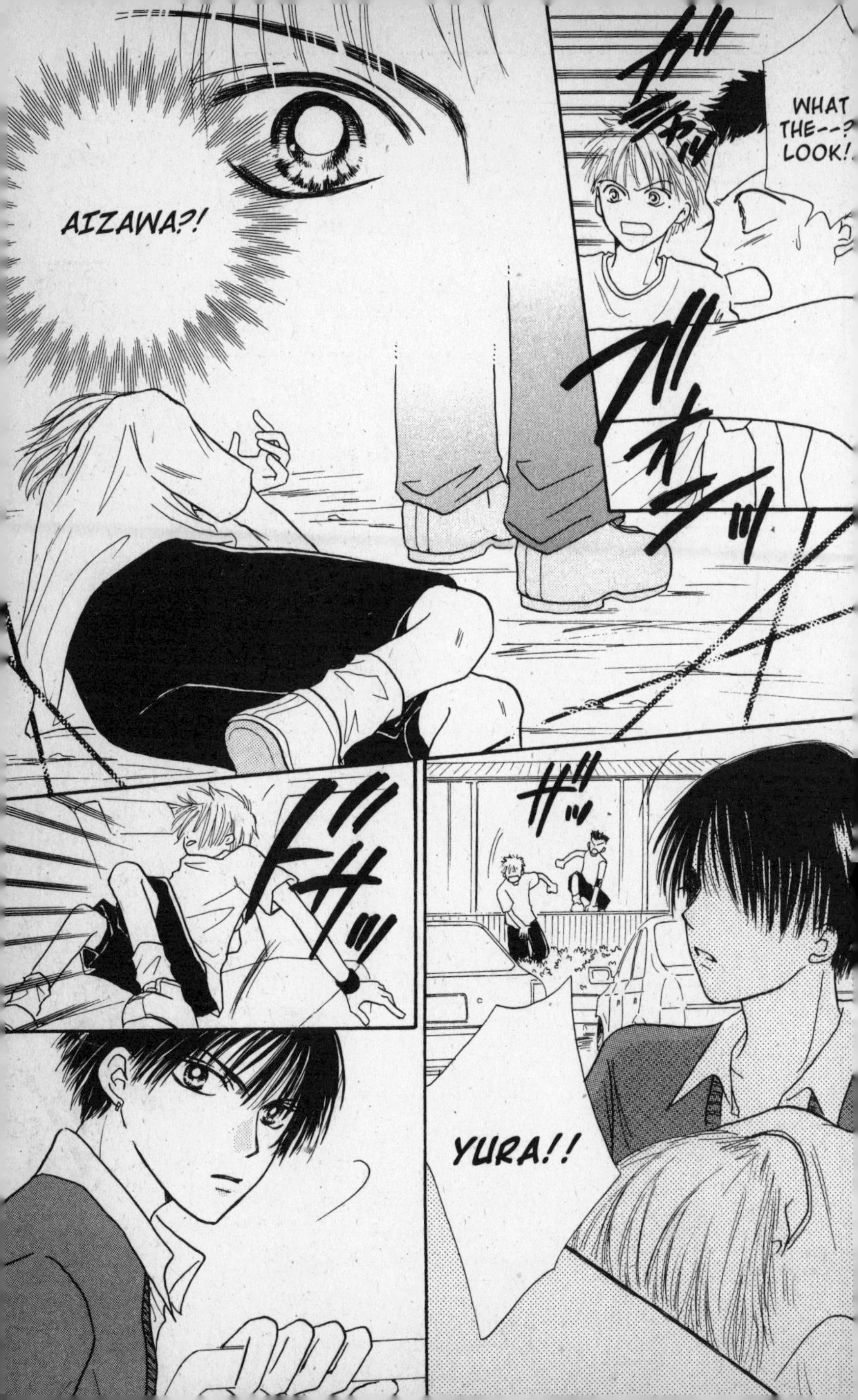
WHAT THE--? LOOK!
AIZAWA?!
YURA!!

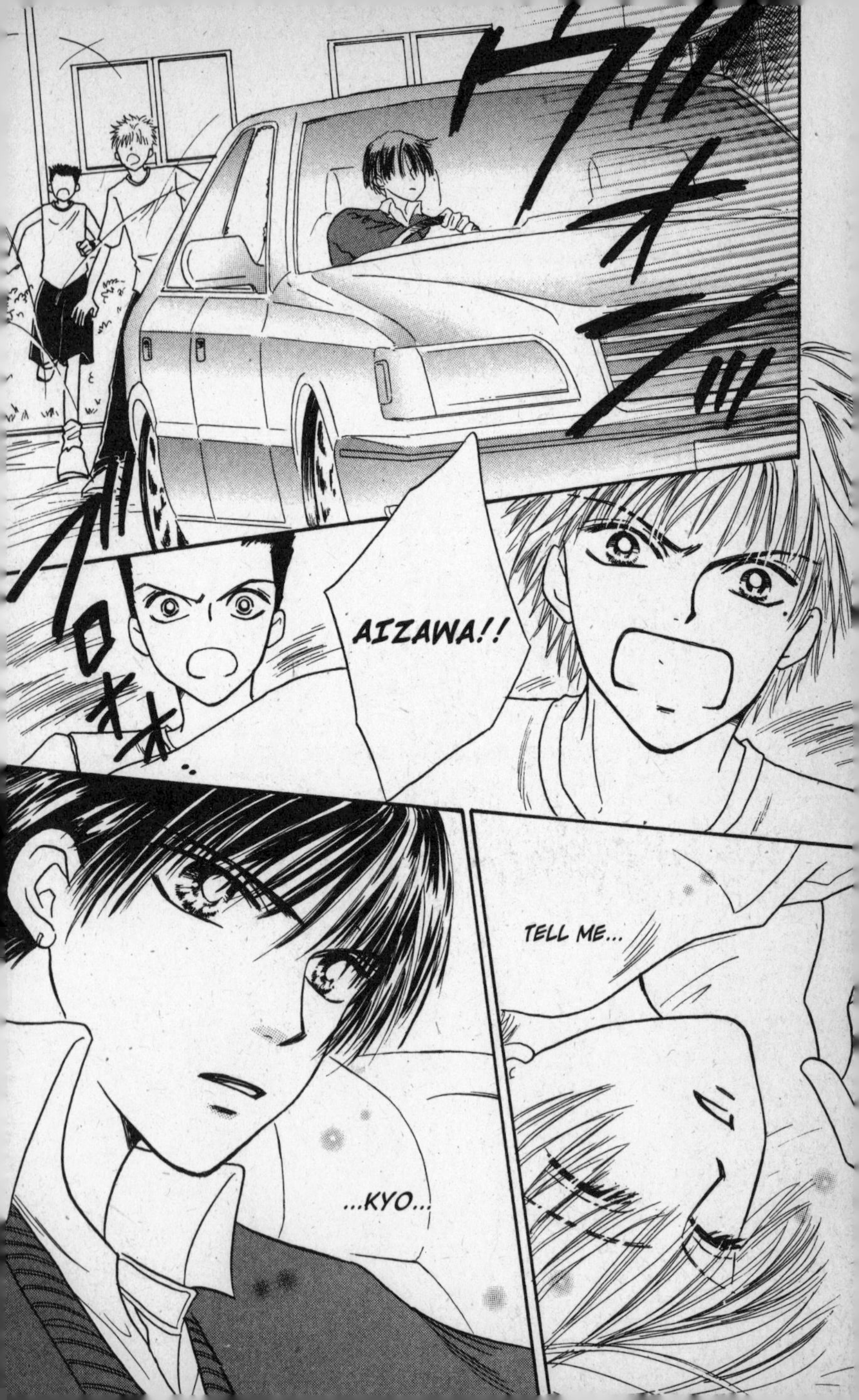
AIZAWA!!
TELL ME...
...KYO...

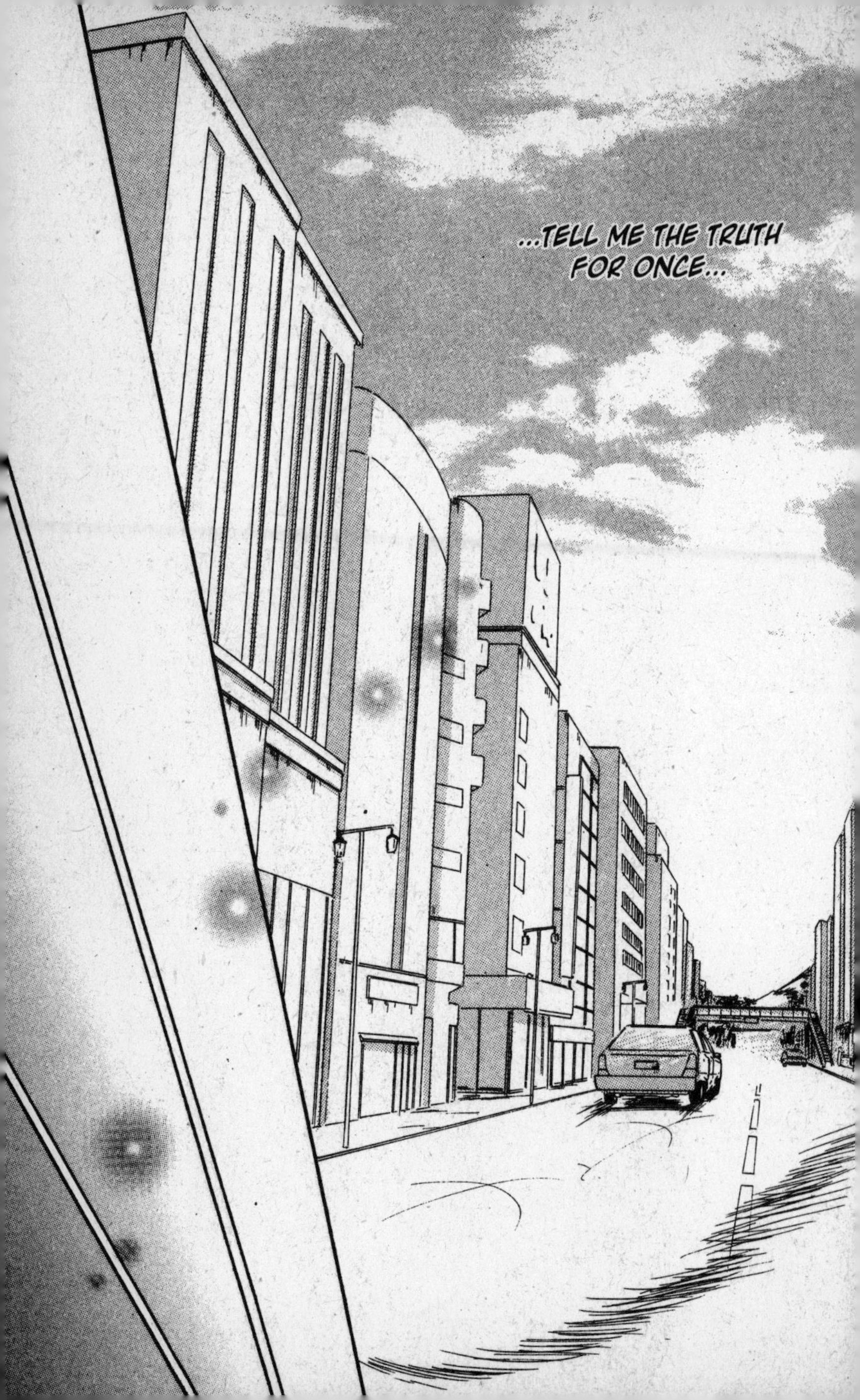
...TELL ME THE TRUTH FOR ONCE...

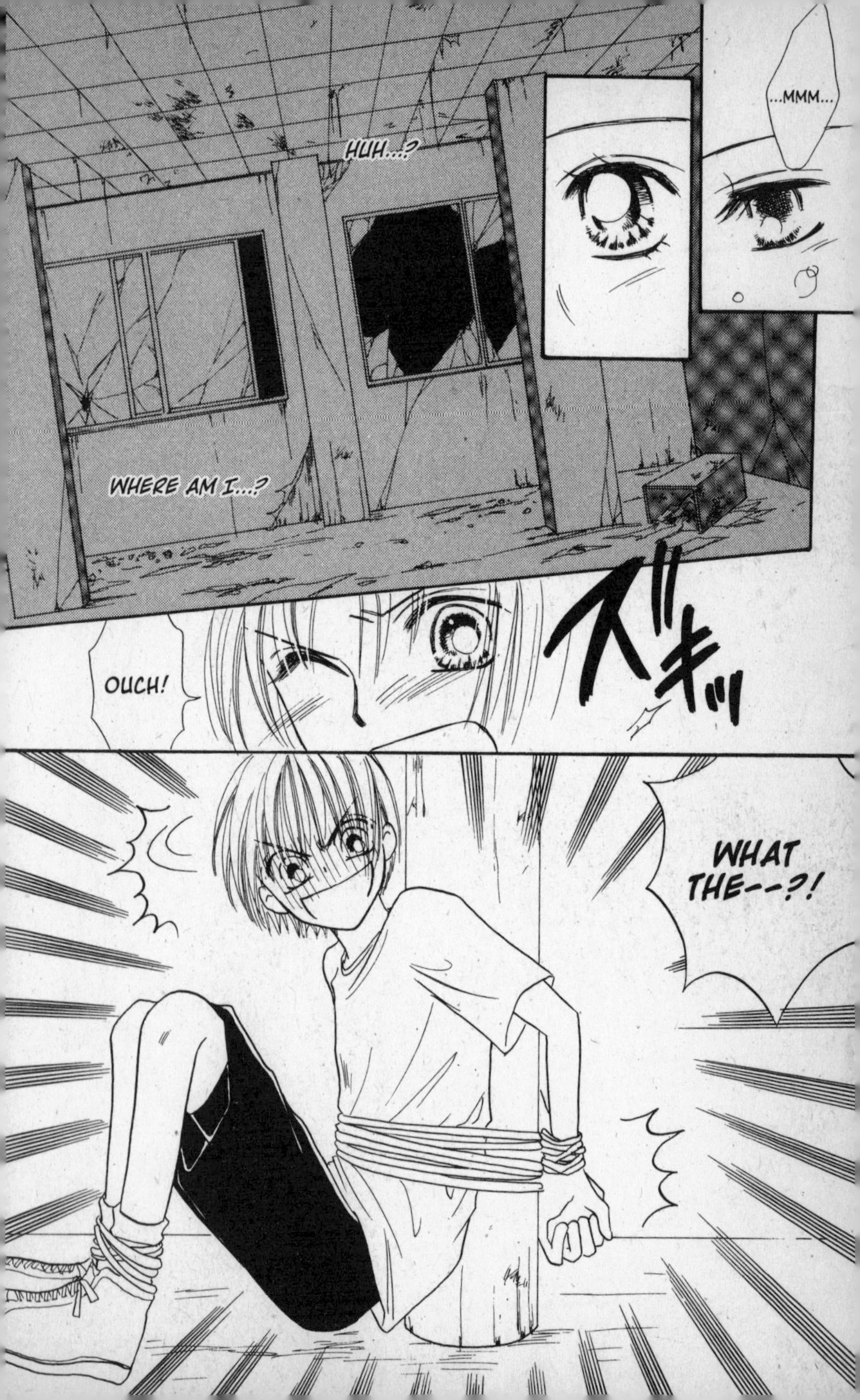
...MMM...
HUH...?
WHERE AM I...?
ズキッ
OUCH!
WHAT THE--?!

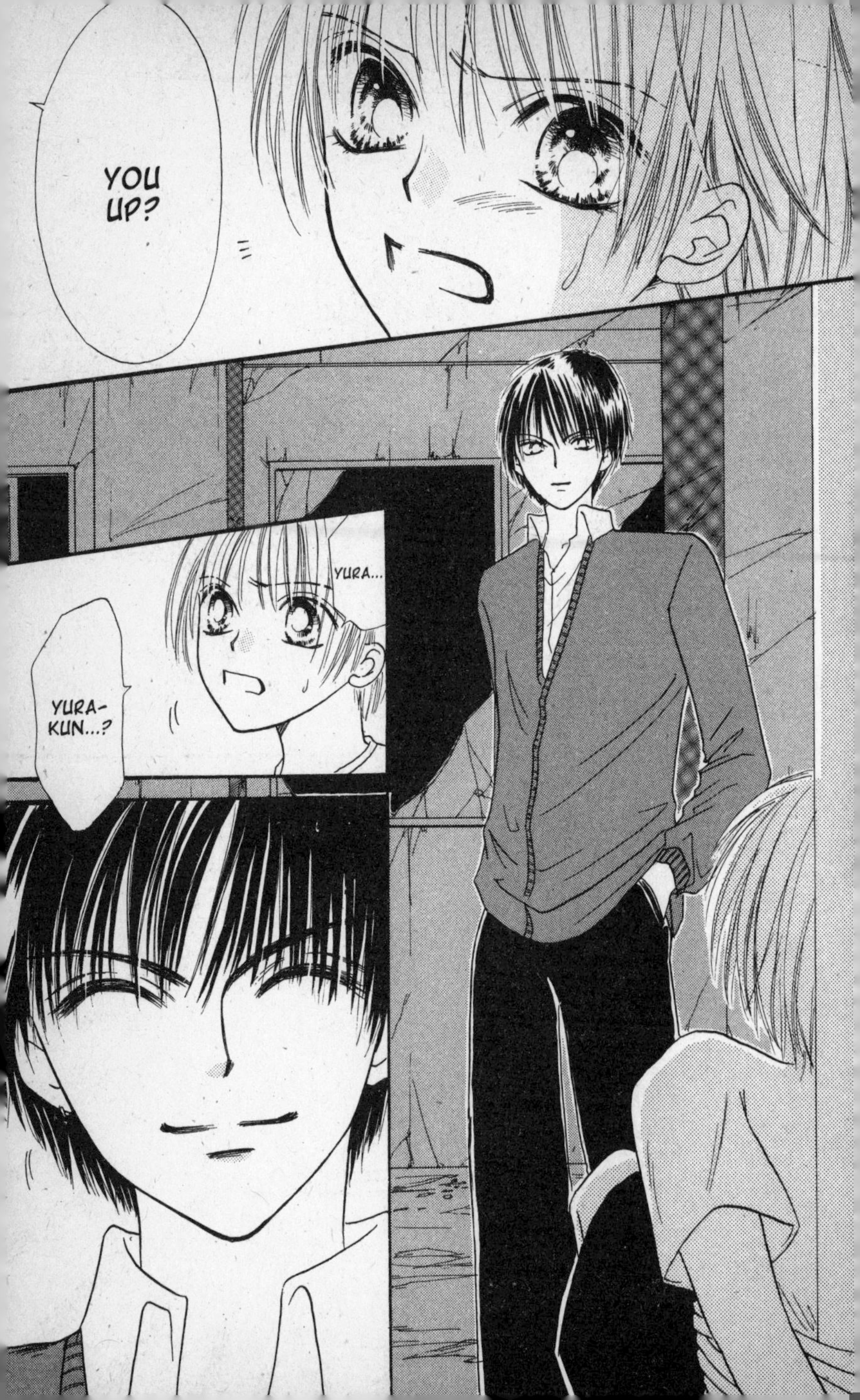
YOU UP?
YURA...
YURA-KUN...?

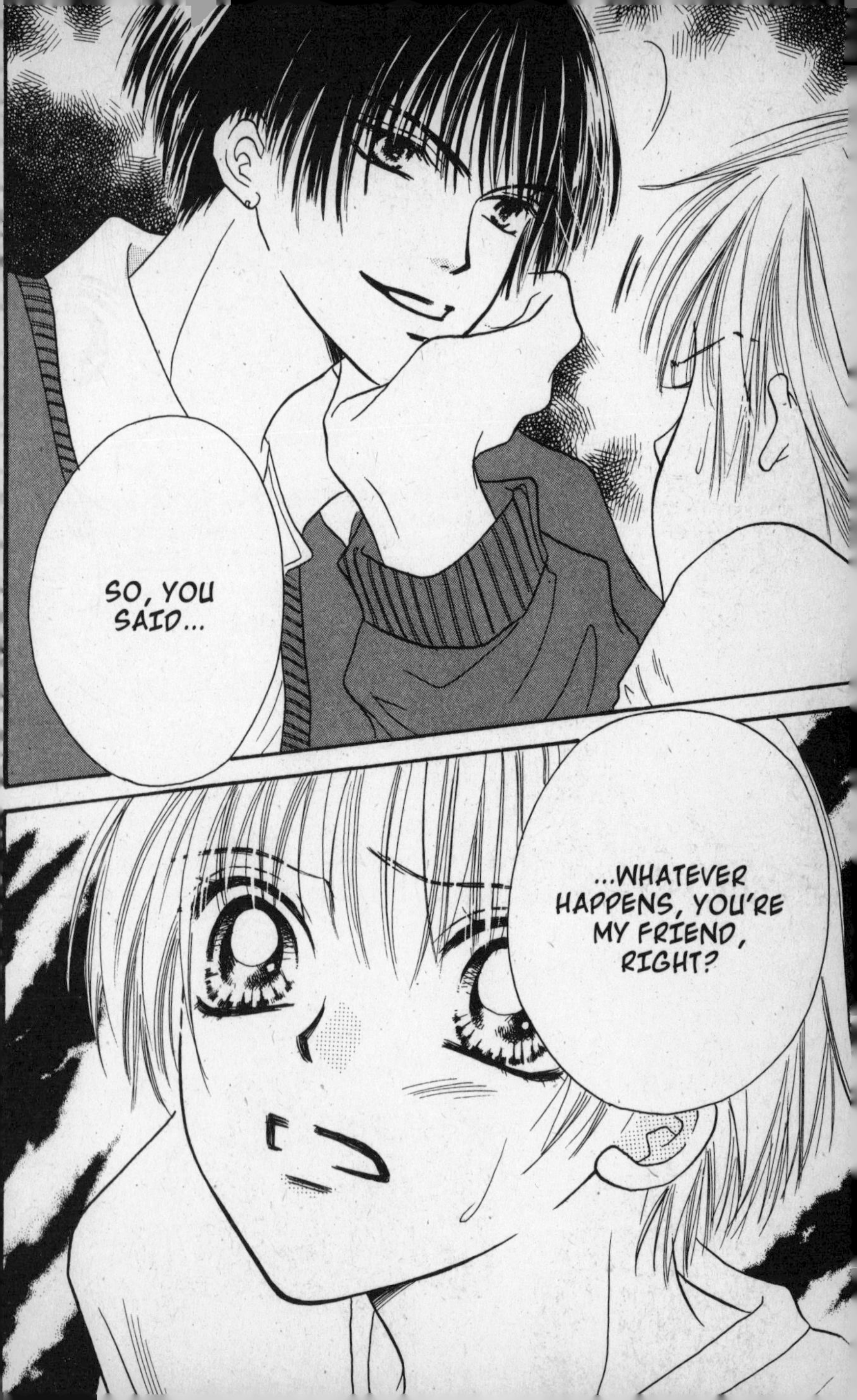
SO, YOU SAID...
...WHATEVER HAPPENS, YOU'RE MY FRIEND, RIGHT?

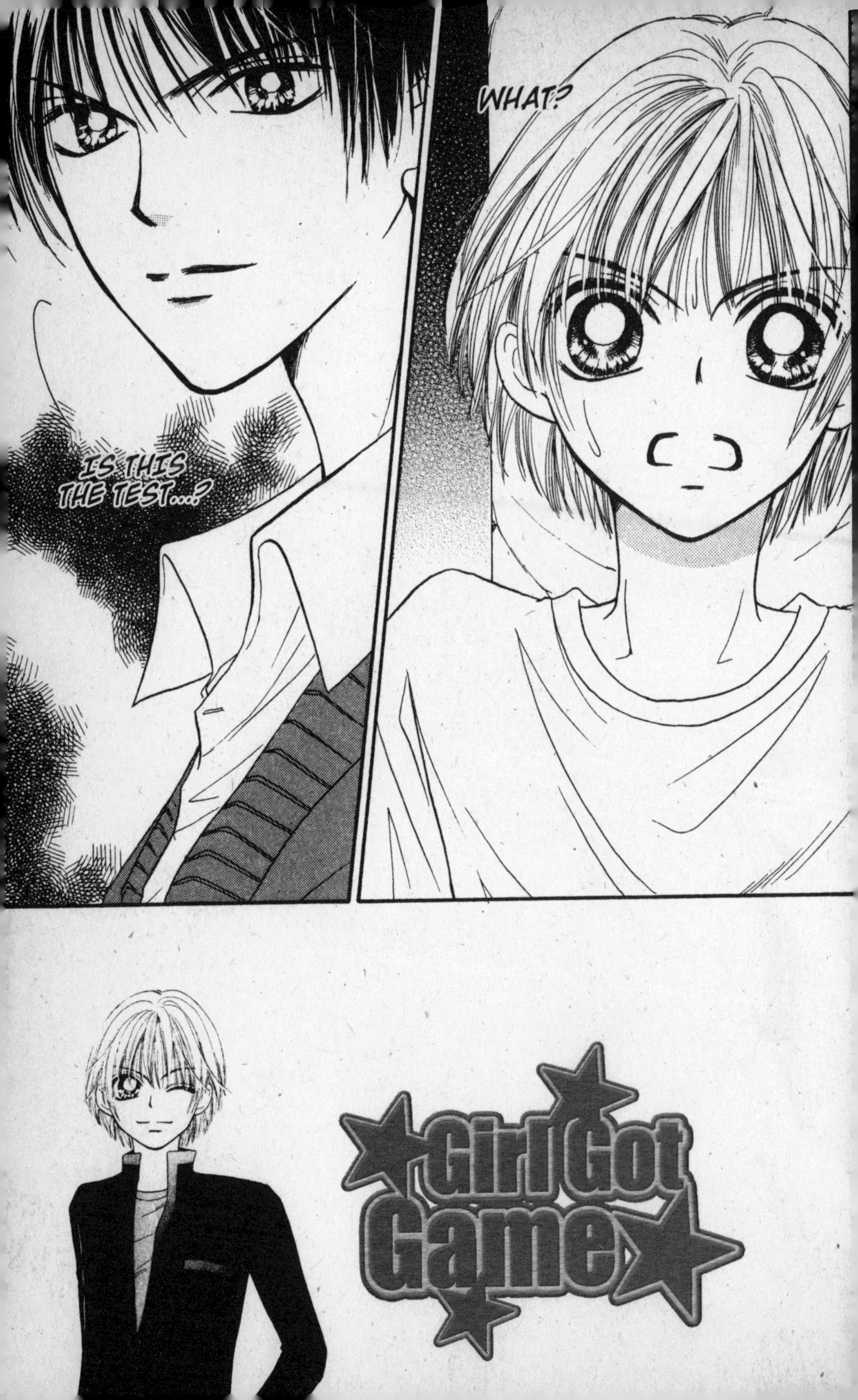
WHAT?
IS THIS THE TEST...?
Girl Got Game

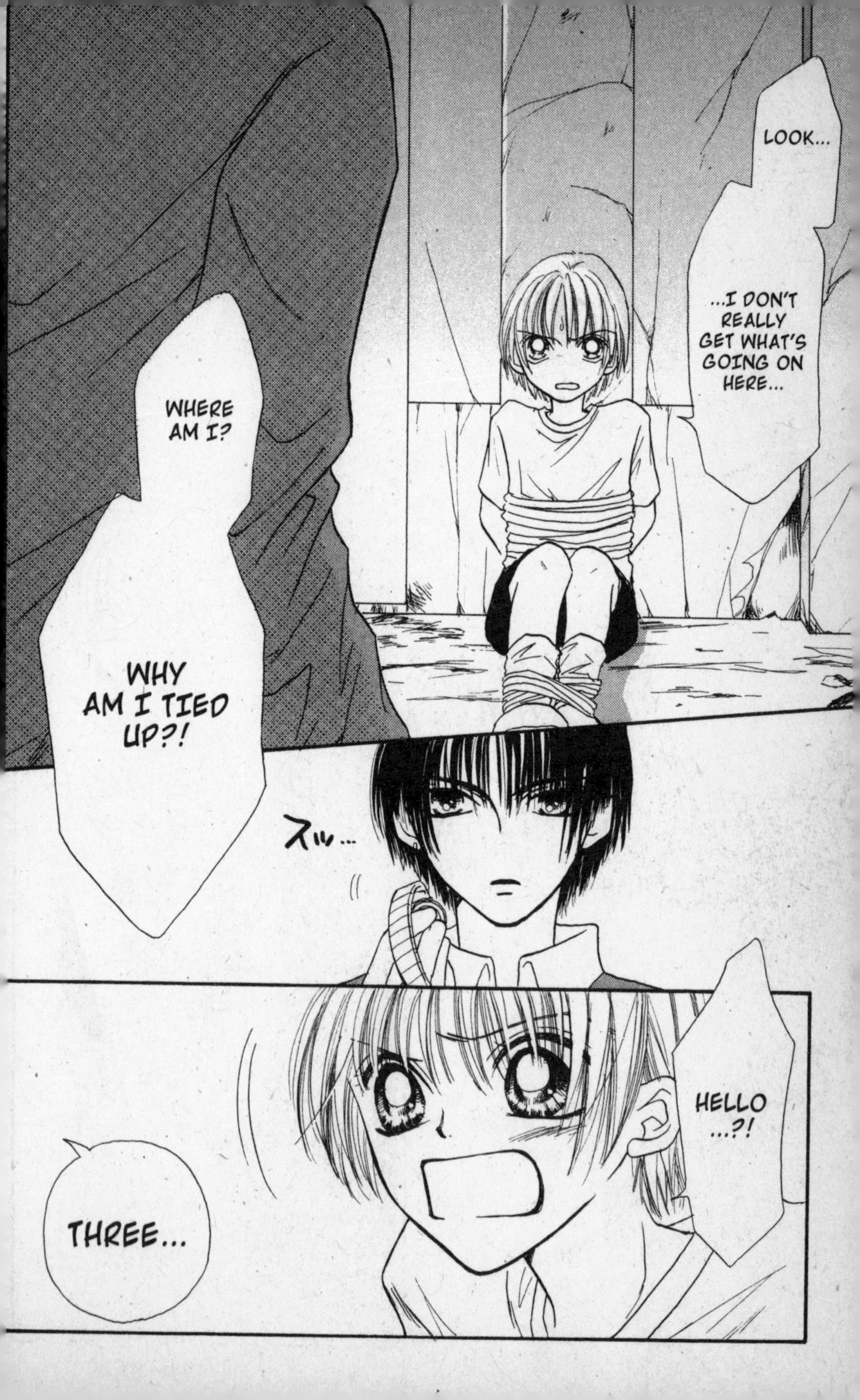
LOOK...
...I DON'T REALLY GET WHAT'S GOING ON HERE...
WHERE AM I?
WHY AM I TIED UP?!
スッ...
HELLO ...?!
THREE...

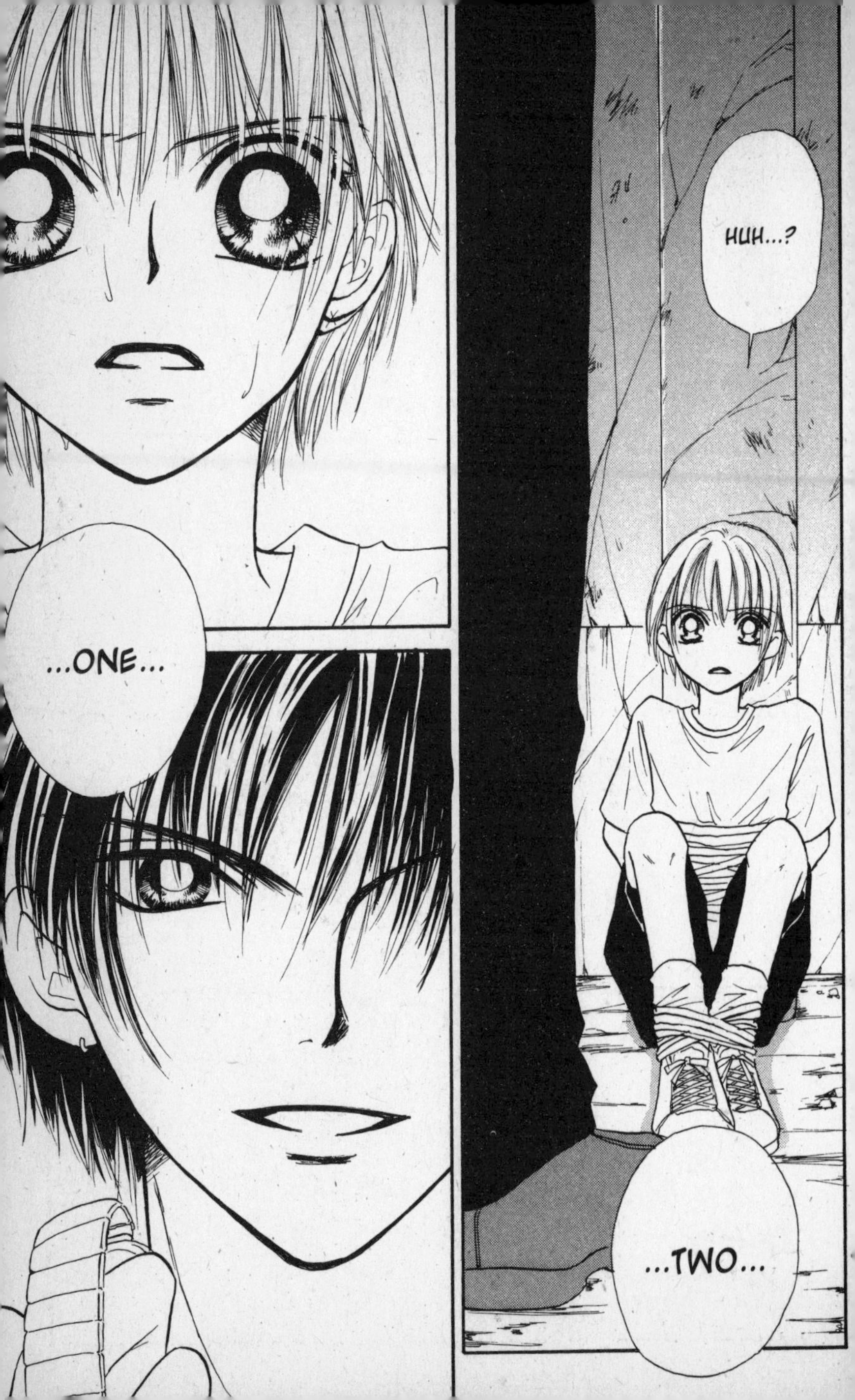
HUH...?
...TWO...
...ONE...

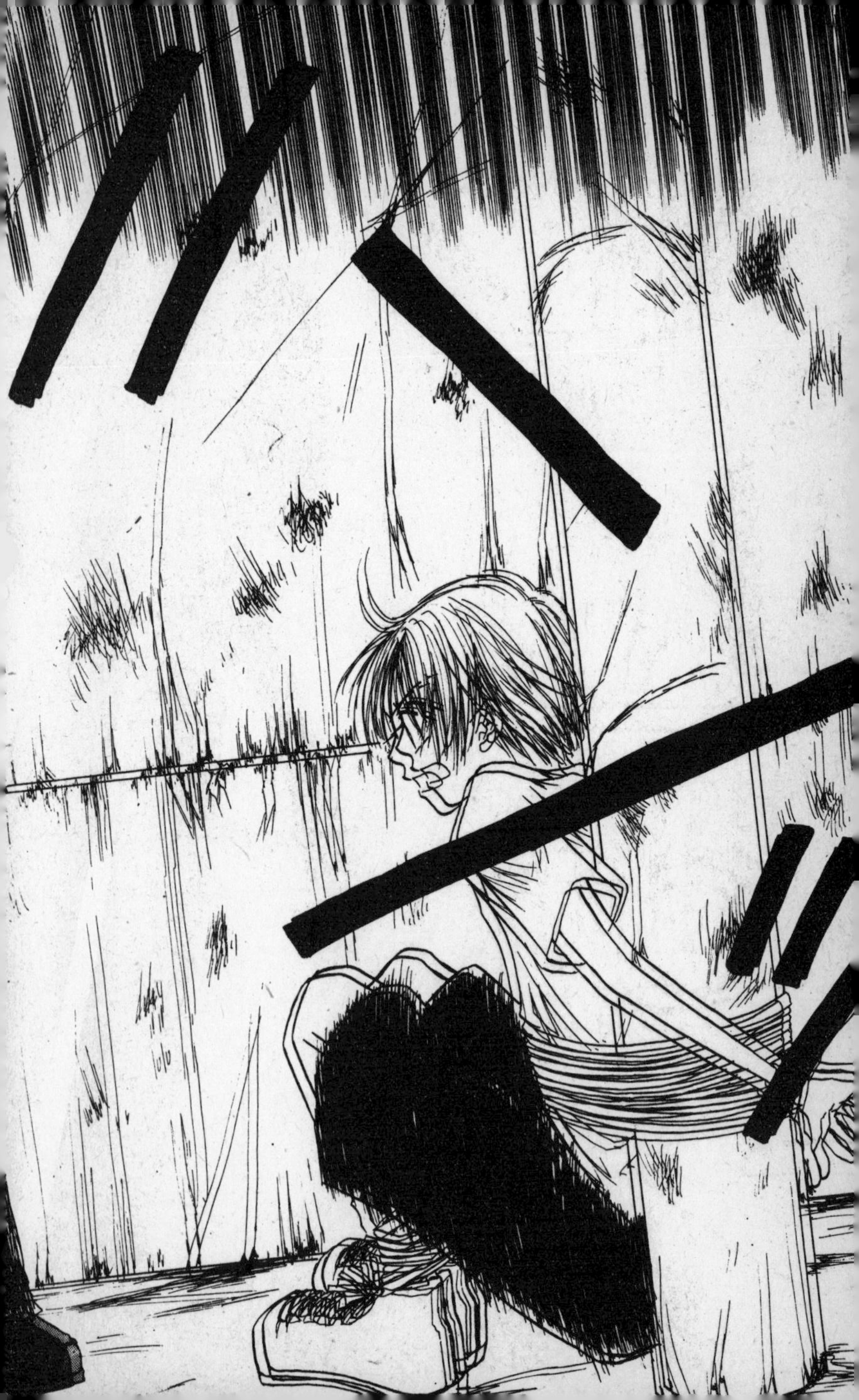

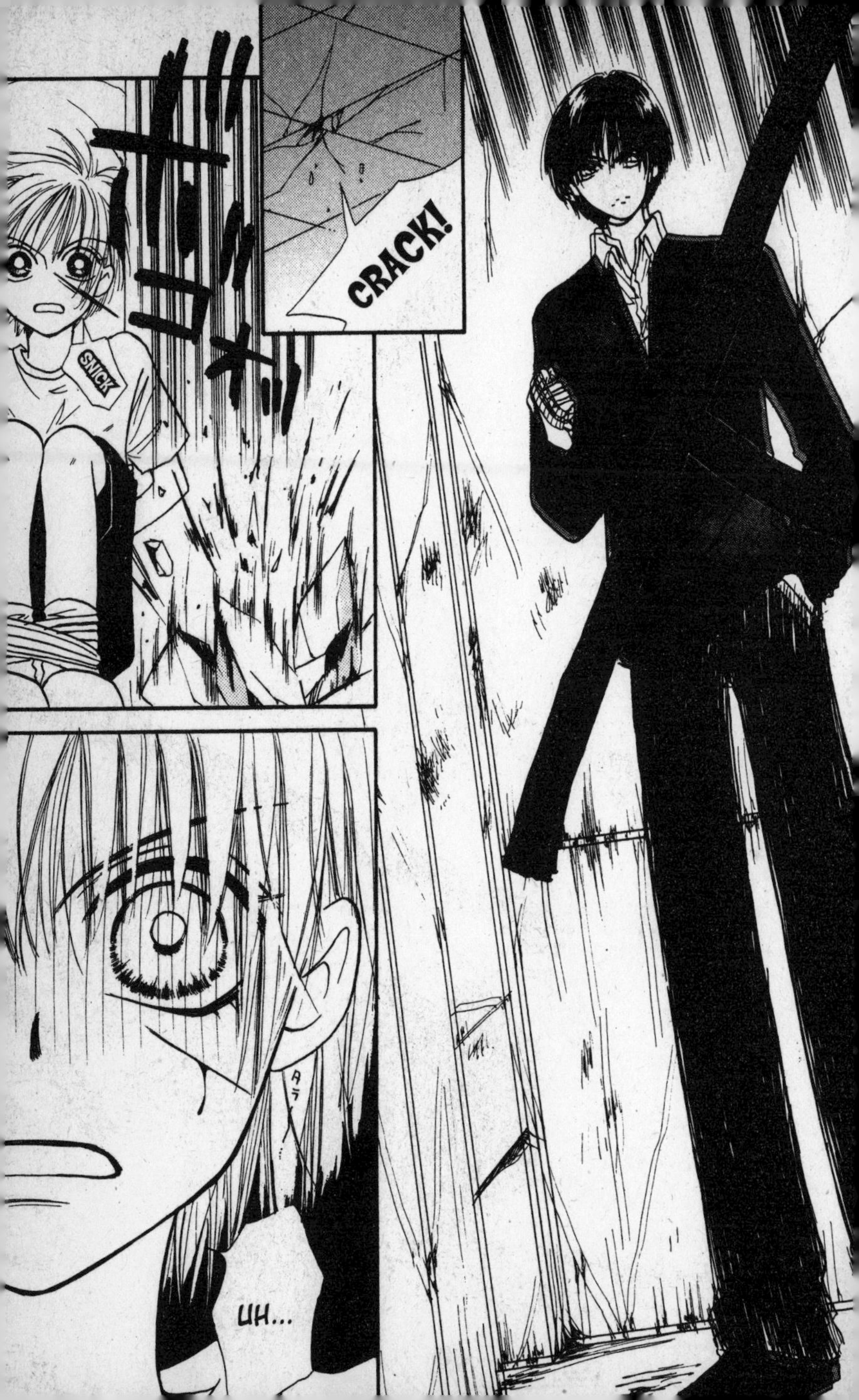
CRACK!
SNICK
UH...

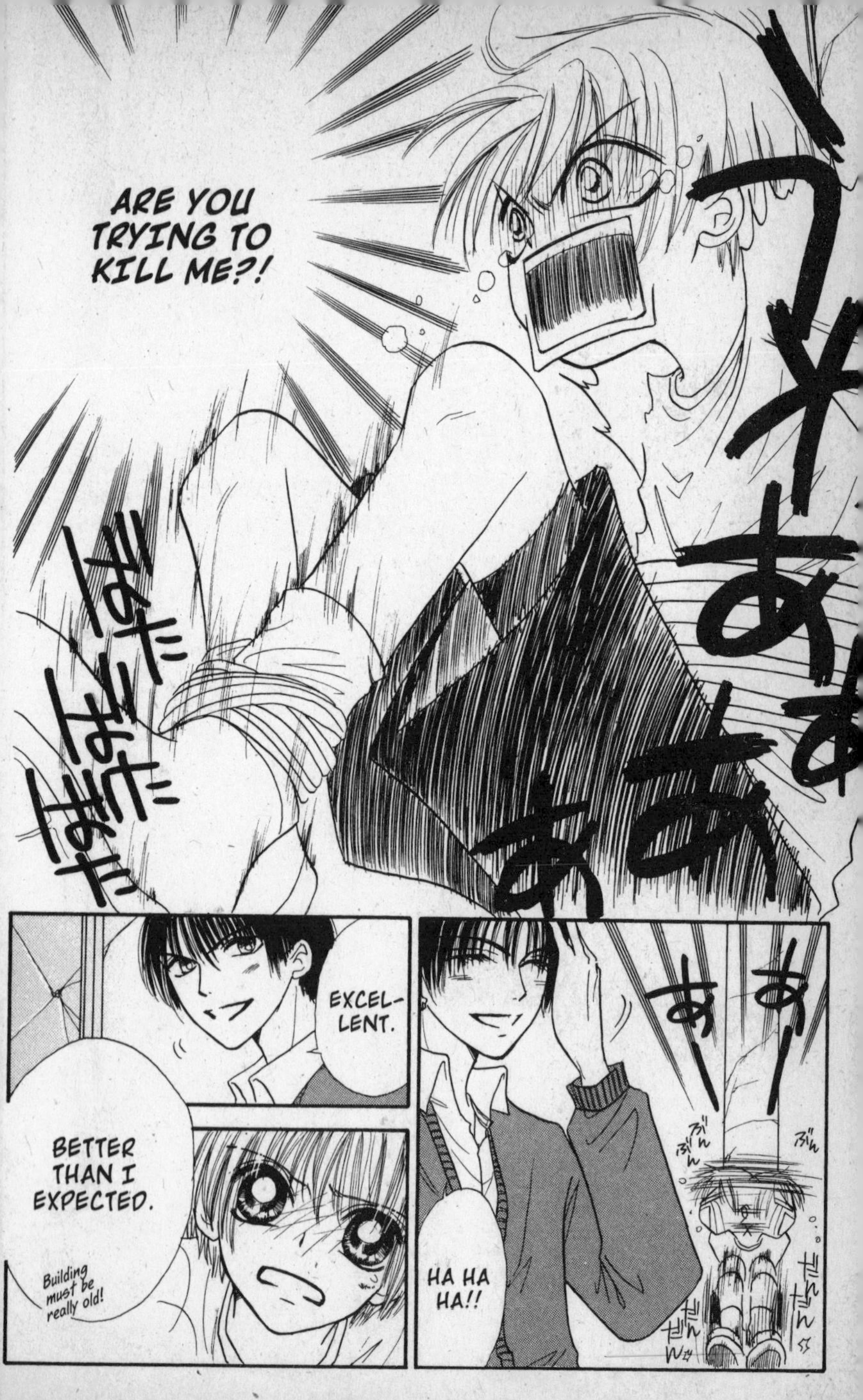
ARE YOU TRYING TO KILL ME?!
HA HA HA!!
EXCEL- LENT.
BETTER THAN I EXPECTED.
Building must be really old!

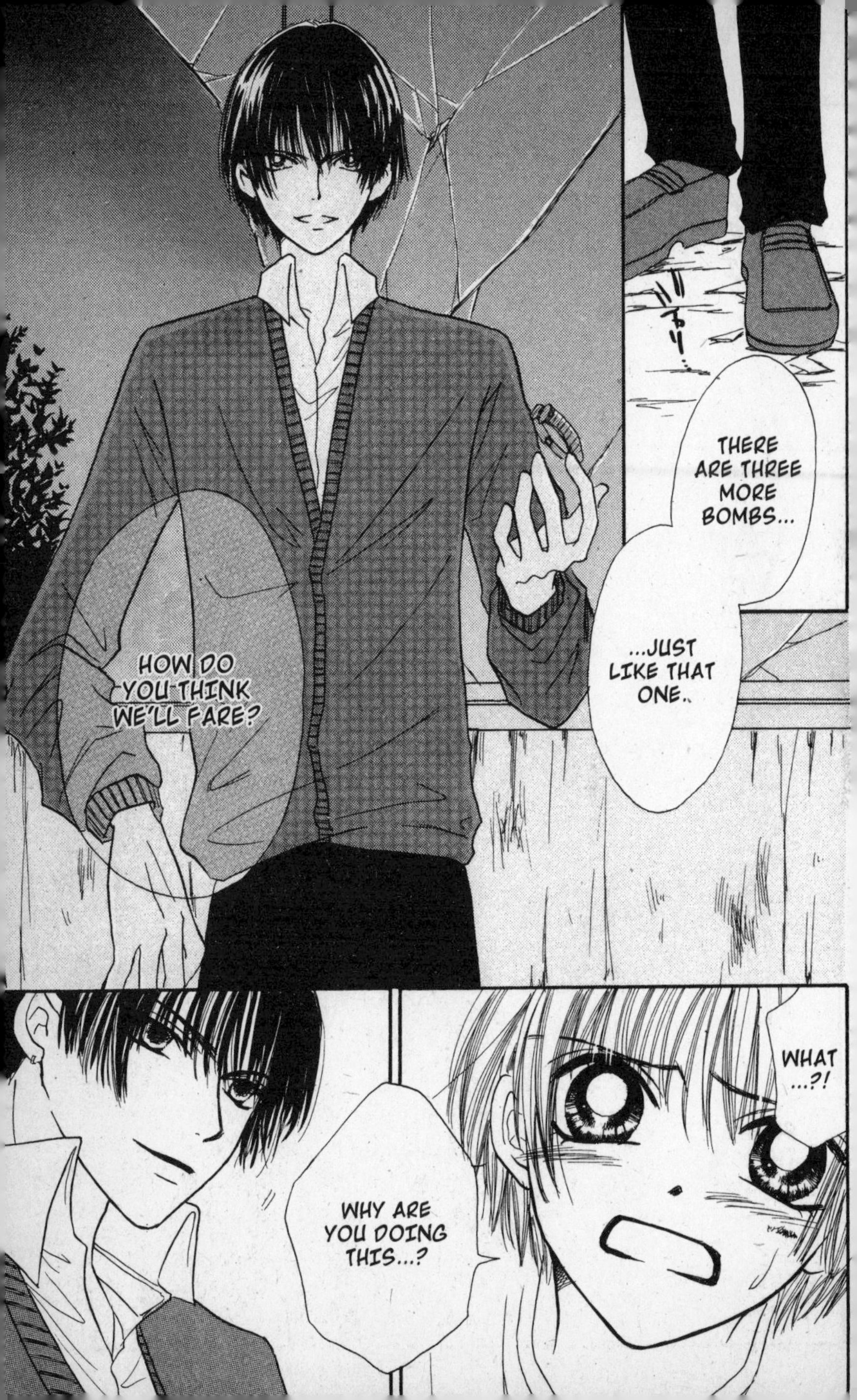
ジャリ…
THERE ARE THREE MORE BOMBS...
...JUST LIKE THAT ONE..
HOW DO YOU THINK WE'LL FARE?
WHAT ...?!
WHY ARE YOU DOING THIS...?

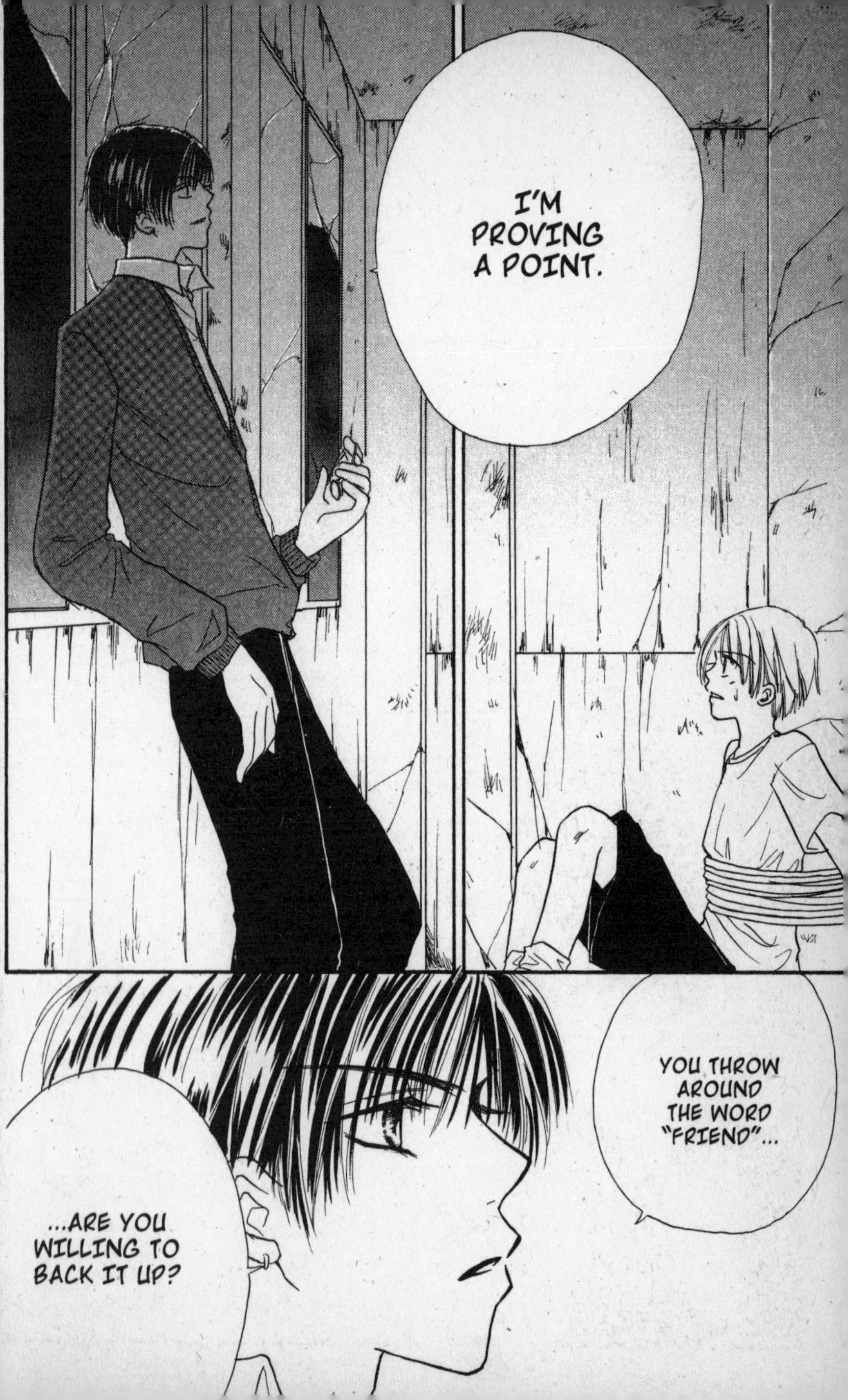
I'M PROVING A POINT.
YOU THROW AROUND THE WORD "FRIEND"...
...ARE YOU WILLING TO BACK IT UP?

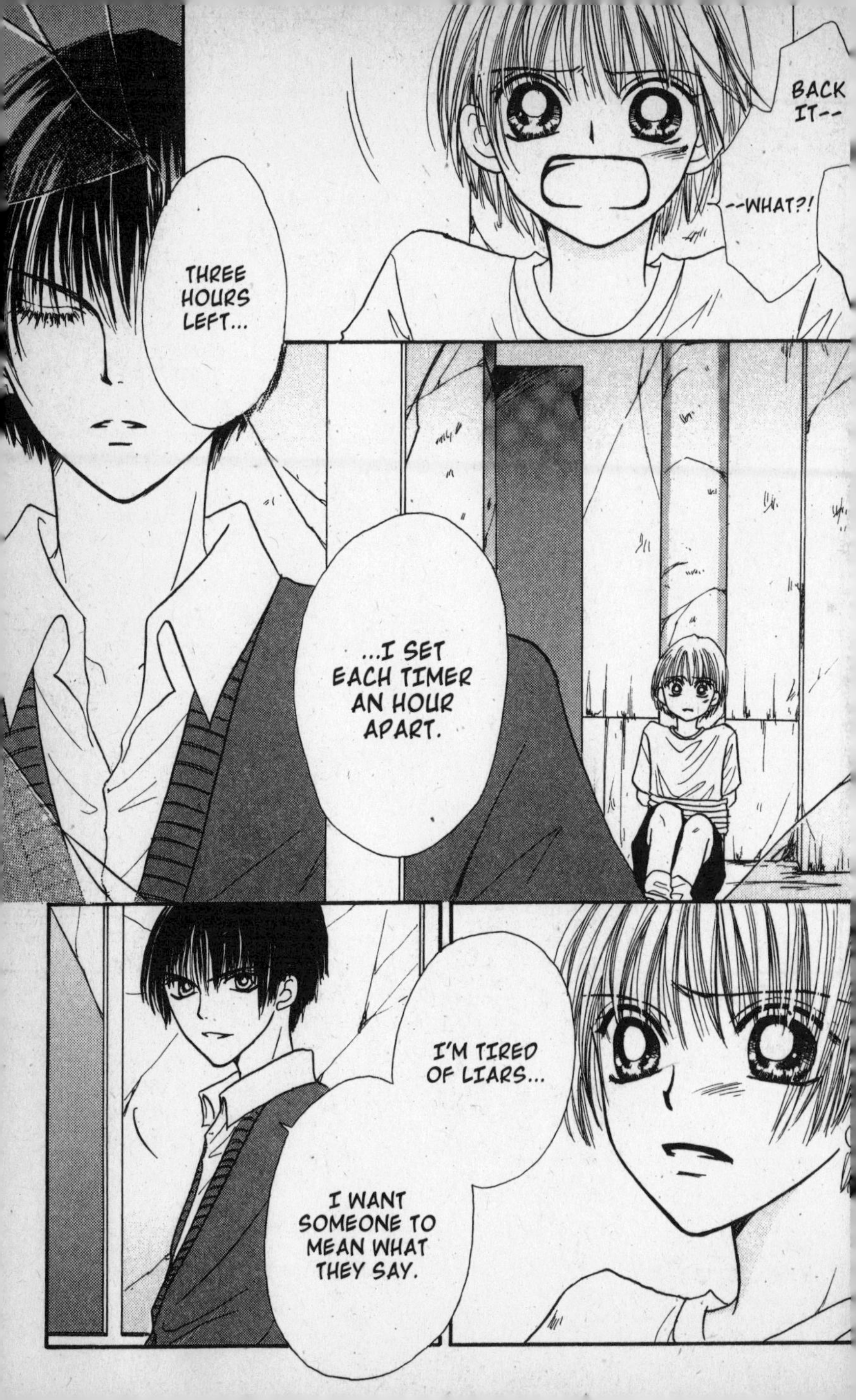
BACK IT--
--WHAT?!
THREE HOURS LEFT...
...I SET EACH TIMER AN HOUR APART.
I'M TIRED OF LIARS...
I WANT SOMEONE TO MEAN WHAT THEY SAY.

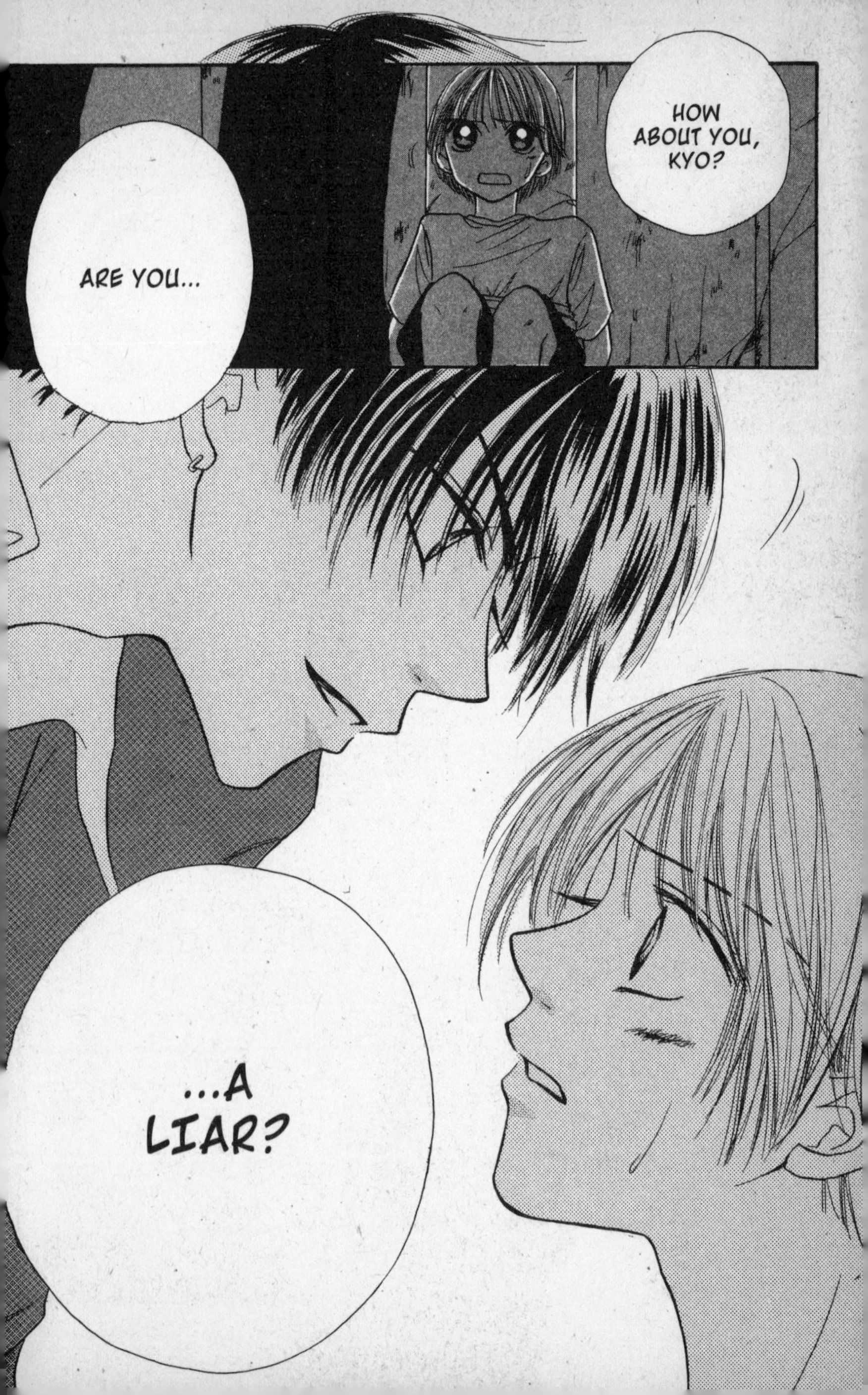
HOW ABOUT YOU, KYO?
ARE YOU...
...A LIAR?

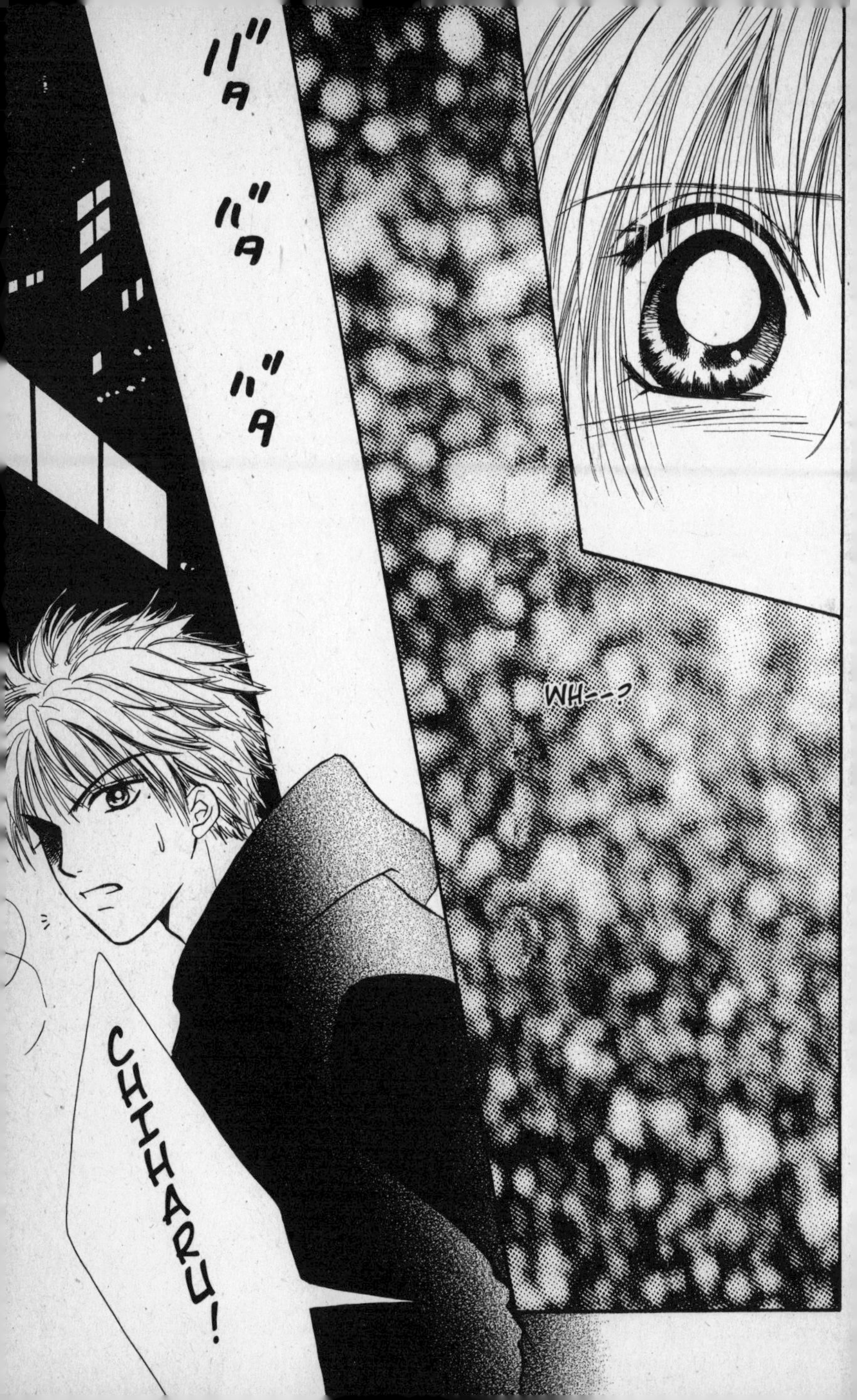
WH--?
バタ バタ バタ
CHIHARU!

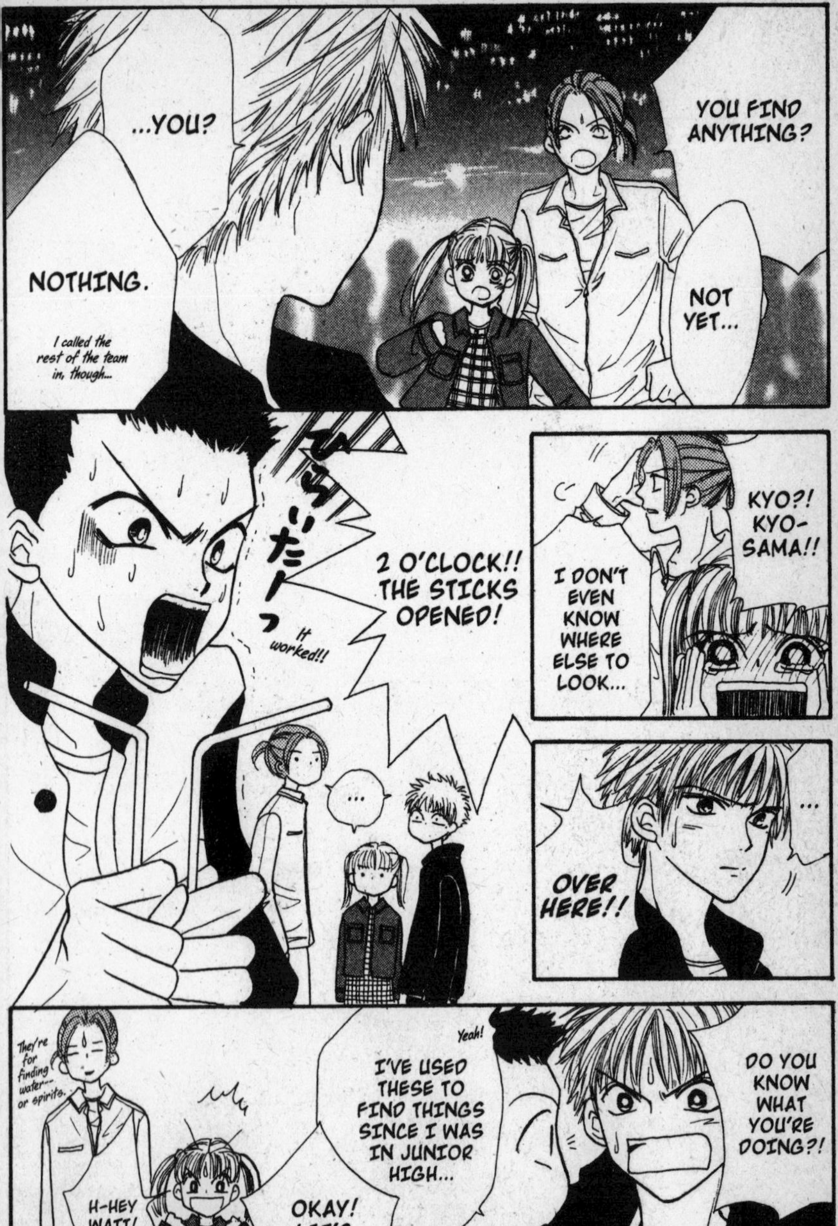
YOU FIND ANYTHING?
NOT YET...
...YOU?
NOTHING.
I called the rest of the team in, though...
KYO?! KYO-SAMA!!
I DON'T EVEN KNOW WHERE ELSE TO LOOK...
...
OVER HERE!!
2 O'CLOCK!! THE STICKS OPENED!
It worked!!
...
DO YOU KNOW WHAT YOU'RE DOING?!
Yeah!
I'VE USED THESE TO FIND THINGS SINCE I WAS IN JUNIOR HIGH...
OKAY! LET'S GO!!
H-HEY WAIT!
They're for finding water... or spirits.

Kind of like E.S.P.

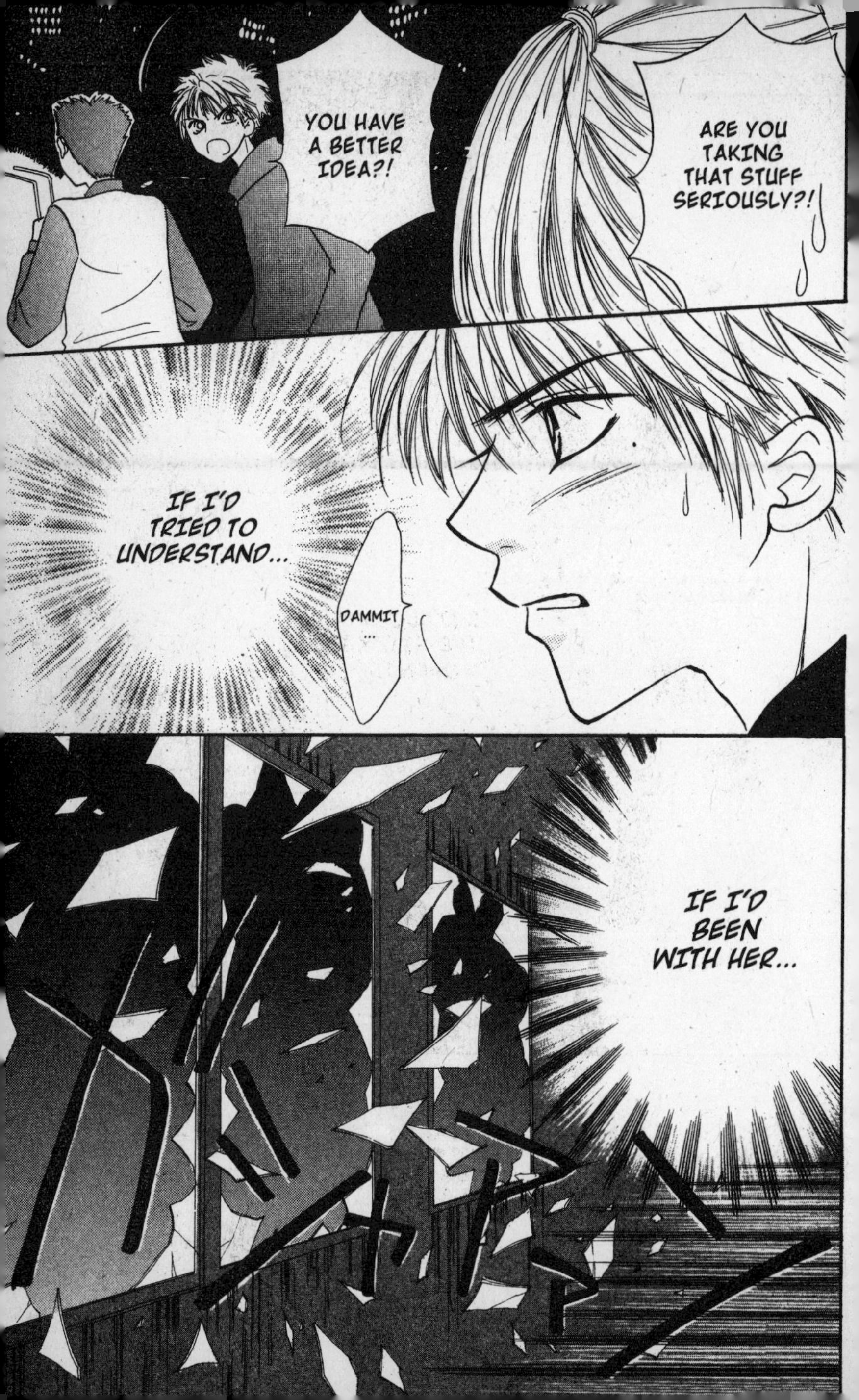
ARE YOU TAKING THAT STUFF SERIOUSLY?!
YOU HAVE A BETTER IDEA?!
DAMMIT ...
IF I'D TRIED TO UNDERSTAND...
IF I'D BEEN WITH HER...

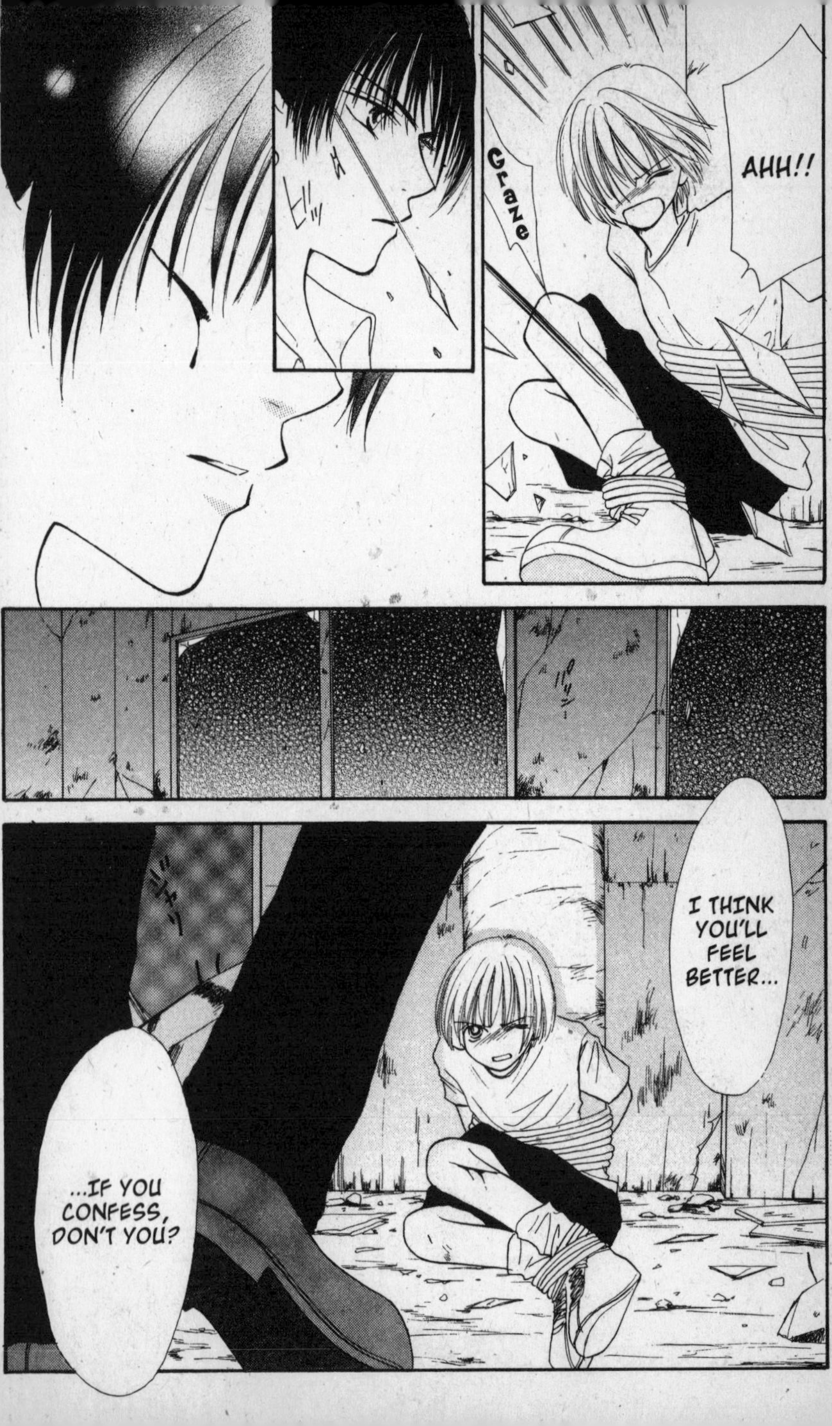
AHH!!
Graze
I THINK YOU'LL FEEL BETTER...
...IF YOU CONFESS, DON'T YOU?

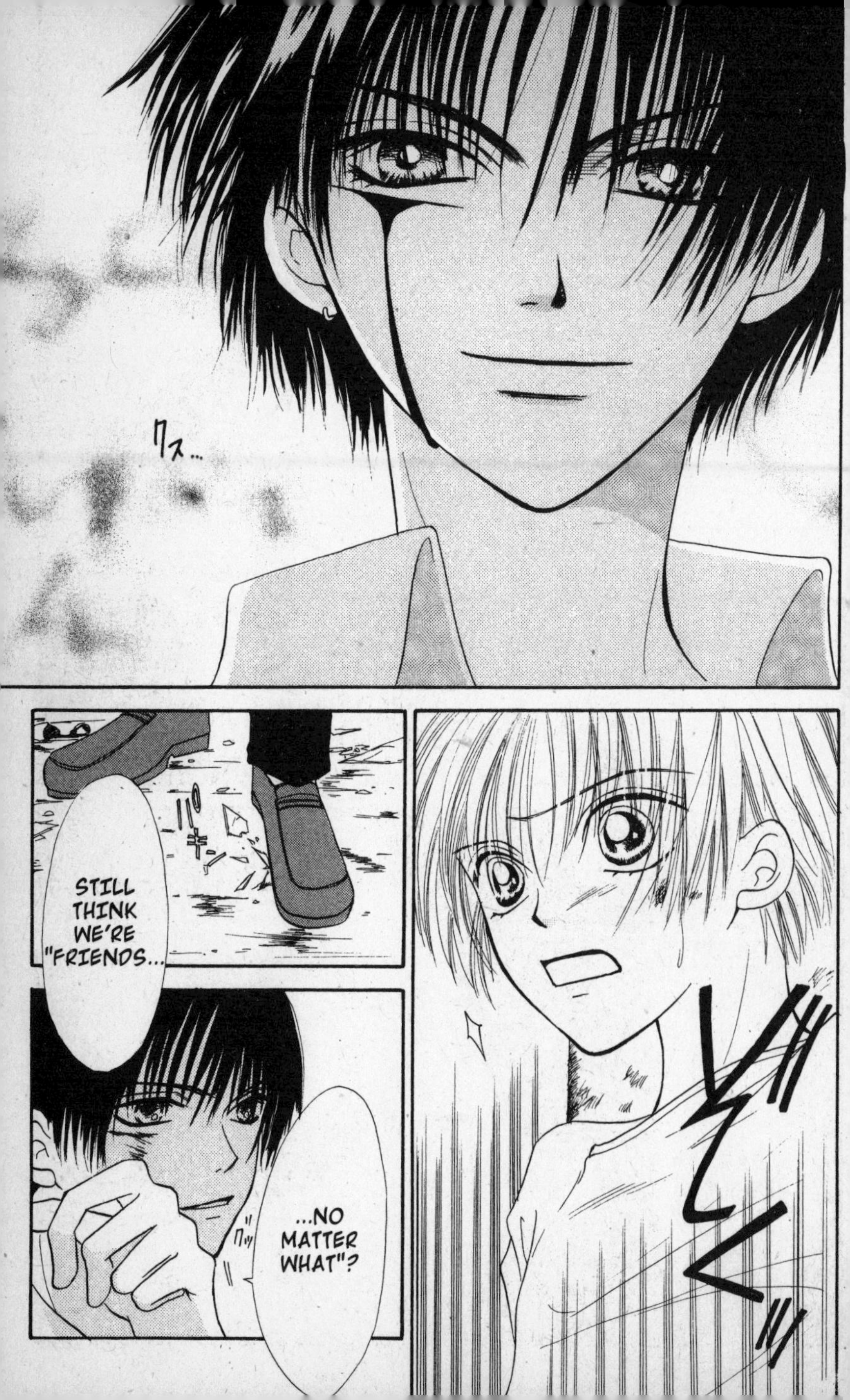
クス...
STILL THINK WE'RE "FRIENDS...
...NO MATTER WHAT"?

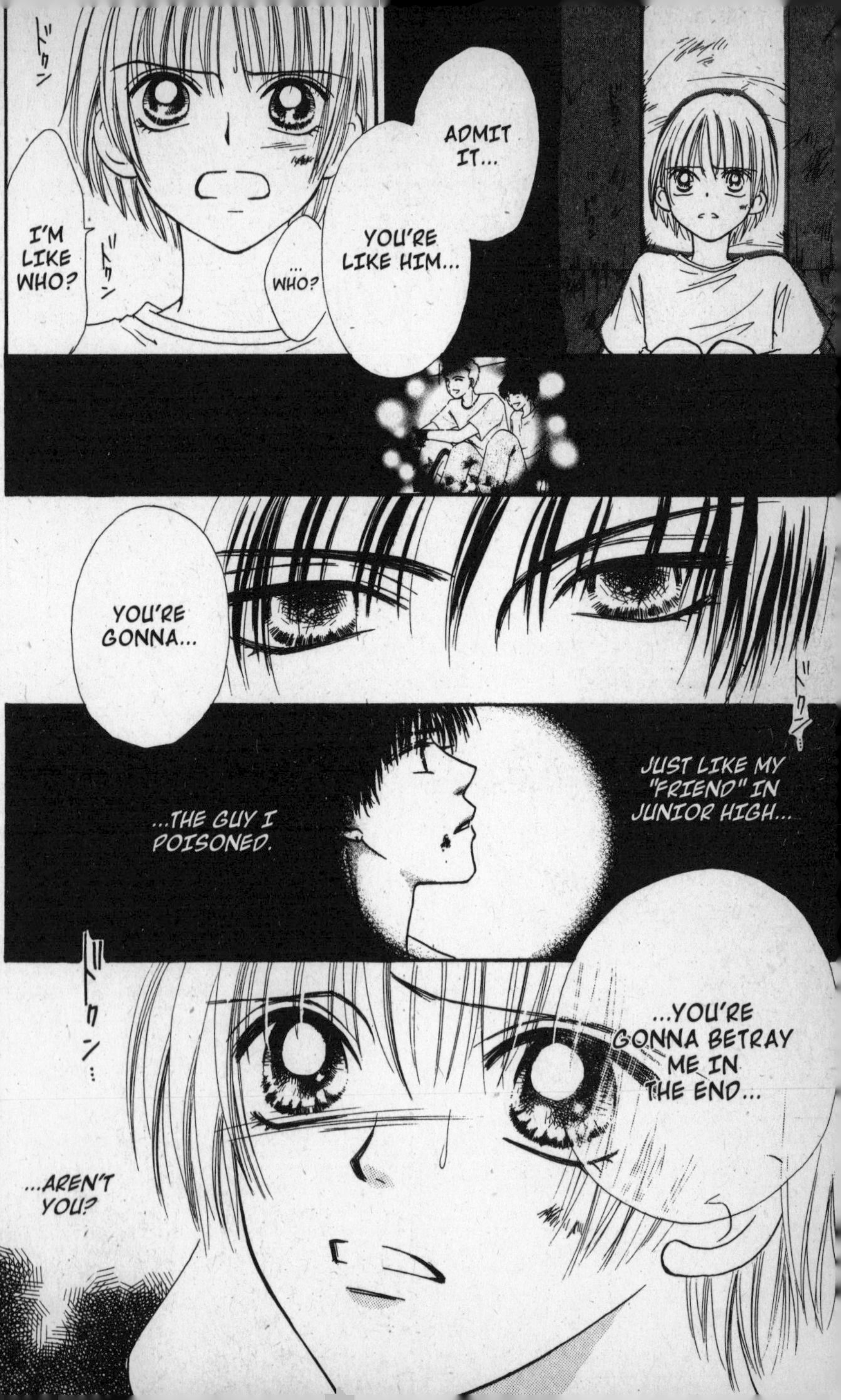
ADMIT IT...
YOU'RE LIKE HIM...
... WHO?
I'M LIKE WHO?
YOU'RE GONNA...
JUST LIKE MY "FRIEND" IN JUNIOR HIGH...
...THE GUY I POISONED.
...YOU'RE GONNA BETRAY ME IN THE END...
...AREN'T YOU?

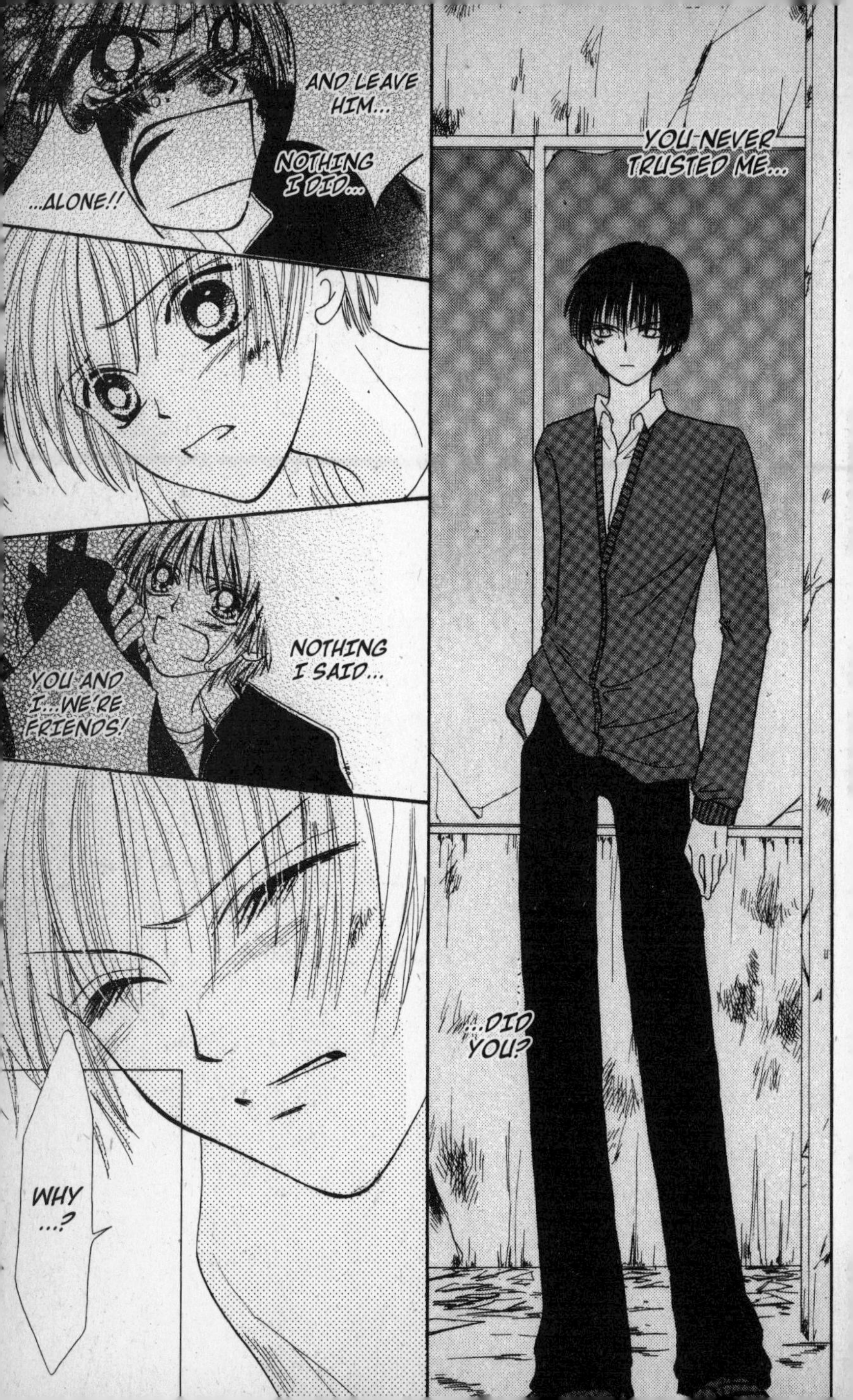
YOU NEVER TRUSTED ME...
...DID YOU?
AND LEAVE HIM...
NOTHING I DID...
...ALONE!!
NOTHING I SAID...
YOU AND I...WE'RE FRIENDS!
WHY ...?

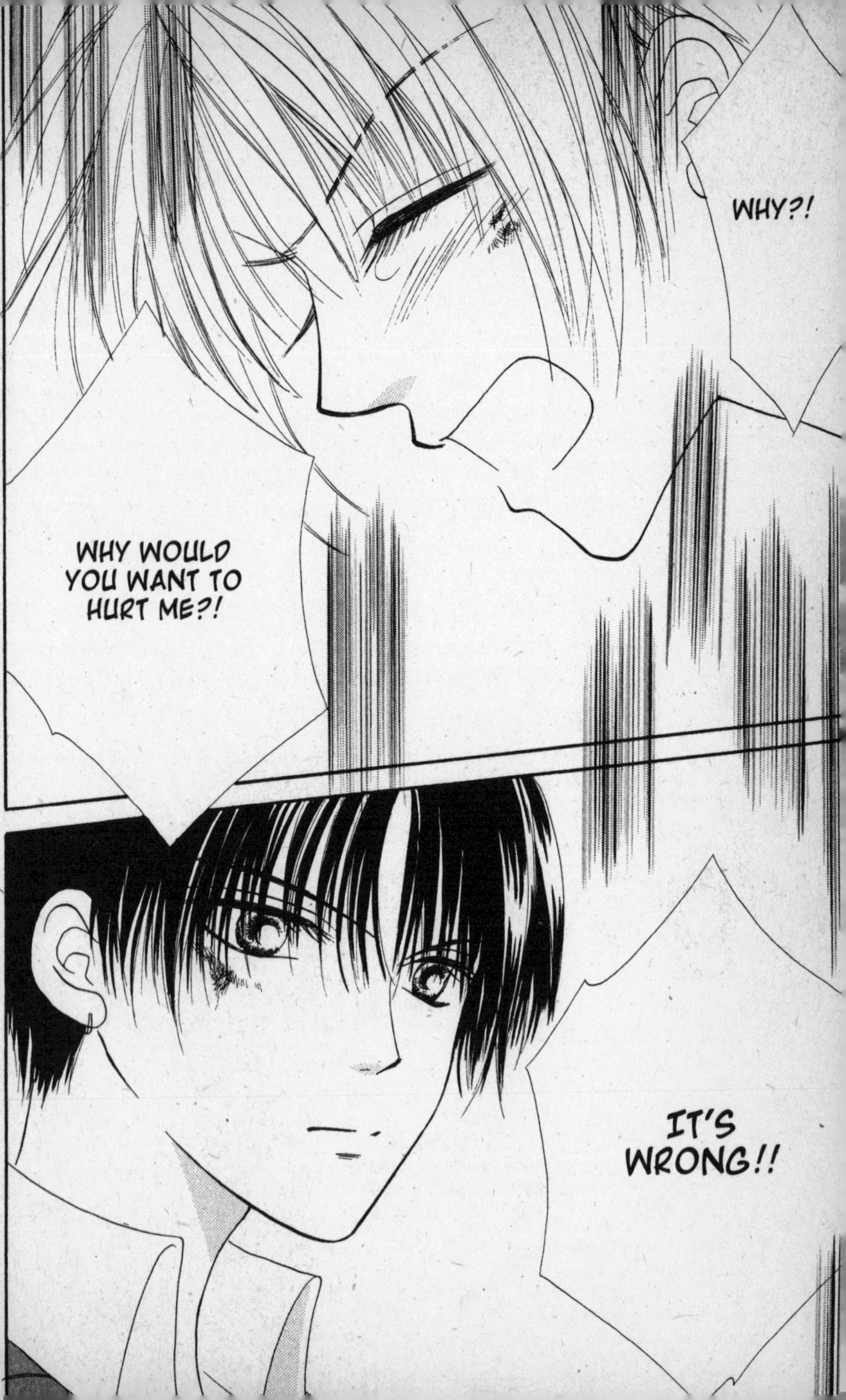
WHY?!
WHY WOULD YOU WANT TO HURT ME?!
IT'S WRONG!!

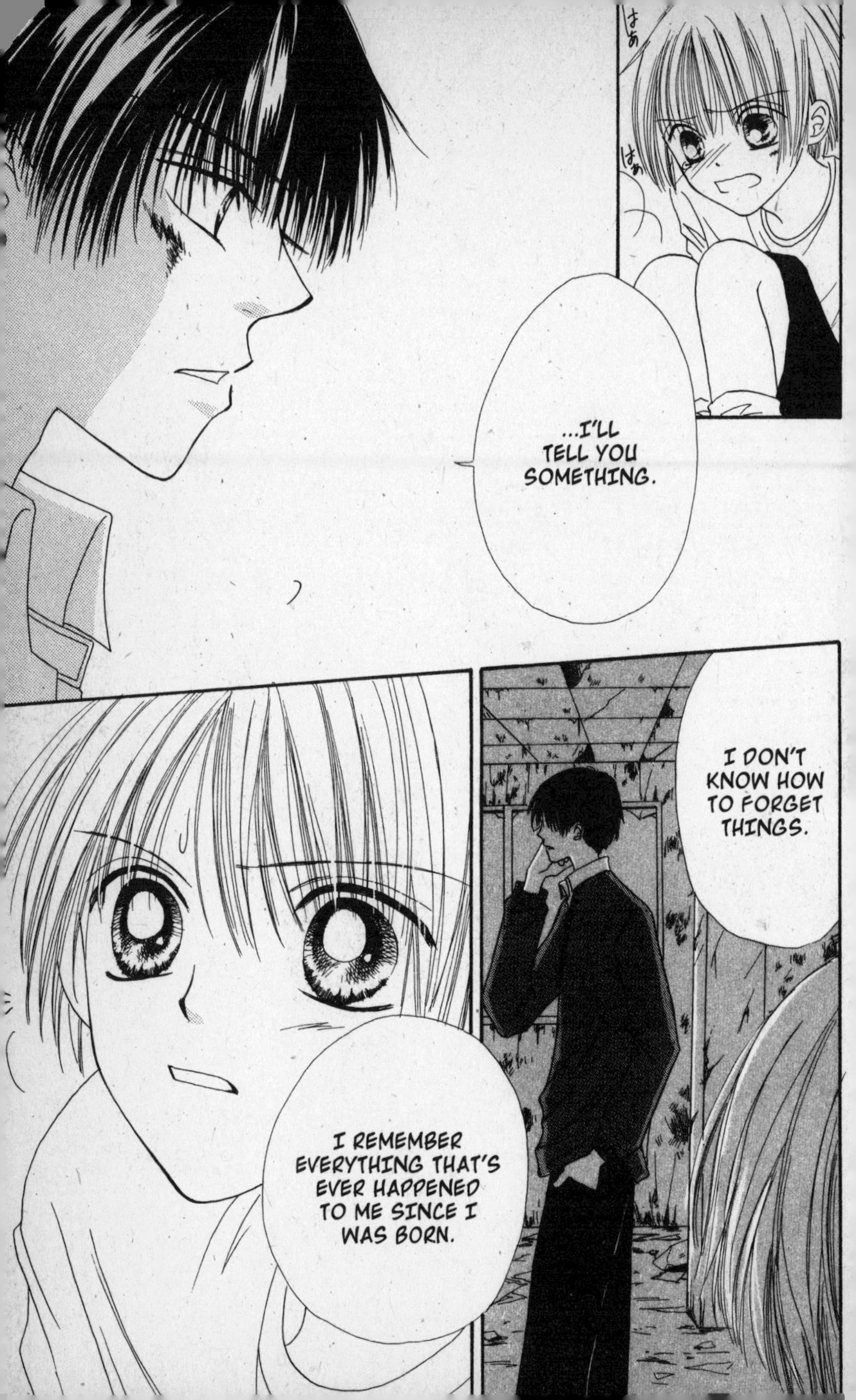
はあ
はあ
...I'LL TELL YOU SOMETHING.
I DON'T KNOW HOW TO FORGET THINGS.
I REMEMBER EVERYTHING THAT'S EVER HAPPENED TO ME SINCE I WAS BORN.

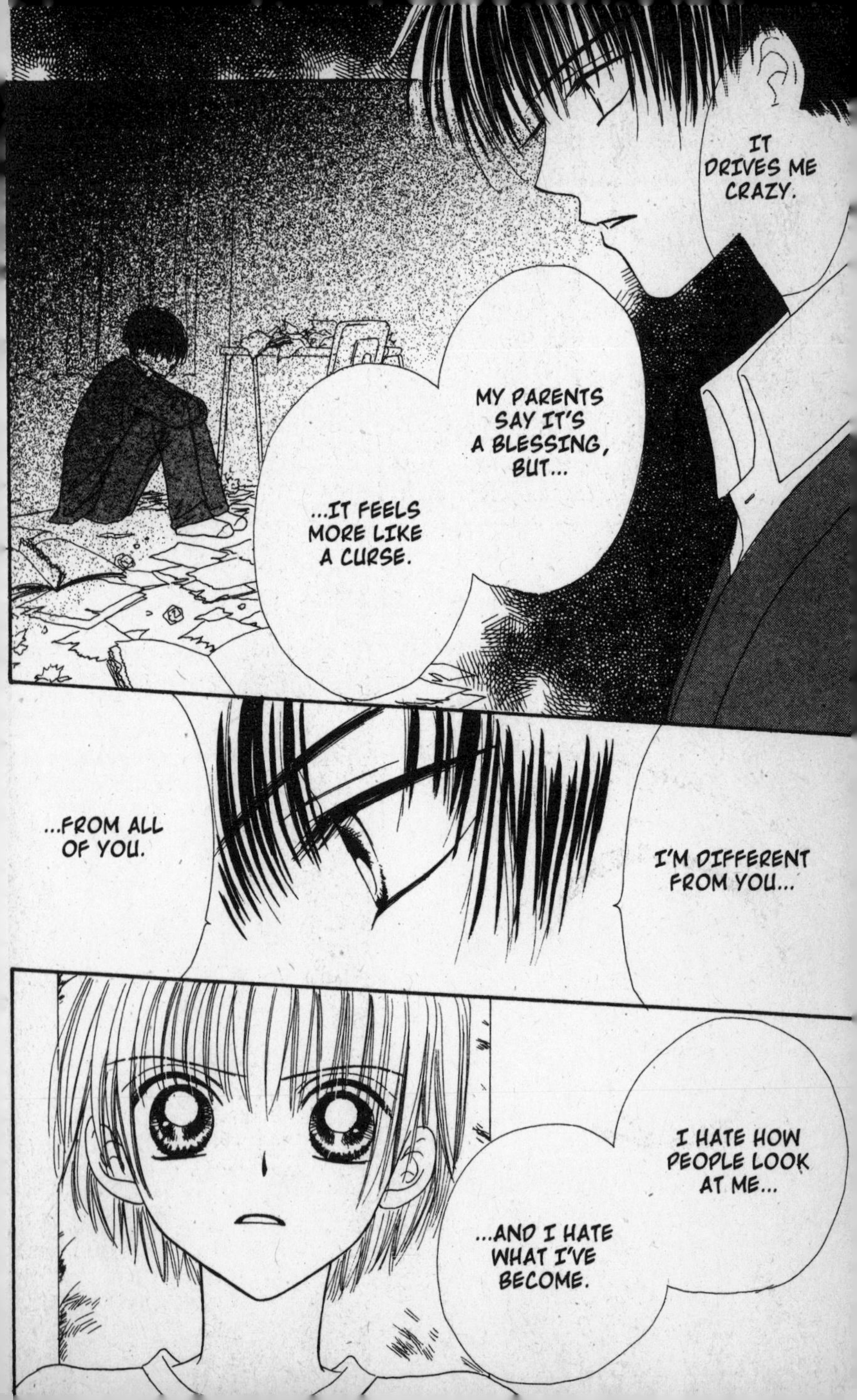
IT DRIVES ME CRAZY.
MY PARENTS SAY IT'S A BLESSING, BUT...
...IT FEELS MORE LIKE A CURSE.
I'M DIFFERENT FROM YOU...
...FROM ALL OF YOU.
I HATE HOW PEOPLE LOOK AT ME...
...AND I HATE WHAT I'VE BECOME.

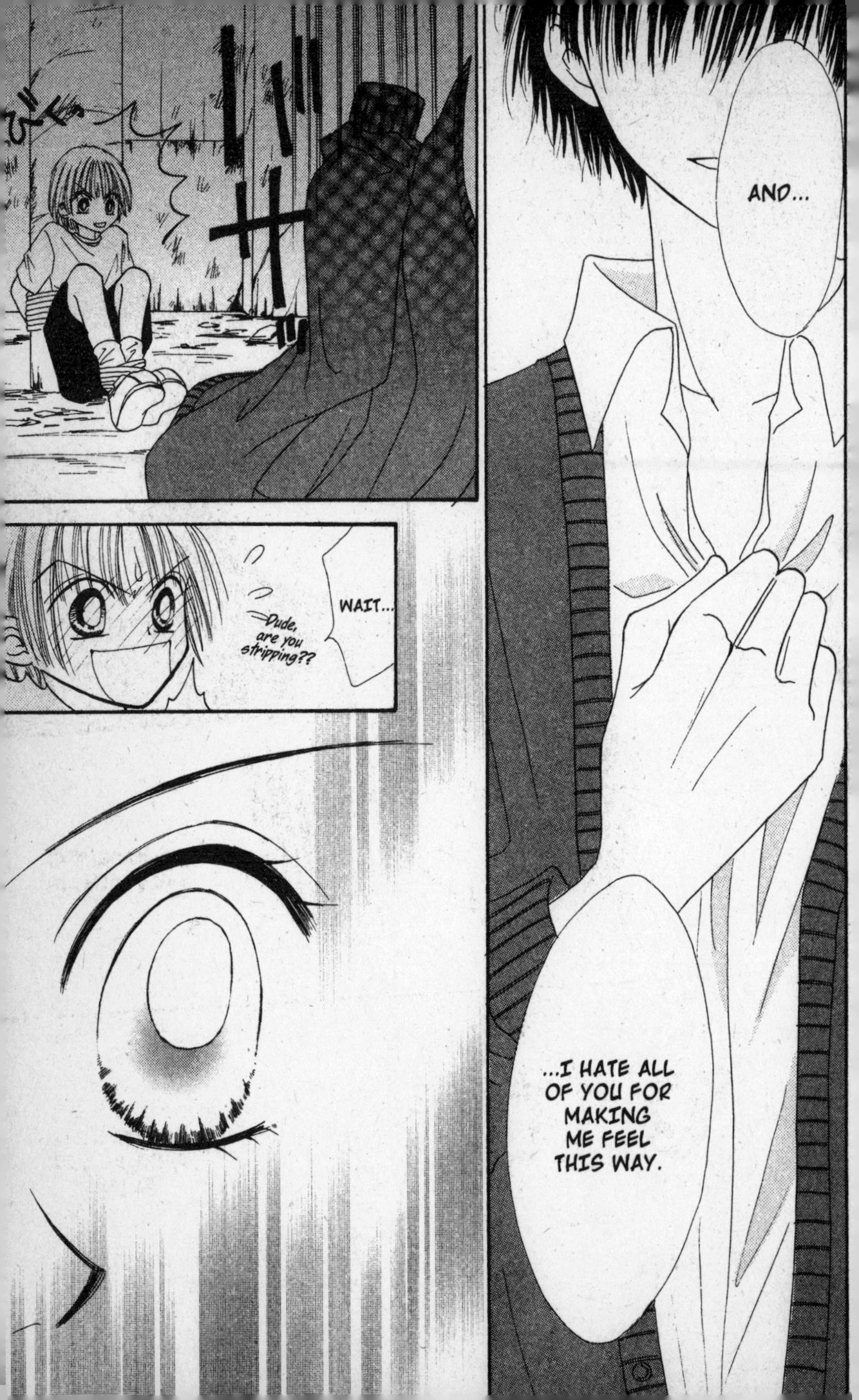
AND...
...I HATE ALL OF YOU FOR MAKING ME FEEL THIS WAY.
WAIT...
Dude, are you stripping??

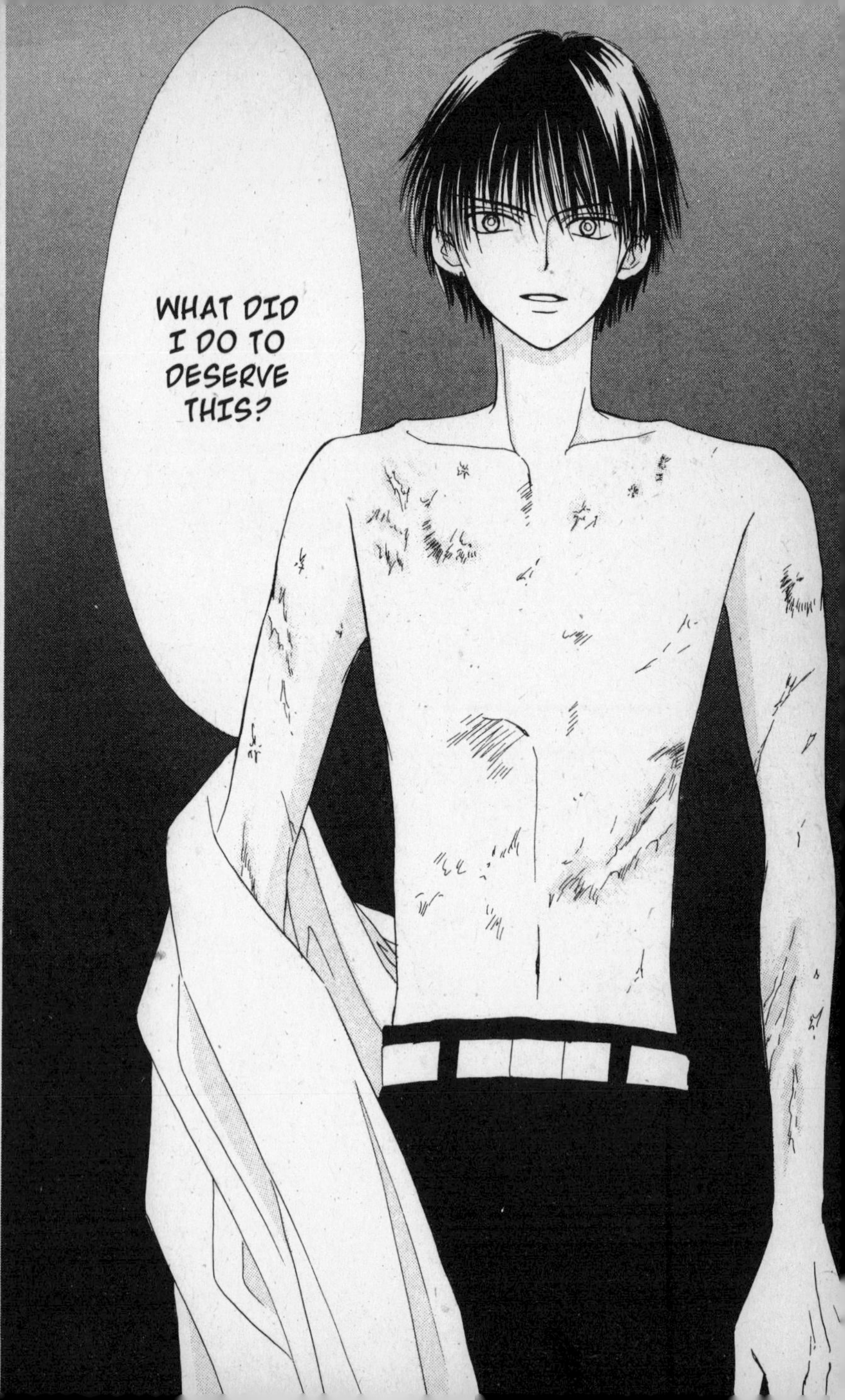
WHAT DID I DO TO DESERVE THIS?

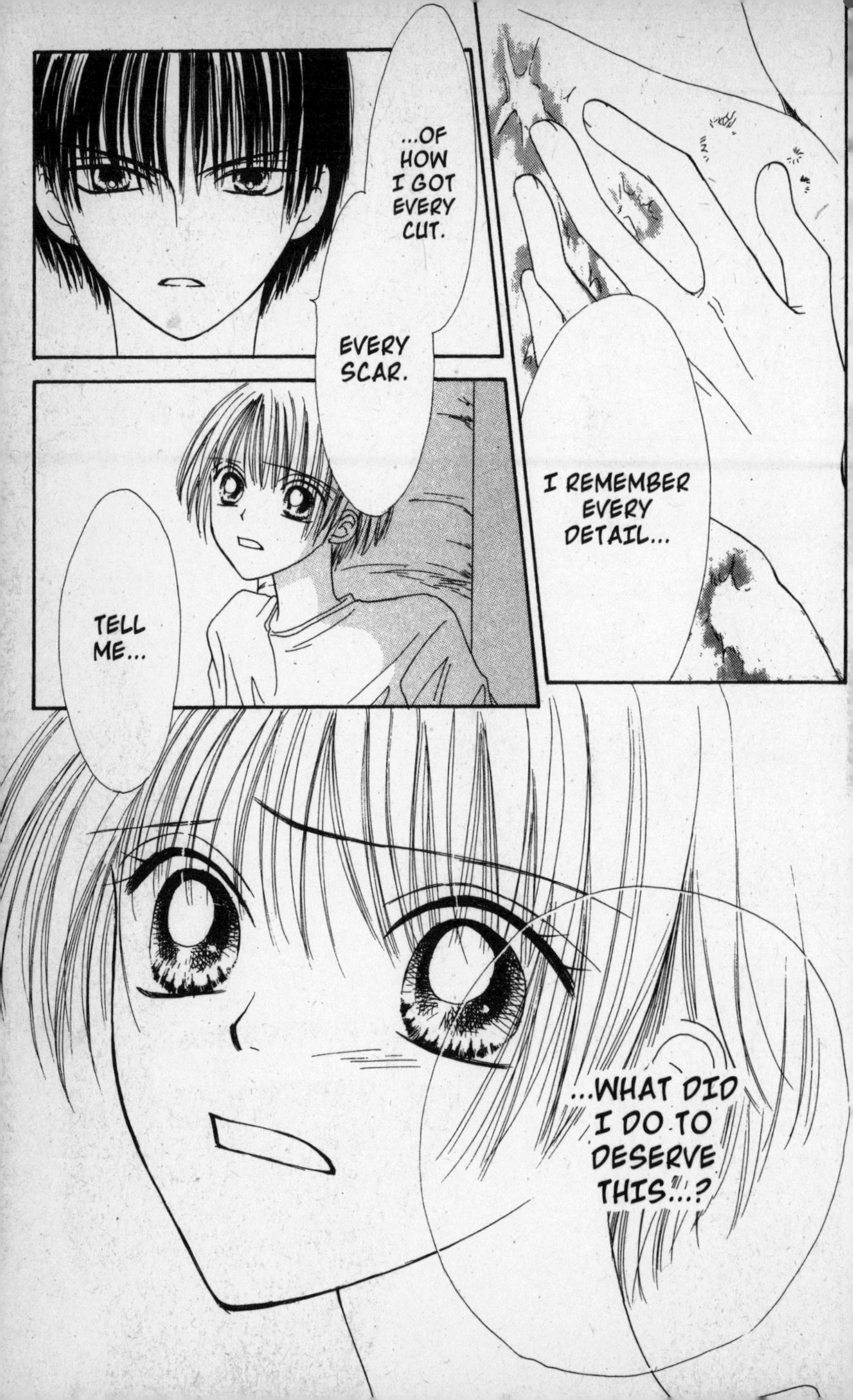
I REMEMBER EVERY DETAIL...
...OF HOW I GOT EVERY CUT.
EVERY SCAR.
TELL ME...
...WHAT DID I DO TO DESERVE THIS...?

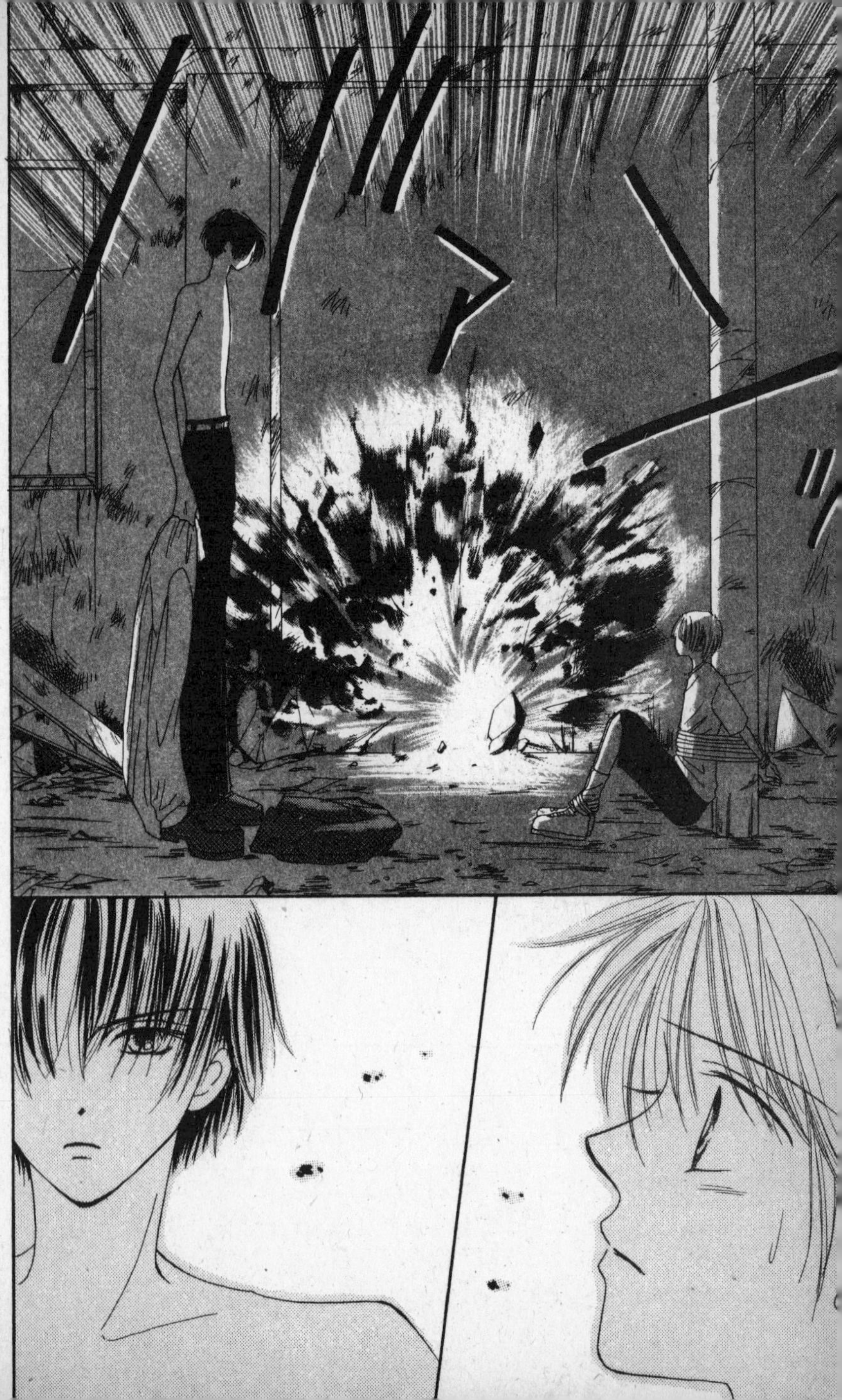

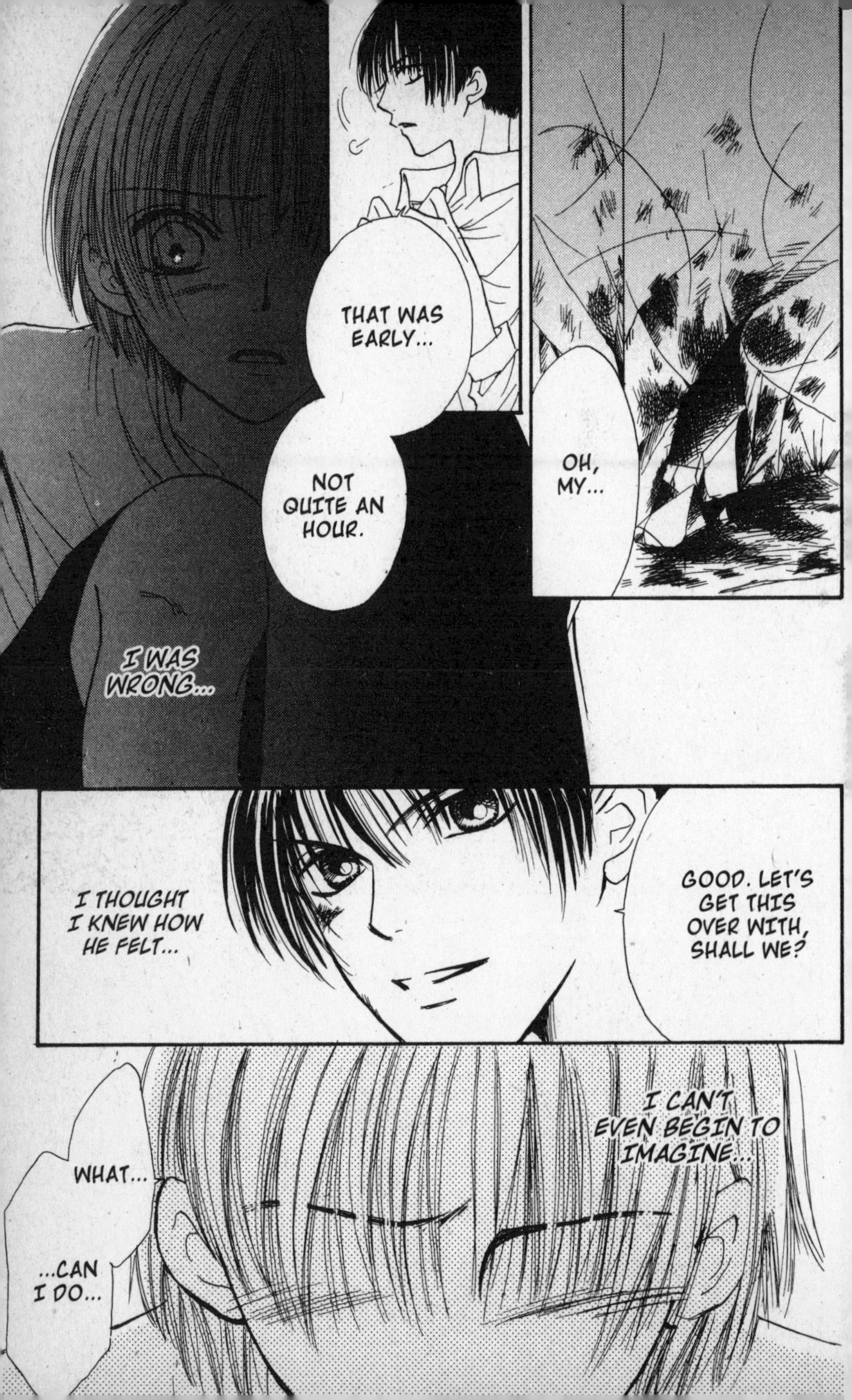
OH, MY...
THAT WAS EARLY...
NOT QUITE AN HOUR.
I WAS WRONG...
GOOD. LET'S GET THIS OVER WITH, SHALL WE?
I THOUGHT I KNEW HOW HE FELT...
I CAN'T EVEN BEGIN TO IMAGINE...
WHAT...
...CAN I DO...

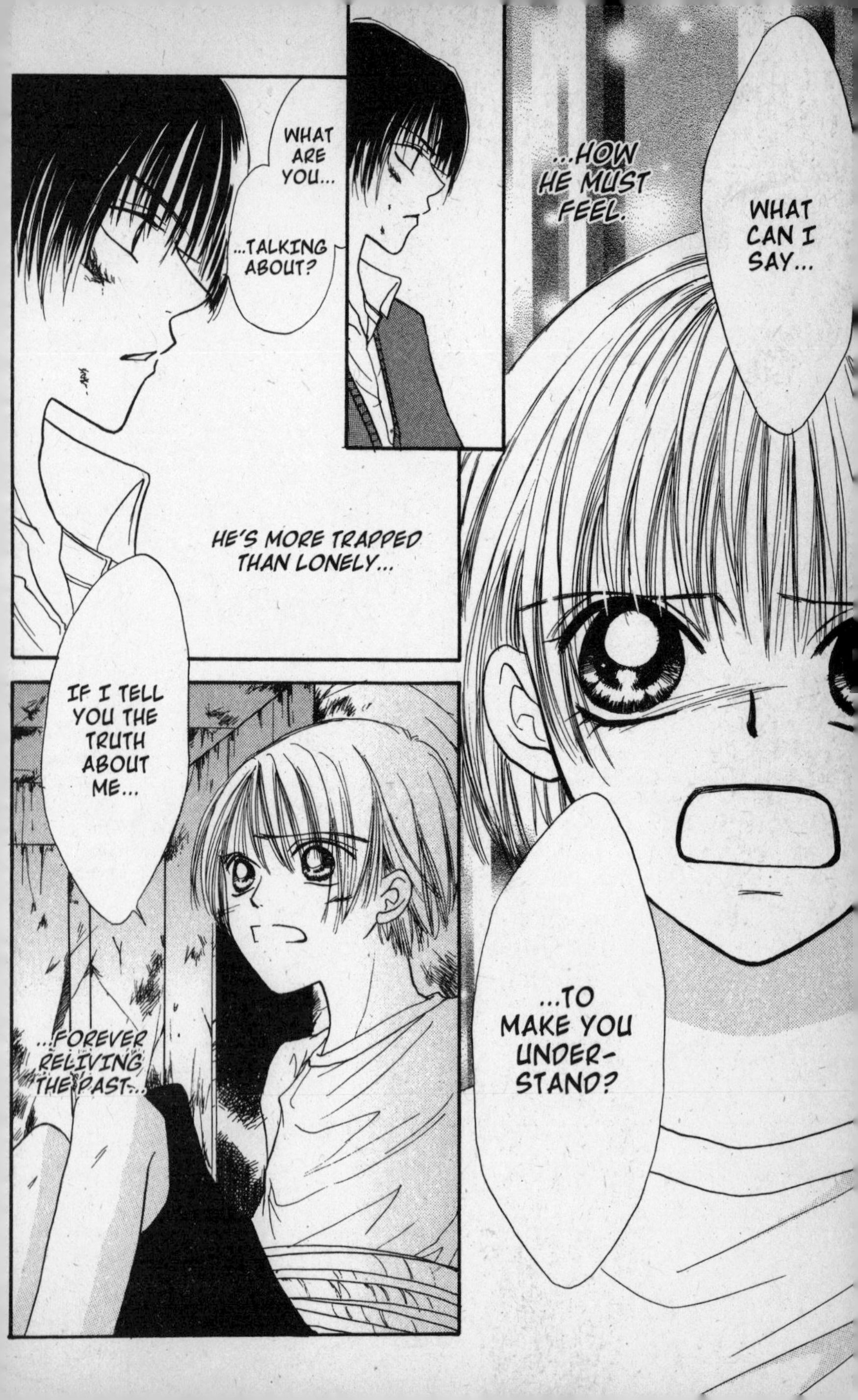
...HOW HE MUST FEEL.
WHAT CAN I SAY...
...TO MAKE YOU UNDER-STAND?
WHAT ARE YOU...
...TALKING ABOUT?
HE'S MORE TRAPPED THAN LONELY...
IF I TELL YOU THE TRUTH ABOUT ME...
...FOREVER RELIVING THE PAST...

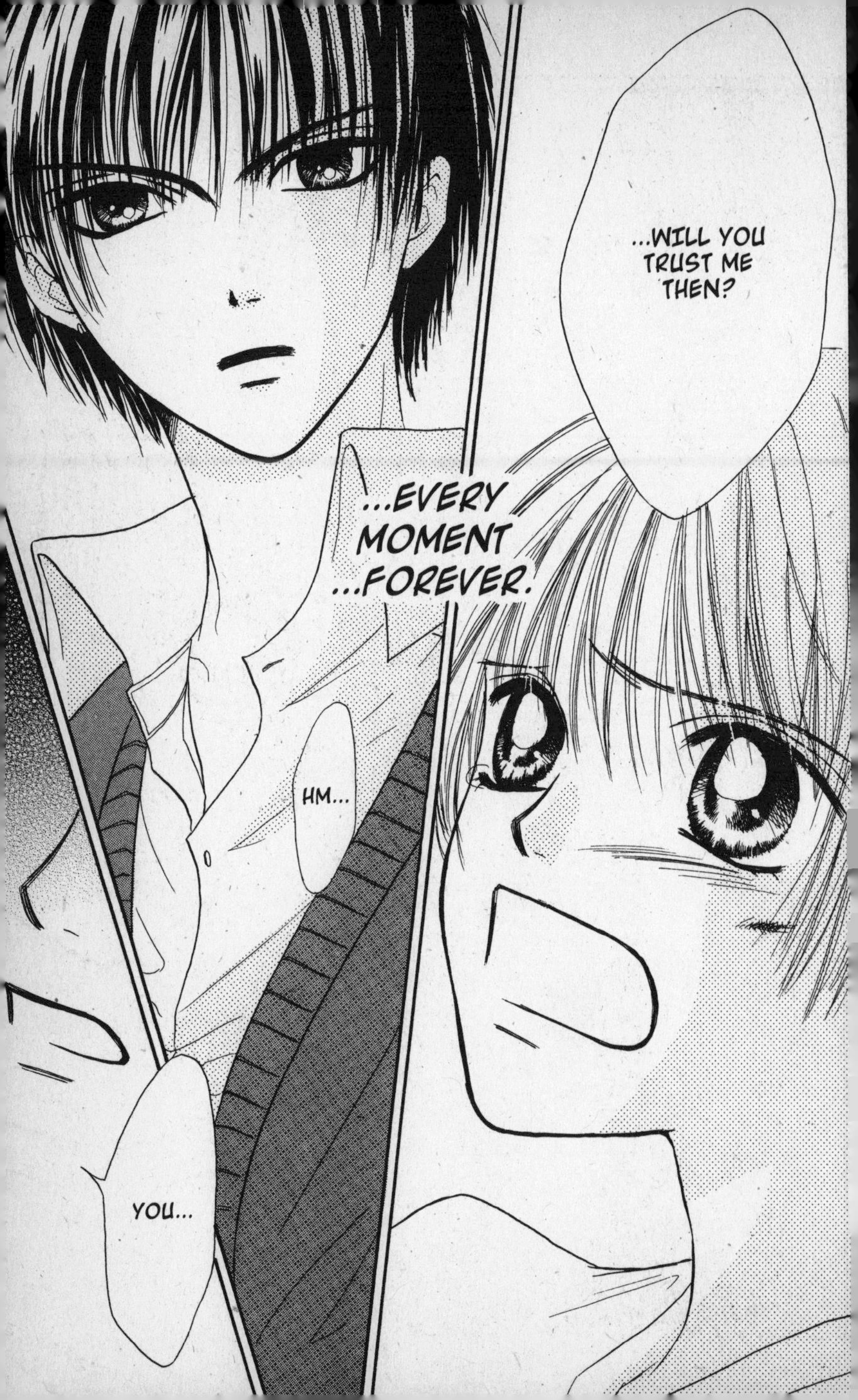
...WILL YOU TRUST ME THEN?
...EVERY MOMENT ...FOREVER.
HM...
YOU...

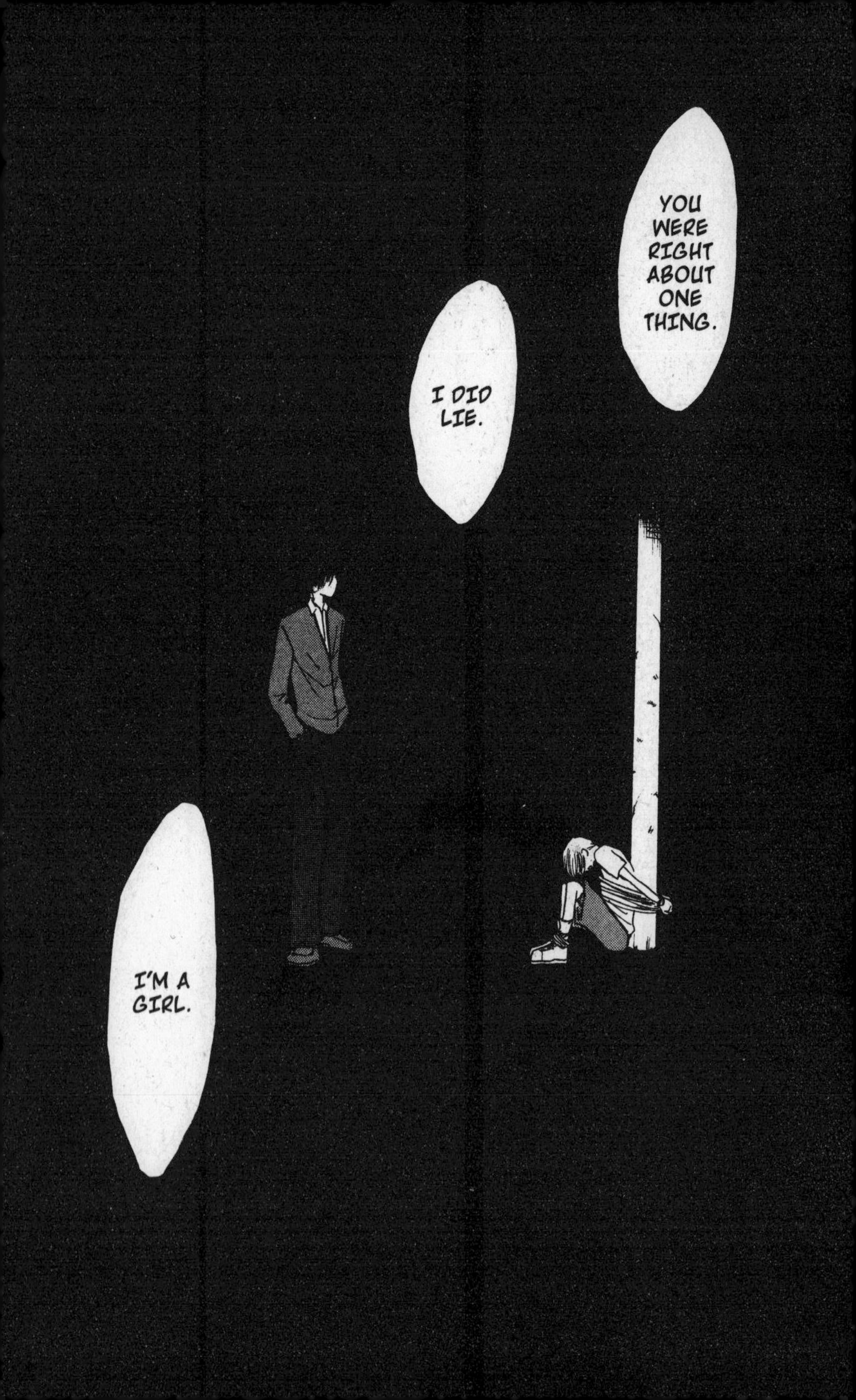
YOU WERE RIGHT ABOUT ONE THING.
I DID LIE.
I'M A GIRL.

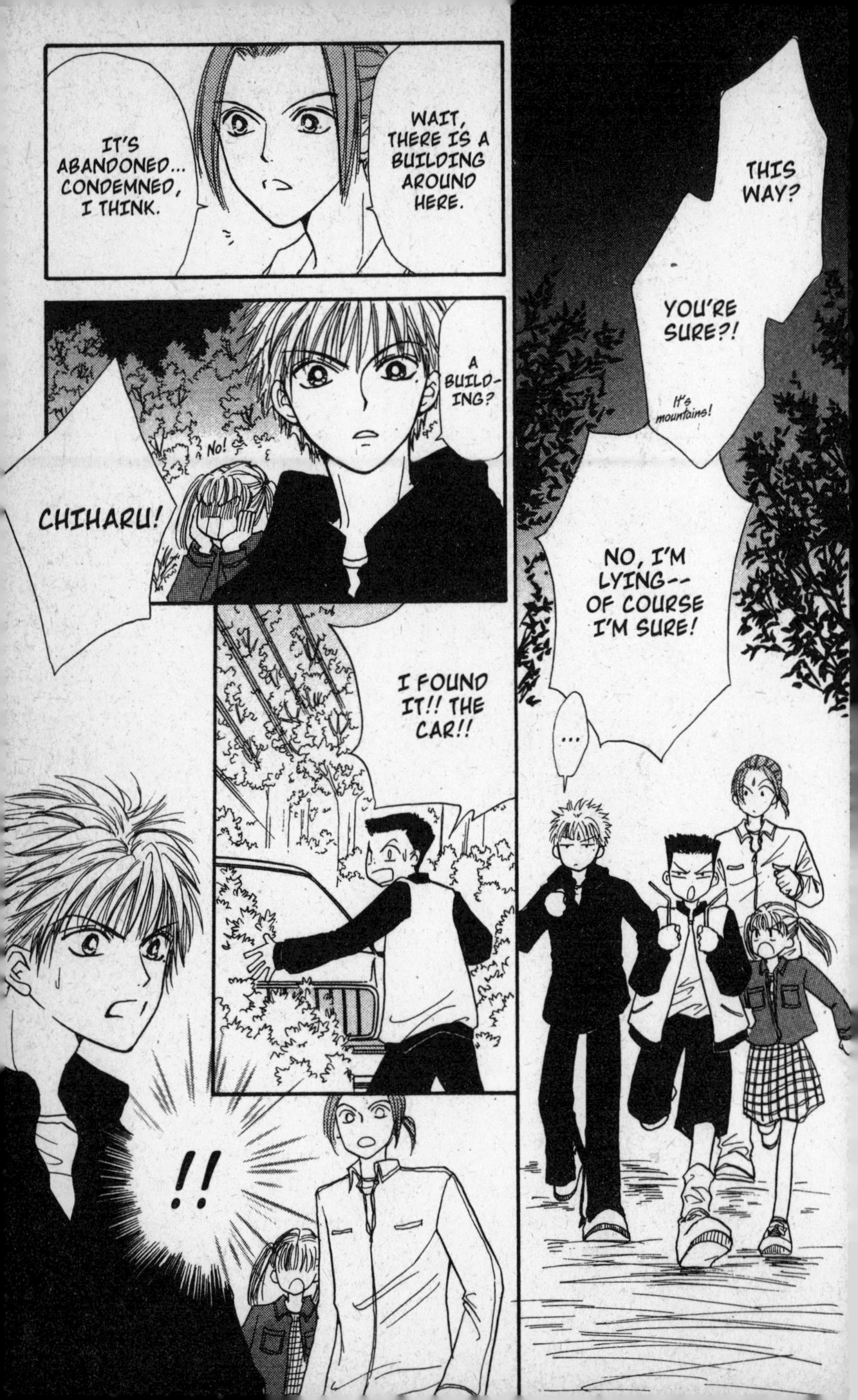
THIS WAY?
YOU'RE SURE?!
It's mountains!
NO, I'M LYING-- OF COURSE I'M SURE!
...
WAIT, THERE IS A BUILDING AROUND HERE.
IT'S ABANDONED... CONDEMNED, I THINK.
A BUILDING?
No!
CHIHARU!
I FOUND IT!! THE CAR!!
!!

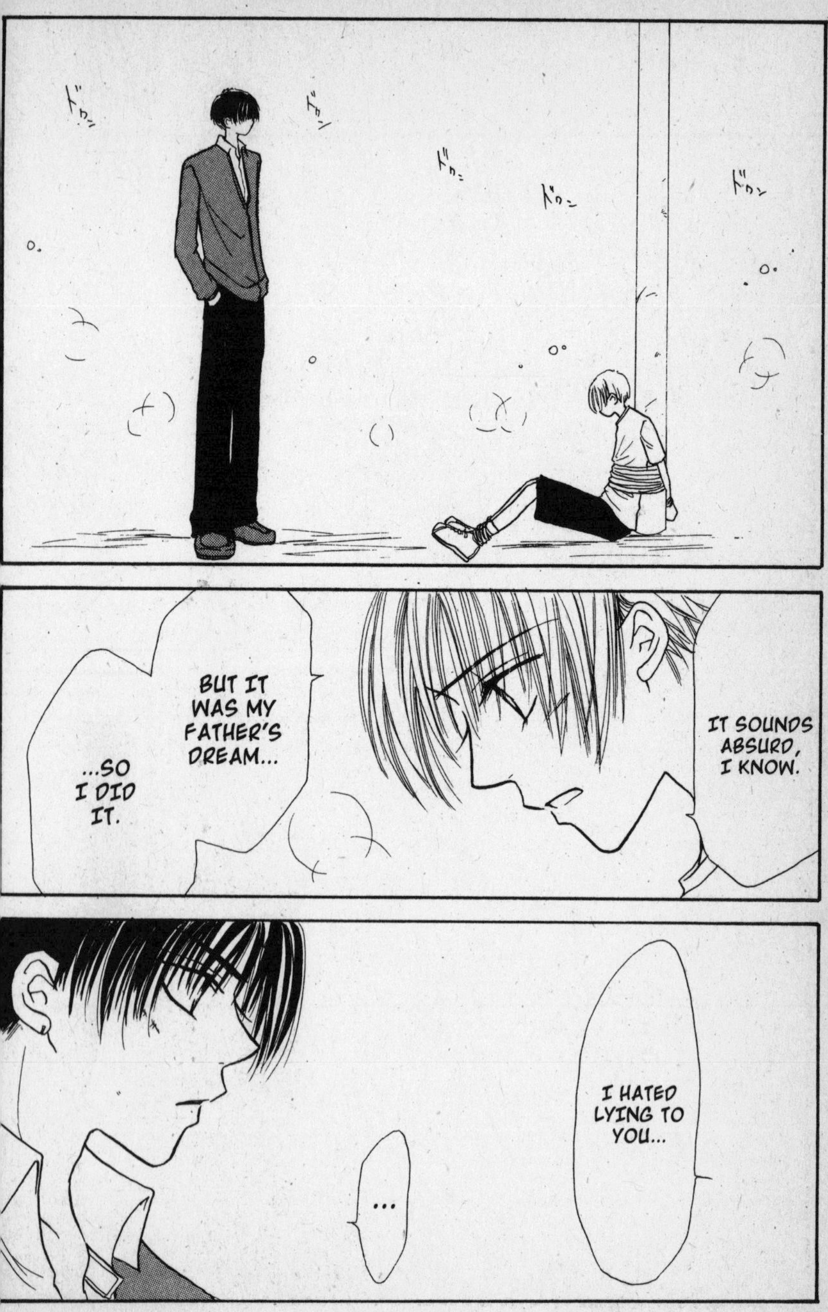
IT SOUNDS ABSURD, I KNOW.
BUT IT WAS MY FATHER'S DREAM...
...SO I DID IT.
I HATED LYING TO YOU...
...

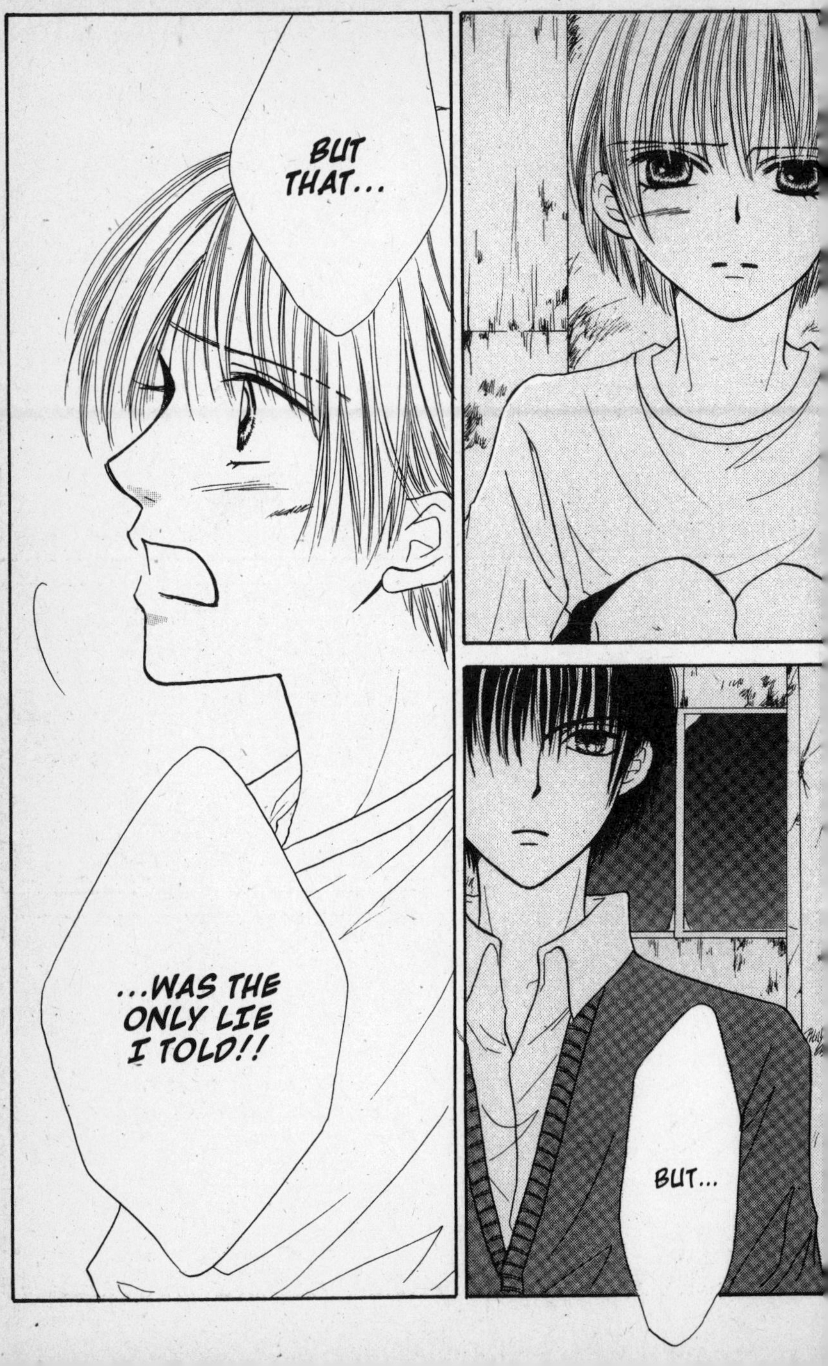
BUT...
BUT THAT...
...WAS THE ONLY LIE I TOLD!!

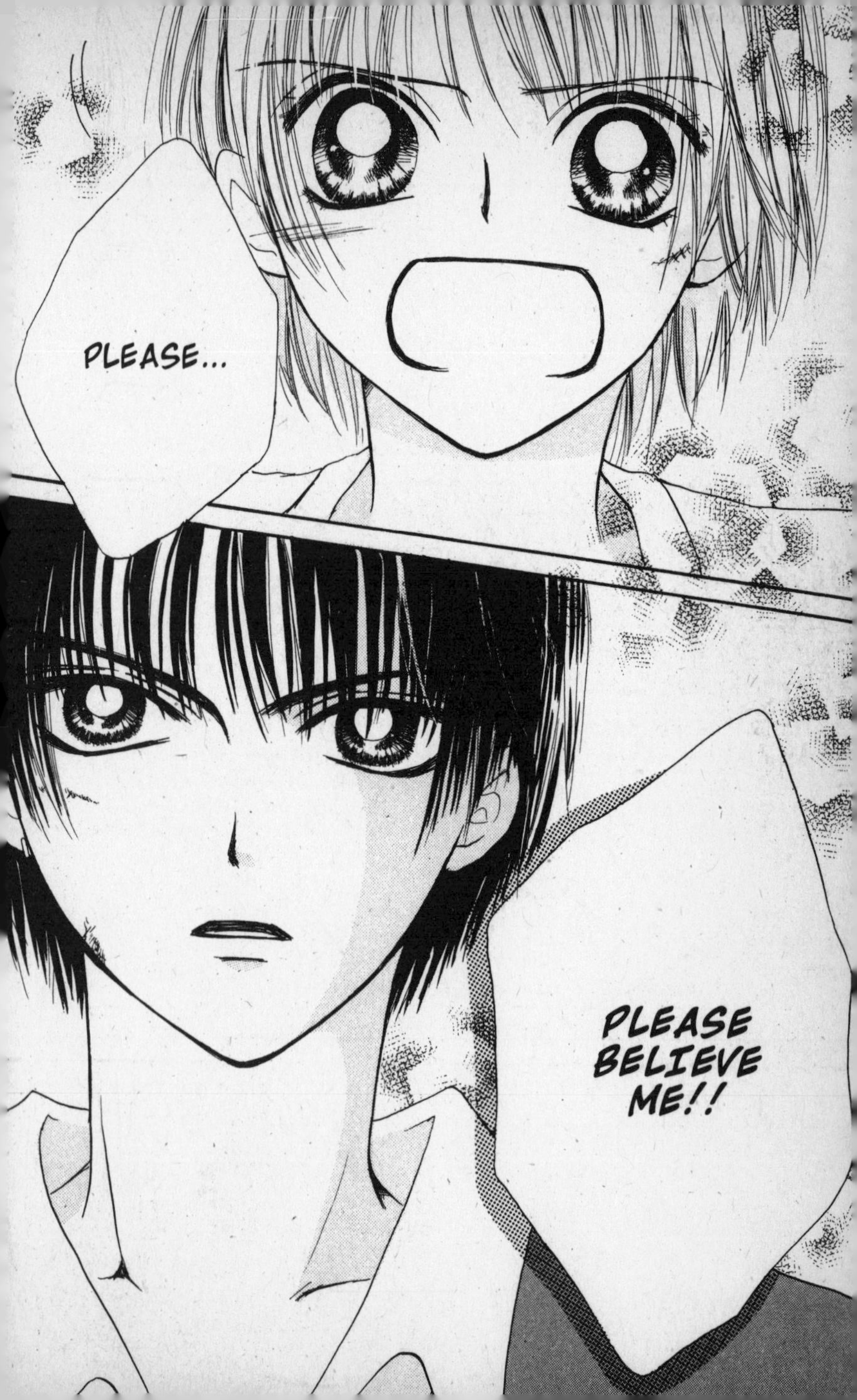
PLEASE...
PLEASE BELIEVE ME!!

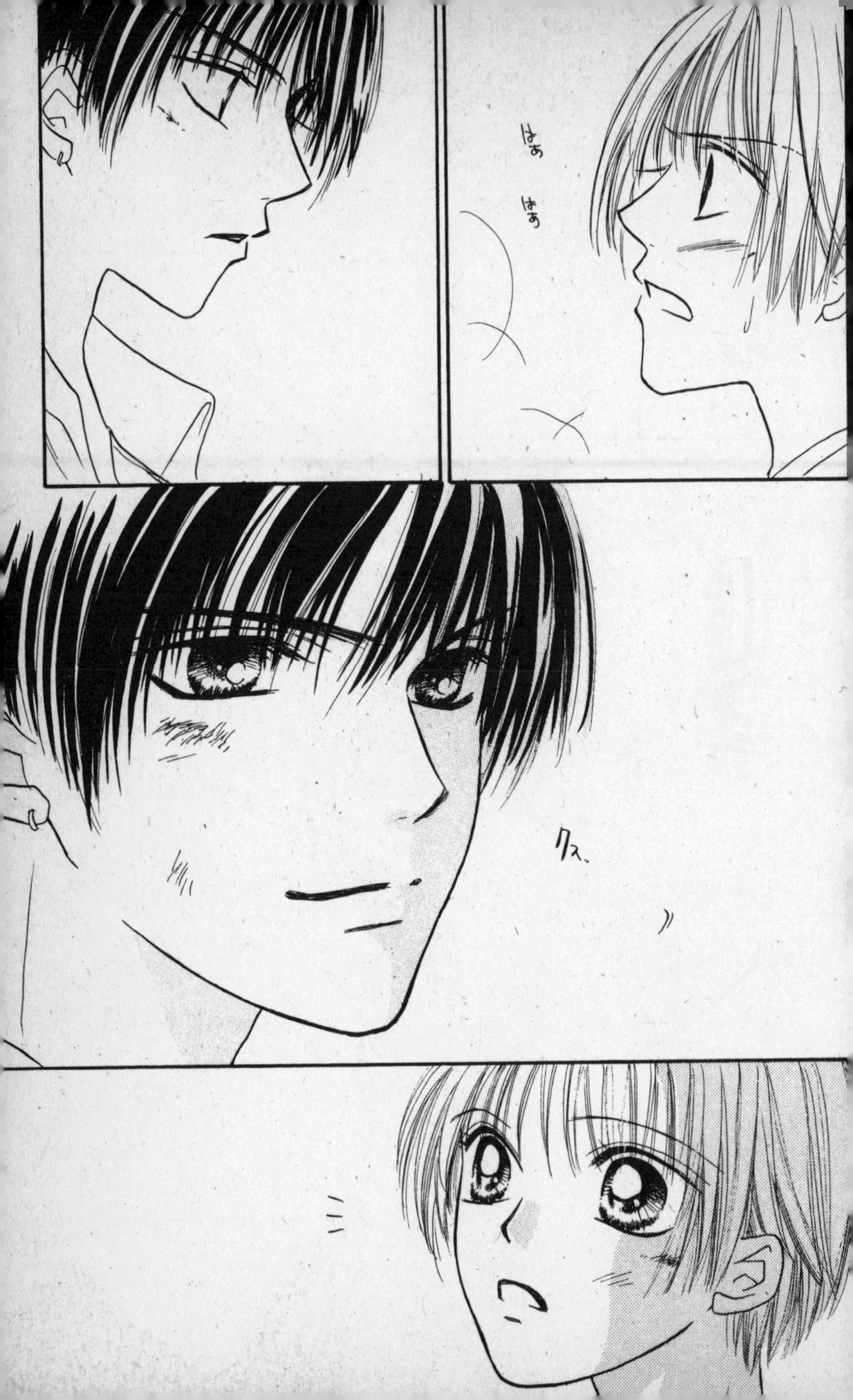
はぁ
はぁ
クス..

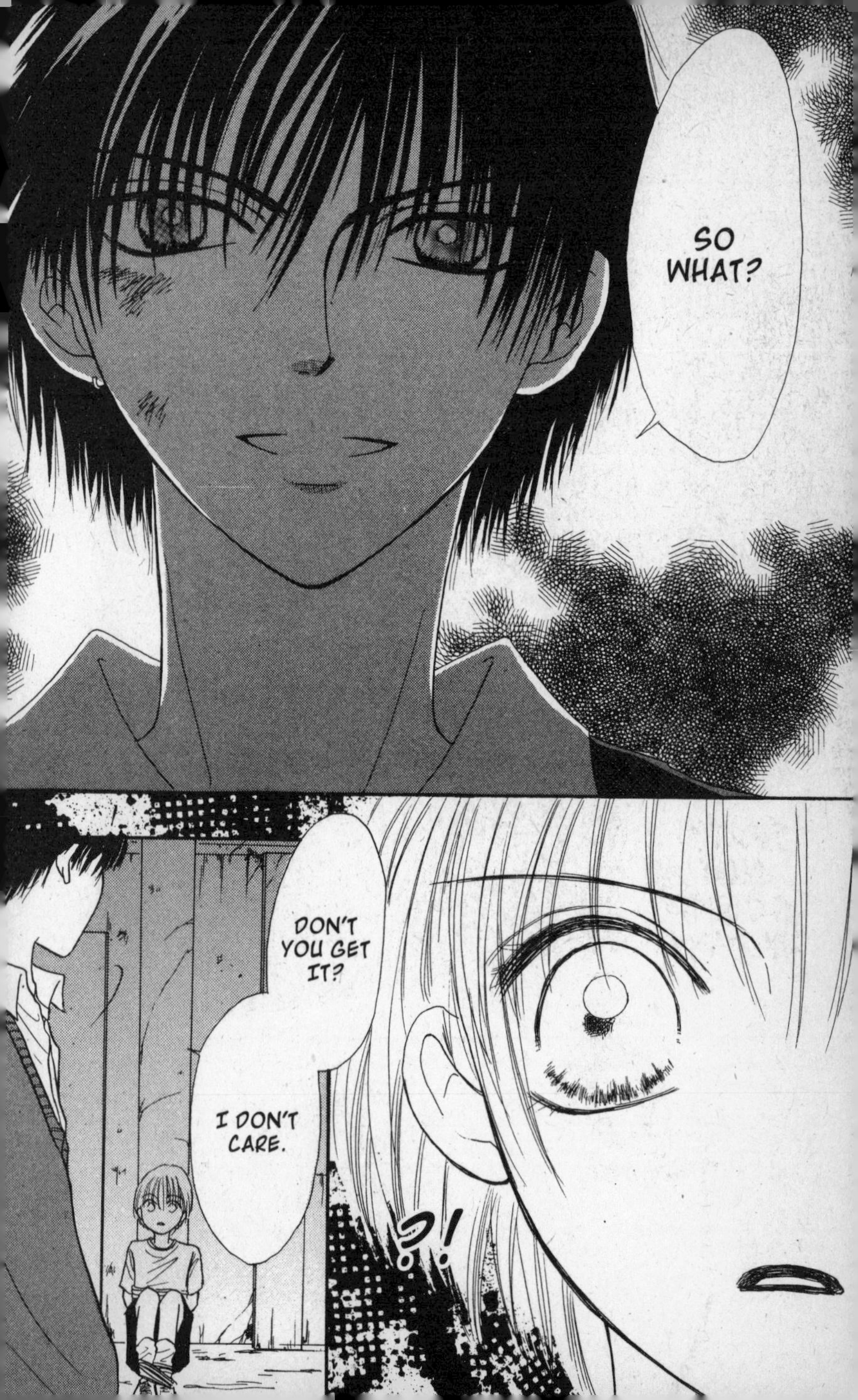
SO WHAT?
DON'T YOU GET IT?
I DON'T CARE.
?!

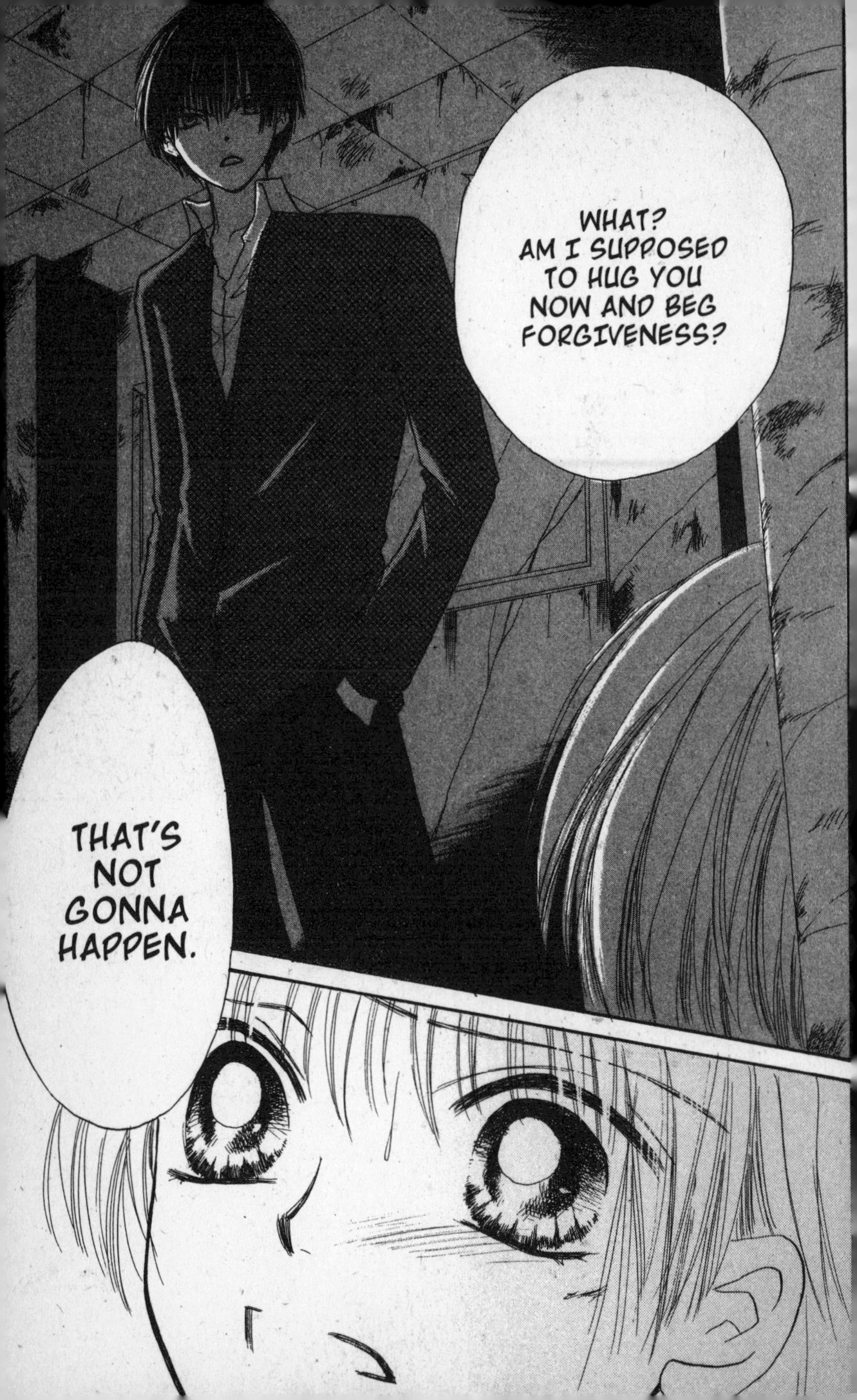
WHAT? AM I SUPPOSED TO HUG YOU NOW AND BEG FORGIVENESS?
THAT'S NOT GONNA HAPPEN.

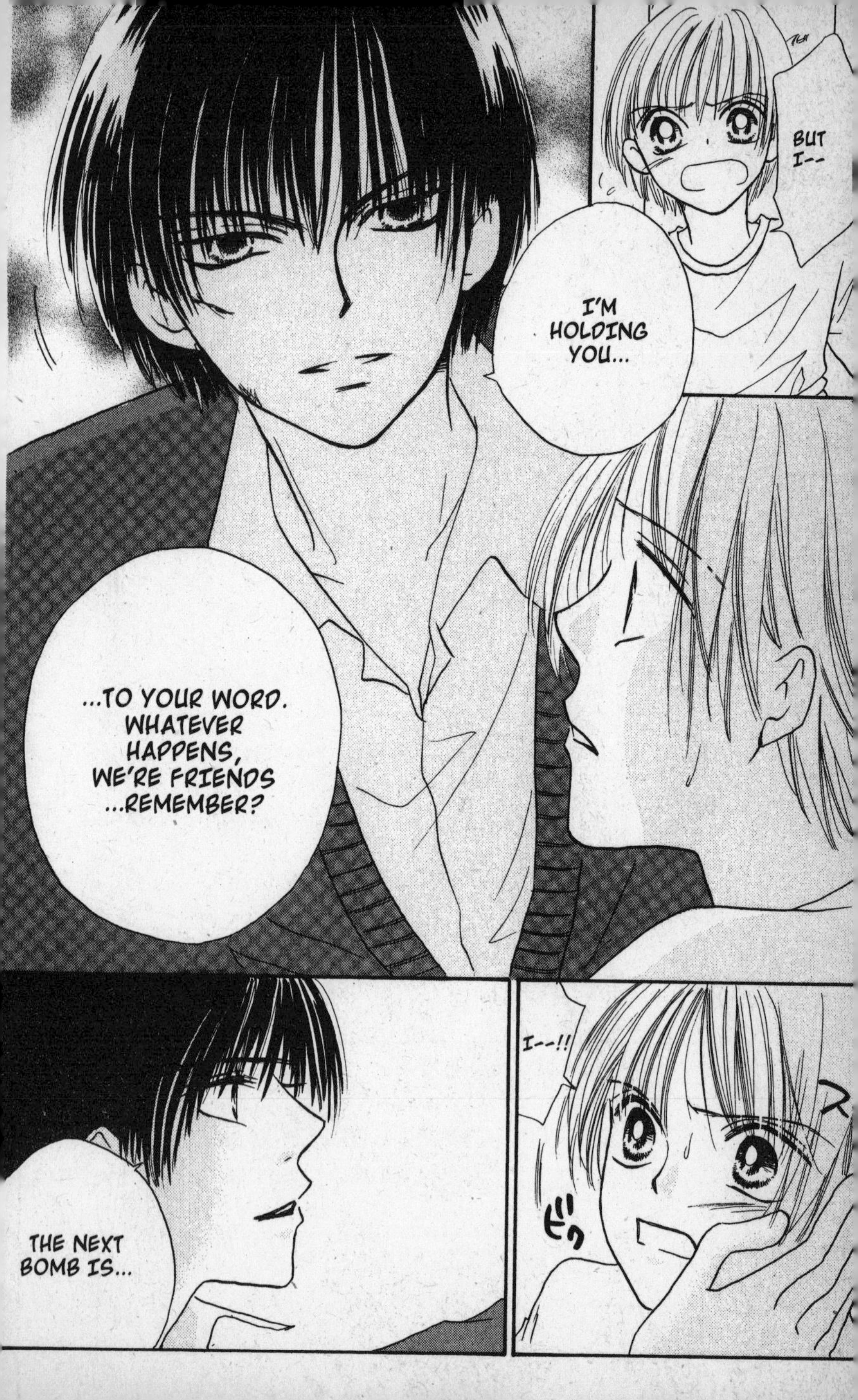
BUT I--
I'M HOLDING YOU...
...TO YOUR WORD. WHATEVER HAPPENS, WE'RE FRIENDS ...REMEMBER?
I--!!
THE NEXT BOMB IS...

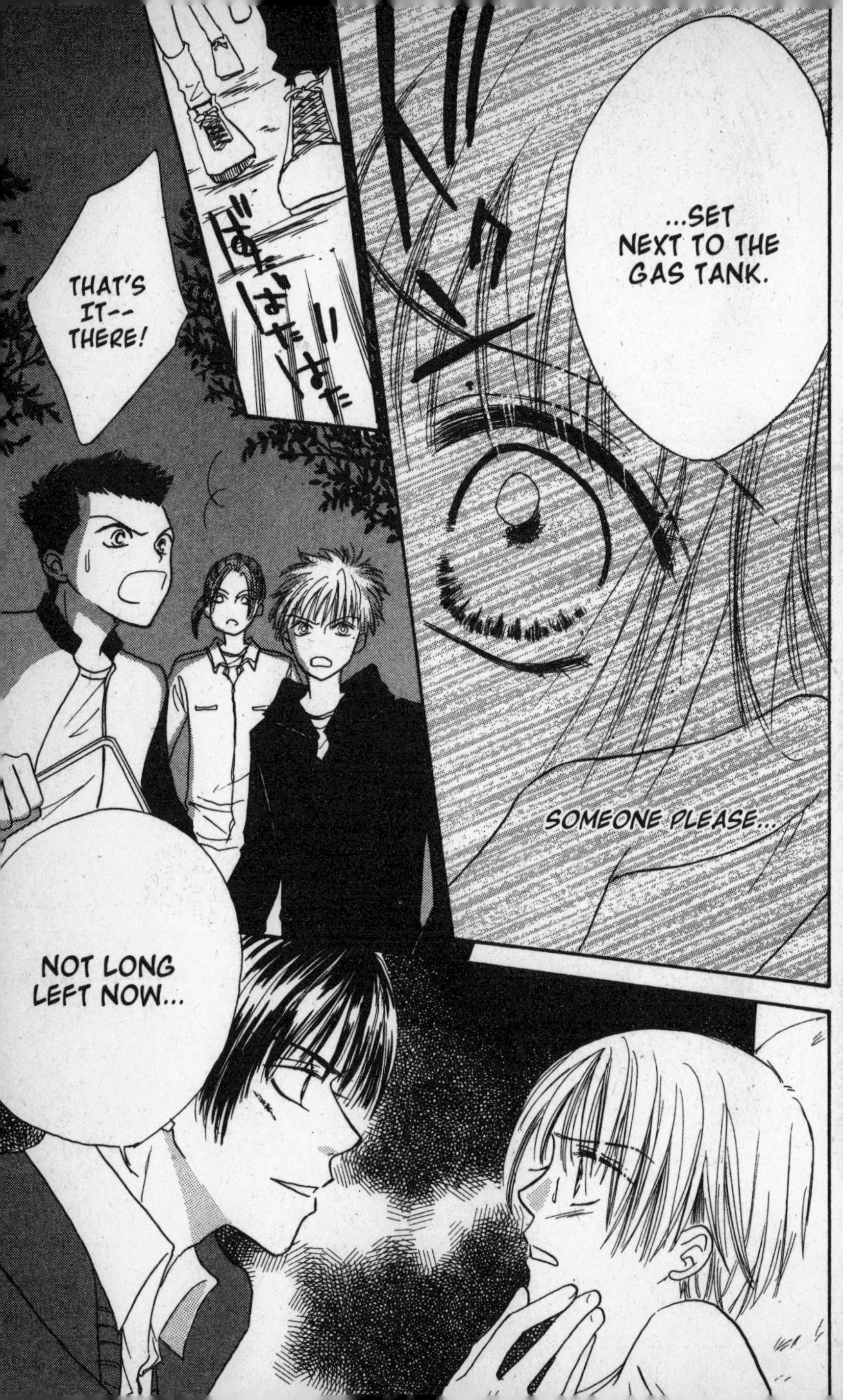
...SET NEXT TO THE GAS TANK.
SOMEONE PLEASE...
THAT'S IT-- THERE!
NOT LONG LEFT NOW...

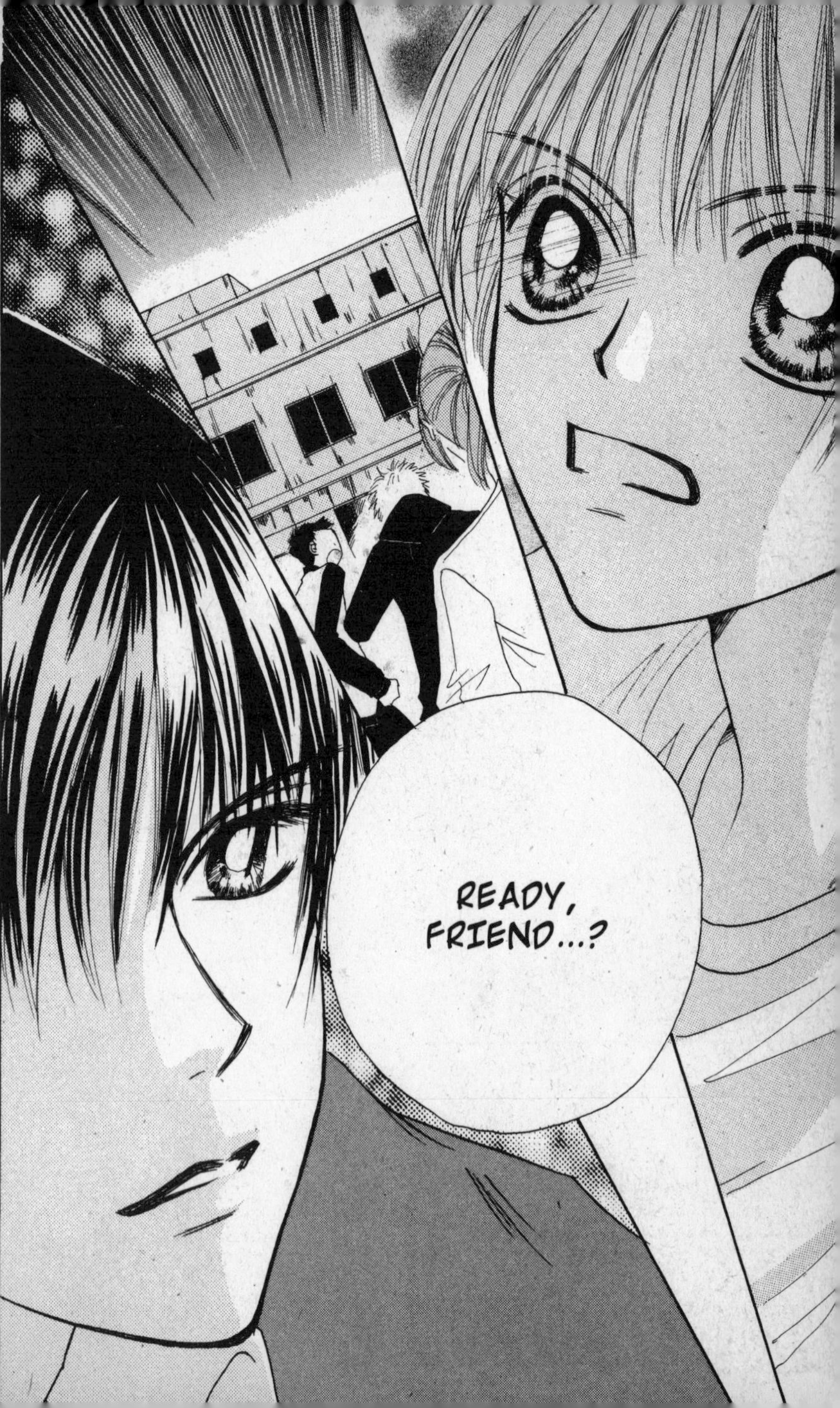
READY,
FRIEND...?

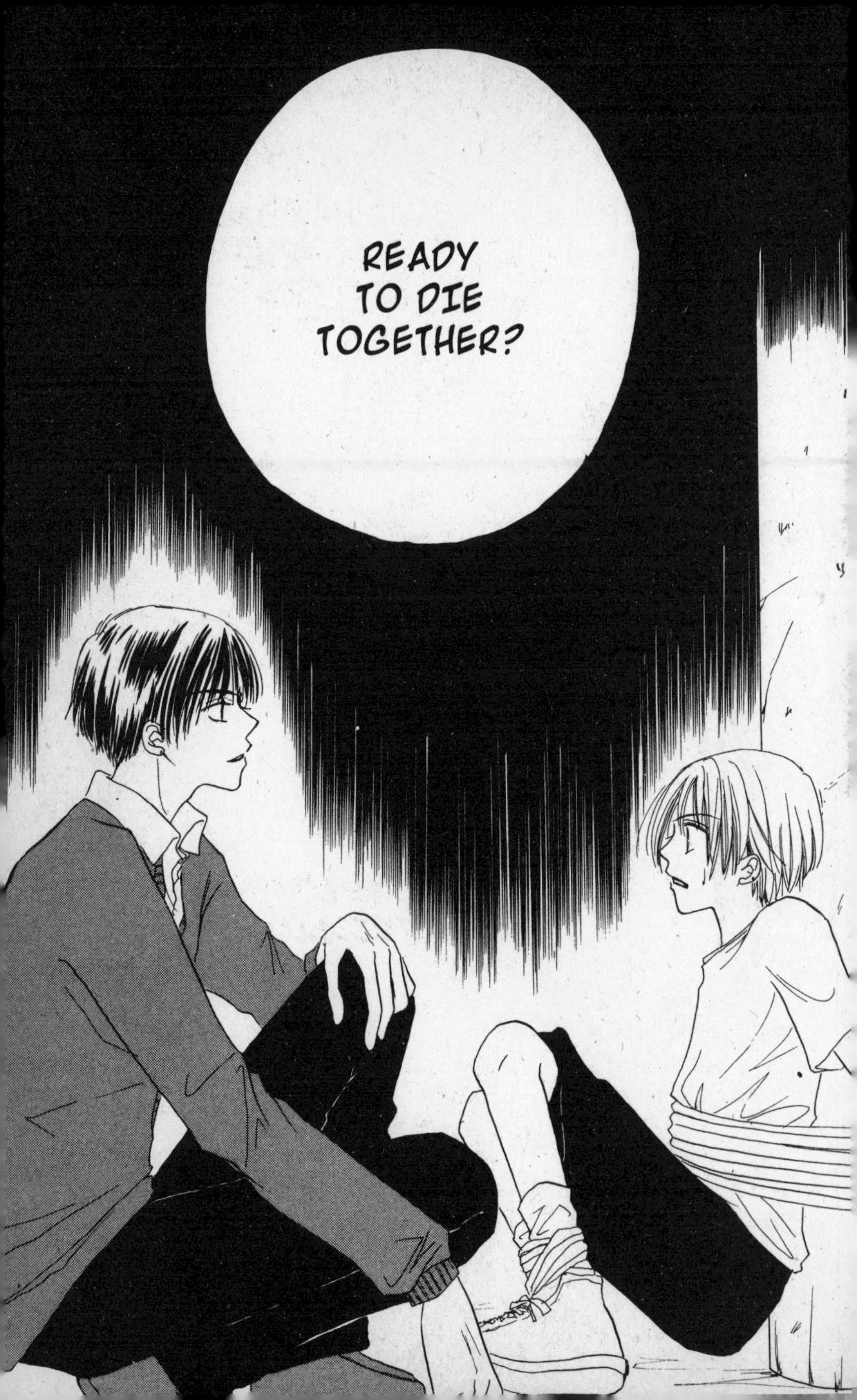
READY TO DIE TOGETHER?

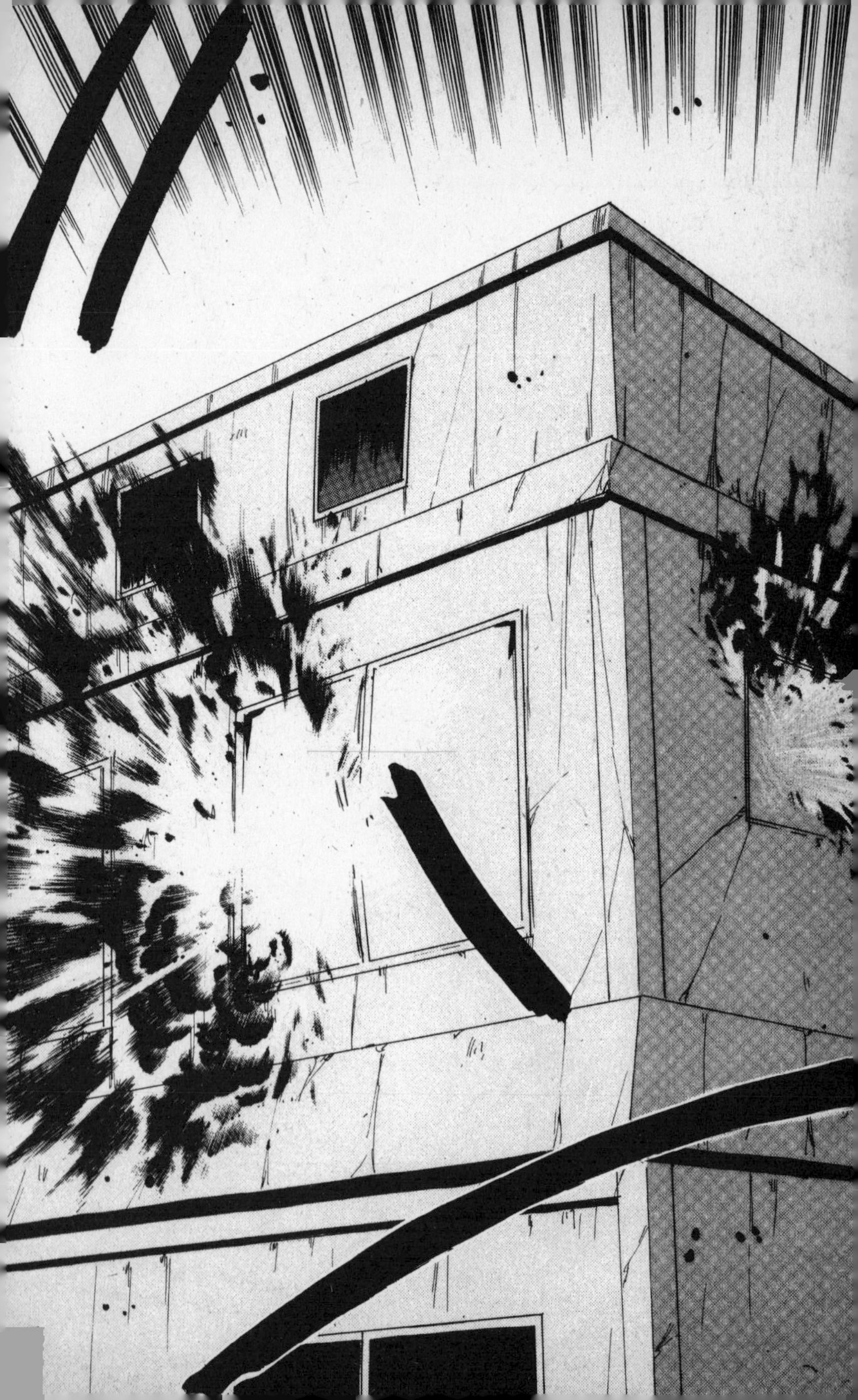

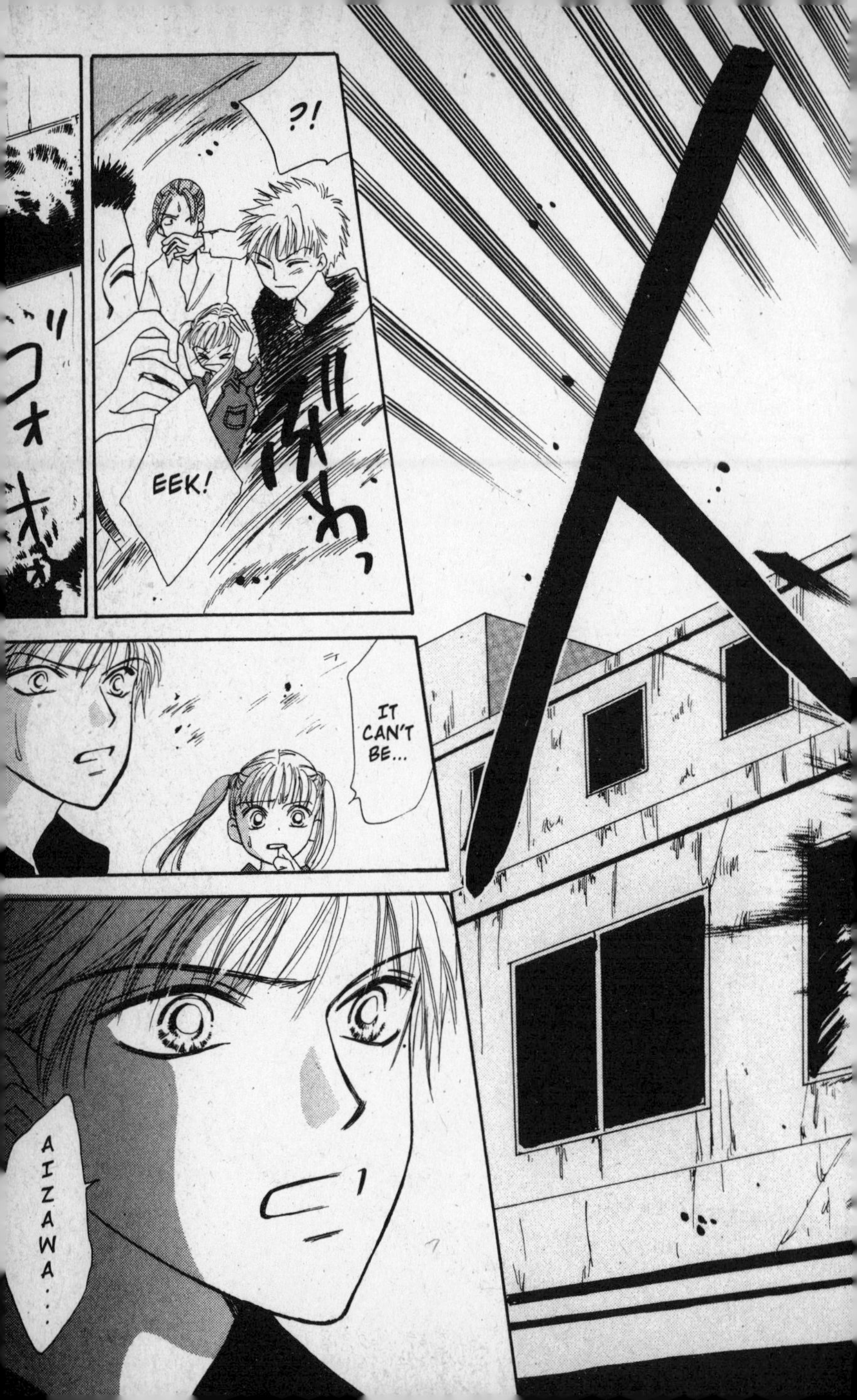
?!
EEK!
ざわっ
IT CAN'T BE...
AIZAWA...

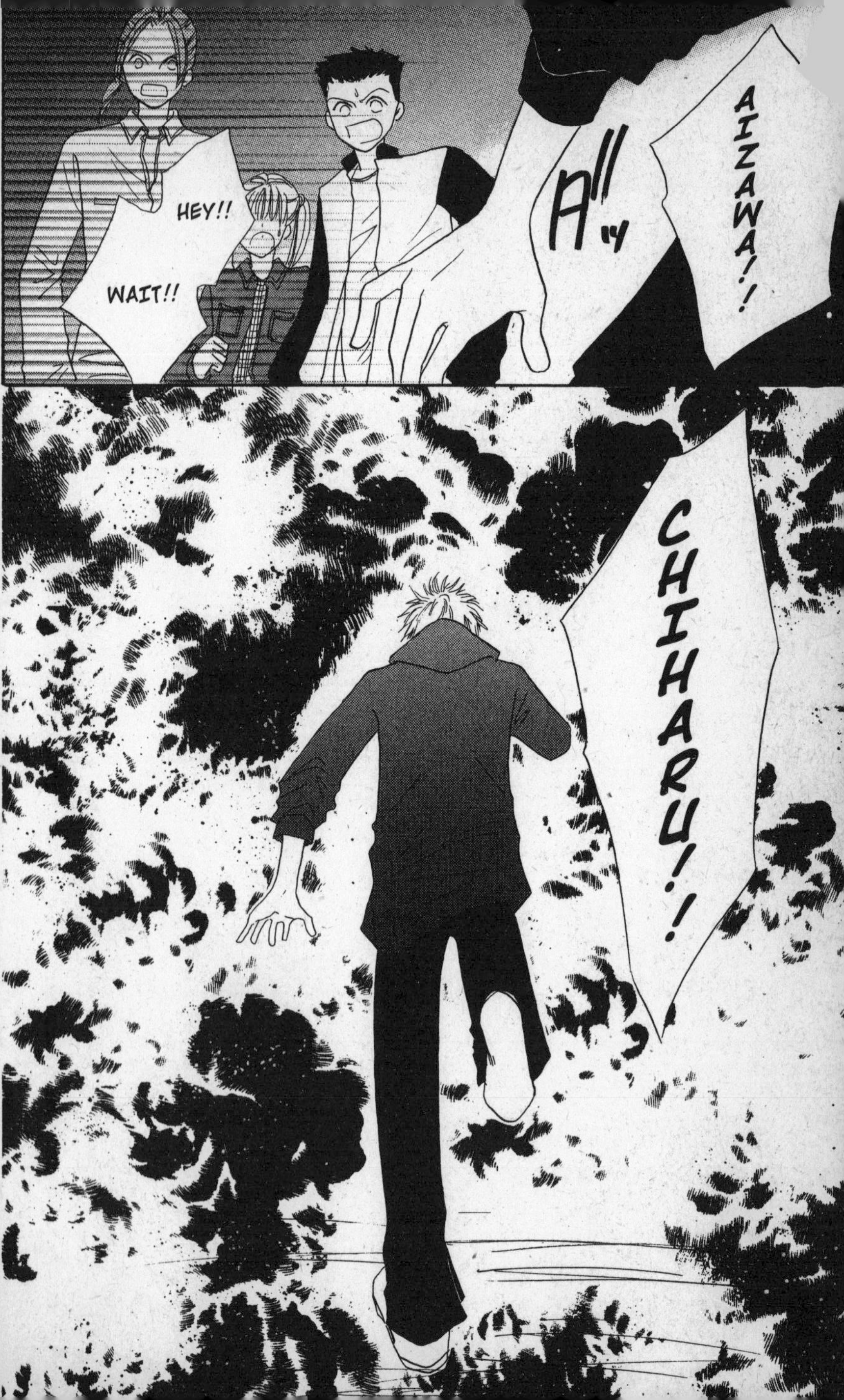
AIZAWA!!
A!!
HEY!!
WAIT!!
CHIHARU!!!

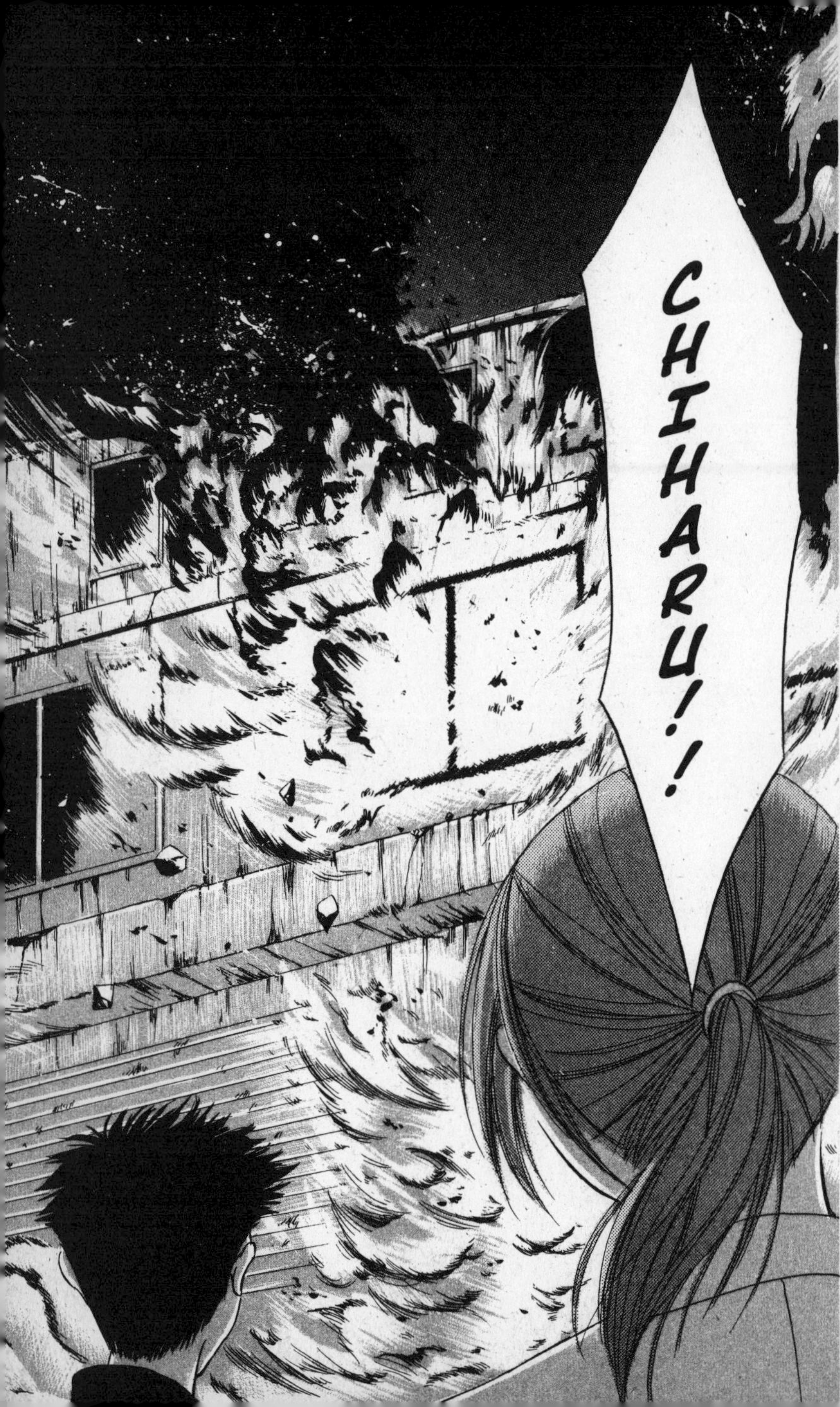
CHIHARU!!

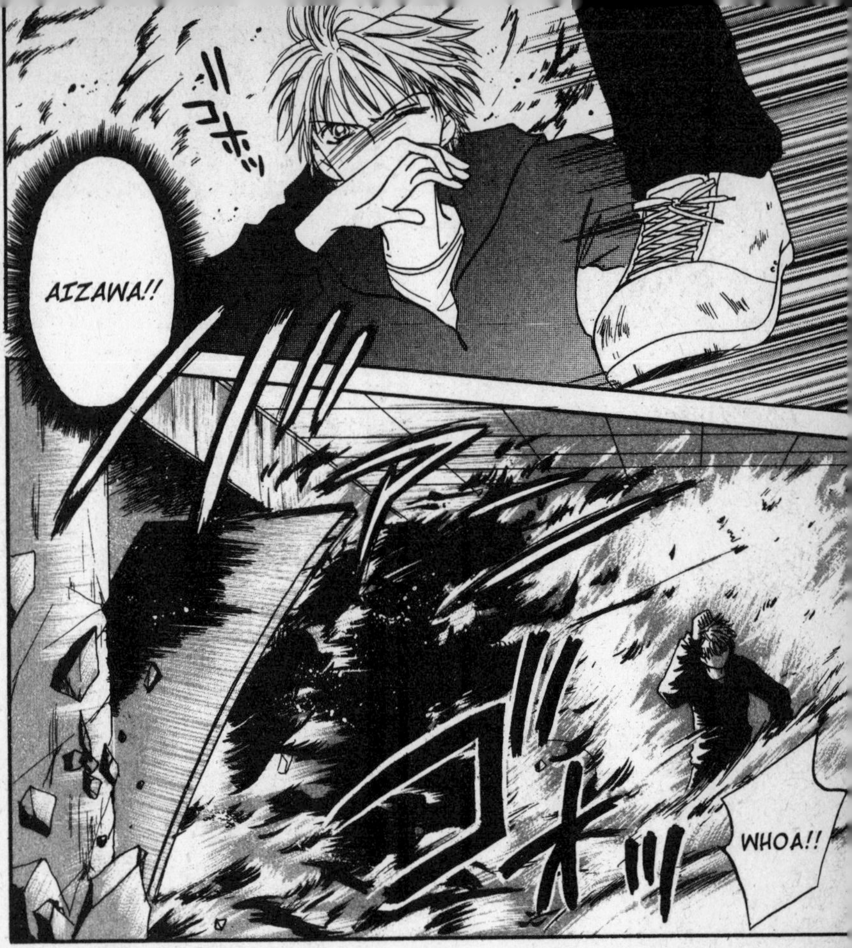
AIZAWA!!
WHOA!!

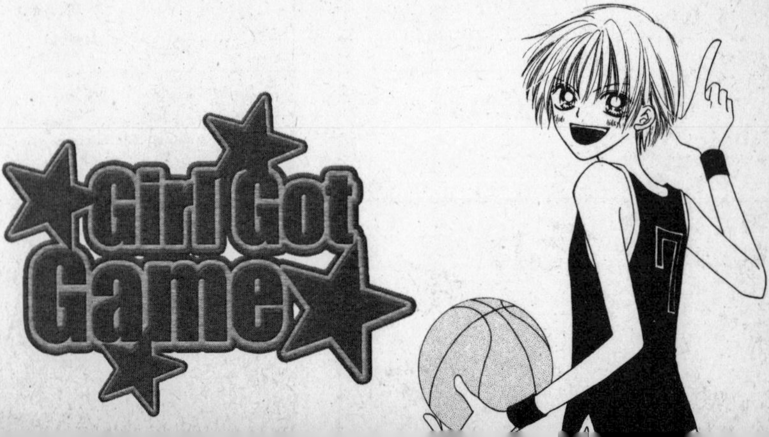
Girl Got Game

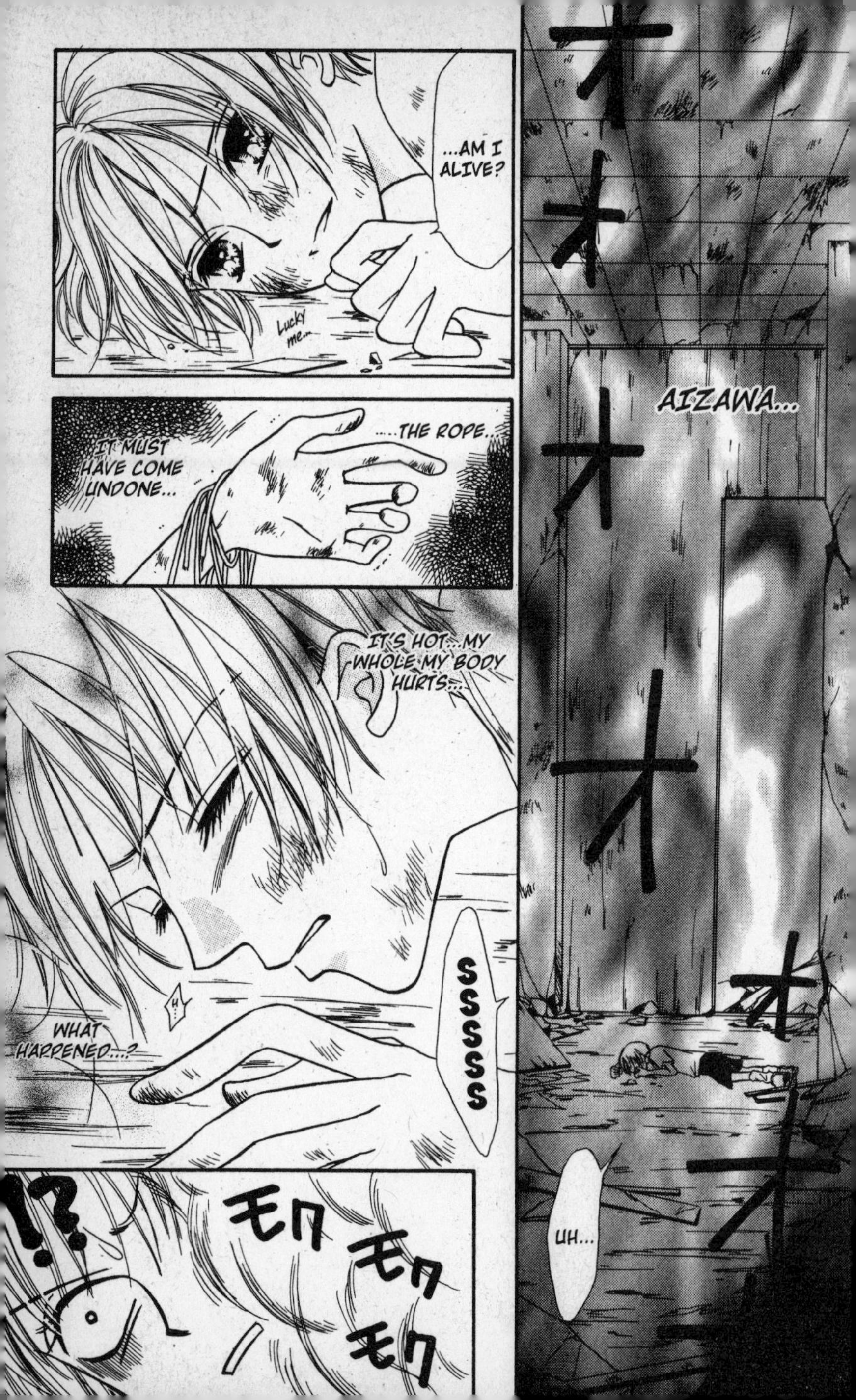
AIZAWA...
UH...
...AM I ALIVE?
Lucky me...
.....THE ROPE...
IT MUST HAVE COME UNDONE...
IT'S HOT...MY WHOLE MY BODY HURTS...
SSSSS
WHAT HAPPENED...?
!?
モワ モワ モワ

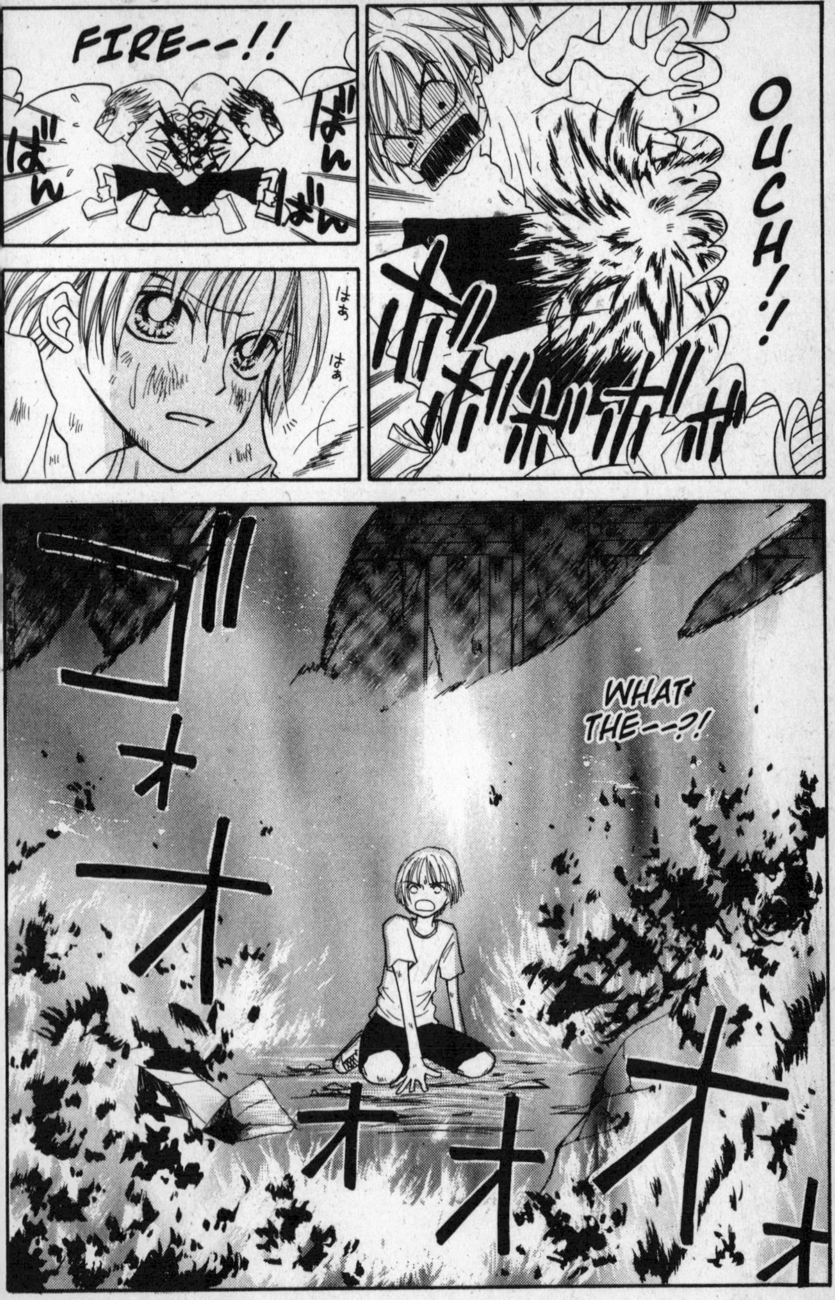
OUCH!!
ボボボボボボ
FIRE--!!
ばんばん
ばんばん
はぁ
はぁ
ゴオオオオ
WHAT THE--?!

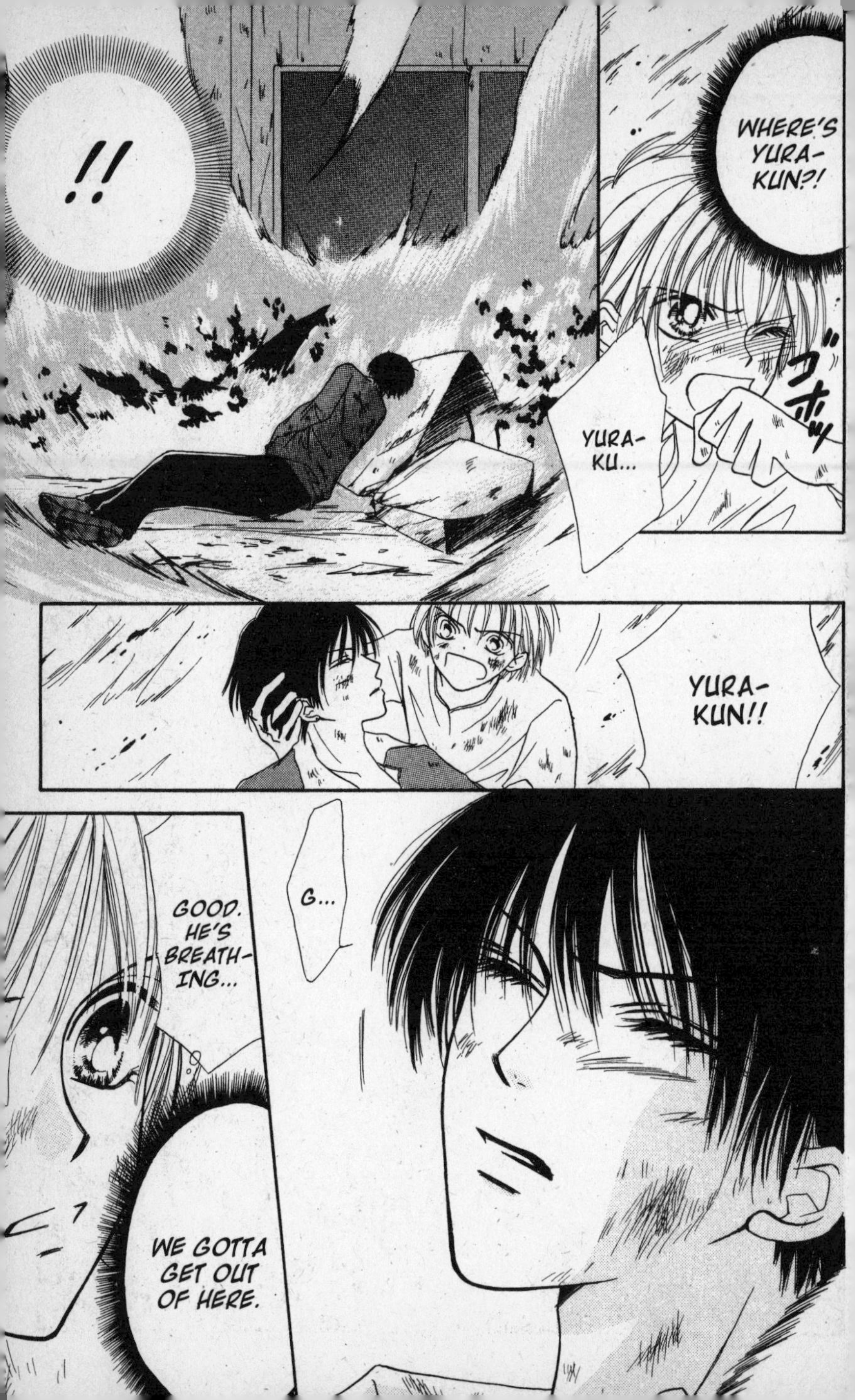
WHERE'S YURA-KUN?!
ゴホッ
YURA-KU...
!!
YURA-KUN!!
G...
GOOD. HE'S BREATHING...
WE GOTTA GET OUT OF HERE.

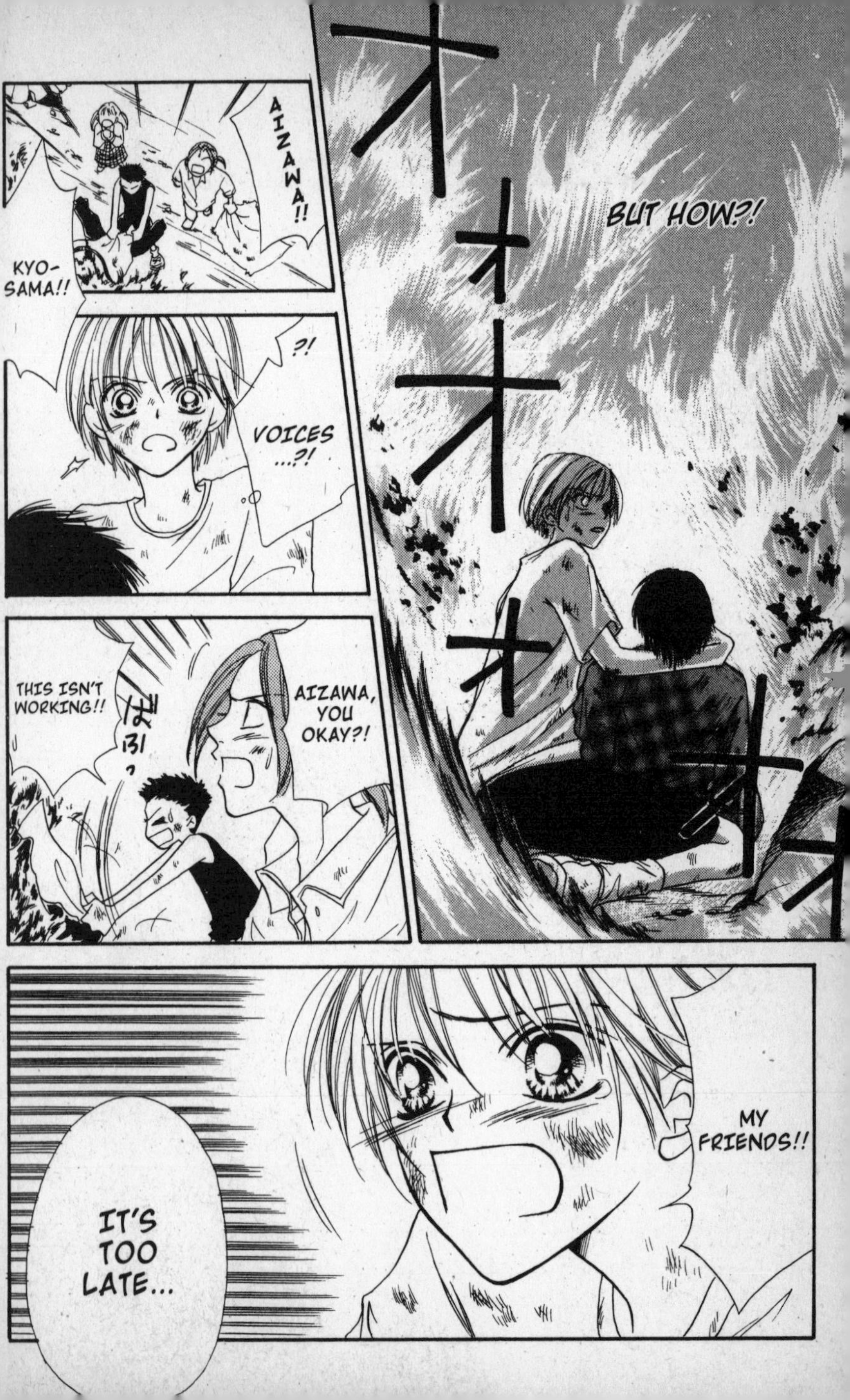
オオオオ
BUT HOW?!
AIZAWA!!
KYO-SAMA!!
?!
VOICES ...?!
AIZAWA, YOU OKAY?!
ばふっ
THIS ISN'T WORKING!!
MY FRIENDS!!
IT'S TOO LATE...

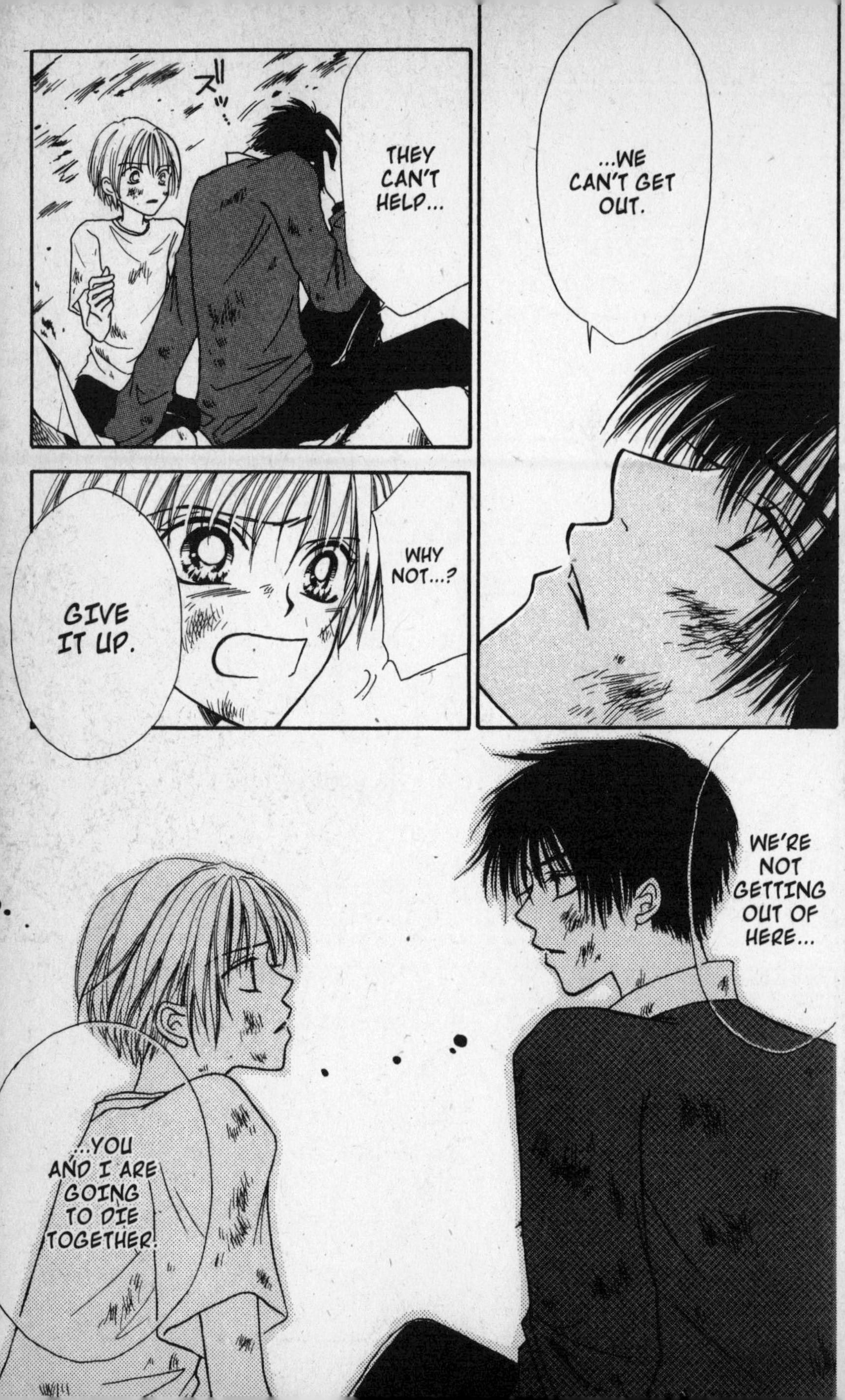
...WE CAN'T GET OUT.
THEY CAN'T HELP...
ズッ…
WHY NOT...?
GIVE IT UP.
WE'RE NOT GETTING OUT OF HERE...
...YOU AND I ARE GOING TO DIE TOGETHER.

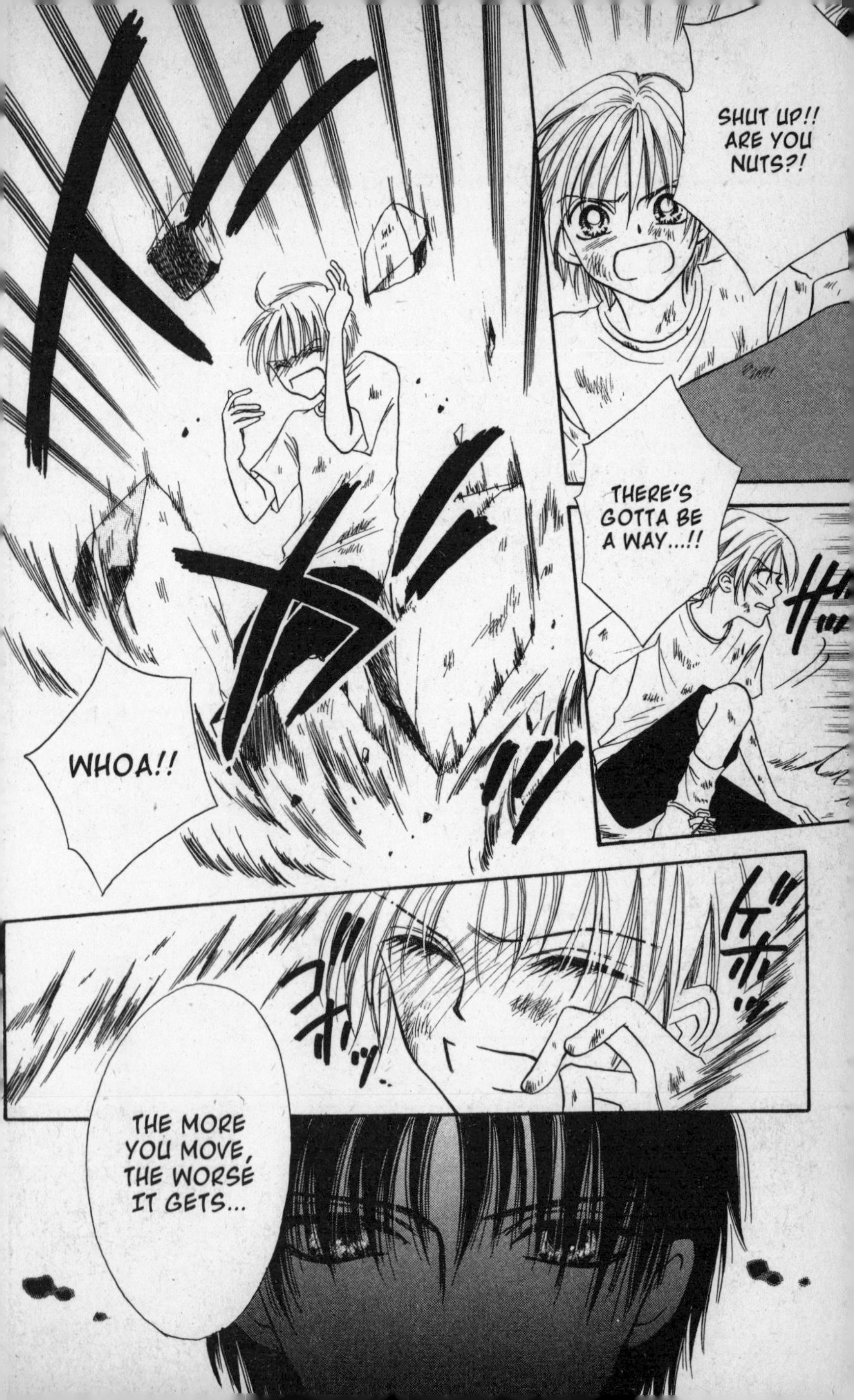
SHUT UP!! ARE YOU NUTS?!
THERE'S GOTTA BE A WAY...!!
WHOA!!
THE MORE YOU MOVE, THE WORSE IT GETS...

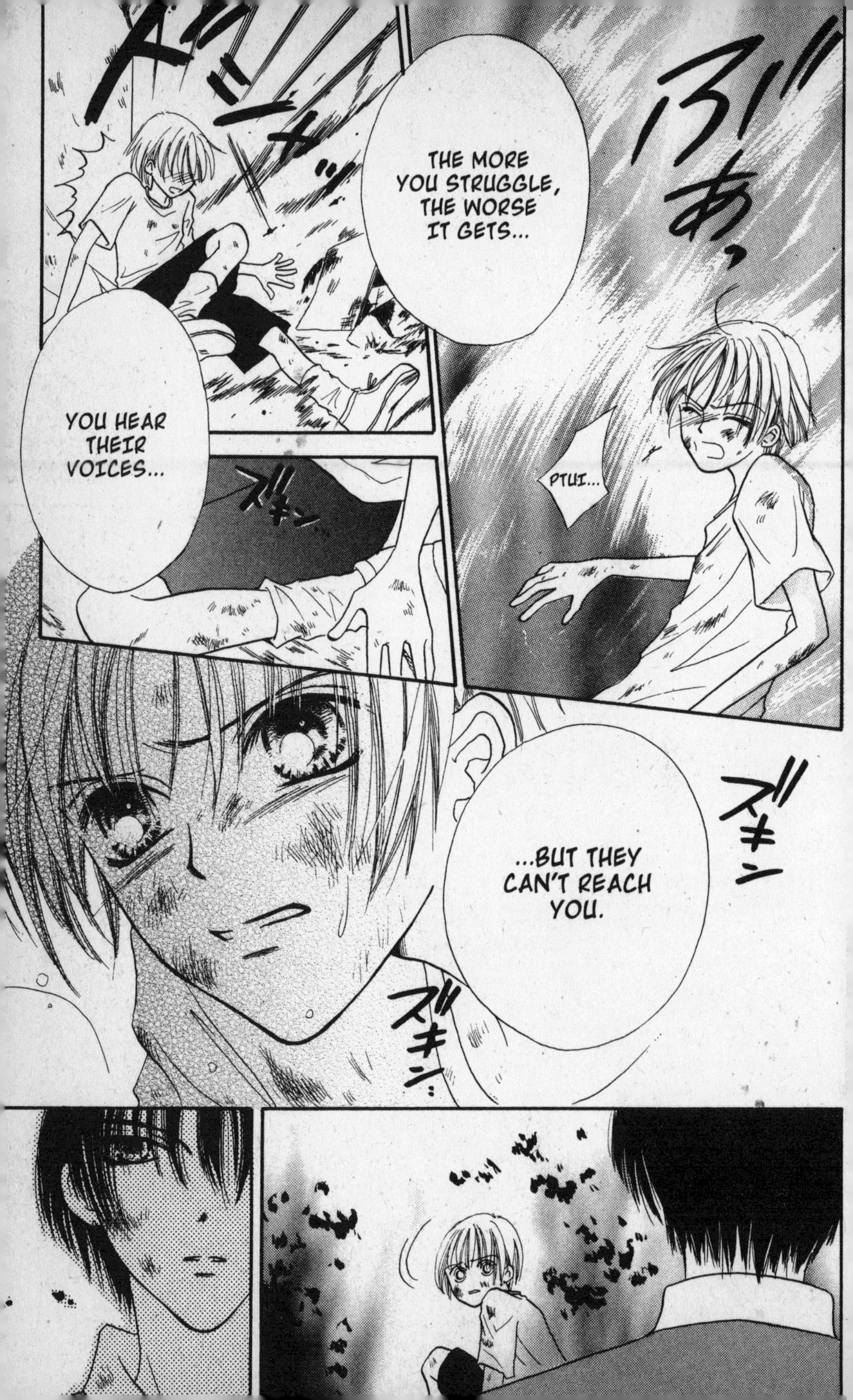
THE MORE YOU STRUGGLE, THE WORSE IT GETS...
PTUI...
YOU HEAR THEIR VOICES...
...BUT THEY CAN'T REACH YOU.

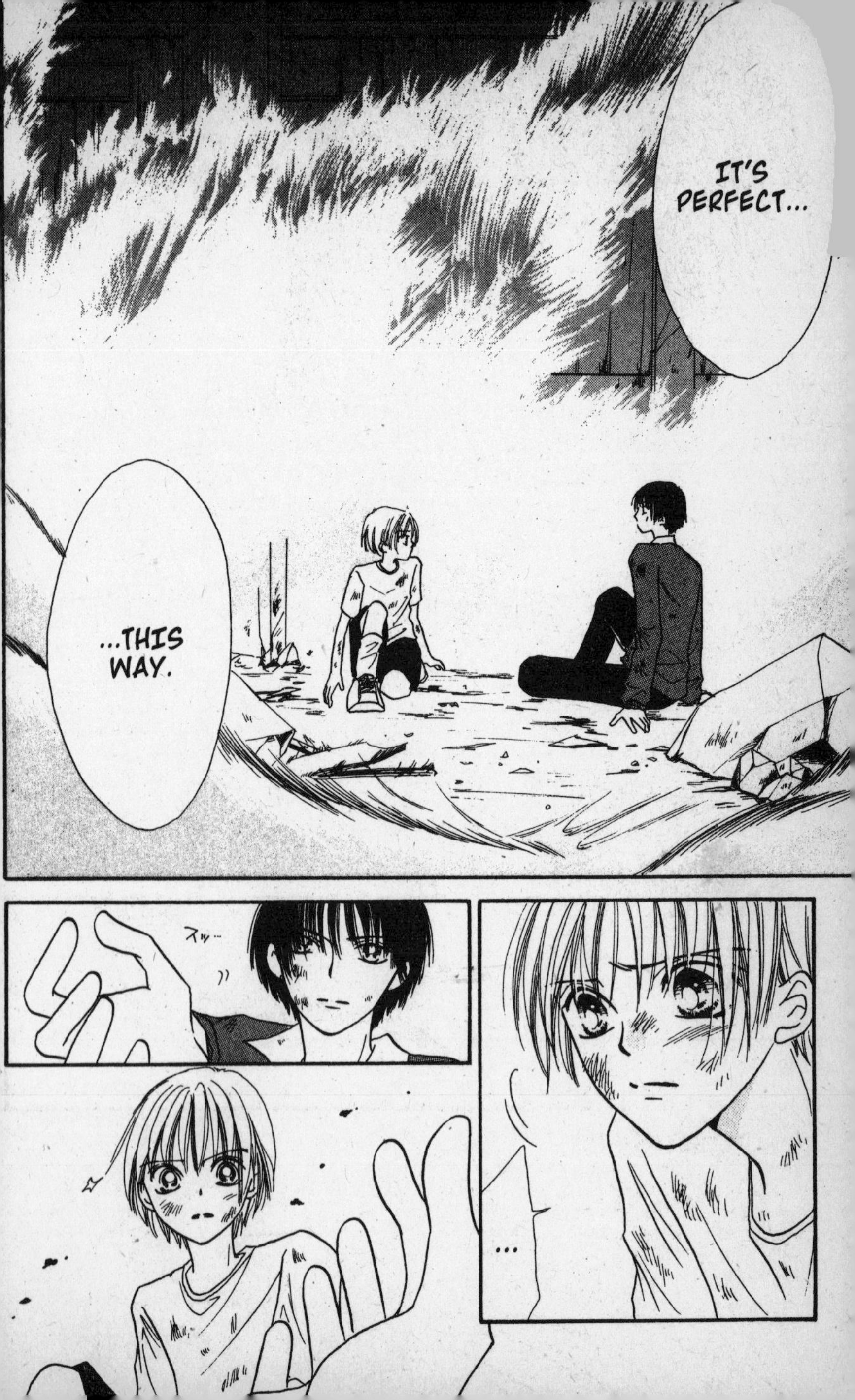

IT'S PERFECT...
...THIS WAY.
...
スッ…

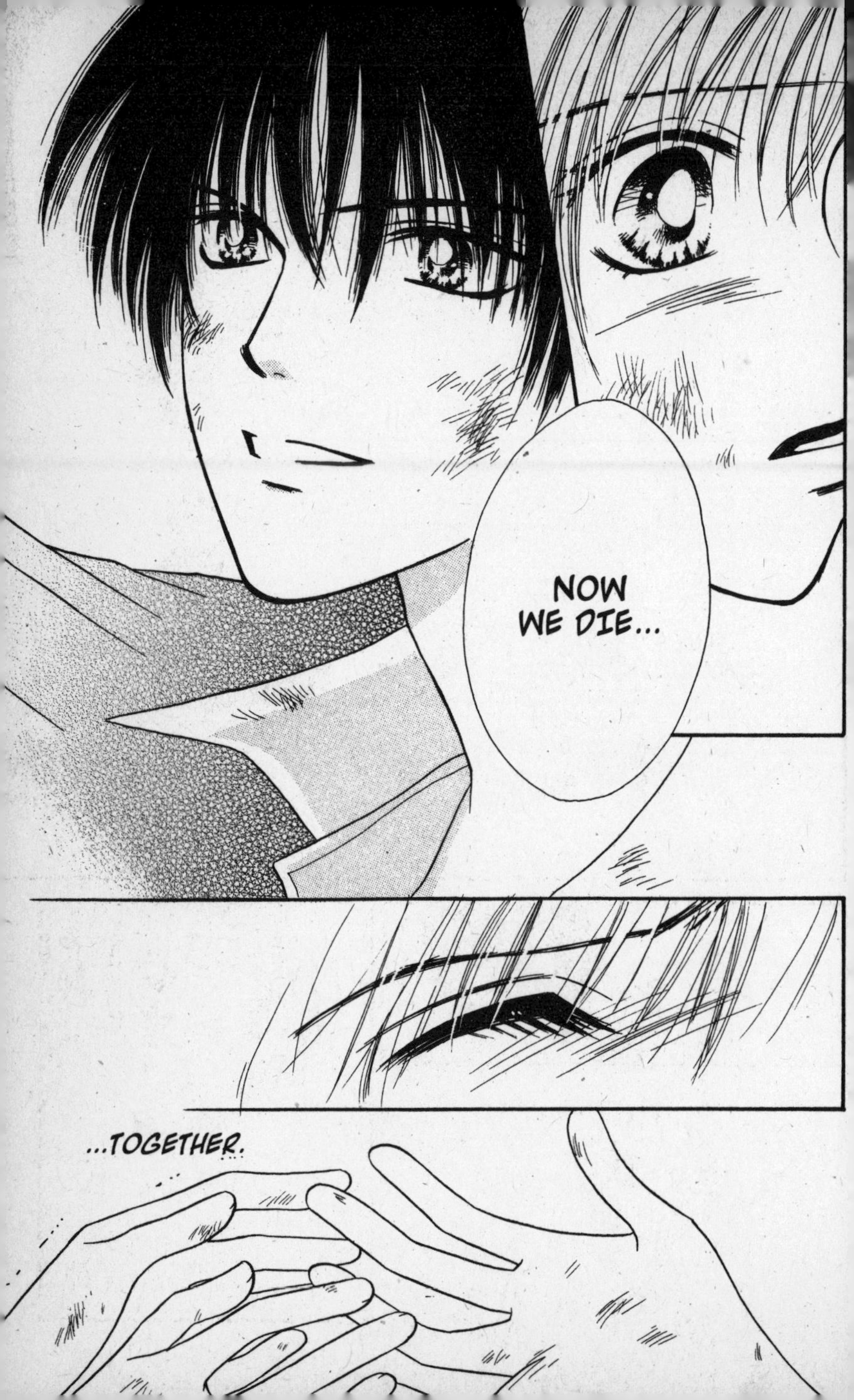
NOW WE DIE...
...TOGETHER.

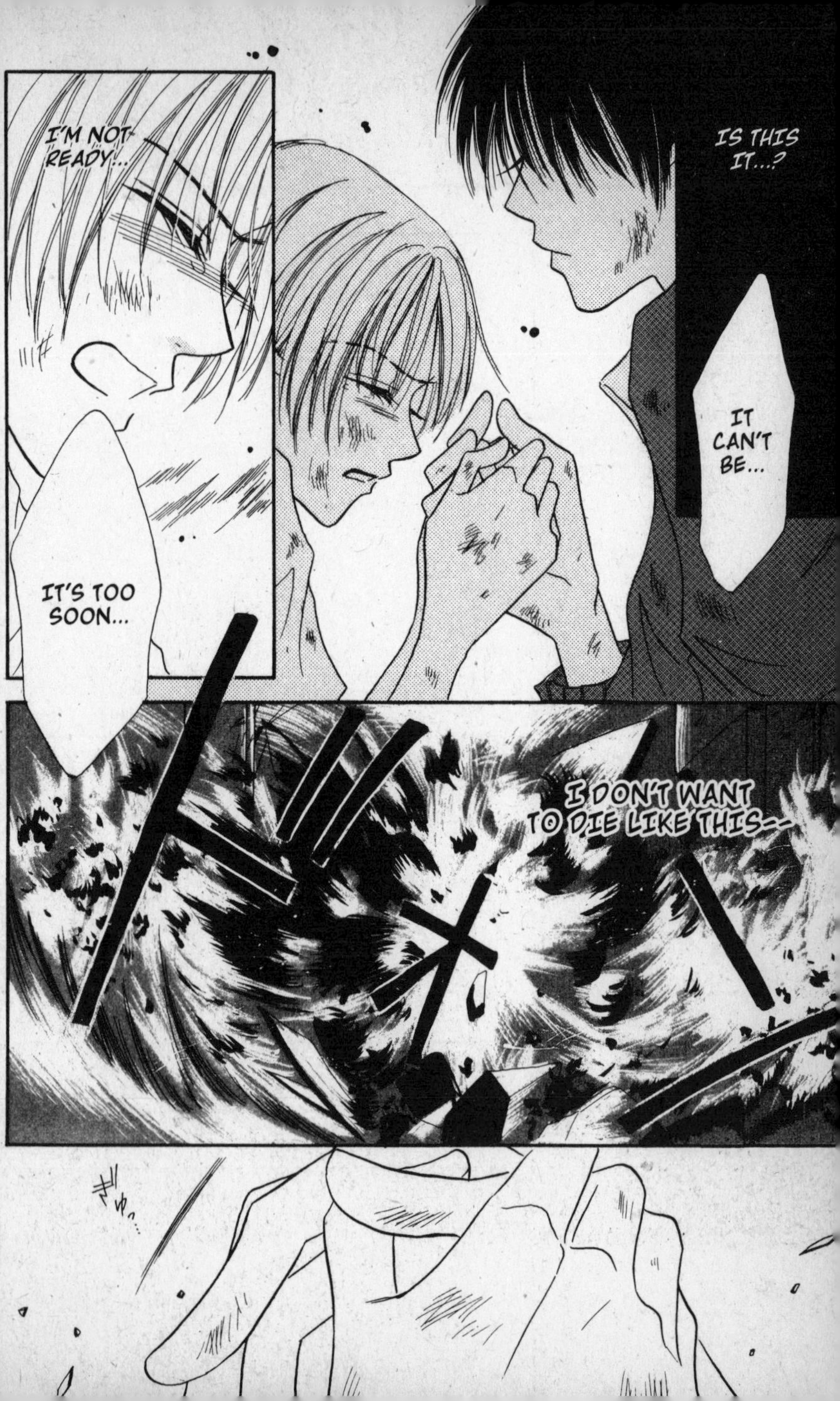
IS THIS IT...?
IT CAN'T BE...
I'M NOT READY...
IT'S TOO SOON...
I DON'T WANT TO DIE LIKE THIS--
ぎゅっ...

THIS CAN'T BE IT...   IT CAN'T BE...

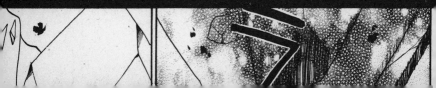

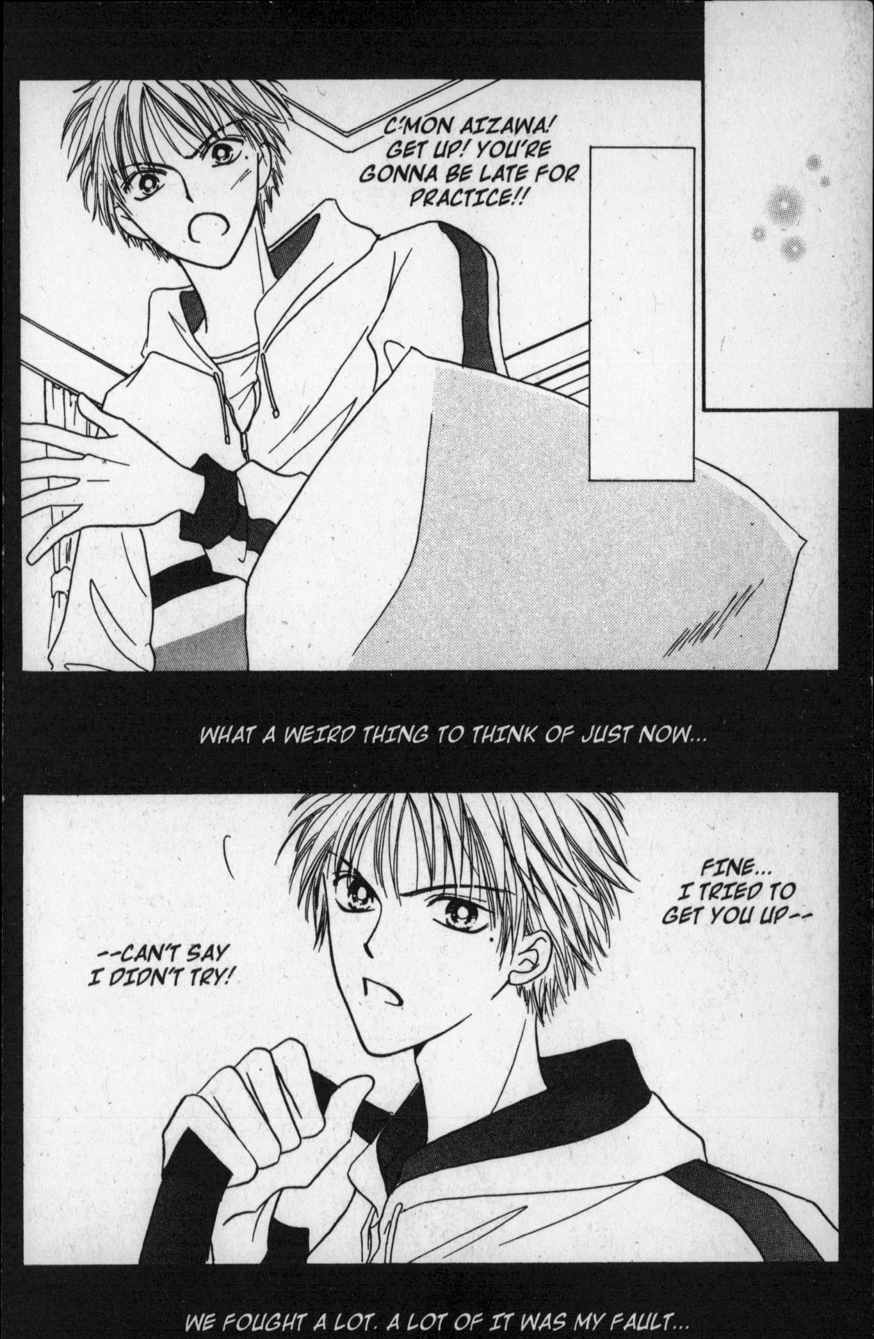
C'MON AIZAWA! GET UP! YOU'RE GONNA BE LATE FOR PRACTICE!!
WHAT A WEIRD THING TO THINK OF JUST NOW...
FINE... I TRIED TO GET YOU UP--
--CAN'T SAY I DIDN'T TRY!
WE FOUGHT A LOT. A LOT OF IT WAS MY FAULT...

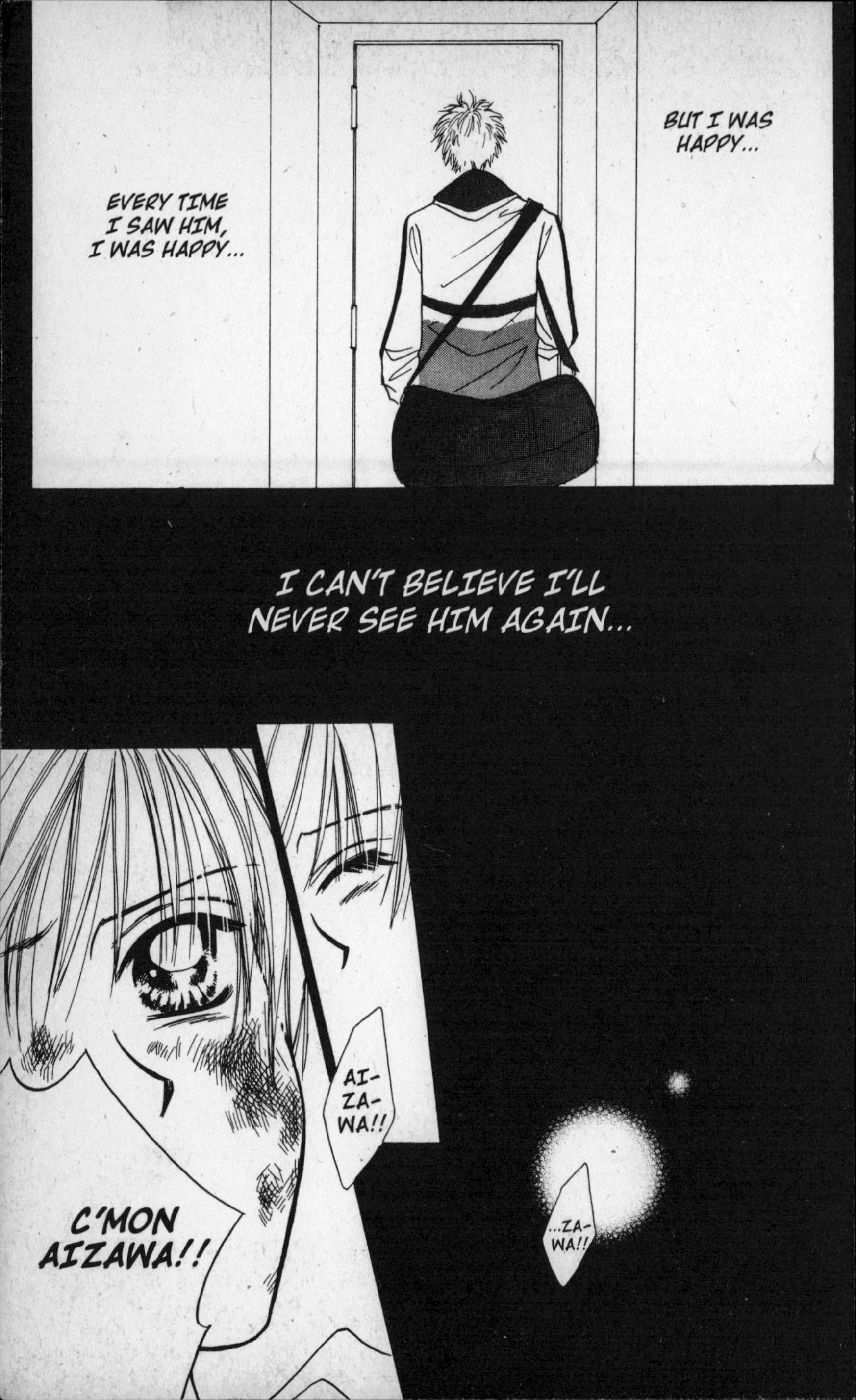
BUT I WAS HAPPY...
EVERY TIME I SAW HIM, I WAS HAPPY...
I CAN'T BELIEVE I'LL NEVER SEE HIM AGAIN...
...ZA-WA!!
AI-ZA-WA!!
C'MON AIZAWA!!

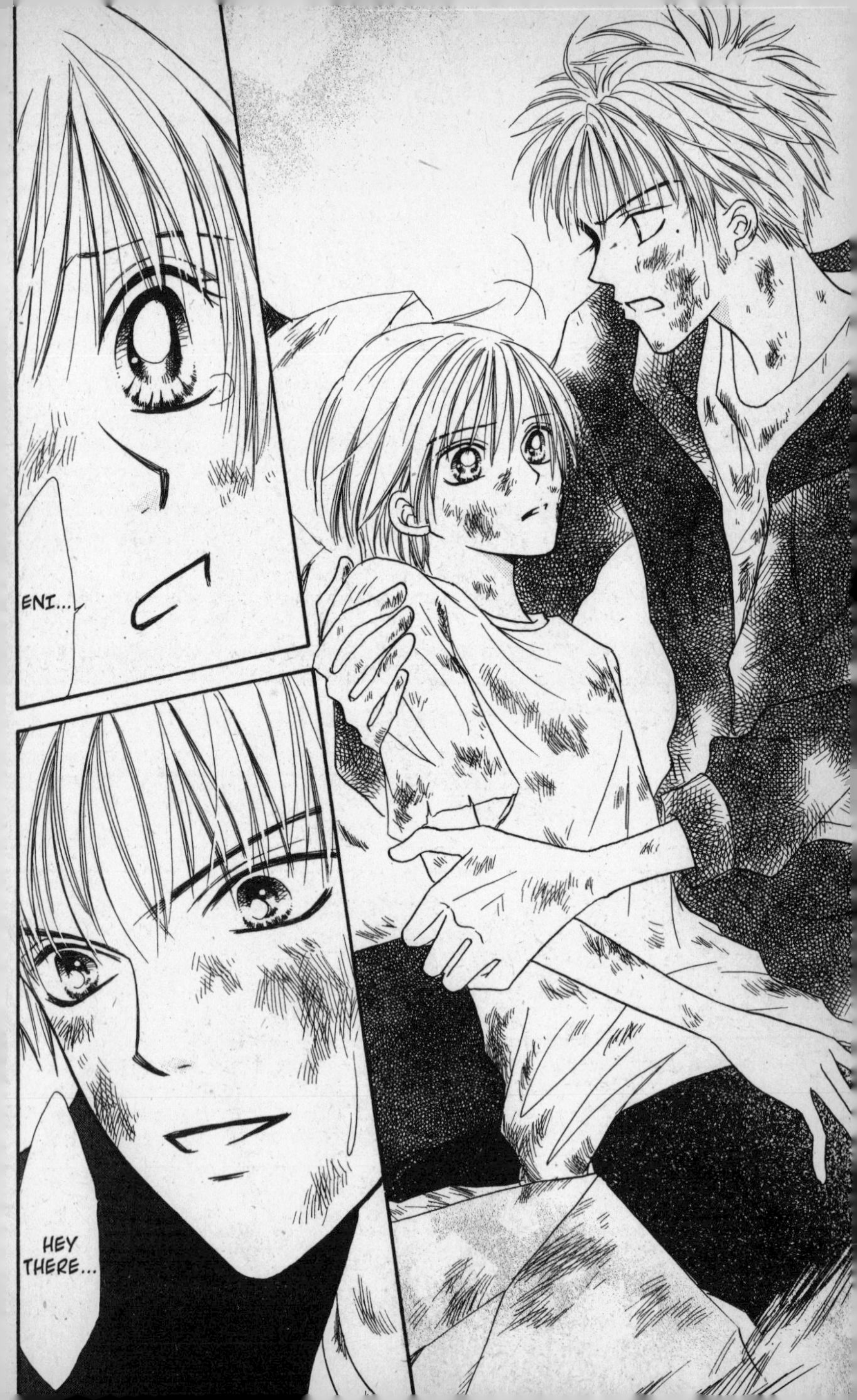
ENI...
HEY THERE...

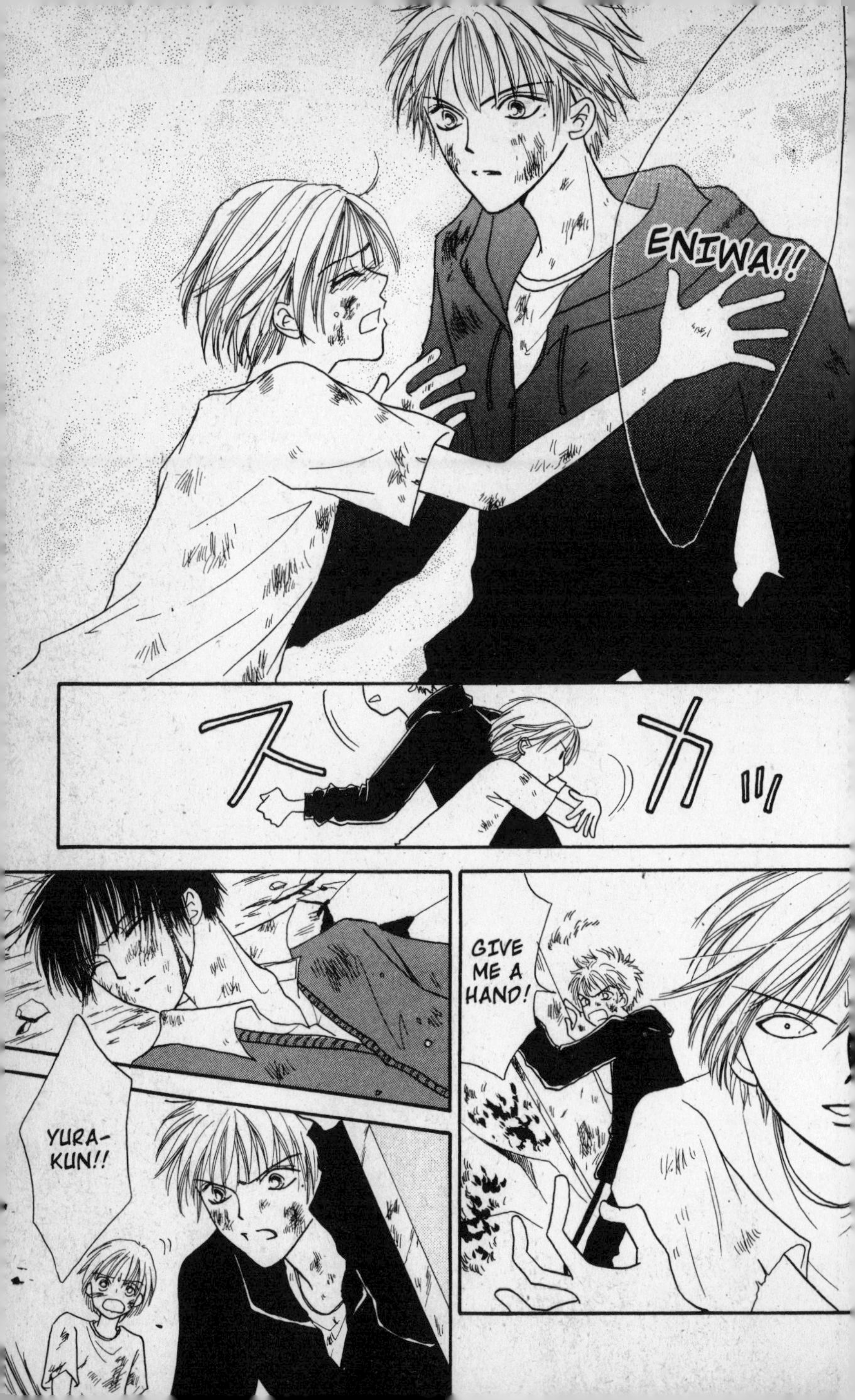
ENIWA!!
スカッ
GIVE ME A HAND!
YURA-KUN!!

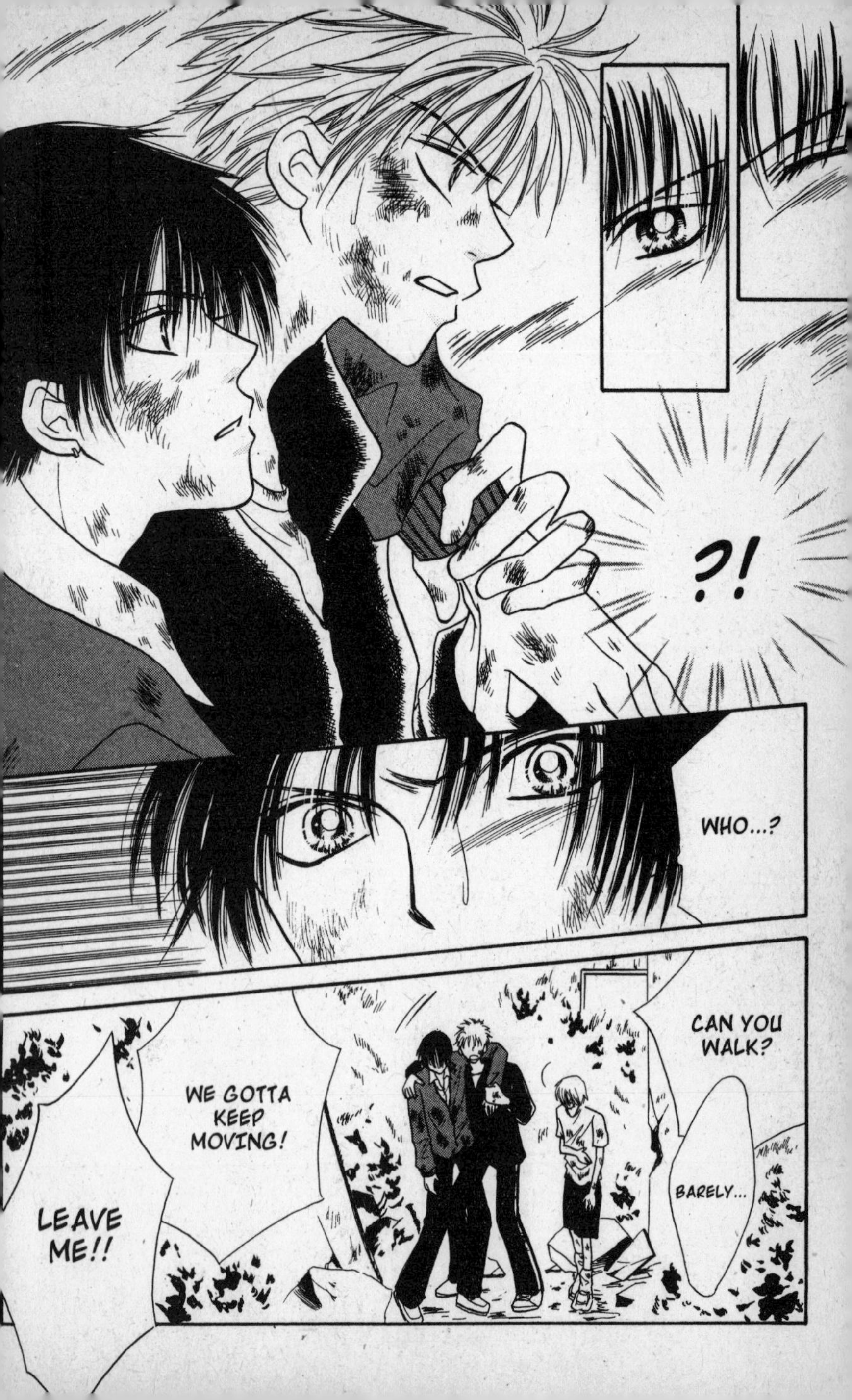
?!
WHO...?
CAN YOU WALK?
BARELY...
WE GOTTA KEEP MOVING!
LEAVE ME!!

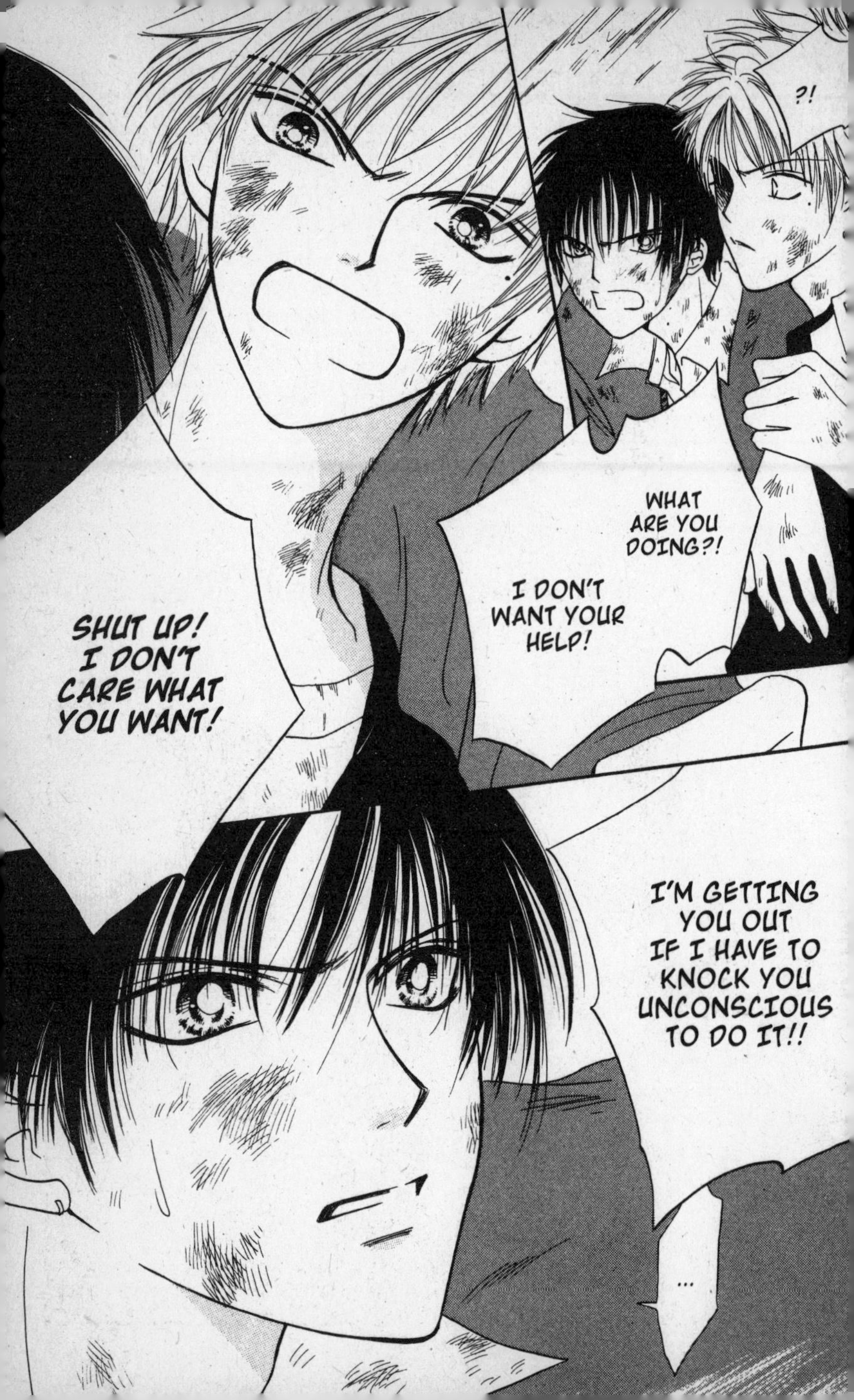
?!
WHAT ARE YOU DOING?!
I DON'T WANT YOUR HELP!
SHUT UP! I DON'T CARE WHAT YOU WANT!
I'M GETTING YOU OUT IF I HAVE TO KNOCK YOU UNCONSCIOUS TO DO IT!!
...

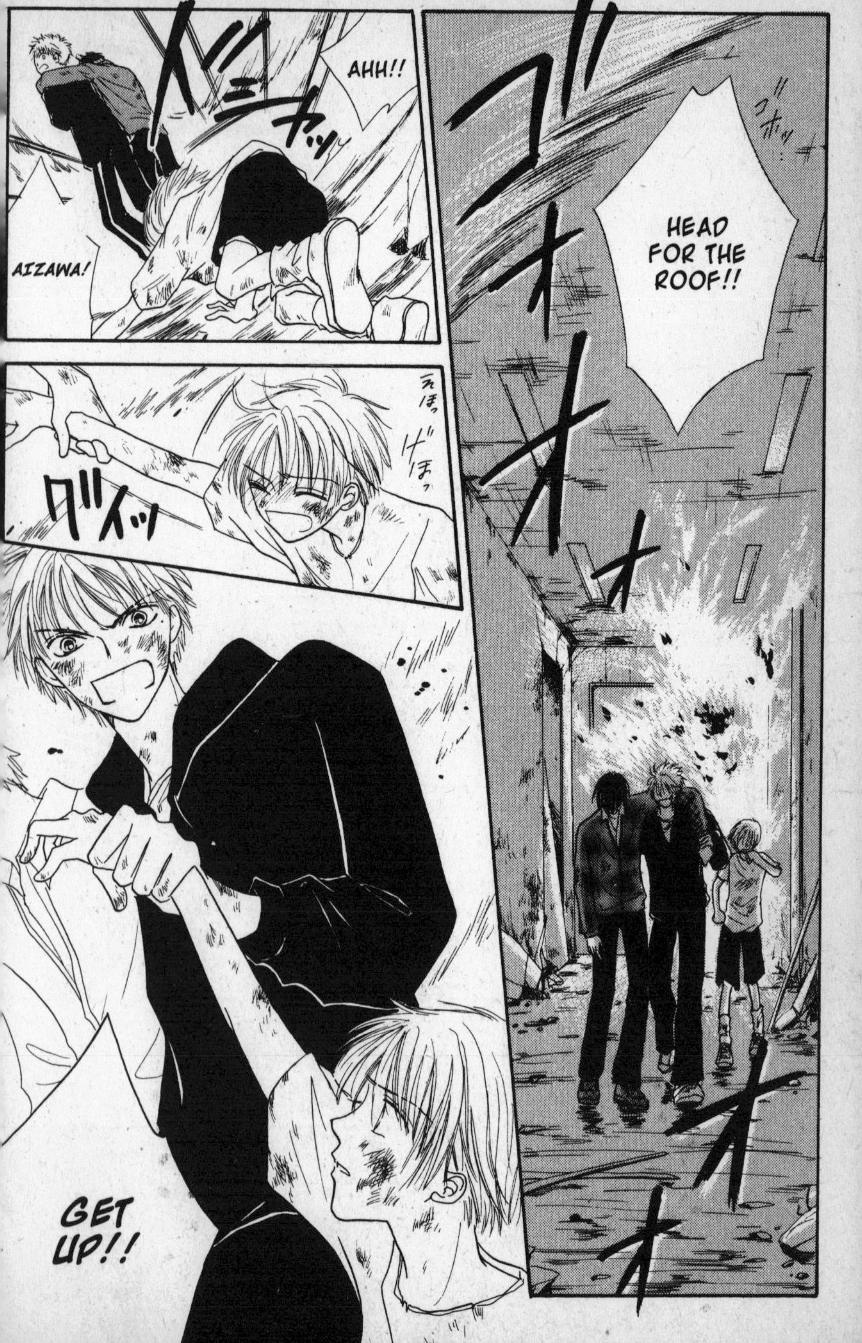
ゴォォォォォ
ゴボッ
HEAD FOR THE ROOF!!
ドシャッ
AHH!!
AIZAWA!
グイッ
えほっ げほっ
GET UP!!

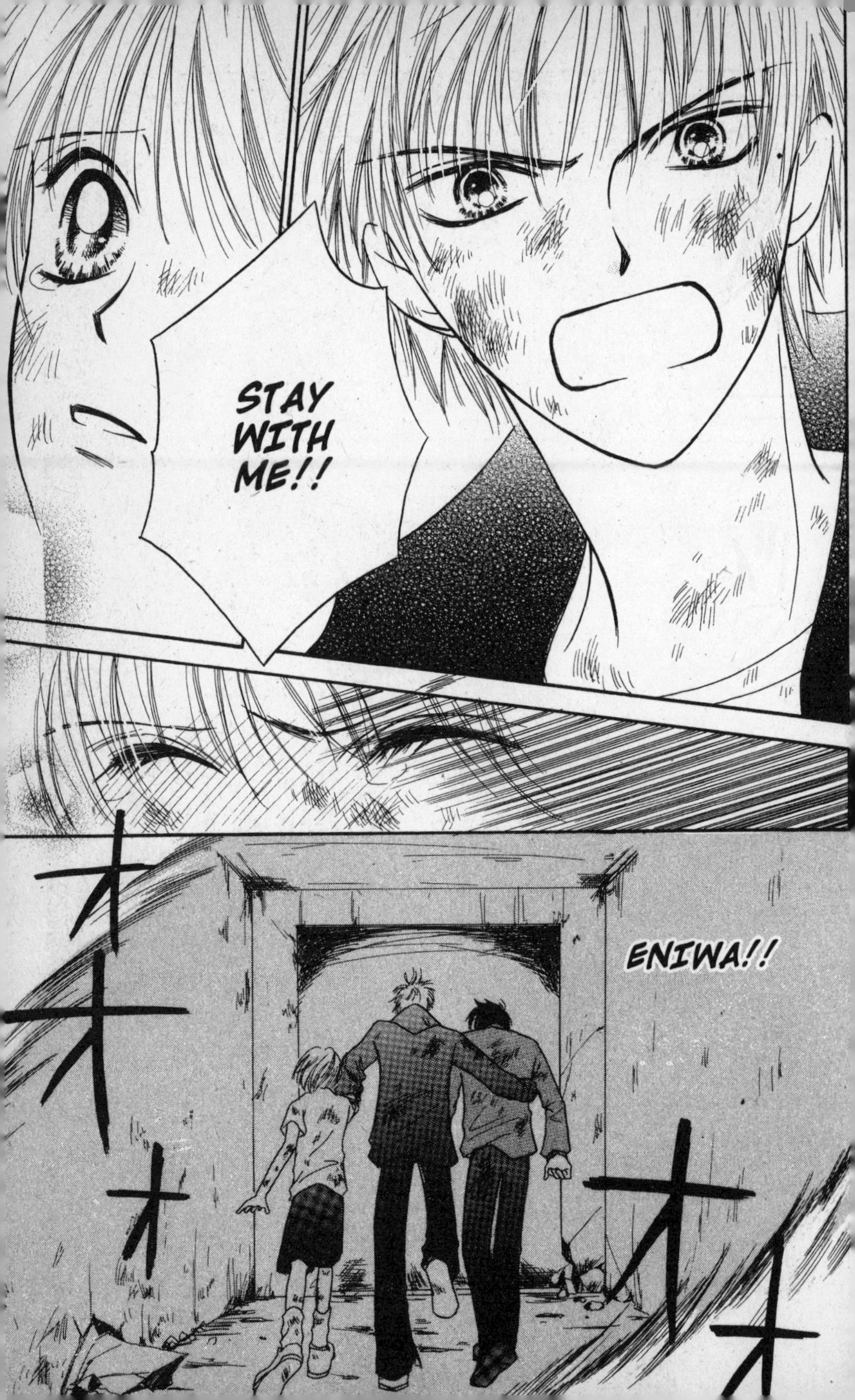
STAY WITH ME!!
ENIWA!!
オオ
オオ

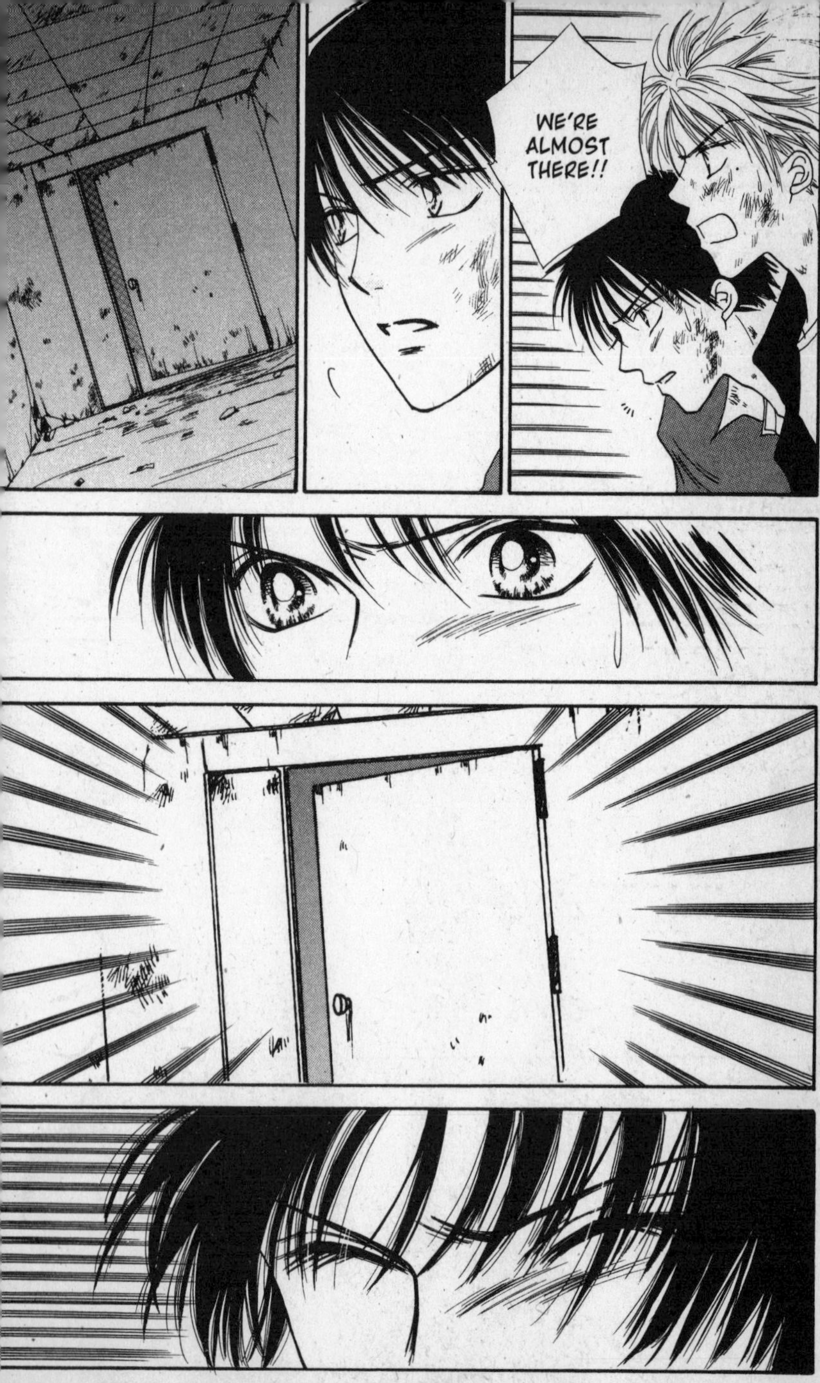
WE'RE ALMOST THERE!!

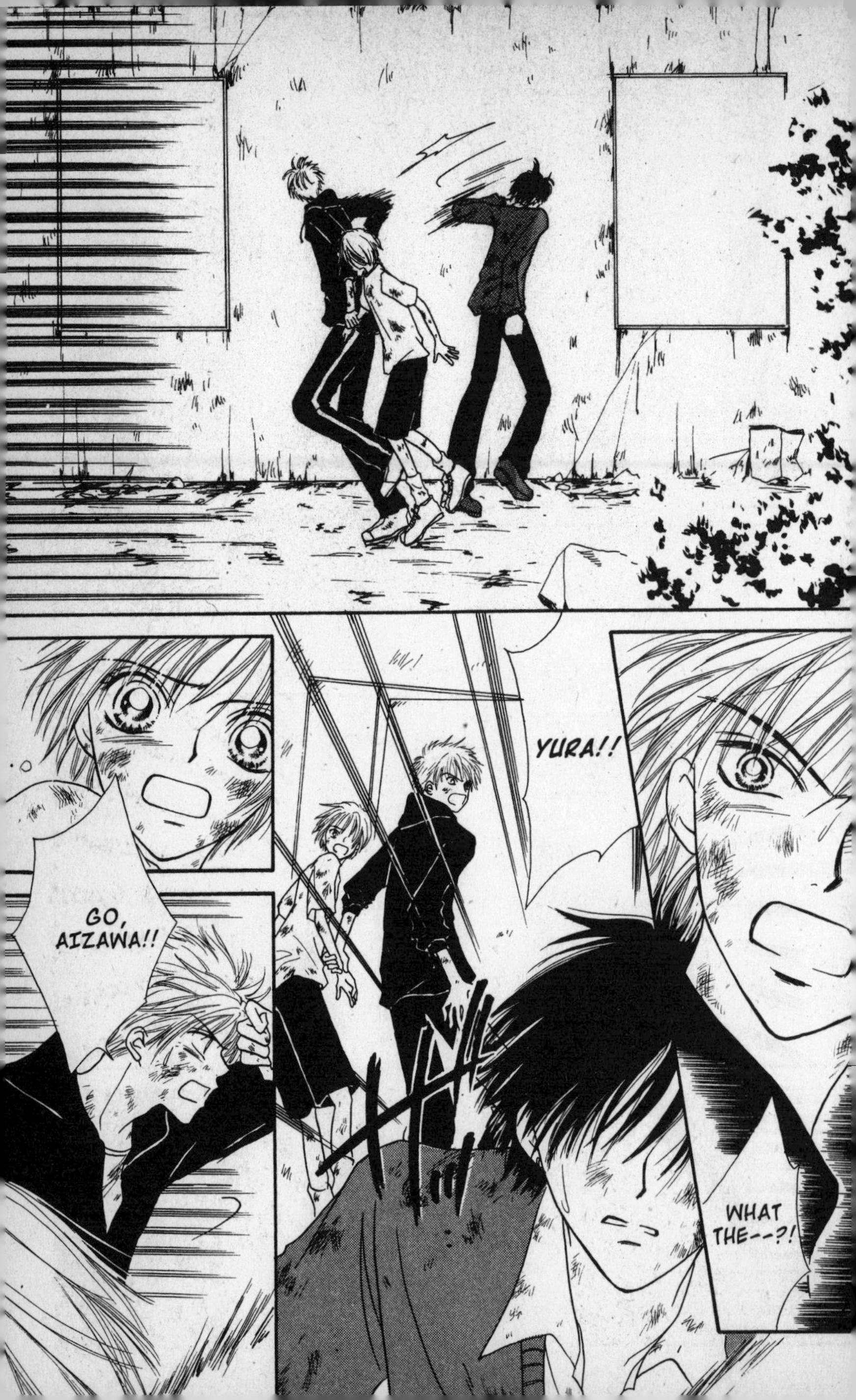
YURA!!
WHAT THE--?!
GO, AIZAWA!!

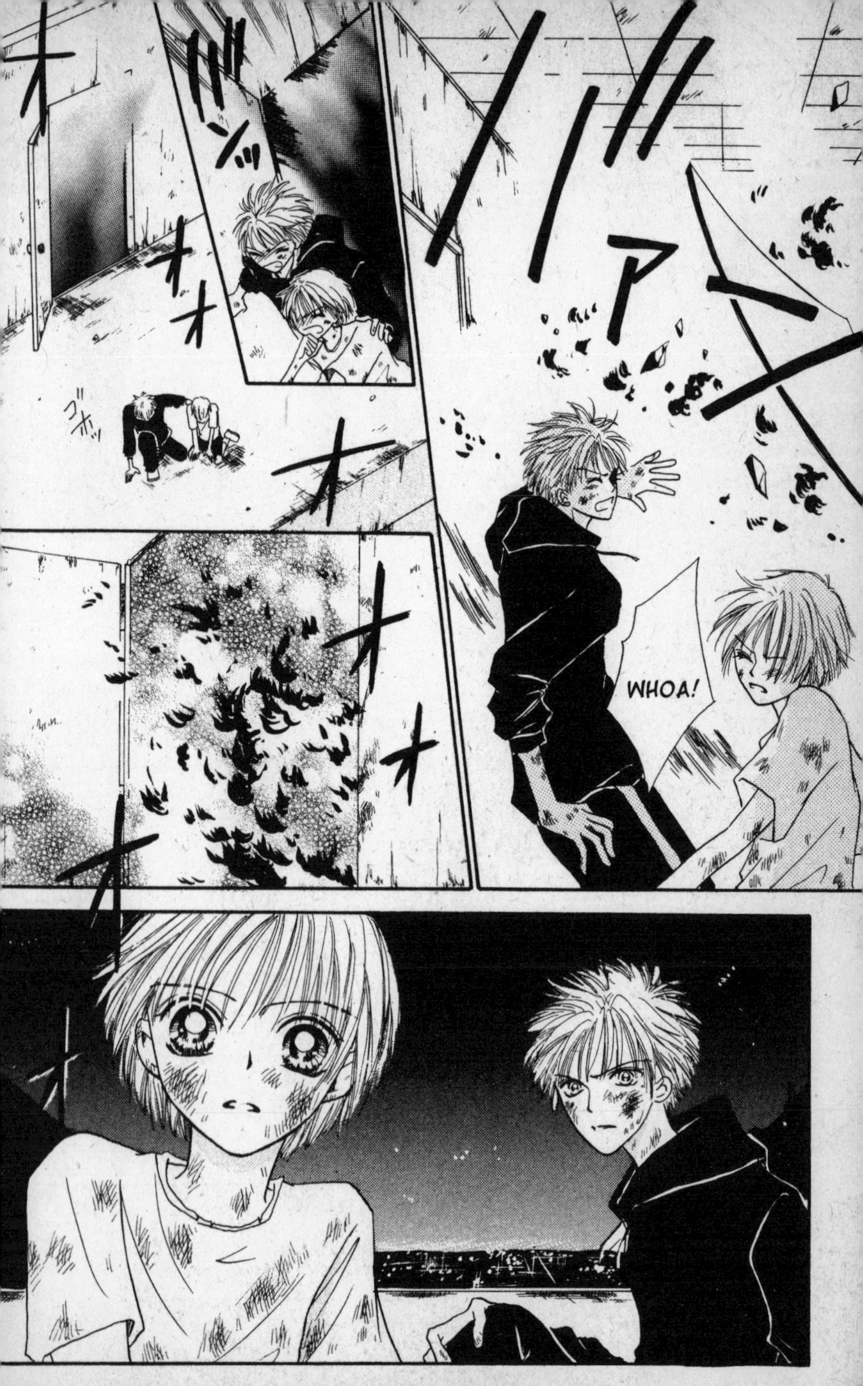
WHOA!

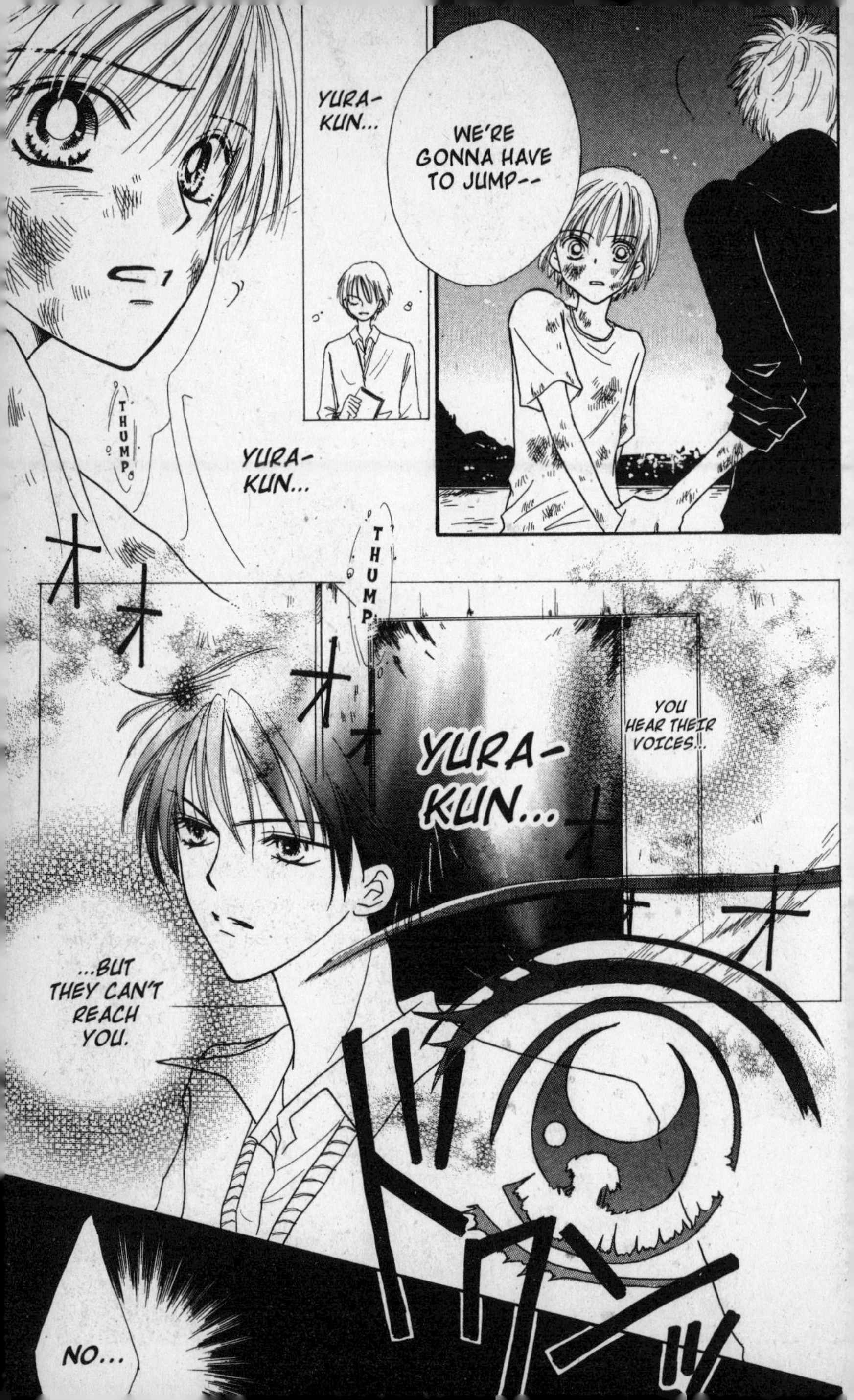
WE'RE GONNA HAVE TO JUMP--
YURA-KUN...
THUMP
YURA-KUN...
THUMP
YOU HEAR THEIR VOICES...
YURA-KUN...
...BUT THEY CAN'T REACH YOU.
NO...

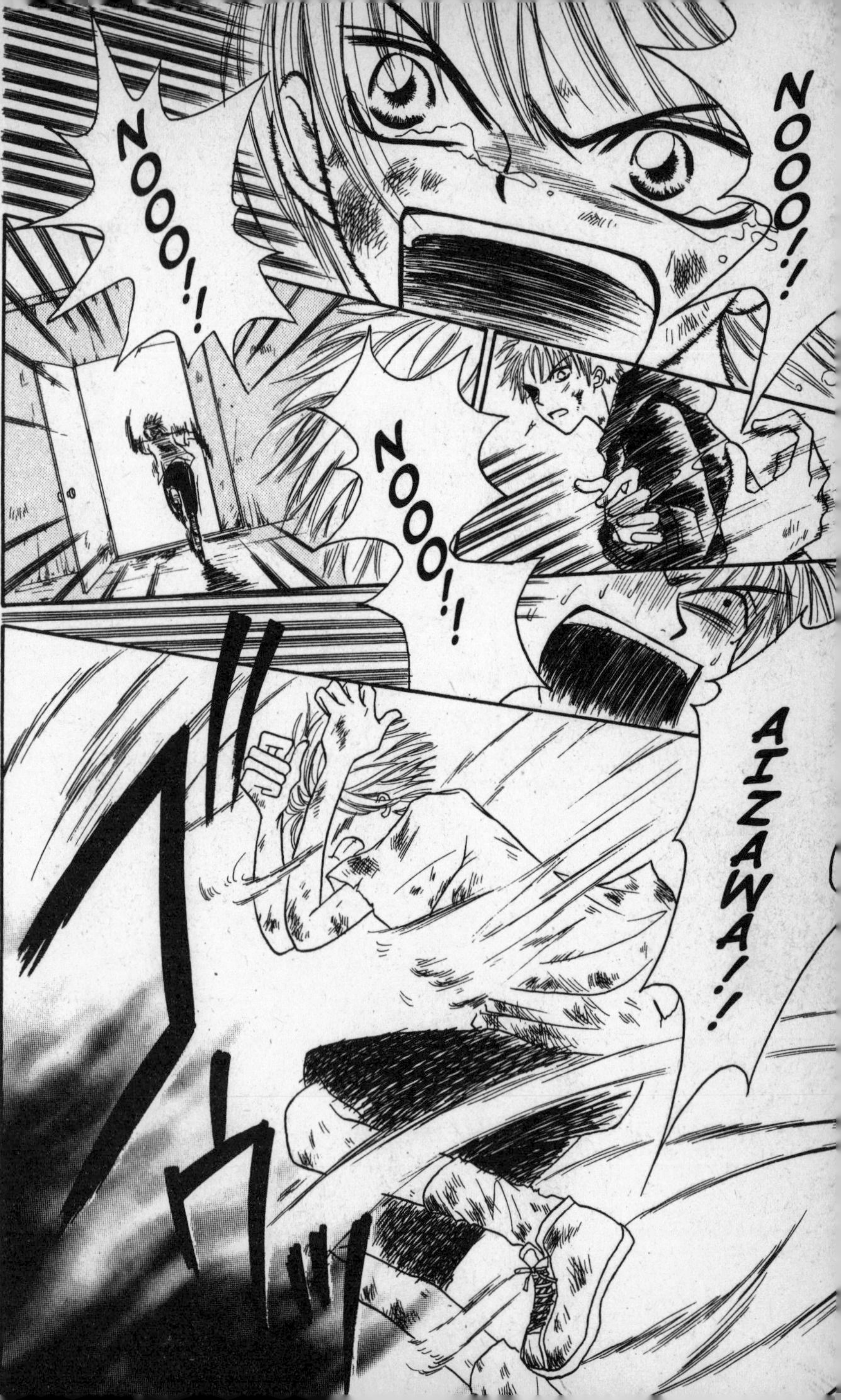
NOOOO!!
NOOOO!!
NOOOO!!
AIZAWA!!

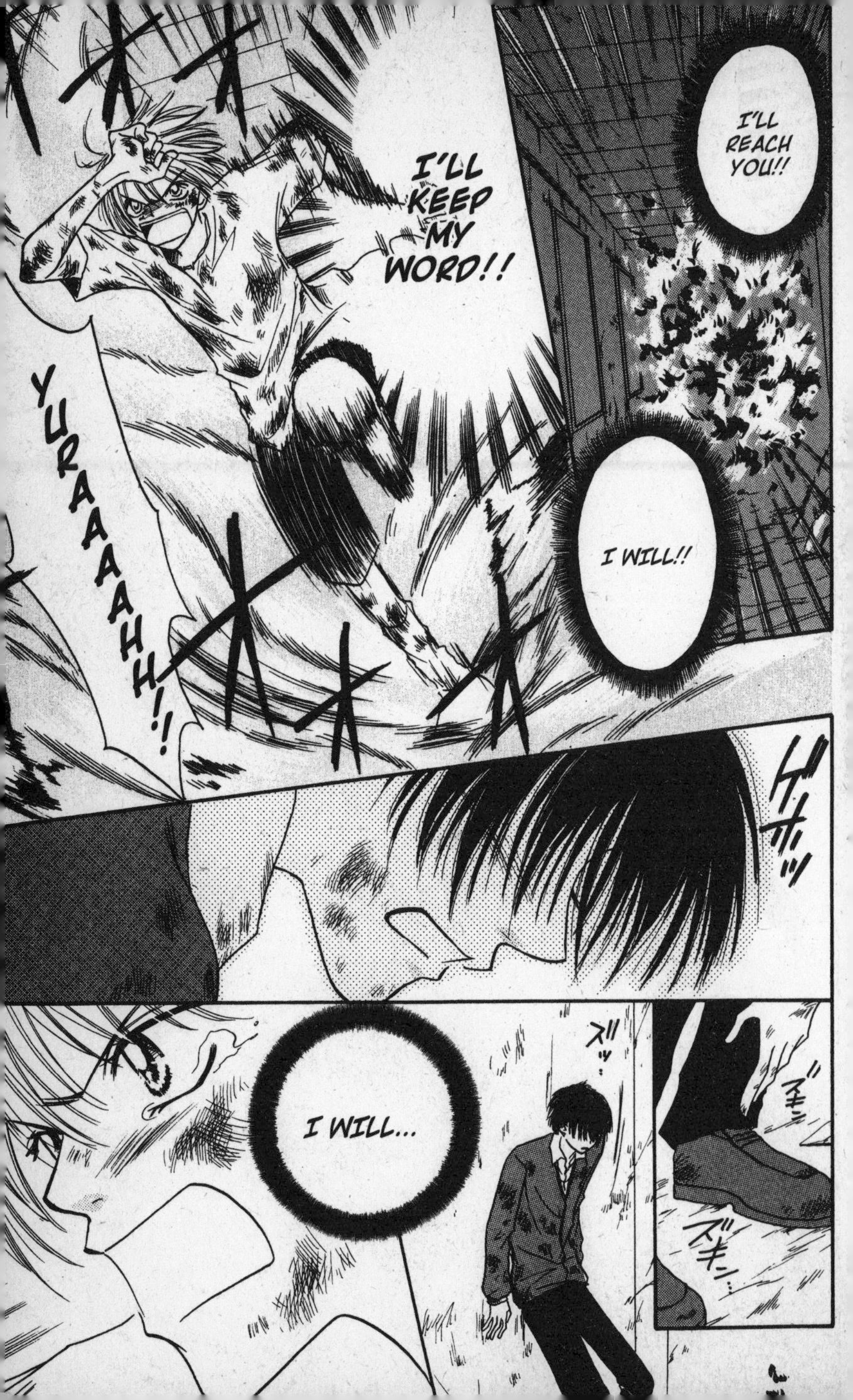
I'LL REACH YOU!!
I WILL!!
I'LL KEEP MY WORD!!
YURAAAAAHH!!
I WILL...

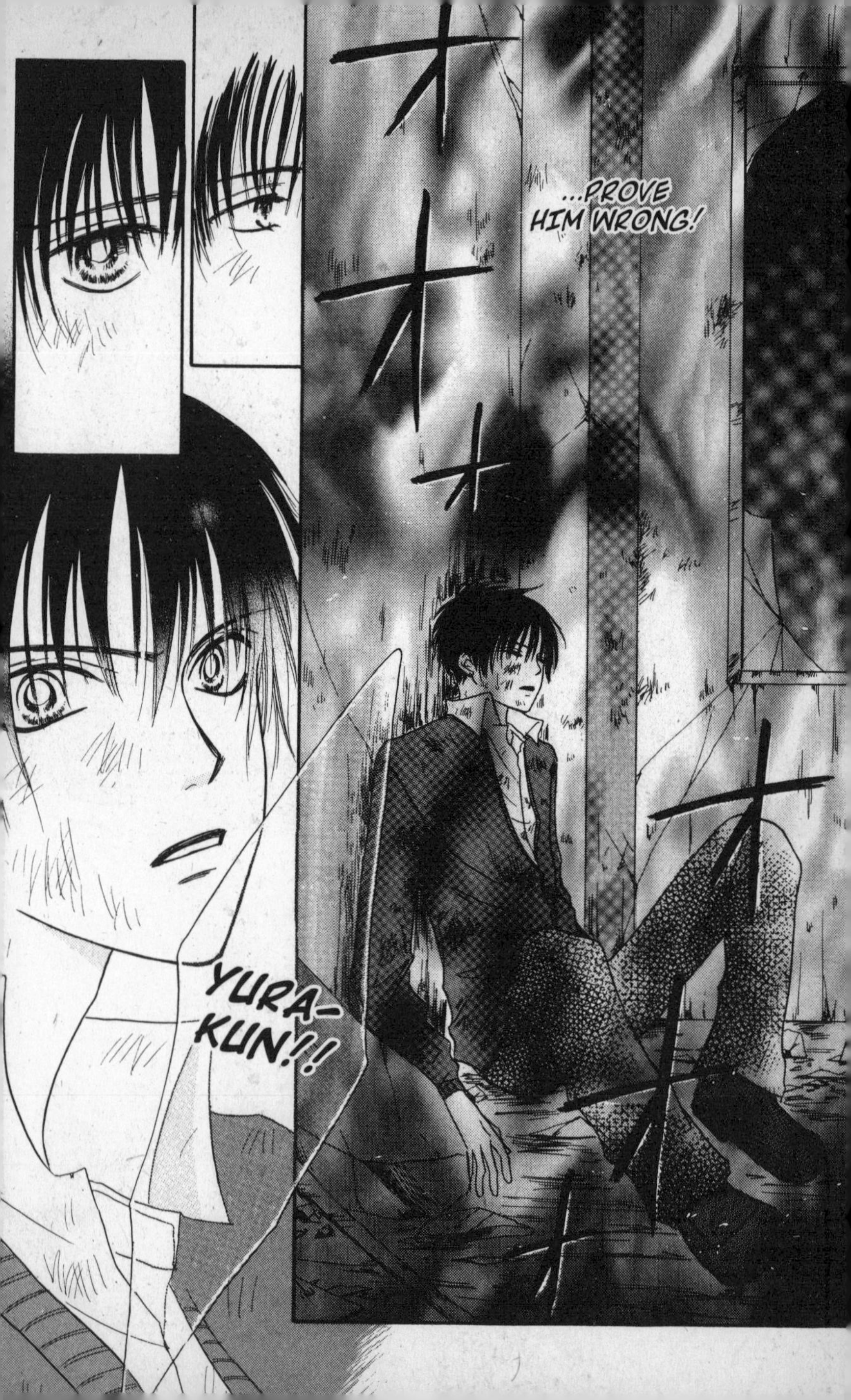
...PROVE HIM WRONG!
YURA-KUN!?!

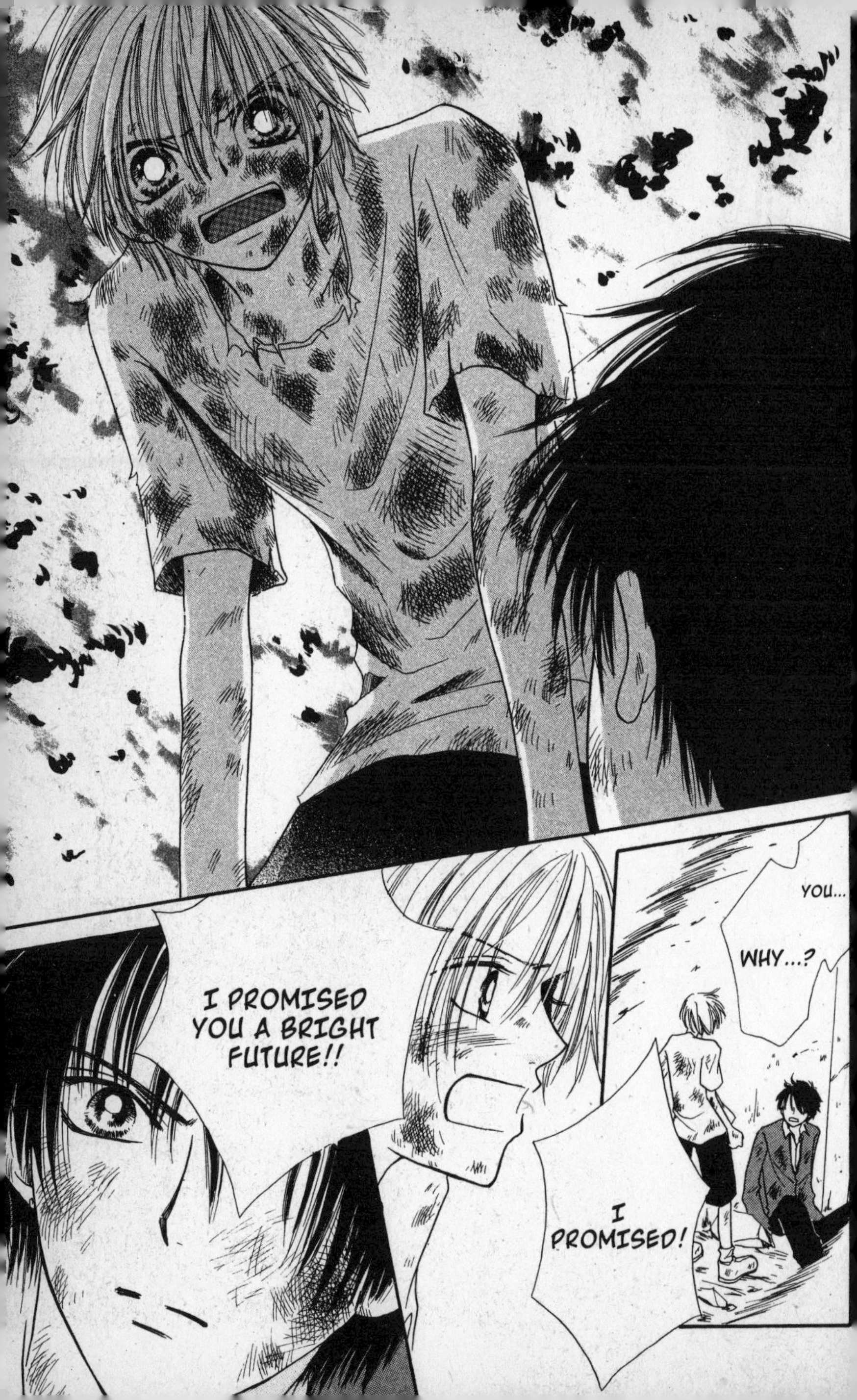
YOU...
WHY...?
I PROMISED YOU A BRIGHT FUTURE!!
I PROMISED!

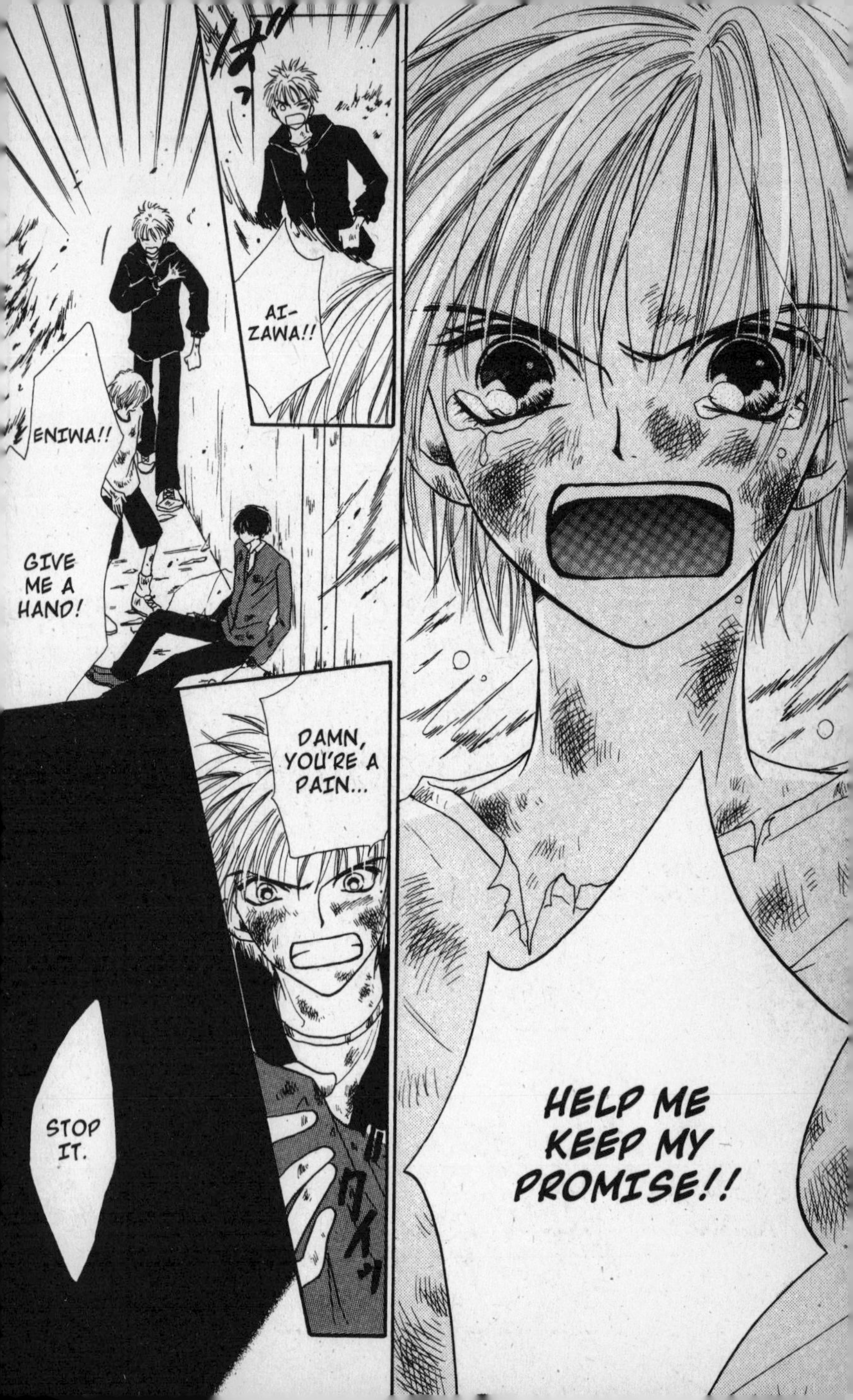
HELP ME KEEP MY PROMISE!!
AI-ZAWA!!
ENIWA!!
GIVE ME A HAND!
DAMN, YOU'RE A PAIN...
STOP IT.

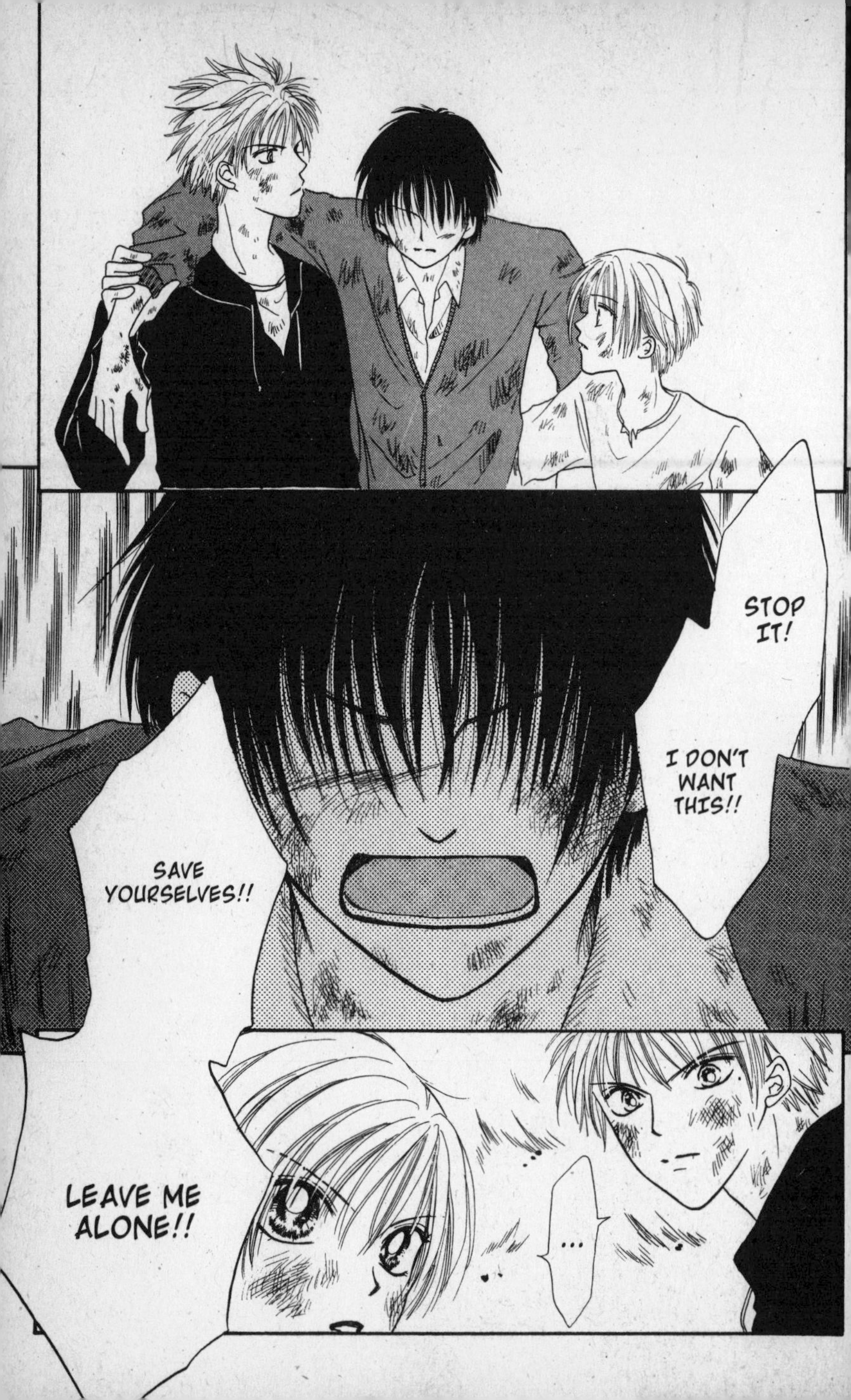
STOP IT!
I DON'T WANT THIS!!
SAVE YOURSELVES!!
LEAVE ME ALONE!!
...

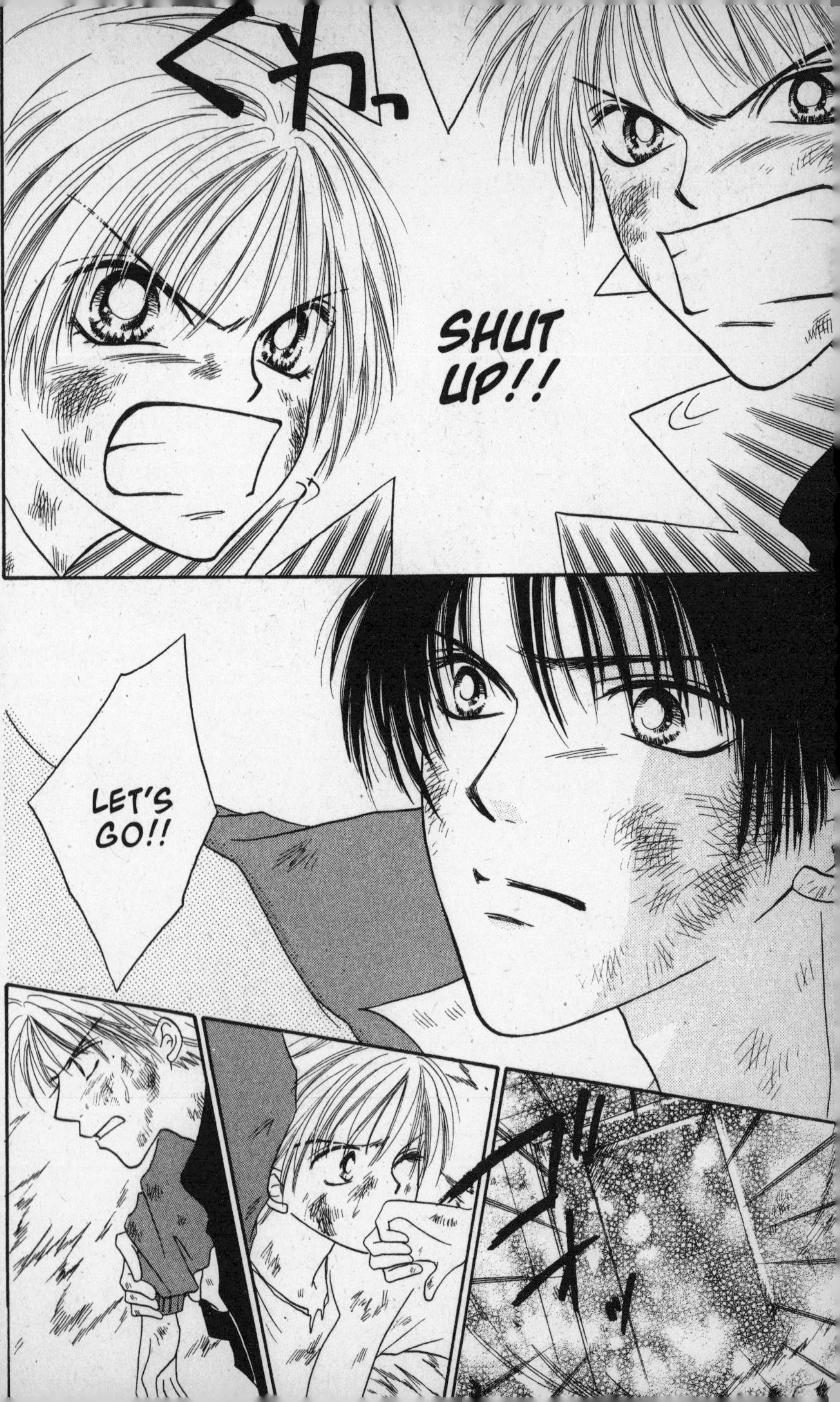
くわっ
SHUT UP!!
LET'S GO!!

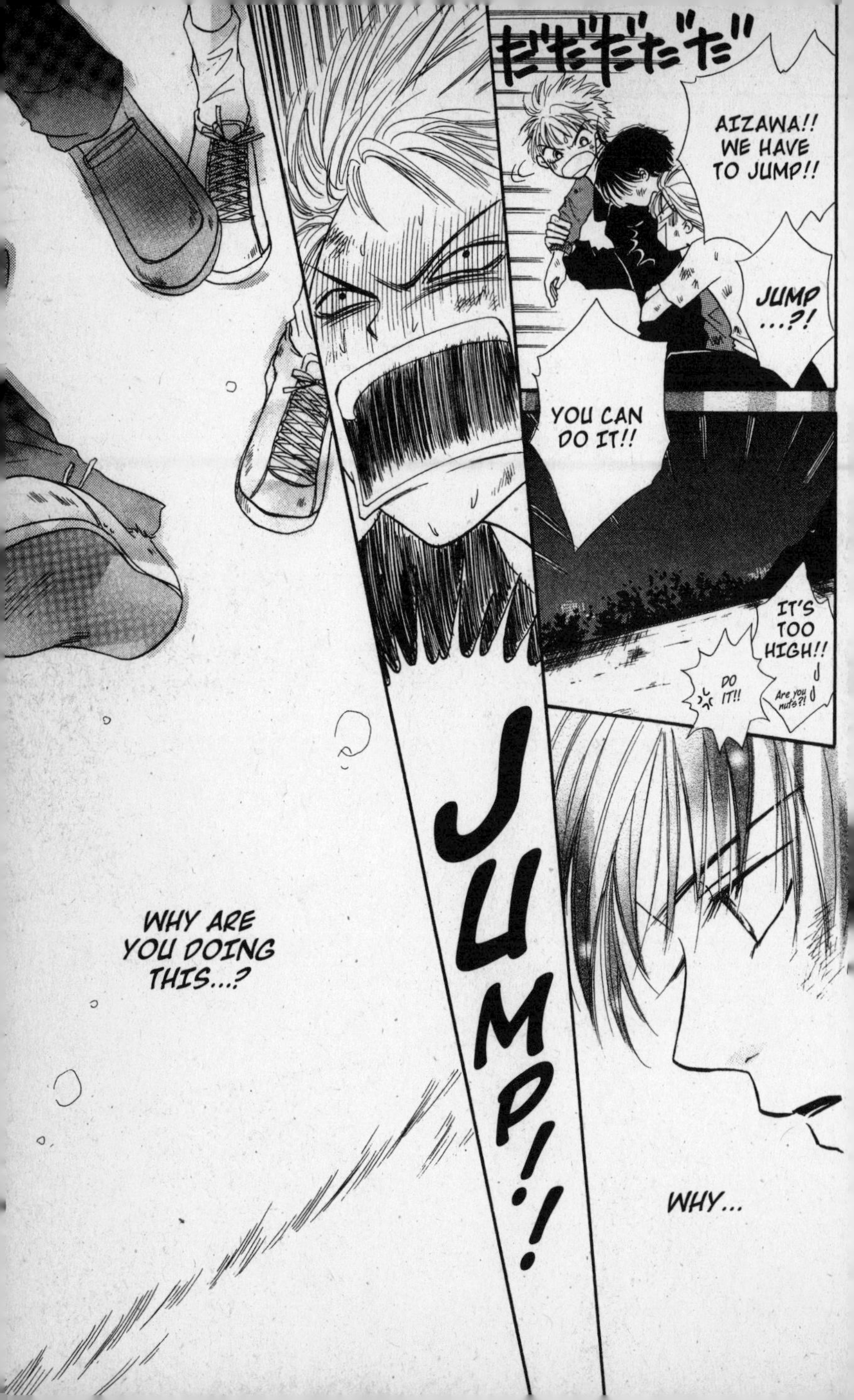
だだだただ
AIZAWA!! WE HAVE TO JUMP!!
JUMP ...?!
YOU CAN DO IT!!
IT'S TOO HIGH!!
Are you nuts?!
DO IT!!
WHY...
JUMP!!
WHY ARE YOU DOING THIS...?

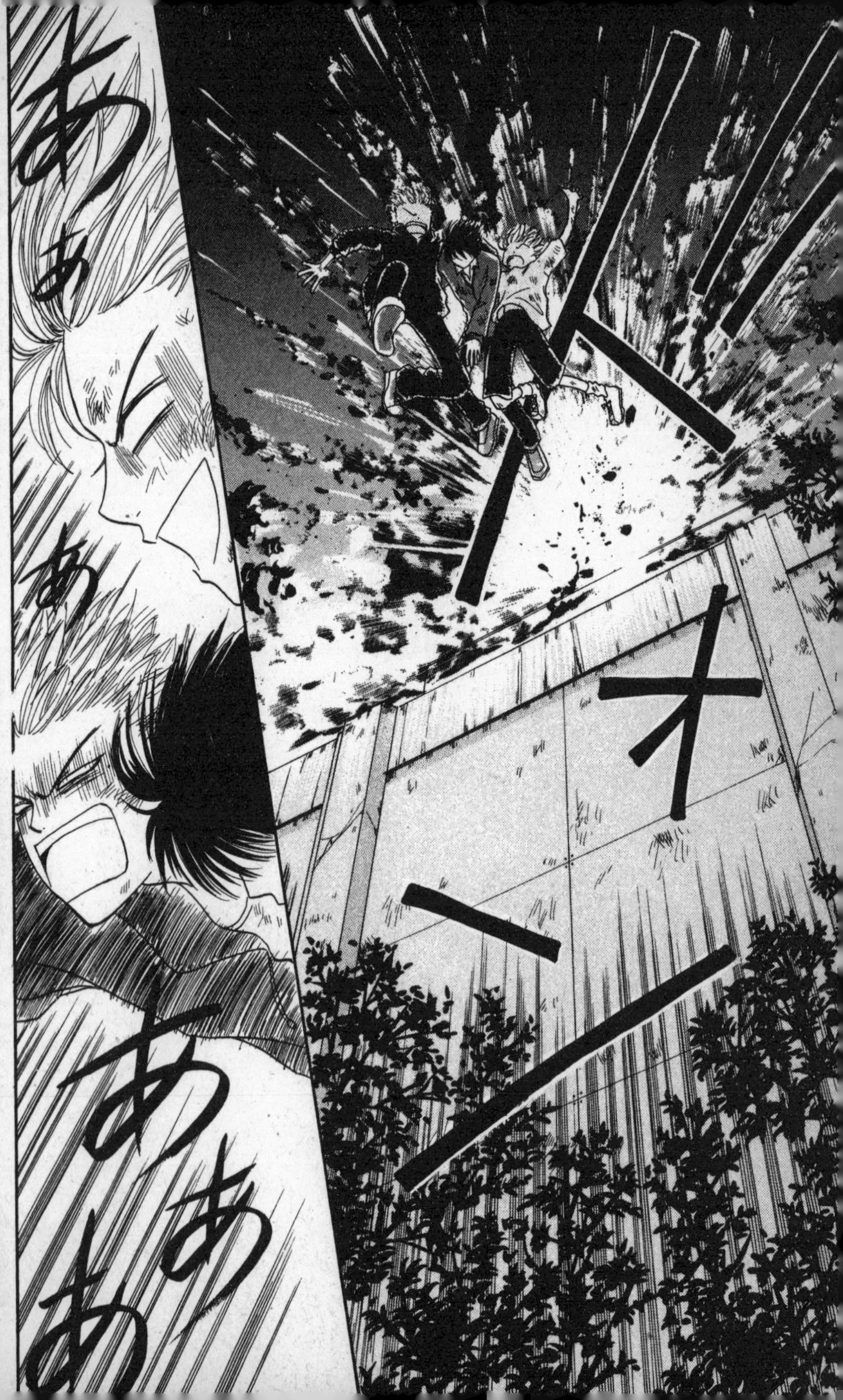

ドオーー
ああああああ

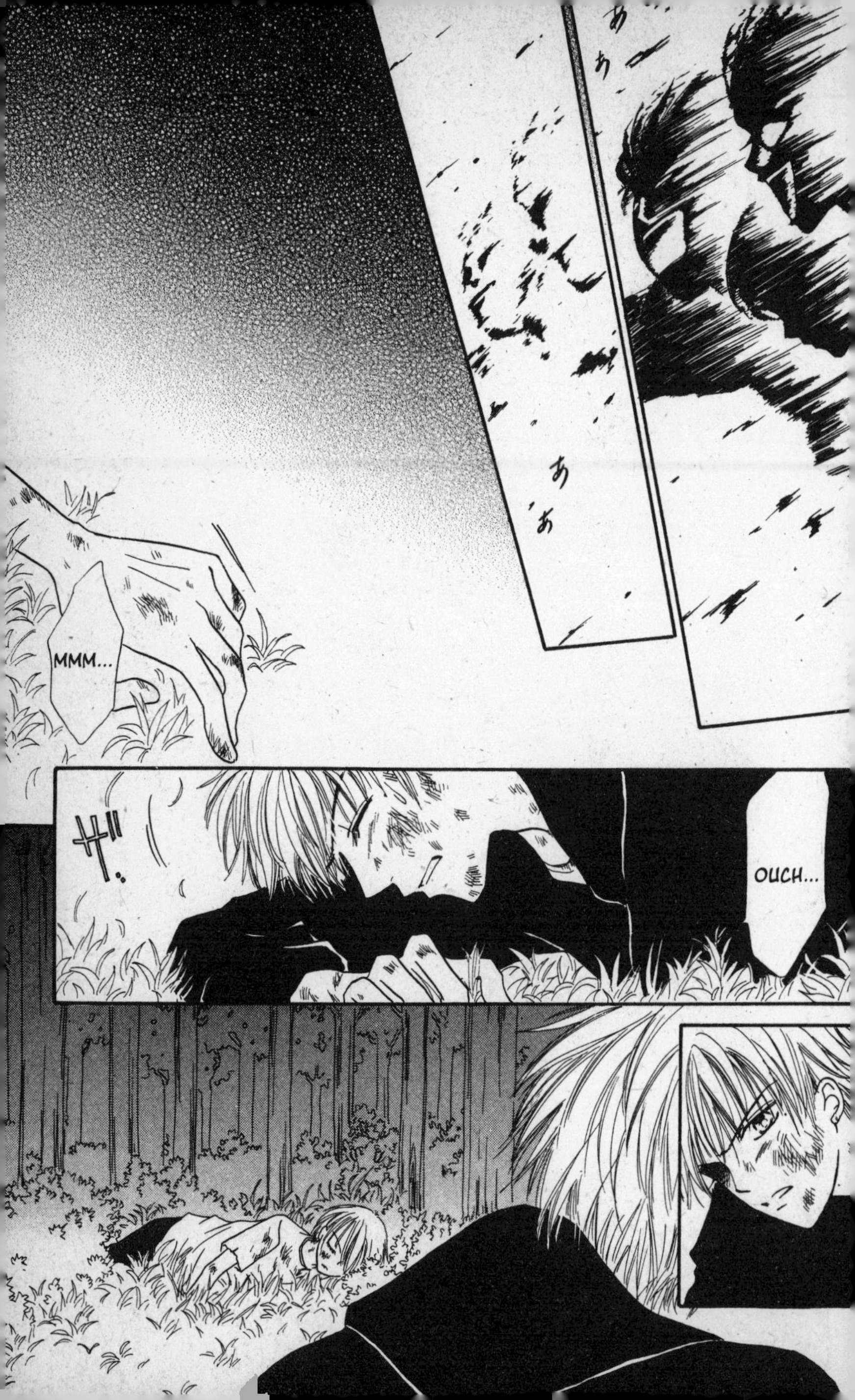

ああ
ああ
MMM...
OUCH...
ザ

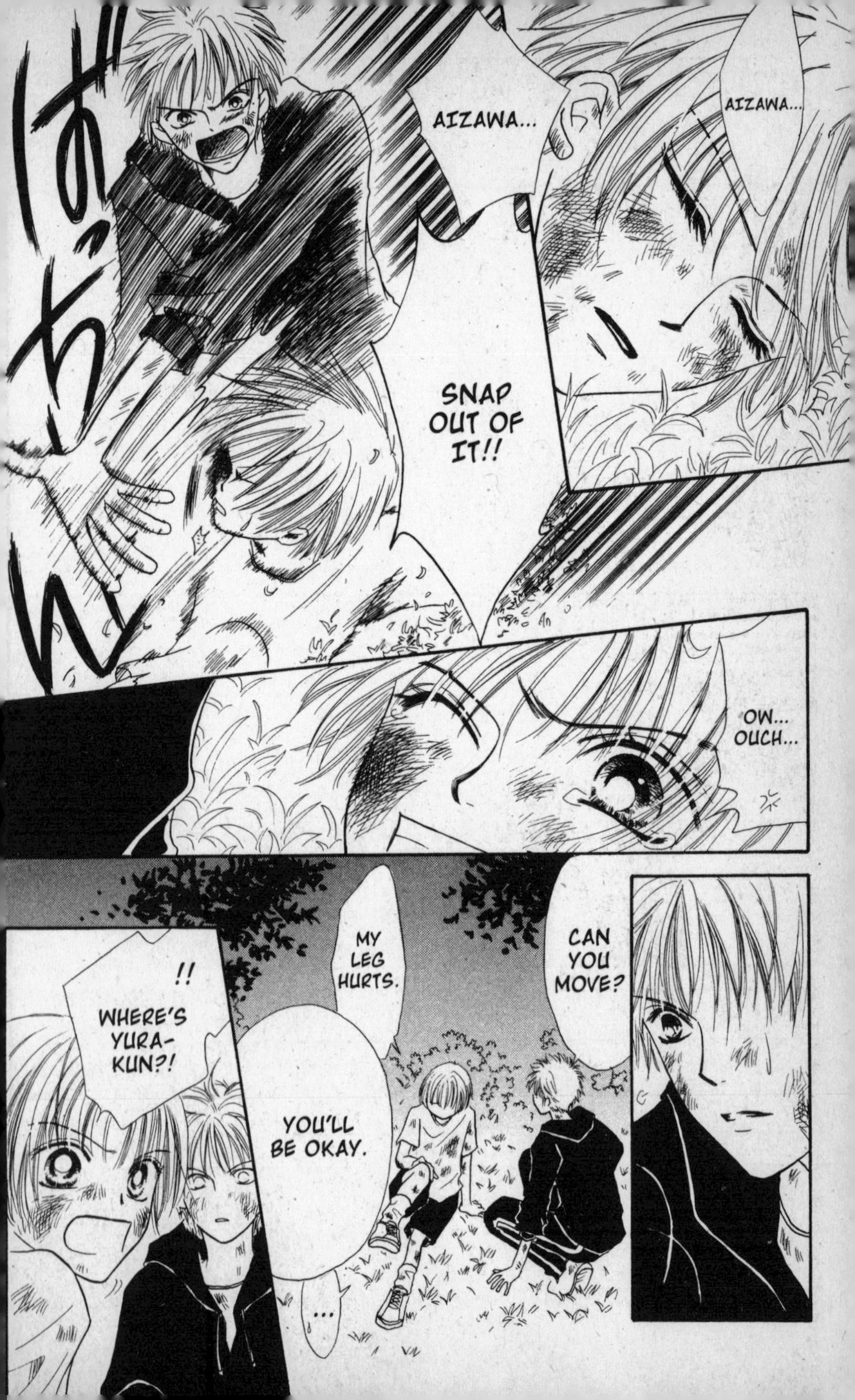
AIZAWA...
AIZAWA...
SNAP OUT OF IT!!
OW... OUCH...
CAN YOU MOVE?
MY LEG HURTS.
YOU'LL BE OKAY.
!!
WHERE'S YURA-KUN?!
...

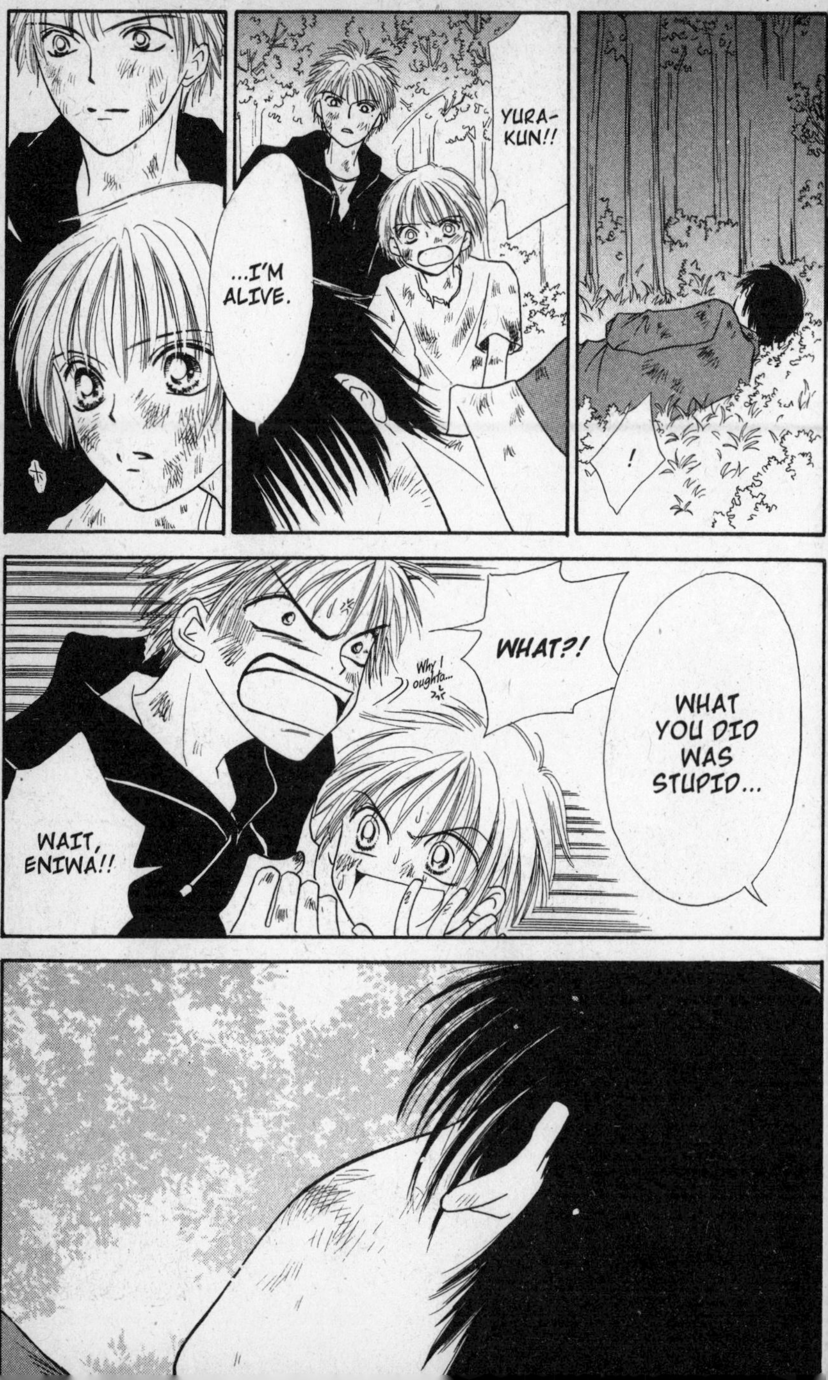
!
YURA-KUN!!
...I'M ALIVE.
WHAT YOU DID WAS STUPID...
WHAT?!
Why I oughta...
WAIT, ENIWA!!

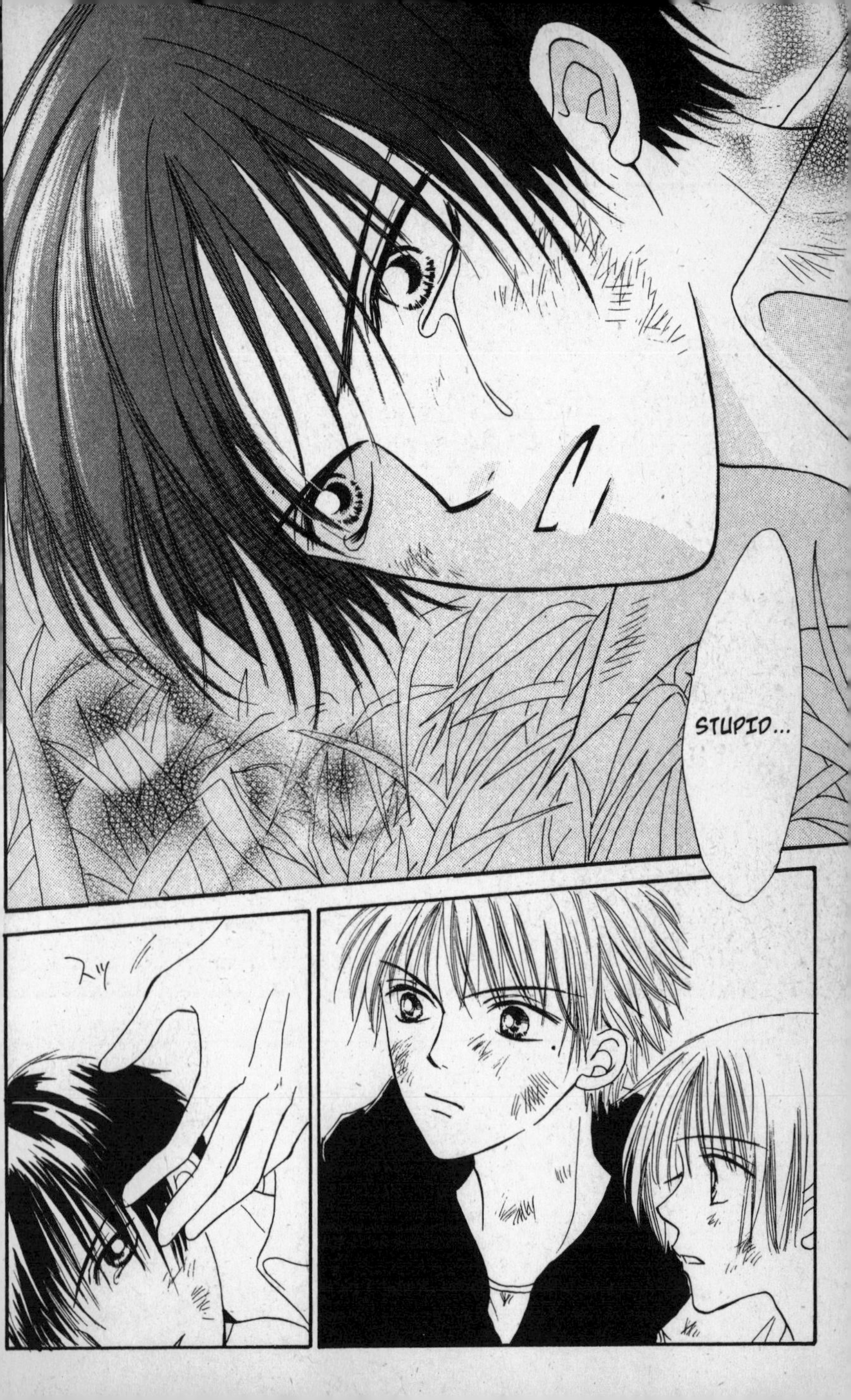
STUPID...
スッ

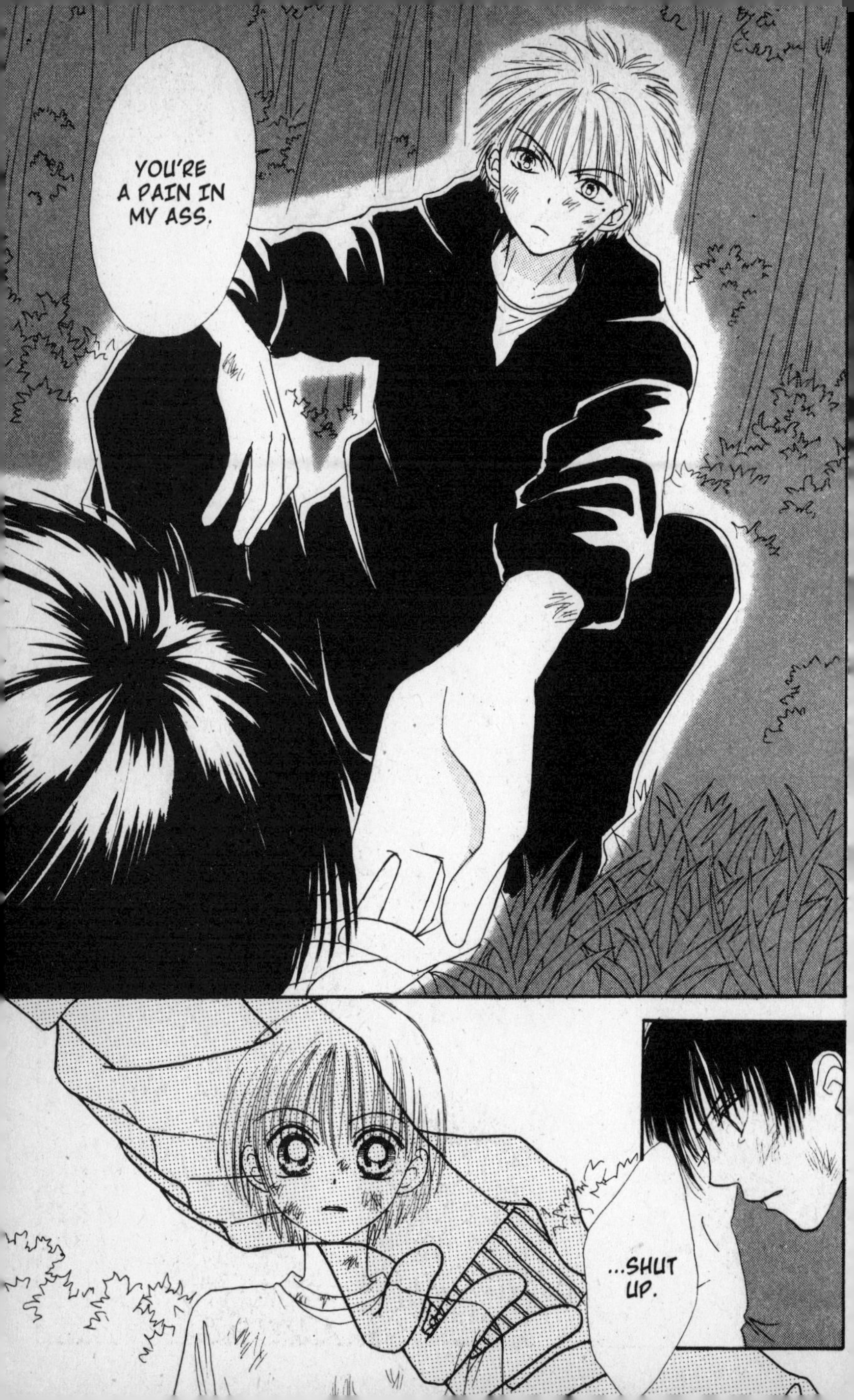
YOU'RE A PAIN IN MY ASS.
...SHUT UP.

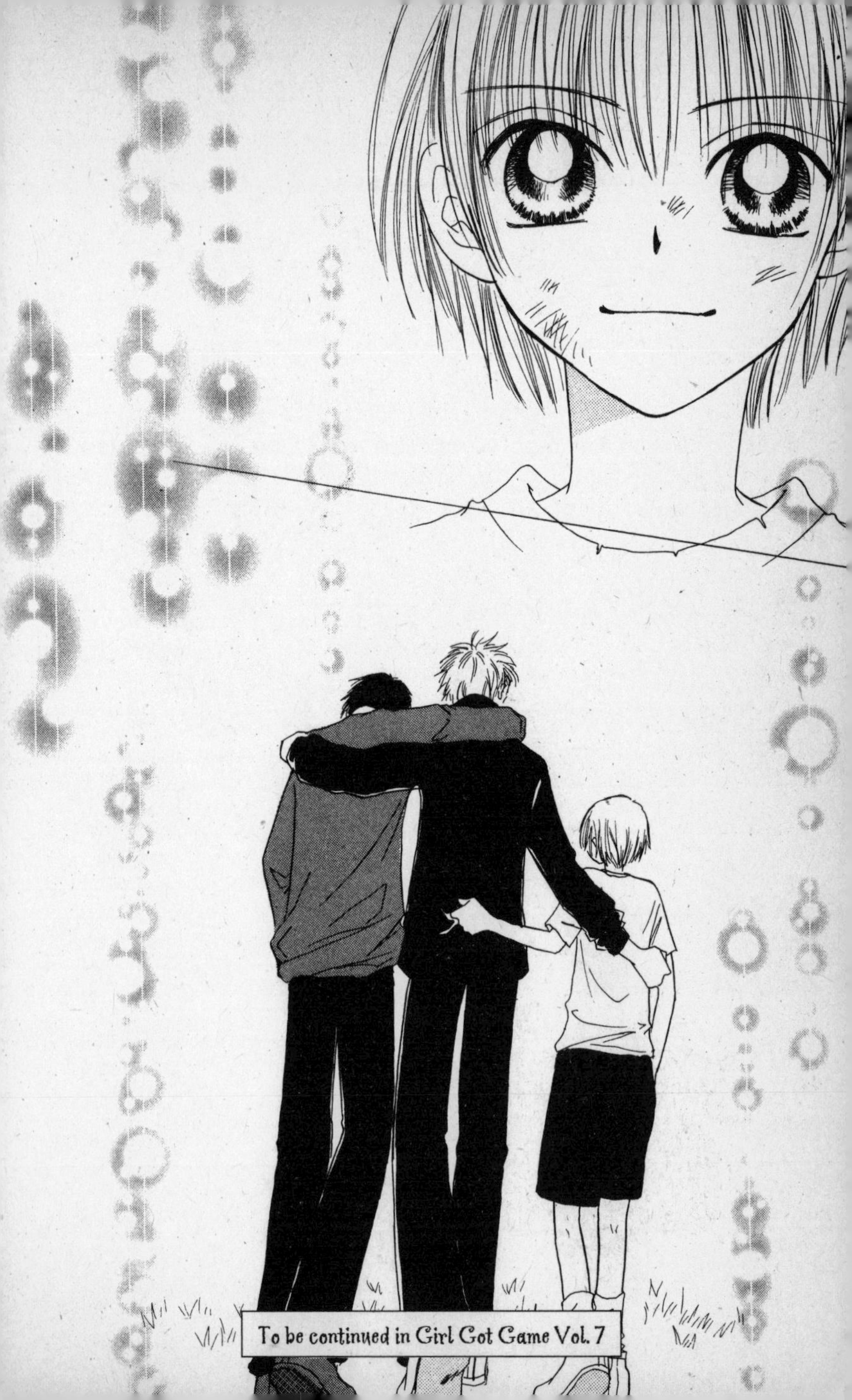
To be continued in Girl Got Game Vol. 7

Girl Got Game

Replay!

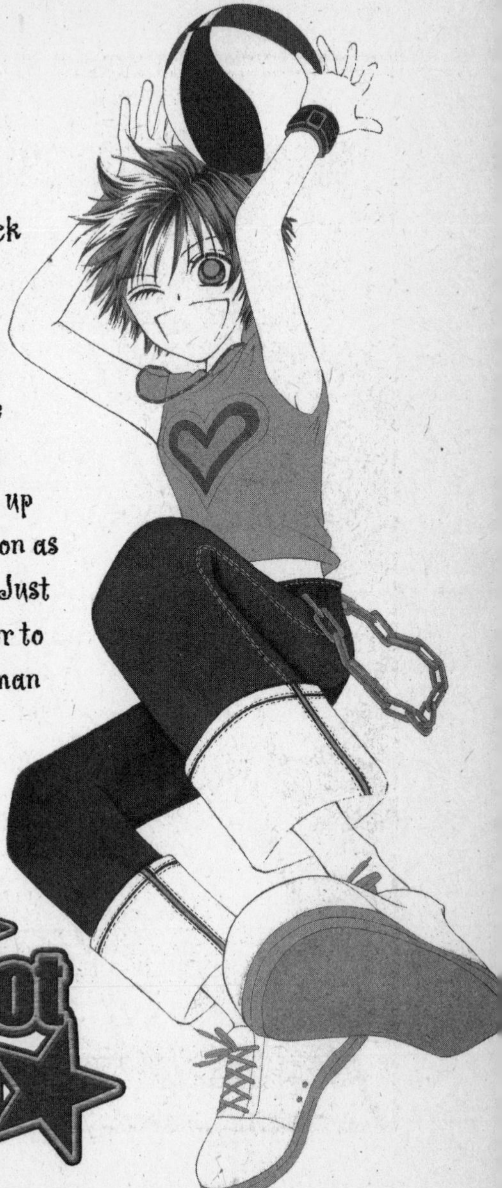

Things finally get back to normal...but is that a good thing? Chiharu moves back in with Kyo, but only because he doesn't think of her as a girl! Not long ago, Kyo put so much time and effort into pretending to be a boy that she ended up earning herself a reputation as a depraved male pervert! Just how far will she go in order to prove that she's still a woman to Chiharu?

All in the next...

Girl Got Game

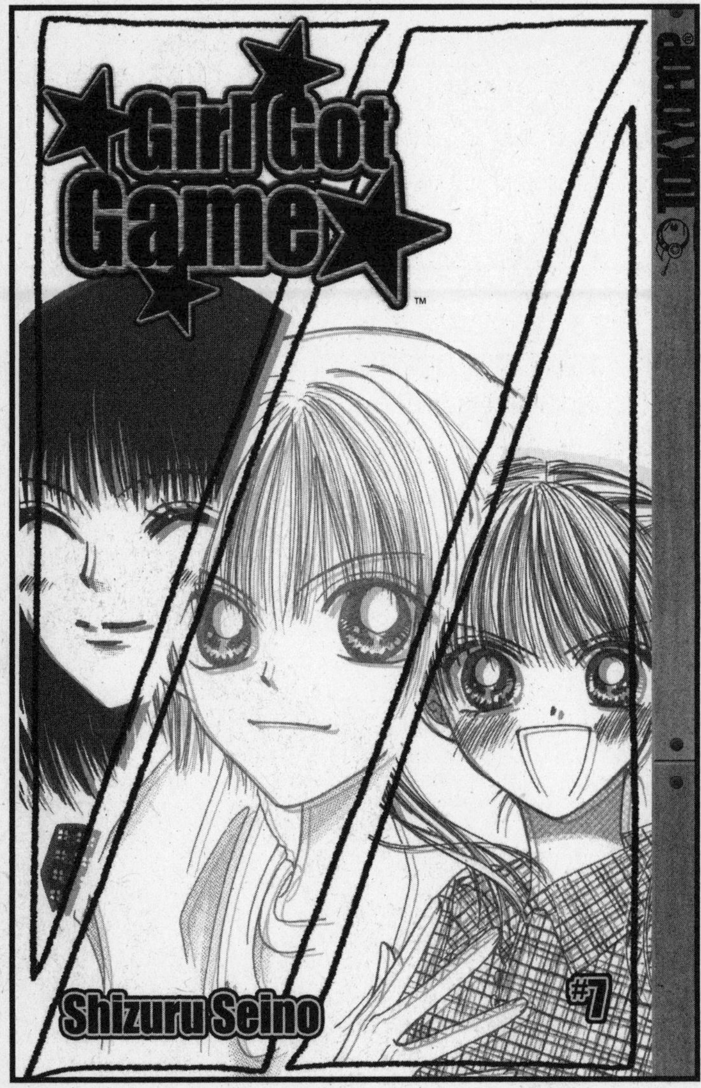
Girl Got Game™
Shizuru Seino
#7
TOKYOPOP®

ALSO AVAILABLE FROM  TOKYOPOP®

PLANETES
PRESIDENT DAD
PRIEST
PRINCESS AI
PSYCHIC ACADEMY
QUEEN'S KNIGHT, THE
RAGNAROK
RAVE MASTER
REALITY CHECK
REBIRTH
REBOUND
REMOTE
RISING STARS OF MANGA
SABER MARIONETTE J
SAILOR MOON
SAINT TAIL
SAIYUKI
SAMURAI DEEPER KYO
SAMURAI GIRL REAL BOUT HIGH SCHOOL
SCRYED
SEIKAI TRILOGY, THE
SGT. FROG
SHAOLIN SISTERS
SHIRAHIME-SYO: SNOW GODDESS TALES
SHUTTERBOX
SKULL MAN, THE
SNOW DROP
SORCERER HUNTERS
STONE
SUIKODEN III
SUKI
TAROT CAFÉ, THE
THREADS OF TIME
TOKYO BABYLON
TOKYO MEW MEW
TOKYO TRIBES
TRAMPS LIKE US
UNDER THE GLASS MOON
VAMPIRE GAME
VISION OF ESCAFLOWNE, THE
WARCRAFT
WARRIORS OF TAO
WILD ACT
WISH
WORLD OF HARTZ
X-DAY
ZODIAC P.I.

NOVELS

CLAMP SCHOOL PARANORMAL INVESTIGATORS
SAILOR MOON

ART BOOKS

ART OF CARDCAPTOR SAKURA
ART OF MAGIC KNIGHT RAYEARTH, THE
PEACH: MIWA UEDA ILLUSTRATIONS
CLAMP NORTHSIDE
CLAMP SOUTHSIDE

ANIME GUIDES

COWBOY BEBOP
GUNDAM TECHNICAL MANUALS
SAILOR MOON SCOUT GUIDES

TOKYOPOP KIDS

STRAY SHEEP

CINE-MANGA™

ALADDIN
CARDCAPTORS
DUEL MASTERS
FAIRLY ODDPARENTS, THE
FAMILY GUY
FINDING NEMO
G.I. JOE SPY TROOPS
GREATEST STARS OF THE NBA: SHAQUILLE O'NEAL
GREATEST STARS OF THE NBA: TIM DUNCAN
JACKIE CHAN ADVENTURES
JIMMY NEUTRON: BOY GENIUS, THE ADVENTURES OF
KIM POSSIBLE
LILO & STITCH: THE SERIES
LIZZIE MCGUIRE
LIZZIE MCGUIRE MOVIE, THE
MALCOLM IN THE MIDDLE
POWER RANGERS: DINO THUNDER
POWER RANGERS: NINJA STORM
PRINCESS DIARIES 2
RAVE MASTER
SHREK 2
SIMPLE LIFE, THE
SPONGEBOB SQUAREPANTS
SPY KIDS 2
SPY KIDS 3-D: GAME OVER
TEENAGE MUTANT NINJA TURTLES
THAT'S SO RAVEN
TOTALLY SPIES
TRANSFORMERS: ARMADA
TRANSFORMERS: ENERGON

ALSO AVAILABLE FROM 🐾TOKYOPOP

MANGA

.HACK//LEGEND OF THE TWILIGHT
@LARGE
ABENOBASHI: MAGICAL SHOPPING ARCADE
A.I. LOVE YOU
AI YORI AOSHI
ALICHINO
ANGELIC LAYER
ARM OF KANNON
BABY BIRTH
BATTLE ROYALE
BATTLE VIXENS
BOYS BE...
BRAIN POWERED
BRIGADOON
B'TX
CANDIDATE FOR GODDESS, THE
CARDCAPTOR SAKURA
CARDCAPTOR SAKURA - MASTER OF THE CLOW
CHOBITS
CHRONICLES OF THE CURSED SWORD
CLAMP SCHOOL DETECTIVES
CLOVER
COMIC PARTY
CONFIDENTIAL CONFESSIONS
CORRECTOR YUI
COWBOY BEBOP
COWBOY BEBOP: SHOOTING STAR
CRAZY LOVE STORY
CRESCENT MOON
CROSS
CULDCEPT
CYBORG 009
D•N•ANGEL
DEARS
DEMON DIARY
DEMON ORORON, THE
DEUS VITAE
DIGIMON
DIGIMON TAMERS
DIGIMON ZERO TWO
DOLL
DRAGON HUNTER
DRAGON KNIGHTS
DRAGON VOICE
DREAM SAGA
DUKLYON: CLAMP SCHOOL DEFENDERS
EERIE QUEERIE!
ERICA SAKURAZAWA: COLLECTED WORKS
ET CETERA
ETERNITY
EVIL'S RETURN
FAERIES' LANDING
FAKE
FLCL
FLOWER OF THE DEEP SLEEP, THE
FORBIDDEN DANCE
FRUITS BASKET

G GUNDAM
GATEKEEPERS
GETBACKERS
GIRL GOT GAME
GRAVITATION
GTO
GUNDAM SEED ASTRAY
GUNDAM WING
GUNDAM WING: BATTLEFIELD OF PACIFISTS
GUNDAM WING: ENDLESS WALTZ
GUNDAM WING: THE LAST OUTPOST (G-UNIT)
HANDS OFF!
HAPPY MANIA
HARLEM BEAT
HYPER RUNE
I.N.V.U.
IMMORTAL RAIN
INITIAL D
INSTANT TEEN: JUST ADD NUTS
ISLAND
JING: KING OF BANDITS
JING: KING OF BANDITS - TWILIGHT TALES
JULINE
KARE KANO
KILL ME, KISS ME
KINDAICHI CASE FILES, THE
KING OF HELL
KODOCHA: SANA'S STAGE
LAMENT OF THE LAMB
LEGAL DRUG
LEGEND OF CHUN HYANG, THE
LES BIJOUX
LOVE HINA
LOVE OR MONEY
LUPIN III
LUPIN III: WORLD'S MOST WANTED
MAGIC KNIGHT RAYEARTH I
MAGIC KNIGHT RAYEARTH II
MAHOROMATIC: AUTOMATIC MAIDEN
MAN OF MANY FACES
MARMALADE BOY
MARS
MARS: HORSE WITH NO NAME
MINK
MIRACLE GIRLS
MIYUKI-CHAN IN WONDERLAND
MODEL
MOURYOU KIDEN: LEGEND OF THE NYMPHS
NECK AND NECK
ONE
ONE I LOVE, THE
PARADISE KISS
PARASYTE
PASSION FRUIT
PEACH GIRL
PEACH GIRL: CHANGE OF HEART
PET SHOP OF HORRORS
PITA-TEN
PLANET LADDER

08.20.04

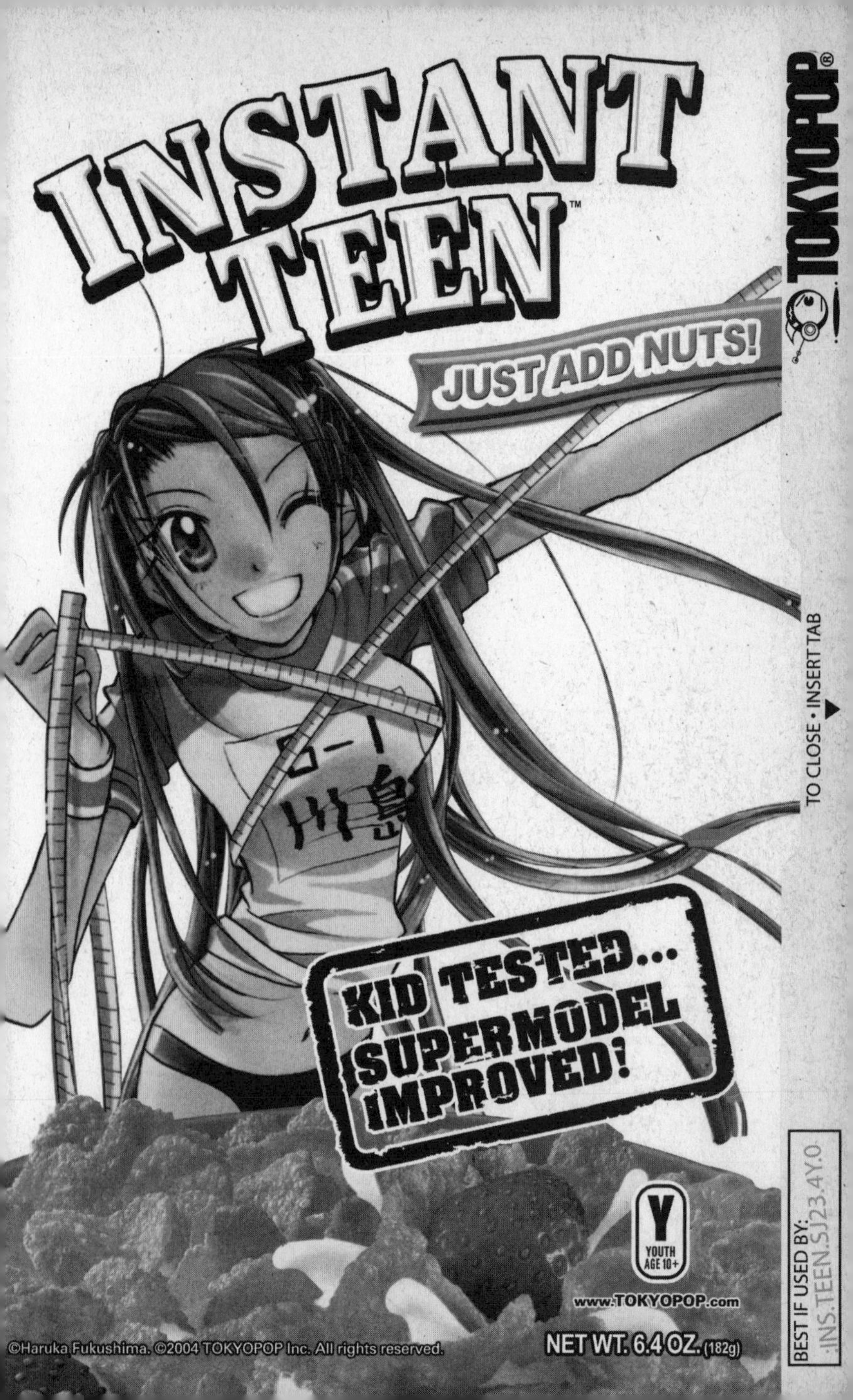
INSTANT TEEN™
JUST ADD NUTS!
TOKYOPOP®
TO CLOSE • INSERT TAB
KID TESTED... SUPERMODEL IMPROVED!
Y
YOUTH AGE 10+
www.TOKYOPOP.com
NET WT. 6.4 OZ. (182g)
©Haruka Fukushima. ©2004 TOKYOPOP Inc. All rights reserved.
BEST IF USED BY:
INS.TEEN.SJ23.4Y.O

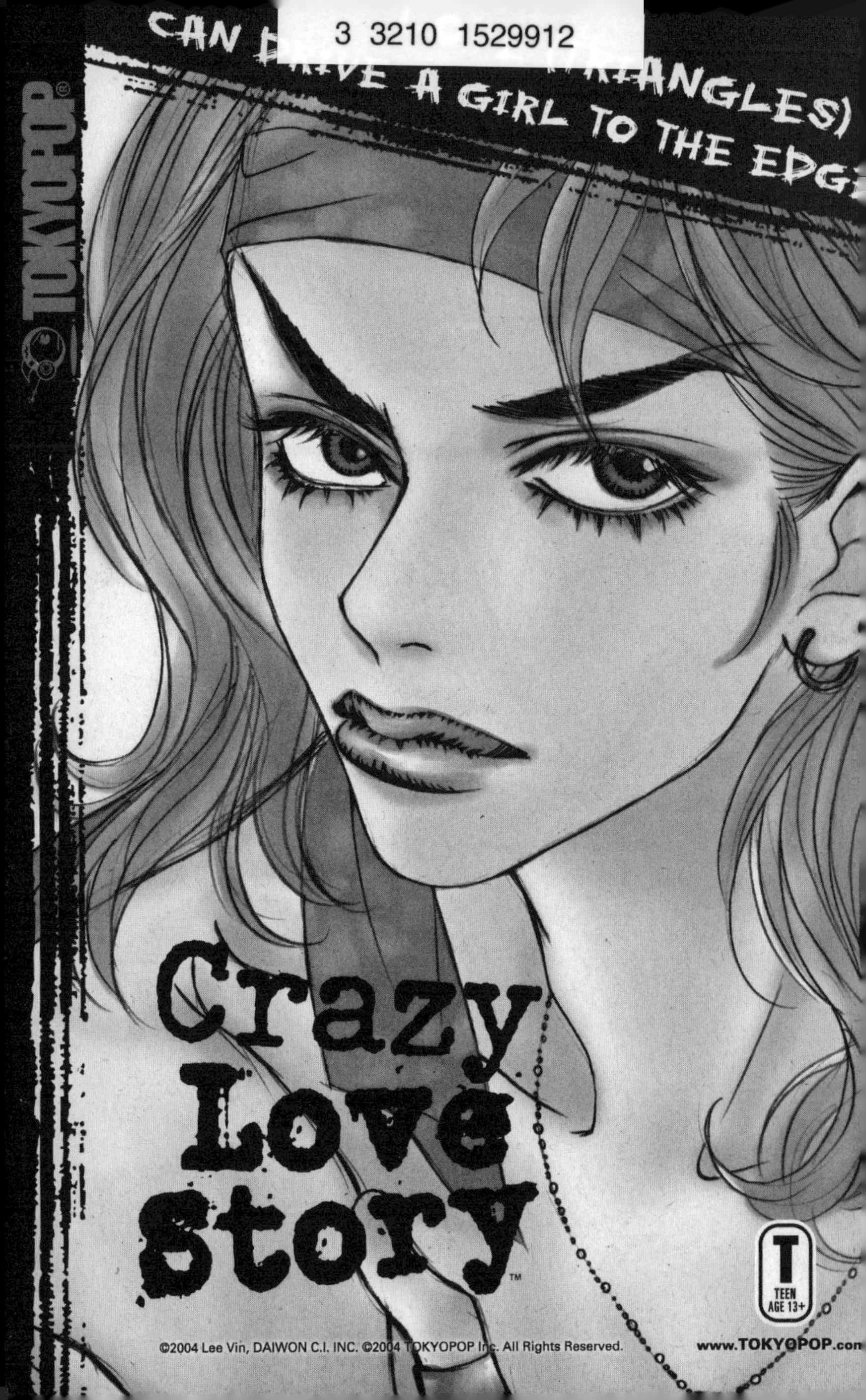
CAN
ANGLES)
RIVE A GIRL TO THE EDG
TOKYOPOP
Crazy Love Story™
T TEEN AGE 13+
www.TOKYOPOP.com

LEGAL DRUG™

When no ordinary prescription will do...

FROM CLAMP
CREATORS OF
CHOBITS
& TOKYO
BABYLON

OT
OLDER TEEN
AGE 16+

www.TOKYOPOP.com

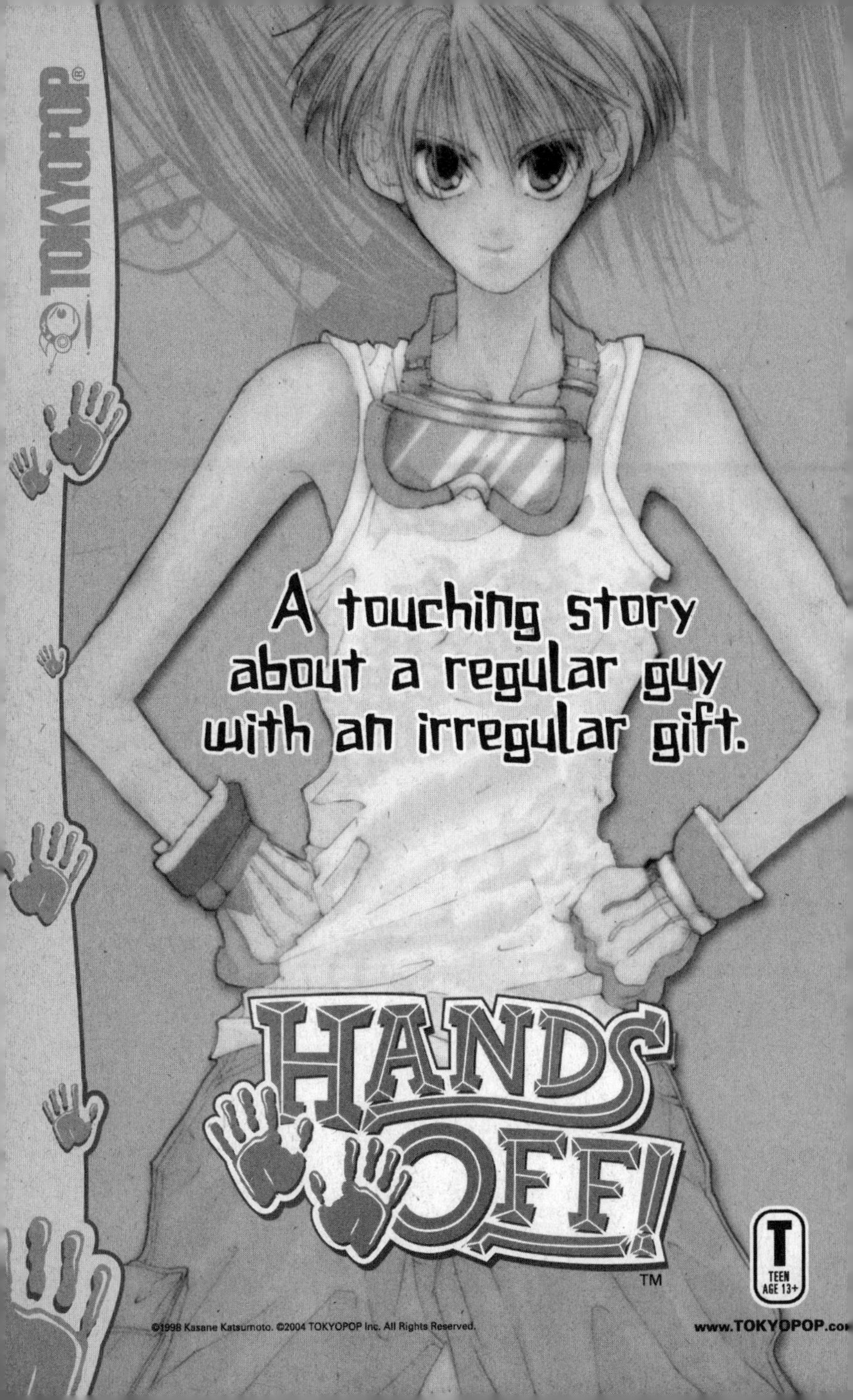

STOP!

This is the back of the book.
You wouldn't want to spoil a great ending!

This book is printed "manga-style," in the authentic Japanese right-to-left format. Since none of the artwork has been flipped or altered, readers get to experience the story just as the creator intended. You've been asking for it, so TOKYOPOP® delivered: authentic, hot-off-the-press, and far more fun!

DIRECTIONS

If this is your first time reading manga-style, here's a quick guide to help you understand how it works.

It's easy... just start in the top right panel and follow the numbers. Have fun, and look for more 100% authentic manga from TOKYOPOP®!